# Passion, Death, and Spirituality

# Sophia Studies in Cross-cultural Philosophy of Traditions and Cultures

The Sophia Studies in Cross-cultural Philosophy of Traditions and Cultures fosters critical and constructive engagement of the intellectual and philosophical dimensions – broadly construed – of religious and cultural traditions around the globe. The series invites innovative scholarship, including feminist, postmodern, and postcolonial approaches.

For further volumes:
http://www.springer.com/series/8880

Kathleen Higgins • David Sherman
Editors

# Passion, Death, and Spirituality

## The Philosophy of Robert C. Solomon

 Springer

*Editors*
Kathleen Higgins
Department of Philosophy
The University of Texas
Austin, TX, USA

David Sherman
Department of Philosophy
University of Montana
Missoula, MT, USA

ISBN 978-94-007-4649-7        ISBN 978-94-007-4650-3 (eBook)
DOI 10.1007/978-94-007-4650-3
Springer Dordrecht Heidelberg New York London

Library of Congress Control Number: 2012940193

Printed on acid-free paper

Springer is part of Springer Science+Business Media (www.springer.com)

# Acknowledgments

The papers in this collection were, for the most part, originally presented in conferences and memorial sessions in honor of Bob. We are grateful to many others who made these conferences and sessions possible. We owe particular thanks to John Bishop, the head of the Philosophy Department at the University of Auckland in 2007, for arranging for a memorial conference in Bob's honor there in July of that year and to Robert Wicks, who organized the conference; and to David Sosa, chair of the Philosophy Department at the University of Texas at Austin, for initiating the idea of a conference in Bob's honor at the University of Texas and supporting this venture throughout its planning stages. We are also grateful to the staffs in the two departments who did much to make these conferences a success. In connection with the University of Texas conference, which occurred in February 2008, we also wish to thank Clancy Martin for sharing our work as co-organizers and for his suggestion that we publish essays from the various conferences and memorial sessions on Bob as a book. Special thanks are due to Jennifer Westrom Sheperd, who volunteered her expertise in organizing conferences to make this conference a reality. We are also grateful to the members of the Philosophy Department staff who were involved in conference details, particularly Nadia Caffesse (who designed a spectacular poster and program) and Laura Elwood; and Amy Bryant and Megan Rickel, who ensured that the conference was preserved in video form.

Sessions in honor of Bob were held at the meetings of a number of learned societies. We wish to thank Jenefer Robinson for organizing a session at the Central Division meeting of the American Philosophical Association in Chicago in April 2007; Agneta Fischer for devoting her Presidential Session at the meeting of the International Society for Research on the Emotions in Coolum, Australia in July 2007 to memorial papers in honor of Bob; Edwin Hartman, for organizing a session at the Society for Business Ethics meeting in Philadelphia in August 2007; Christa Davis Acampora and Lanier Anderson for organizing a session of the North American Nietzsche Society at the American Philosophical Association Meeting in Pasedena, California, in March 2008; Stephen Davies for organizing a session of the American Society for Aesthetics at Asilomar, California, in March, 2008; Purushottama Bilimoria for organizing a session at the Australasian Society for

Asian and Comparative Philosophy meeting in Melbourne in July 2008; and Martha Nussbaum and John Deigh for organizing the Royal Conference at the University of Texas at Austin in February 2009, devoted to philosophy of the emotions, in memory of Bob.

We wish also to acknowledge the speakers and discussants in these diverse venues, many of whom are represented in this volume: Joanne Ciulla, Jesse Prinz, Jenefer Robinson, and Richard Schacht at the American Philosophical Association session; Agneta Fischer, Lisa Feldman-Barrett, Batja Gomes de Mesquita, and Ronald de Sousa at the International Society for Research on the Emotions session; Roger Ames, John Bishop, Ray Bradley, Tim Dare, Ruth Irwin, Fred Kroon, Jeremy Seligman, Christine Swanton, and Koji Tanaka at the University of Auckland conference; Robert Audi, Joanne Ciulla, Daryl Koehn, and Richard Nielsen at the Society for Business Ethics session; Katherine Arens, Amelie Benedikt, Jessica Berry, Steve Best, Joanne Ciulla, Katie Cooklin, Stephen Davies, Ronald de Sousa, Elaine Engelhardt, Betty Sue Flowers, Roger Gathmann, Mitchell Ginsberg, Benjamin Gregory, Douglas Kellner, Pierre Lamarche, Clancy Martin, Chad McCracken, Janet McCracken, Thomas Miles, Iain Morrisson, Kelly Oliver, James Pennebaker, Stephen Phillips, Irene Price, Jesse Prinz, Gregory Reimann, Jenefer Robinson, Henry Rosemont, Richard Schacht, Garret Sokoloff, Shari Starrett, Ariela Tubert, Markus Weidler, Patricia Werhane, and David Zimmerman at the Robert C. Solomon Memorial Conference at the University of Texas; Jessica Berry, Daniel Conway, Paul S. Loeb, Shari Starrett, and Tracy Strong at the North American Nietzsche Society session; Stephen Davies, Peter Goldie, and Jenefer Robinson at the American Society for Aesthetics session; Cheshire Calhoun, Padmasiri de Silva, and Koji Tanaka at the Australasian Society for Asian and Comparative Philosophy session; and Noël Carroll, John Deigh, Owen Flanagan, Charles Nussbaum, Martha C. Nussbaum, Robert Roberts, Nancy Sherman, Michael Stocker, and Paul Woodruff at the 2009 Royal Conference.

Great thanks go to Purushottama Bilimoria, who has enthusiastically supported the publication of this book in the Sophia Studies in Cross-Cultural Philosophy of Traditions and Cultures, which he edits. We are also grateful to Willemijn Arts, Anita Fei van der Linden, Marleen Moore and other members of the editorial and production staff at Springer who have helped to make this book a reality.

# Contents

# Introduction

**Kathleen M. Higgins**

The philosophy of Robert C. Solomon ("Bob" as we will call him in this book) is wide-ranging. As the table of contents of this book suggests, he made contributions to the philosophy of the emotions, ethics, aesthetics, comparative philosophy, the history of Western philosophy, and the philosophy of religion. His participation in so many different fields might suggest the scattered attention of a dilettante. But this is to miss the core commitments that motivated his work across its many manifestations.

In the introduction of his book *From Hegel to Existentialism*, Bob calls himself an existentialist. For Bob "existentialism" did not mean to stay within a narrow tradition. Instead, he was concerned to traverse all things human, by multiplying perspectives on all the things he thought were important in a well-lived life. His description of himself as an existentialist is a useful summary of this philosophical outlook. The term points to the coherent vision that integrated Bob's philosophical endeavors, a vision that is one with his cosmopolitan approach to being a human being in the world.

The essays in this volume address different facets of the prism that is Bob's work. They are grouped thematically, but the reader will observe that some themes recur across thematic groupings, a pattern that reflects Bob's consistent concerns across the range of topics he addressed. In particular, Bob's interest in emotion and its role in human life permeates his thought on all topics. Accordingly, emotion is central to all of the contents of this volume. Nevertheless, the first of our thematic groups includes essays that address Bob's groundbreaking contribution to the philosophy of the emotions.

Bob's book *The Passions*, which appeared in 1976, argued that contrary to the view that has dominated much of Western philosophical history, emotions are intelligent. Popular culture by now has embraced this idea; but in 1976 it was radical. *The Passions* in effect launched the contemporary field of the philosophy of the emotions. Over the next several decades, Bob's view that emotion involves

K.M. Higgins
The University of Texas at Austin, USA

cognitive judgment became the dominant view. Subsequently, however, in light of new evidence about the biological aspects of emotion, a new generation of critics reasserted a version of the view that Bob had challenged, the non-cognitive interpretation of emotions as feelings, which had been defended by William James.

Jesse Prinz represents this younger generation. In "Sensational Judgmentalism: Reconciling Solomon and James," he articulates the issues in the debate over cognitivism in emotion. As his title suggests, Prinz contends that one can endorse James's position that emotions are essentially bodily feelings while still accepting key features of Bob's position, specifically the views that emotions involve judgments, have intentional objects, can occur in the absence of feelings, and amount to strategies. Ultimately, according to Prinz, Bob's version of cognitivism and Prinz's version of non-cognitivism are not as far apart as they superficially seem to be.

Bob's views on emotion and his brand of existentialism are tightly linked, as is particularly evident in one of Bob's more controversial claims, the idea that we have a remarkable degree of choice regarding emotions. Ronald de Sousa and David Sherman both consider this existentialist side of Bob's account of emotion. In "Biology and Existentialism," de Sousa discusses the apparent contradiction between Bob's contention that emotions are largely voluntary and a biological view of humanity. de Sousa argues that properly understood, these views are not in conflict; Bob's existentialist view about our freedom to choose emotion is consistent with the view that our genes shape our goals to a considerable extent.

David Sherman takes a critical stance toward Bob's position that emotions are significantly voluntary. Describing the transformation of Bob's specific position over time, he contends that Bob rightly came to recognize that he had not provided an account of the grounds for one's choices (including those involving emotions), and that in his later writings he laid greater stress on the way in which social and cultural factors mediate the choices one makes in constructing a self. Sherman argues, however, that a difficulty with this position is that it does not indicate how one gains sufficient distance from one's culture to be able to criticize its practices. He concludes that one of Bob's aims in emphasizing the voluntary character of emotion was admonitional: Bob sought to remind us that we have real choices and that we are able to subject social practices to critique and creative revision.

Bob took other controversial stances on emotion in addition to his cognitivism and his view that emotions are voluntary. One of these was his contention that emotions cannot be neatly classified by valence, i.e. as intrinsically "positive" or "negative." These classifications do not consider the complex roles that emotions play in our experience, Bob argued. An emotion that is not pleasant to experience, for example, may be valuable in sorting through one's circumstances or in motivating one to constructive action. Such an emotion, he claimed, should not be called "negative" without qualification.

Arindam Chakrabarti's "A Critique of Pure Revenge" and Bob's response concern a politically problematic "negative" emotion, the emotion of vindictiveness, the desire for revenge. Bob held that despite its "nasty" character, the desire for revenge should be acknowledged as basic to our motivational nature. He argues that it is an essential aspect of our way of relating morally to the world, and that it plays a role even in one of our apparently noblest emotions, the desire for justice. Chakrabarti, by contrast, contends that the desire for revenge should never be satisfied, summarizing his view as, "An examined revenge is never worth taking." The essays on revenge included in this volume are those presented in quite literally the last public debate in which Bob participated. Aptly, they are presented here without resolution, as Bob's philosophical work continues to provoke further discussion.

If vindictiveness is on the harsh extreme of the emotional range, another case Bob discussed, sentimentality, is on the other. Sentimentality is often viewed as both a moral and an aesthetic defect, but Bob argued that it was not necessarily either one. Jenefer Robinson, one of Bob's long-term interlocutors in both aesthetics and the philosophy of emotions, challenges these views. While she and Bob agree that realistic literature can help to train the moral sensibilities of the reader, Robinson contends that sentimentality in literature does not sufficiently encourage a reflective response on the part of the reader. Bob, by contrast, finds value in sentimental literature, claiming that it exercises our sympathies without exhausting them, leaving us well equipped for applying them in everyday contexts.

Robinson's consideration of the development of moral sensibilities segues well into the group of essays dealing with Bob's contributions in ethics. The first two essays in this section deal with Bob's applied work on ethics in business. Patricia Werhane and David Bevan offer an appreciative account of Bob's Aristotelian approach to business ethics, which emphasizes the importance of cultivating virtue and recognizing one's participation in a larger community. Werhane and Bevan see Bob's views on emotion—in particular his cognitivism and his view that we have some control over our emotions—as of a piece with his Aristotelian emphasis on virtue. Developing virtue involves altering habits, and Werhane and Bevan emphasize cognitive habits, or mindsets, that prevail within business. Bob's defense of an Aristotelian model of commerce, they argue, in and of itself effectively persuades readers to transform their perspective on business. This model does not oppose the ideal of profitability in business, but repositions it as part of a more encompassing aim, that of the flourishing human life.

Robert Audi also considers Bob's Aristotelian perspective on business ethics. In "Virtues, Styles, and Rules in Business Ethics: Reflections on the Contributions of Robert C. Solomon," Audi considers the virtue ethical cast of Bob's approach. Drawing attention to some of the virtues that Bob sees as essential to good practice in business, and praising Bob's conception of diverse "ethical styles" that various individuals exemplify, Audi takes up the question of whether virtue ethics offers sufficient guidance for action. Audi submits that it does not, but he suggests that Bob might see the contrast between virtue ethics and theories that focus on right actions as a false dichotomy. Audi concurs with Bob in embracing Aristotle's point that we should optimally cultivate character so that doing the right thing comes to seem natural.

While Audi emphasizes the relationship of Bob's business ethics to Aristotelian theory, Christine Swanton brings out Bob's connection to Nietzsche in his formulation of a virtue ethical model. In "Robert Solomon's Aristotelian Nietzsche," she observes that Bob saw Nietzsche as much more closely related to Aristotle than

Nietzsche saw himself. Swanton elaborates a Nietzschean virtue ethics based on this Aristotelian reading of Nietzsche. She shares Bob's view that while Nietzsche tended to see some virtues as optimal for everyone, he relativized some virtues to particular types of individuals. However, she disagrees with Bob on the relevance of will to power for Nietzschean ethics, on the importance of the passionate, "overflowing" virtues in Nietzsche's account, and on whether the virtues of the herd constitute real virtues for Nietzsche.

Kelly Oliver considers Bob's ethical theory from the standpoint of a particular pair of emotions that he considered in depth, grief and gratitude. She focuses on Bob's view that grief is a continuation of love and his contention that we produce memorials as means for expressing that love. She raises the issue of how we relate to the deaths of those whom we do not know and never met, and who may be on the other side of the world. Do we have an obligation to mourn for them? Oliver shows that Bob's views on such personal emotions as grief and gratitude can have important political implications.

Bob took up the idea that we should look beyond our immediate neighborhood, both emotionally and theoretically, in his consideration of non-Western philosophy. He rejected arbitrary intradisciplinary distinctions that tend to dichotomize between the West and the rest, and he recognized how many of the issues that arise within the Western tradition are also dealt with elsewhere. To come up with a more enriched perspective on these issues, he did not hesitate to explore the philosophical traditions of the non-Western world. Accordingly, unlike many American philosophers, he proselytized on behalf of comparative philosophy, the focus of our third group of essays. The theme of grief, interestingly, is the focus of several authors in this group, which relate to Oliver's essay in this respect as well as in their insistence that we transcend philosophical parochialism.

In "Grief and the Mnemonics of Places: a Thank You Note," Janet McCracken contemplates the role that commemorations play in honoring the dead. She compares the Zoroastrian tradition's approach to funerary rites with those of the ancient Greeks. She suggests that the Greeks performed their rites—including the performance of funerary games—with the aim of offering a place for remembering the dead. The Zoroastrians, by contrast, did not inter the bodies of their dead; instead, they honored the deceased by having a dog look upon the corpse, which was supposed to free the soul of the deceased from the place at which death occurred. McCracken sees this Zoroastrian ritual as highly symbolic, drawing on dogs' loyalty to their human companions and their ability to witness and move on. Nevertheless, she suggests that the impulses behind both kinds of rituals are evident in the responses of those who mourn Bob.

Prompted by loss in his personal life, Purushottama Bilimoria explores the gap between philosophical accounts of grief and the powerful feelings it involves. He acknowledges Bob as an interlocutor, but he is dissatisfied with the approaches to grief taken in the philosophical literature, including Bob's. In particular, Bilimoria rejects any philosophical theory that would equate grief with a propositional judgment. While he acknowledges that Bob increasingly moved away from extreme cognitivism and emphasized the importance of affect and the phenomenology of emotion, Bilimoria nevertheless thinks that Bob's theory under-emphasizes the feeling dimension of grief. He explores the ways that the practices and literature from various cultures deal with the painful and disruptive feelings involved in grief.

Bilimoria also challenges one of Bob's more theoretical claims about grief, the suggestion that in some circumstances it is not only appropriate, but morally obligatory. While it may indeed be appropriate, Bilimoria argues, to grieve solely because it is morally mandated would be highly undesirable; and the actual experience involves more improvisational responses than any "required" mourning behavior. Nevertheless, he concludes that theoretical accounts are still called for, and he encourages further philosophical work on the subject.

Like Bilimoria, Padmasiri de Silva engages with Bob's perspective on grief. In his essay, "The Lost Art of Sadness," he situates the consideration of grief within a broader discussion of sadness. He credits Bob as an influence on his thinking about emotion, particularly about "the rhythms of our emotional life." de Silva considers these rhythms in connection with the Buddhist practice of mindfulness, and he discusses the approach to sadness taken by the mindfulness-based emotion focused therapy to which he has devoted himself as a practicing clinician for many years. He utilizes this therapeutic perspective as a basis for disputing the common view within the psychiatric community that sadness amounts to a mental disorder. Instead, de Silva argues, sadness is part of the human condition that can, in its own way, enrich one's life.

Shifting to a consideration of emotion in the thick of political activity, Henry Rosemont draws on Bob's emphasis on the importance of emotion to discussions of justice and analyses the truth and reconciliation commissions that have been used in many nations in efforts to recover from violence between ethnic, racial, and religious subgroups within their populations. Rosemont observes that the goals of such commissions—to set the record straight about who has victimized whom and to effect reconciliation—have been inconsistent. Truth and reconciliation commissions will be hindered in achieving reconciliation, he argues, so long as they are premised on the notion of society as constructed of free, autonomous individuals. Rosemont commends Bob's emphasis on the need to transform our sense of the self if we are to properly understand justice. He sees Bob's perspective as bearing some resemblance to the Confucian tradition, which understands human beings as essentially related to each other. By comparison with models that consider society the aggregation of autonomous individuals, a relational approach would serve as a better theoretical basis for structuring the work of truth and reconciliation commissions so that they actually achieve reconciliation.

The relational emphasis of Bob's work is evident throughout the final grouping of essays, which conjoins some of Bob's work in the history of philosophy with his relatively late writings on spirituality. These essays, despite their various topics, all accentuate the stress Bob placed on the importance of recognizing one's individual life in the context of something much larger than oneself.

Shari Neller Starrett draws attention to the theme of human interconnectedness in Bob's innovative interpretation of Hegel. She contends that his many startling themes cohere around a view of Hegel's dialectic as a metaphor, not a method.

The upshot of Bob's interpretation is that Hegel's philosophy is more art than science and the dialectic more about growth and development in experience than about logical relations. Starrett draws attention to Bob's controversial views that Hegel did not posit the Absolute as literally attainable and that the Hegelian Spirit, our collective presence in the world, never reaches a final goal. In keeping with this idea, Starrett suggests, we can see Bob's spirit as continuing beyond his physical death, for it is part of Spirit writ large.

Richard Schacht also takes up Bob's relationship to Hegel and his understanding of Hegel's notion of *Geist,* the term usually translated as "Spirit." Schacht points out that the term *Geist* in German is much richer than "spirit" or "mind" (alternative translations) are in English, and he urges us to leave the term untranslated. He concurs with Bob that Hegel's *Geist* is not an otherworldly concept, and like Bob, he is unwilling to dispense with the idea, as many contemporary philosophers are happy to do. Schacht relates the conception of *Geist* to Bob's conception of a naturalized spirituality, developed in his book *Spirituality for the Skeptic.* Although Schacht doubts that the many features of spiritual life that Bob indicates are genuinely necessary for spirituality, he views Bob's account as a welcome invitation to think further about spirituality, spirit, and *Geist* in naturalistic terms.

Markus Weidler considers Bob's contention that gratitude is essential to spirituality, whether or not there is really any God or gods to be thanked. Weidler interprets this stance in light of Bob's criticism of what he called "death fetishism," a delusory view that sees death as endowing one's life with its true significance. Weidler analyzes fanaticism as a manifestation of death fetishism, for fanaticism seeks to manifest devotion so extreme that one is willing to die for one's cause. The fanatic is so uncompromising in his insistence on his own dogma that he violates his own highest values, even imposing his demands on his god(s). Bob's proposal of gratitude without dogma, even about that gratitude's possible recipient, according to Weidler, offers a salutary spiritual alternative to fanaticism, which from time to time represents a dangerous temptation to all of us.

John Bishop considers Bob's idea of spirituality in relation to revisionary theism that rejects the notion of an all-powerful, all-knowing, and all-benevolent God ("the omniGod" in Bishop's parlance) and seeks an alternative conception of God. Bishop sees a certain commonality between Bob's naturalized spirituality and the kind of revisionary theism he embraces, particularly with respect to the question of how appropriate it is to commit oneself to a certain spiritual vision of reality in the absence of compelling evidence. Bob analyzes spirituality in terms of central spiritual passions, including reverence, love, gratitude, and trust, all of which involve taking the world to be fundamentally deserving of such attitudes despite the fact that we lack evidence that this belief is justified. Bishop argues that both the attitudes entailed by the spiritual passions and belief in a God as conceived by revisionary theism can be defended as epistemically responsible. He also concludes that Bob's account of spirituality is rooted in similar motivations to those of the revisionary theist, for both seek a spiritually optimistic outlook toward the world without a controlling deity who runs things.

In the concluding essay, "Bob on Meaning in Life and Death," Kathleen Higgins picks up on Bob's spirit of optimism in the face of death, despite his skepticism about personal experience beyond it. Appropriately, given the character of his philosophy, Bob's solution to the problem of finding meaning in life in the face of death is emotional as well as philosophical. His claims that spirituality is "the thoughtful love of life" and that gratitude is the best response to tragedy summarize his life as well as his philosophy.

# Part I
# Emotions

# Chapter 1
# Sensational Judgmentalism: Reconciling Solomon and James

Jesse J. Prinz

**Abstract**  Robert Solomon is responsible for developing one of the most influential and sophisticated cognitive theories of emotion in recent philosophy. In his own work, and in commentaries, this theory is often contrasted with the non-cognitive theory of William James. For James, emotions are felt sensations of changes in the body. For Solomon, emotions are judgments that have intentional objects and can occur without feelings. Solomon also says that emotions, unlike usual sensations, are strategic choices rather than automatics responses. This chapter argues that, despite this apparent contrast, the Jamesian view can be adapted to satisfy the basic tenets of Solomon's theory, and the resulting hybrid may have been anticipated in Solomon, despite his reservations about James.

No one contributed more to contemporary philosophical discussions of emotion that Bob Solomon. His seminal work in the 1970s helped set the agenda for decades to come, and the arguments he offered in those early works remain as relevant today as they were when they were originally penned. Those of us who came to this discussion in recent years revere Solomon as an intellectual hero. But many of us have also used him as a foil. As so often happens in academe, newcomers try to kill the father, and often then resurrect the grandfather as an alternative. In this case, the grandfather is William James. The last two decades have witnessed a Jamesian turn in emotion theory, and Solomon's views are often seen as the polar opposite. Solomon authored some of the most penetrating critiques of the Jamesian approach, and his positive

J.J. Prinz (✉)
Department of Philosophy, CUNY Graduate Center, City University of New York,
365 5th Avenue, New York, NY 10016, USA
e-mail: jesse@subcortex.com

K. Higgins and D. Sherman (eds.), *Passion, Death, and Spirituality*,
Sophia Studies in Cross-cultural Philosophy of Traditions and Cultures 1,
DOI 10.1007/978-94-007-4650-3_1, © Springer Science+Business Media Dordrecht 2012

theory of the emotions often looks like a systematic inversion of James's core tenets. As a Jamesian, this is how I'd seen things, and despite receiving unbelievably gracious support and encouragement from Solomon during my early forays, I'd thought of his work as more of a foil than a foundation. I realize now that this was a mistake. Many of Solomon's most controversial views strike me as plausible now, not because James was wrong, but because there is room for a reconciliation. Solomon was a leading force in bringing together different disciplines (psychology, anthropology, and philosophy), different generations (historical and contemporary sources of influence), and different philosophical traditions (analytic and continental). It turns out that he was also prescient in seeing how the most ostensibly antithetical theories of emotion might find some common ground. This is the most important of many philosophical lessons I learned from him, not only because it is crucial for understanding emotions, but because it serves as a reminder, in this polarizing field, that the best solution to many of our debates is collaboration.

In what follows, I begin by presenting some of the central themes in Solomon's theory of the emotions, focusing on his groundbreaking 1973 paper, but updating where appropriate. I indicate how these themes depart from the position advanced by James. Then, in the second part, I argue that the Jamesian should not reject Solomon's arguments, but rather accommodate them, and I will suggest that his considered view can be regarded as integrative as well.

## Solomon Contra James

In 1884, James published his first and most influential discussion of the emotions. There he defends a view that is sometimes called *sensationalism*. According to James, emotions are felt sensations of changes that take place in the body. When we experience an emotionally evocative event, our bodies prepare for a behavioral response, and the feeling of those preparations is the emotion. When we encounter a bear in the wilderness, to use a Jamesian paradigm case, our bodies prepare for flight, our hearts race, we perspire, and we get goose bumps (a vestige from hairier ancestors whose goose bumps caused hair to erect, giving rise to a larger appearance in the eyes of predators). The emotion of fear is a sensation comprising this somatic pattern.

James based this account on two central observations. The first is phenomenological. James asks readers to imagine an intense emotion, such as rage or terror, and then systematically subtract in our minds all its bodily symptoms. If we try this exercise, James says, we will find that there is nothing left that we would recognize as an emotion. The phenomenology of emotion is fundamentally bodily. The second observation is more or less empirical—it was speculative in James's time but has since been tested and confirmed. When we change the configuration of our bodies, our emotions seem to change as well. James combated his own depression by adopting an erect posture and a smile, methods known now to enhance mood. If bodily changes can change our emotions, then, James concludes, emotions may be sensations of such changes. These arguments continue to persuade some contemporary emotion researchers and have been buffered by empirical work linking emotional responses to brain structures that are involved in the perception of bodily changes (Damasio 1994; Prinz 2004).

James's theory of the emotions captivated philosophers and psychologists when it first appeared, and it became a dominant theory until 40 years later, when Walter Cannon (1927) authored an eviscerating critique. Cannon argued that emotions cannot be bodily sensations, because bodily nerves are too slow and insensitive to explain the immediacy and intensity of our emotional responses. He also argued that bodily responses cannot differentiate the emotions, and that stimulation of visceral nerves does not cause people to have experiences that they mistake for emotions, as James might have predicted. Solomon (1976) endorses this critique, which has often received inadequate attention by contemporary followers of James.

It should be noted, however, that the critique is less decisive than it may appear. First, some forms of bodily perception, such as heart rate, can be quite accurate and fast. Second, the fact that some visceral nerves are slow does not undermine the Jamesian theory, because emotions sometimes come on slowly, and because emotional experiences may begin as soon as the brain anticipates changes in the body, even if such changes have not yet taken place or been perceived. Third, the fact that stimulating an organ does not cause an emotional sensation can be explained by the fact that emotions involve whole patterns of bodily change. The stimulation of one organ alone would not suffice. This also speaks to the questions of differentiation. A rapid heart rate would not be enough to distinguish fear and euphoria, since both involve cardiovascular acceleration. But fear also characteristically involves a muscle tension (part of the freezing response), widened eyes, and tingling spine. And euphoria causes flushing rather than pallor, and the lips turn upward rather than down. Inducing such global patterns of change can indeed cause felt changes in the emotions. Indeed, facial expressions (Laird 1984; Zajonc et al. 1989) and respiratory changes (Philippot et al. 2002) may be enough to differentiate basic emotions. So the case against James cannot hang on Cannon's critique. Solomon certainly wouldn't make this mistake. His central objections to James have little to do with physiology. Rather, he defends a positive theory of his own, which seems to conflict with sensationalism in multiple ways.

Solomon's approach to the emotions is inspired by Sartre rather than James. His overarching claim is that emotions are judgments, not sensations. James is a noncognitivist. That is, he thinks cognitive states are unnecessary for emotions. An emotion can be triggered by a perceptual experience (seeing a bear), and consist in somatic sensations. A creature without thoughts could emote. For Solomon, emotions are fundamentally cognitive: they are judgments about states of affairs in the world, such as the judgment that the bear is dangerous. This can be called *judgmentalism*. Like James, Solomon cites phenomenological evidence. His paradigm case is anger, which he associates with the judgment that there has been an offense. He invites us to imagine being angry with no such judgment, and concludes that this impossible. It would be paradoxical, in a Moorian way, to say, "I am angry at you, but I don't think you've done anything wrong."

Solomon's judgmentalism is welded to four other supporting planks, which further reveal his departures James. The first of these can be given the awkward name *feeling contingentism*. This is the view that emotions need not occur with any characteristic feelings. There is no feeling that is unique to anger and found in all instances of it. No feelings can be used to differentiate the emotions. Where James says that emotions *are* feelings, Solomon says that emotions need not even occur with feelings. One can be angry, he claims, without feeling angry.

Another plank of Solomon's account can be called *intentional essentialism*. On this view, emotions have intentional objects, and they have them essentially. One cannot just be angry. One must be angry about something. Anger always has an object. This is an intentional object and not merely a cause. Anger might be caused by a bad day at work, but directed at something entirely different. The object of anger may not even be real. I may get angry at an offense that is merely imagined, perhaps because of that bad day at work. Like intentional objects in general, the objects of our emotions are opaque or subjective (what Solomon sometimes calls surreal). I may be frightened of Mr. Hyde, but not of Dr. Jekyll, even though they are one and the same person.

It is famously difficult for sensationalists to accommodate the fact that emotions represent, since we don't usually think of sensations as having intentional objects; we don't use that-clauses when ascribing tickles or twinges. Sensationalists sometimes respond by proposing that emotions are sensations *plus* representations of precipitating events. Solomon rejects this, saying that it doesn't account for the non-separability of an emotion and his object. This non-separability cuts both ways. Solomon says that the fear of something cannot persist without its object, and the object too is presented as fearful. Thus, emotions do not consist of representations of cool facts appended to feelings, or even appended to evaluative judgments. Rather, those judgments permeate our way of experiencing their objects. This is an interesting thesis that has been neglected in the emotion literature, especially within cognitive science. Such non-separability is especially challenging for Jamesians, who explain emotional objects as representations that trigger felt bodily changes, rather than seeing such objects as inextricably bound to the emotions they evoke.

Solomon's most provocative plank is intimated in the title of his 1973 paper: "Emotions and Choice." For him, emotions are mental acts, and, as acts, they can be regarded as choices that we make, and for which we have responsibility. This can be called *voluntarism* about the emotions. Voluntarism is at odds with common sense; we think emotions are things that happen to us. But Solomon says we have agency over them. We fail to realize this because emotions are not consciously or deliberatively chosen. We are unaware of our complicity. Emotions are also urgent judgments, so we experience them in a way that makes them feel like they have taken hold of us, disrupting our normal activities. That is because emotions are responses to unusual circumstances. Swept up by the exigency of a situation, we fail to appreciate that emotions are in some sense voluntary. This view contrasts with the position of James who is a functionalist, in the psychological sense of that term. He sees emotions as ancient and automatic, evolved responses—bioprograms designed for coping with life's challenges in a way that bypasses our more recent capacity for choice.

Voluntarism is also at odds with sensationalism more broadly, since sensations are passive mental events. We don't choose our chills and twinges.

The final plank that I will mention is closely related to voluntarism. Emotions have a strategic function. They fit in with our goals, and expressing them advances our purposes. Solomon explains this *purposivism* with an example. A man may get angry at his romantic partner over some trivial event in an effort to avoid going out with her on evening when he'd rather be watching television. The anger stirs up a fight, which makes an evening out unlikely, even though the anger is not about going out. In such cases, we are blind to the purposes of our emotions (or emotional expressions). If we realized these ulterior motives, the emotions would dissipate. But the fact that such motives exist can be explained by agentic nature of the passions, and would be deeply puzzling if emotions were merely involuntary sensations.

In all these ways, Solomon's approach to the emotions contrasts sharply with James's. On the face of it, his view systematically rejects sensationalism and all of its implications. Two views could hardly be more opposed. Or so it might seem. I now want to suggest that there is room for a reconciliation. Solomon's views can be used to rehabilitate sensationalism, and such a rehabilitation is actually in line with his considered account of what emotions really are.

## Towards a Sensational Judgmentalism

A diehard Jamesian might try to rebut Solomon by challenging the central tenets of his theory. This would be a courageous strategy, and perhaps even foolhardy. Solomon is a magnificent observer, and his discussions of the emotions are so rich, and so faithful to human life that it is hard to resist his conclusions without looking anemic. Jamesians are reductive; they try to find the most basic constituents of emotions. Solomon begins with emotions in their most florid, social, manifestations. If the Jamesian pleads for physiology without any resources for scaling up, the account will lose appeal. Jamesians should aspire to accommodate Solomon's insights rather than treating emotions as reptilian responses that have no connection to the most sophisticated aspects of our psychology.

Toward this end, I want to revisit the planks of Solomon's account to see whether they can be incorporated into a sensationalist framework. The resulting picture will, of necessity, depart from James, but it will preserve his emphasis on bodily sensations. The aim is to articulate a sensational judgmentalism.

Let's begin with Solomon's claim that emotions are judgments. On the face of it, judgments and sensations seem to be very different kinds of mental states. For Solomon, we cannot be angry without judging something to be offensive, and, for James, anger is a perception of a bodily preparation for action—presumably a preparation to aggress. One might try to bring these two together in a causal sequence. Perhaps judgments about offenses cause our bodies to change, and we feel the resulting perturbations. This would be a major concession for the Jamesian, since it would imply that emotions depend on cognitive states that are prior to bodily responses, and that would be one small step away from the view that the felt bodily responses are dispensable. But there is an alternative. One can say that the bodily feelings *constitute* a judgment.

Imagine that you experience an offense, whether real or imaginary. Some one might shout an obscenity at you, step on your toe without apology, show up late to your all-important meeting, or endorse a tax cut that you consider irresponsible. Immediately upon experiencing these acts, your body reacts; blood flows to your extremities, your heart races, your brow lowers, your fists clench. When you perceive this pattern of changes, your sensation can be described as representing your body, but this is not all it represents. Sensations always occur when the body undergoes a transformation, but they often also represent things that go beyond the body. For example, visual sensations depend on changes in the retina caused by light, but they also represent lions, lizards, and lounge chairs; likewise, auditory sensations depend on cochlear vibrations, but they inform us about creaks, cries, and crunches. Sensations use the body to tell us about the world, or our place in it. They do so with such immediacy and familiarity that we find it difficult to focus on the medium rather than the message. We say, "There's a lion," not "there's a pattern of light reflecting off the lion's surface onto my retina."

From a psychosemantic perspective, sensations get their meaning from their usual causes and effects. The shape sensation caused by seeing a lion is similar to other sensations caused by lions, and is thus a reliable indicator that a lion is present. If you experience a sensation like that, you are probably in proximity to a lion or at least a picture of one. This sensation will also lead you to react in certain ways. You will draw inferences and make decisions. If you see the lion while hiking in the wilderness, you might choose to take flight, but a similar experience in a zoo will promote approach behaviors rather than avoidance. Your sensation represents the lion because it is of a type that generally has lions as causes and leads to lion-relevant effects. In a similar way, if you experience your body preparing for aggression, then chances are you have encountered something offensive, and the experience of such a sensation may lead you to respond aggressively, if retaliation seems feasible, or to bite your tongue, if you think retaliation would make things worse. In that way, your bodily sensation represents offensiveness—it is of a type that has offensiveness as a usual cause, and it leads to offense-relevant effects. One can say that the bodily sensation is a kind of judgment. It is a psychological state with the semantic content: there has been an offense. I call this the embodied appraisal theory of emotions (Prinz 2004).

This suggests that emotions can be sensations and judgments at the same time, a major step towards reconciling Solomon and James. But the next tenet of Solomon's theory may seem impossible to accommodate by the Jamesian: feeling contingentism. That is the view that emotions are not necessarily felt. One can be angry without feeling angry. On the face of it, this is a direct contradiction of sensationalism. James says that emotions *are* feelings, and that implies that they are essentially felt. There is, however, another interpretation. It is important to recall that sensations are perceptual states. They are episodes in our sensory input systems. An emotion, for James, is a complex interoceptive state. Within perceptual psychology, it is axiomatic that perception can occur below the threshold of consciousness. This is the case in subliminal vision, for example. Equating feelings with conscious episodes, then, we can say that sensations can occur unfelt. An unfelt sensation is one of which we are not conscious. Since sensations can, in general, occur without consciousness, it follows that there can be unfelt emotions, even if emotions are sensations. Those would be perceptions of bodily changes that do not make it into consciousness.

Indeed, it is fairly easy to see how this might occur. Consciousness depends on attention (Prinz 2012). One can undergo a bodily change without attending to it. This may be especially common in the case of emotions, because we tend, when emoting, to focus on the object of the emotion, rather than the emotion itself. If frightened by a sound at night, for example, we focus intently on the source of the sound, not on the racing heart. In this case, I may even know that I am afraid, while at the same time not feeling my fear, just as an athlete might surmise that her body is in pain, while not feeling this pain, because she is too focused on her strides towards victory. It follows that emotions can go unfelt and this may be relatively common.

What then of James's claim that emotions are feelings? In a sense, James is still right. After all, when emotions are felt, the feelings are the emotions; it is just that James did not appreciate the fact that emotions can occur unconsciously. Thus, one can accept James's equation of emotions and feelings while embracing Solomon's thesis that feelings are contingent, as paradoxical as this might sound (Prinz 2005).

Turn next to Solomon's intentional essentialism, the view that emotions have their objects essentially, and that there is a sense in which the object, too, is inseparable from the emotion. In my own work on the emotions, I have said too little about intentional objects, which have always been at the center of Solomon's discussions. The embodied appraisal approach entails that emotions represent things, such as offenses and losses and dangers; but how do they come to represent specific things, such as the offensiveness of a pundit's diatribe, or the loss of a friend, or the (surreal) danger of flying? My own thinking about this has invoked counterfactuals. An emotion represents its particular object if the emotion would not have occurred had that object not been represented. This trivially accommodates one aspect of intentional essentialism. If the emotion depends counterfactually on (the representation of) its intentional object, then any given emotion has its object essentially. Contra Solomon, I think an emotion can linger after one stops thinking about its object, but such lingering feelings might best be called moods, and Solomon (1973) is agnostic about the relationship between moods and intentional objects. So there is clearly room for intentionally essentialist sensationalism.

So far, however, this story doesn't capture Solomon's deep observation that the essential link between emotion and object cuts both ways. For even if I could not have had a particular emotion without its object, it does not follow that I cannot have represented that object without the emotion. In fact, on the story just suggested, the object representation precedes the emotion and is, to that extent, independent of it. This presents a predicament for the Jamesian. Either the object cannot precede the emotion, in which case the counterfactual strategy for explaining intentional essentialism will fail, or the object cannot be dependent on the emotion, in which case Solomon's deep insight will go unmet.

To accommodate Solomon's insight, I think the Jamesian should say that the object that precipitates an emotional response is transformed once that response is initiated. Following Solomon, one might even invoke Sartre's notion of magic here (invoked in the latter's claim that emotions are "magical transformations of the world"). The object may begin as neutrally represented before the emotion begins, but then it is magically transformed by the emotion, becoming hot, rather than cold. We project our emotions onto the world. We see things as offensive, dangerous, and tragic, even though these properties do not exist objectively out there, but depend instead on our responses.

But what is it to see something as offense? How does affect infuse object? These questions are challenging for the Jamesian, because emotions are bodily sensations, and representations of objects are usually not somatic. How can a bodily state infuse a disembodied representation? To answer this question, we need to involve a pair of phenomena that have been neglected by Jamesians. First of all, emotions usher in changes in how we process information, including patterns of attention and cognitive styles. In joy we experience the world holistically. In fear attention becomes highly acute. In despair we are inundated by negative thoughts about the future. Thus the way an object is represented can change depending on what emotion we are experiencing, and those changes may explain one sense in which objects depend on emotions. These changes are not sensational, nor are they judgmental. Both judgmentalists and sensationalist need to explain their theories by recognizing that emotions are not merely states, but ways of seeing.

The second aspect of affect infusion is more Jamesian. When the body undergoes changes, those changes are object-specific. When enraged we don't simply form a generalized disposition to aggress. Rather our bodies militate against a specific offender. Correlatively, once the emotion sets in, the offended takes on what J. J. Gibson called an affordance. In perceiving or reflecting on the offender we register the action that we are inclined to take. Think about the experience of a friend as huggable, or a delicious food as demanding to be devoured. These behavioral responses are not experienced as after-effects—something above and beyond the perception of friend and food. Rather we perceive the affordances as properties of the objects that afford them. We project our bodies onto the world. This move is Jamesian in nature, but it has been missed because Jamesians tend to ignore intentional objects. Solomon's focus on objects, and his ideas about subjective or magical transformations, point towards an enriched sensationalism. And this enrichment further narrows the gap between the sensational approach and the idea that emotions are ways of construing the world.

We can turn now to the most controversial aspect of Solomon's account, one that most cognitivists would probably reject: the idea that emotions are voluntary choices. In an appendix to "Emotions and Choice," Solomon (1980) weakens his voluntarism a bit, saying that he moved too quickly in his early formulations from the view that emotions are actions to the conclusion that emotions are chosen.

Solomon also notes that culture exerts a strong influence on emotions, which seems to count against emotions being chosen, since that is an external influence. It might also be added that judgments are not always chosen. They are often passive responses to situations that present themselves. In fact, whether we can ever simply choose to judge something is controversial. If you don't think the moon is made of cheese, you cannot simply judge that it is.

For all that, I think there is something importantly right about Solomon's early voluntarism—something that the Jamesian should accommodate. Emotions can come unbidden, but we can also play an active role in changing emotional attitudes. For example, we can reconstrue life events. A loss that may be experienced with great sadness may also be an opportunity to reflect, reprioritize and renew. An offense may actually be sign that you have done something that hurt the offending party's feelings. A danger may also be a challenge through which one can grow. The contours of an emotion can change, when we reconstrue, and in some cases, one sentiment can give way to another. Whenever we have an emotion, there is an element of choice in so far as we can choose to acquiesce or we can look for ways to change perspective.

Even the decision to stay with an emotion, like Sisyphus and his rock, can be thought of as voluntary. Sisyphus could not do otherwise, but he could choose to identify with his activity, making his life his own, and overcoming alienation. We sometimes think of emotions as things that happen to us, like invasive forces. We feel stressed by work, and we suffer from depressive disorders. Instead, we can acknowledge that we thrive on stress and that we feel at home in our gloom. We might find those who lead stress-free lives dull, and those who are not depressed myopic. Embracing these pathologized sentiments is always an option when opting out fails.

Given the link between choice and construal, voluntarism may seem difficult to square with sensationalism. Construal is a very cognitive activity. We don't think of construal as impacting perception. I cannot reconstrue that green tomato as red, and thereby see it as ripe. On the other hand, there is a way of reconstruing that is very familiar in perceptual psychology. We can reconstrue by shifting attention. We cannot see green as red, in this way—there are constraints—but we can see a duck-rabbit as fuzzy or fowl. Ambiguous inputs are amenable to attentional alteration. The sting of the cold can be seen as painful or exhilarating by focusing on different aspects of our somatic response (the adrenal lift or the agonized grimace). Jamesians should not deny that cognitive construals can influence our emotions, but they can also insist that some construals are perceptual. By staring out of the air plane window and seeing the distant ground below, the phobic may exacerbate fear. But one can also stare at the beautiful clouds or feel the stability of the chair or the music in one's headphones. Perception is not passive. We chose where to look. Consequently, emotional voluntarism is not incompatible with sensationalism.

This brings us, at last, to purposivism. Can sensations be strategic? In his Appendix, Solomon (1980) notes that his (1973) discussion of purposes conflated emotions and their expressions. His example of the man who gets angry to avoid going out, might better be described as a man who expresses anger to avoid going out.

After all, had the emotion gone unexpressed, it would not have the desired effect. This adds a complication for standard forms of judgmentalism, since expression and emotion are divorced. If emotions are ordinary judgments, they can occur without changes in the body, and can thus easily exist without being expressed. For the Jamesian, expression and emotion are linked. Since emotions are bodily sensations, they will usually be accompanied by bodily changes, including expressions. Emotions will be perceivable to others, in posture, face, and vocal intonation. It would take effort to conceal anger. Since the body is perceivable, it follows that emotions convey information to others; they are fundamentally, even if unwittingly, communicative. They are fundamentally social. This fits well with the strategic view of emotions. Bodily changes serve a dual function. They prepare us for action, but they also indicate to others that we are so prepared. We bear our teeth, we cower, and we stare lustfully. Every smile is a welcome sign, and every tear a supplication. Since these communicative displays influence others, emotions cannot be understood without taking their social impact seriously. The question, "Why did you feel X?" is often best answered by asking what effect you wanted to have on another person. It is unsurprising that the unconscious mechanisms that determine when we feel doomed or delighted take this into account, and the likelihood of an emotional episode may depend on the extent to which its expression will advance our ends. This Solomonian insight invites a Jamesian implementation.

In summary, the major planks of Solomon's judgmentalism can be accommodated within a Jamesian framework. The resulting sensational judgmentalism differs from James's own account (he failed to emphasize the meaning of emotions), but it preserves the idea that emotions are sensations of bodily changes. They are that, but also much more. Solomon's account can be seen as a set of desiderata that any theory must meet. These may look incompatible with the Jamesian approach, but there is room for a reconciliation.

## Solomon's Wisdom

By way of conclusion, I want to suggest that the hybrid I have been describing may not be far from Solomon's own considered account of the emotions. As a newcomer to emotion research, I was inclined to interpret Solomon as the archrival of James. That impression was fuelled by Solomon's explicit critiques of the standard sensationalist program, but also by a prejudice I brought with me in thinking about the nature of judgments. Trained in contemporary philosophy of mind, I had come to think that anyone who talks about judgments must be imaging something like sentences in a language of thought. On prevailing views, a judgment is a sentence in the head. So, on reading his claim that emotions are judgments, I assumed that Solomon must have a sentential view about the passions, a view that I found difficult to digest. But this impression was based on a mistake. The sentential theory of thought was not the default for Solomon, who was coming out of the continental tradition. Heidegger compares thinking to building, and Merleau-Ponty tries to collapse the distinctions between thinking and perceiving, and between perceiving and acting. It is therefore a mistake to assume that Solomon's account is incompatible with an embodied view of the emotions simply because he equates emotions with judgments.

This possibility—that emotional judgments might be embodied—is already intimated in some of Solomon's early work. Though he criticized James in his 1973 and 1976 discussions, his return to these themes in 1980 underscores the fact that emotional judgments are judgments of personal concern (Solomon 1973, 1976, 1980). The recognition of an offense that characterizes anger is not to be understood as the judgment, "What he said to me was offensive," but rather as the exclamation, "He offended me!" Here already, then, we see Solomon emphasizing that emotions are judgments of a special kind. They have heat, urgency, and a connection to the self that is distinctive. In thinking about the self here, one brings to mind Sartre's prereflective self-consciousness, not the symbolically mediated consciousness that underwrites explicit self-ascription. Or, perhaps, we might think of Merleau-Ponty, who insists that the self is the body. To recognize offensiveness in this personal way is to see it in some prereflective way as a concern for the embodied self.

Solomon's move toward embodiment culminates in his later discussions of the emotions, most explicitly in his 2003 re-visitation of the judgmentalist position (Solomon 2003). There, he likens the judgments that constitute emotions to embodied skills, citing both Merleau-Ponty and Ryle. He offers kinesthetic judgments as an analogy. When ascending a stairwell, the body judges the position of the next step. Most strikingly, he suggests that emotions may involve "judgments of the body," a term that anticipates the notion of embodied appraisals. Solomon humbly acknowledges that the body was underemphasized in his early explorations of passion, but he importantly keeps the core tenets of those early views intact. He does not abandon his judgmentalism, but rather fleshes it out, quite literally. The early work says little about what judgments are, and here, in his most considered treatment, we find Solomon saying that emotional judgments are somatic in nature. In other words, Solomon had arrived at something very much like the rapprochement that I have recommended here.

In late November 2006, I had the privilege of staging a public "debate" about the emotions with Solomon at the University of Pennsylvania, in his former hometown, Philadelphia. I came expecting a battle. I nervously anticipated a head-to-head clash with one of the most sophisticated cognitivists in the world, someone who had thought about the emotions for decades, a *sine qua non* for all of us in the field. I thought I might stand up for James, but also anticipated some bruising, and I was confident I would learn a lot. The last of these predictions was true, but I was wrong to expect a fight. As we conversed in that public setting, the differences between James and Solomon seemed to evaporate, and that was not because Solomon offered any concessions. He was not one to shy away or back down. Rather, it was because his theory did not match the caricature I had sketched in my mind. Under Solomon's influence, I was prepared to admit that James underestimated the intelligence of emotions, and Solomon had long appreciated that standard cognitivism underestimated the body. There in Philadelphia, these two titans of emotion theory,

Solomon and James, found common ground. I came to be a mouthpiece for James, but that was unnecessary, for Solomon had already incorporated the body, and he had theorized how we might think with our hearts. I learned other things from Solomon that weekend, about art and life, and about humility. I saw an intellectual hero as a human being then, and even grander and more heroic in that capacity.

**Acknowledgment** My heartfelt thanks to Kathy Higgins for helpful feedback and for involving me in this celebration of Solomon's contributions to philosophy.

# References

Cannon, W. 1927. The James-Lange theory of emotions: A critical examination and an alternative theory. *American Journal of Psychology* 39: 106–124.

Damasio, A.R. 1994. *Descartes' error: Emotion reason and the human brain*. New York: Gossett/Putnam.

James, W. 1884. What is an emotion? *Mind* 9: 188–205.

Laird, J. 1984. The real role of facial response in the experience of emotion: A reply to Tourangeau and Ellsworth, and others. *Journal of Personality and Social Psychology* 47: 909–917.

Philippot, P., C. Chapelle, and S. Blairy. 2002. Respiratory feedback in the generation of emotion. *Cognition and Emotion* 16: 605–627.

Prinz, J.J. 2004. *Gut reactions: A perceptual theory of emotion*. New York: Oxford University Press.

Prinz, J.J. 2005. Are emotions feelings? *Journal of Consciousness Studies* 12: 9–25.

Prinz, J.J. 2012. *The conscious brain: How attention engenders experience*. New York: Oxford University Press.

Solomon, R.C. 1973. Emotions and choice. *The Review of Metaphysics* 27: 20–41.

Solomon, R.C. 1976. *The passions*. New York: Doubleday.

Solomon, R.C. 1980. Appendix to "Emotions and choice". In *Explaining emotions*, ed. A. Rorty, 271–276. Berkeley: University of California Press.

Solomon, R.C. 2003. Thoughts and feelings: What is a 'cognitive theory' of the emotions and does it neglect affectivity? In *Philosophy and the emotions*, ed. A. Hatzimoysis, 1–18. Cambridge: Cambridge University Press.

Zajonc, R.B., S.T. Murphy, and M. Inglehart. 1989. Feeling and facial efference: Implications of the vascular theory of emotion. *Psychological Review* 96: 395–416.

# Chapter 2
# Biology and Existentialism

Ronald de Sousa

**Abstract** Robert Solomon identified himself as an existentialist, but he did not, unlike some of the key figures associated with that stance, regard it as a reason not to be keenly interested in scientific approaches to emotions and to human life in general. Existentialism is actually an entirely appropriate philosophy for one that takes human beings as biological entities, in which the invention of language results in conversation, debate, and the consequent creation of new and evolving values.

There would seem to be little in common between existentialism, with its affirmation of the absolute freedom of human agents, and the biological view of human reality, with its connotations of determinism, reductionism, and denial of transcendence. But when both are rightly interpreted the latter can, with suitable qualifications, be seen as arising from the former. That is my message in a nutshell.

The tremendous breadth of Solomon's philosophical passions is, of course, attested by the enormous variety of topics he addressed in his books, teaching, and articles. More poignantly, it is attested by the fact that he is probably the only person whose expertise encompassed those of all the contributors to this volume. But it is also beautifully exhibited in the single so-called "field" I shared with him, the philosophy of emotions. To me, emotions are a great topic not just because emotions are, as Bob often pointed out, what life is *all about,* but also because on the theoretical side the study of emotions encompasses pretty much everything: if you are interested in nearly everything in philosophy, you will be interested in emotion because that brings it all in. A look at Bob's anthology of "classics" in the philosophy of emotions, *What is an Emotion* (Solomon 2003; first published as Solomon and Calhoun 1984), illustrates this nicely. I am using that book as a teaching tool at the moment,

R. de Sousa (✉)
Department of Philosophy, University of Toronto,
170 St. George Street, #424, Toronto, ON, Canada M5R 2K7
e-mail: sousa@chass.utoronto.ca

K. Higgins and D. Sherman (eds.), *Passion, Death, and Spirituality,*
Sophia Studies in Cross-cultural Philosophy of Traditions and Cultures 1,
DOI 10.1007/978-94-007-4650-3_2, © Springer Science+Business Media Dordrecht 2012

and I'm again struck with the omnivorous excellence of his selections and the insight of his brief introductions. Bob is at once deeply sympathetic to the various classical accounts—Aristotle, Stoics, Descartes, Spinoza, Hume—and lucid in his analysis of how each needs complementation by the others. Particularly impressive is the way that Bob managed to assimilate the scientific literature on emotions—from evolutionary theory, anthropology and brain science to psychology—and take stock of its importance to the philosophical perspective that was most deeply in tune with his own philosophical temperament, i.e. existentialism.

Many of us will remember Bob's deeply felt plea for existentialism, not only in some of his books and articles, but also in the movie *Waking Life*. I think that through all the sophistication of a professional philosopher's life, existentialism remained his central philosophy of life. Many philosophers nowadays—including me—are left somewhat embarrassed and uncharacteristically mute when non-philosophers ask, "You are a philosopher—so what is *your* philosophy?" Bob's response, I think would be unhesitatingly to answer: "I'm an existentialist." And in a way, perhaps, I want to say I am one too, though I feel I sadly lack the credentials. I have always been more inclined than he was to take a biologically deterministic view. As I will try to explain, however, one can be a determinist reductionist, (and even a genetic determinist, which I am not) and still be an existentialist.

It must be acknowledged that the more extreme Sartrian doctrines about freedom do face some problems exacerbated by findings in neuroscience. Bob Solomon, unlike Sartre, did not, as far as I know, write philosophy exclusively under the influence of corydrane; and I think he would have been willing to renounce the literal interpretation of those more extreme doctrines, because they simply do not accord with the facts of life. Nevertheless, and this is what I want to argue, I think that Bob was right to be an existentialist, and that existentialism is not only compatible with a broadly biological vision of who we are, but a corollary of a certain conception of our biology.

It is a biological fact about us that we transcend biology.

This appears to be a paradox, and indeed people have taken it to be so. Witness a review by a prominent intellectual journalist, Leon Wieseltier, of Dennett's recent book *Breaking the Spell* (Dennett 2006), in which he accuses Dennett of contradicting himself. Wieseltier begins by quoting Dennett:

> Like other animals... we have built-in desires to reproduce and to do pretty much whatever it takes to achieve this goal.... But we also have creeds, and the ability to transcend our genetic imperatives.

Wieseltier comments: "And then more, in the same fine antideterministic vein: 'This fact does make us different'" (Wieseltier 2006)

Notice first in passing that the smooth passage from the idea that we are "different" to the idea of "anti-determinism" is a complete non-sequitur. In the sense intended by Dennett, "transcendence" has strictly nothing to do with determinism.

Wieseltier goes on:

> Then suddenly there is this: "But it is itself a biological fact, visible to natural science, and something that requires an explanation from natural science."... Dennett does not see that he has taken his humanism back. Why is our independence from biology a fact of biology?

And if it is a fact of biology, then we are not independent of biology. If our creeds are an expression of our animality, if they require an explanation from natural science, then we have not transcended our genetic imperatives. The human difference, in Dennett's telling, is a difference in degree, not a difference in kind—a doctrine that may quite plausibly be called biological reductionism (Wieseltier 2006).

But Wieseltier has entirely missed the point. Let me try to explain the mild paradox that has apparently stumped the refined literary mind of Dennett's critic.

In emulation of Bob's broad-minded interest in everything, including religion, let me begin by citing Genesis. The story of Genesis is about the expulsion from the Garden of Eden, earned by Adam and Eve by eating the fruit of the tree of knowledge of right and wrong. We can take the Garden of Eden to be the garden of nature. To be sure, the study of nature might well dissuade anyone from thinking of it as a paradise. Nature is better described as an amoral hell. "Red in tooth and claw" is an understatement: nature was a nasty business long before there was a tooth or a claw to be reddened. In any case, whatever happens in nature, in all its diversity, is determined by just one quasi-teleological principle: that is, simply, the reproduction of patterns. Those patterns are mostly genes; but current controversies about epigenesis, about developmental systems, and more generally the variety of things that can be understood to be inherited are entirely irrelevant to the general point that nothing exists but what has been allowed to pass through the filter of natural selection. What passes through the filter of natural selection is what has been able in the past to reproduce. And those, in turn, are abstract patterns, and not individual organisms— for the simple reason that individual organisms never do survive.

So expulsion from the Garden of Eden represents the break between the natural teleology of reproduction and the individual teleology that is engendered by the capacity to create and formulate individual goals. The point is perhaps best conveyed by comparing it to something David Velleman wrote, which I first thought was much the same idea, but which I now think is better described as its converse or perhaps even its contrary.

On this interpretation, the reason why Adam and Eve weren't ashamed of their nakedness at first is not that their anatomy was perfectly subordinate to the will but rather that they didn't have an effective will to which their anatomy could be insubordinate. In acquiring the idea of making choices contrary to the demands of their instincts, however, they would have gained, not only the effective capacity to make those choices, but also the realization that their bodies might obey their instincts instead, thus proving insubordinate to their newly activated will. Hence the knowledge that would have activated their will could also have opened their eyes to the possibility of that bodily recalcitrance which Augustine identified as the occasion of their shame (Velleman 2001: 34).

I think this is the converse rather than a parallel to the point I'm making, because what I want to stress is not the discovery of the body's recalcitrance to the will, but of the will's recalcitrance in the face of the demands of the genes. As I see it, the body and the will are, or ought to be, on the same side, *against* the tyranny of the genes. And the way I see it, the capacity to form projects that might undermine the genes' replication is the first existential moment. Velleman might be right, at some allegorical level, about the genesis of shame; but I would rather see the expulsion from the Garden as a moment of triumph. From the moment Adam and Eve stepped out of the Garden, we were destined to invent birth control, democracy and individualism.

The capacity to form individual goals is originally part of our biological inheritance. It constitutes what Keith Stanovich (2004) has referred to as long-leashed methods of serving the reproductive imperative. But the important point comes with the development of language, and perhaps, as Daniel Gilbert (2006) has argued, very specifically with the capacity to imagine the future. The ability to think explicitly about one's individual and collective future is entirely different from the capacity of desiring something, despite the fact that satisfaction of a desire is always in the future. With explicit deliberation, thought and emotion are no longer confined to the functional role they play in disposing the body to serve the replication of genes. They are now in the service of individual goals. But those individual goals are not elaborated by individuals in isolation: rather—and this is why language is essential—they result from the elaboration of values in discussion and confrontation. That, in a nutshell, is how it comes to be that it is a biological fact that we can transcend biology. Or to put that in different terms—though I'll take some of this back in a moment—it can be argued that the core doctrine of existentialism, that in humans existence precedes essence, can be seen to follow from biological fact.

To get into a bit more detail about how this works, let me return to the emotions, and to Bob. For this whole drama of the subversion and enactment of biological destiny at the level of individual choice is played out principally on the stage of our emotional life.

When I first encountered Bob's work, it was through the bracing shock of his doctrine about emotion and choice, in his paper of that name (Solomon 1973). As so often happens with the most fruitful philosophical paradoxes, the cascade of paradoxes that Bob dared to put forward in that early paper generates some deep truths.

Solomon claims in that paper that we are *responsible* for our emotions; that emotions are *judgments*, and that emotions are *chosen*. The cascade of paradoxes starts with the first assertion, continues in the tension between the latter two claims, and is heightened by the fact that both the latter claims individually seem counterintuitive. So there are three paradoxical assertions:

1. Some judgments are chosen.
2. Emotions are chosen.
3. Emotions are judgments.

Let me take these one by one.

1. Judgments, it would seem, are not voluntary, and so cannot be chosen. It is only in very special circumstances that we can make sense of the idea that we "choose to believe" something. When we do speak of "choosing to believe," that phrase is usually intended as some sort of idiom or figure of speech that is not intended to be taken literally. Thus 'I choose to believe what you say' usually means that I don't believe it but that I will act, for the moment, as if I did. And 'I can't

believe it' usually means that I do believe it, but find it surprising. For most ordinary beliefs, choosing to believe is not an option.

But there is something one can say in favor of the first paradoxical claim. It goes back to Descartes, the first existentialist, who thought the will could outstrip the understanding, and sought by that doctrine to let God off the hook and show that humans were to blame for their own mistakes. And I think that in a way that is right. If I am (reasonably or unreasonably) convinced that p is true, *I cannot not believe it*. But that is not because I *cannot believe at will*. For in this case I *do* will to believe it. What the case shows is that although I can believe at will, I cannot *want* at will. But that's enough to blame me, if the fact that I am doing what I want is a sufficient condition of being responsible for what I have done.

2. The second point applies specifically to the kinds of evaluative judgments to which Solomon assimilates emotions. Where choosing to believe is not an option, choosing to *assert* something of which one is less than certain may indeed be a choice. And Solomon's insight, inspired by Sartre, is precisely that in many cases having an emotion is more like choosing to assert something than choosing to believe it. For various more or less Machiavellian reasons, we may commit ourselves to an *expression* of emotion, and by so doing—that much seems right about William James's equally paradoxical yet opposite doctrine—we bring it about that we really experience the emotion. But in some sense we did it on purpose.

3. So what of the doctrine that emotions are judgments? Of all the doctrines Solomon asserted, this is probably the one that has been subjected to the heaviest criticism. Several of the heaviest hitters are in this volume, and I wouldn't presume to go over the same ground. I will mention only one more recent essay in the new (and to some still suspect) field of "neuroethics." The essay in question is by Adina Roskies, who provides a very neat demonstration of the relevance of fMRI evidence to the question of what she calls "ethical internalism" (Roskies 2006). Ethical internalism is, I think, more or less equivalent to the view that you cannot *really* believe that *p*, where *p* is an evaluative judgment, without some degree of commitment to behavior consonant with the judgment. No evidence can, of course *prove* that this is true, since it is partly a matter of what *counts* as endorsing such a judgment. But the brain evidence shows that all *other* features of what are normally called belief or judgment are present in cases where the behavioral commitment is entirely lacking. If the judgment is intact in every other way when the presence of certain differences in brain response indicates a lack of motivation, it simply begs the question to claim that a judgment without motivation was not "really" endorsed.

Still, I think the claim that emotions are judgments is an important insight. Judgments are elaborated in the crucible of discussion and debate; and to the extent that emotions are belief dependent, they too, however much they have their roots in biology, are products both of culture and of the individual stories in which each person's repertoire has been forged. The thought was well expressed by Catherine Lutz:

> Talk about emotions is simultaneously talk about society—about power and politics, about kinship and marriage, about normality and deviance…. The calling up of a scenario

by the speaker of emotion words is done in particular contexts for particular ends, to negotiate aspects of social reality and to create that reality. (Lutz 1988, quoted in Solomon 2003: 144, 147).

Some of the central ideas, or better, attitudes of existentialism can be seen as fitting "naturally"—the word is apt—into a biological perspective. But I don't want to go too far. I remain committed to a fundamentally biological picture of our individual destinies. It was Heraclitus, I think, who first said *character is destiny*. We have all known people whose lives were blighted by certain traits of character that restricted their own vision of the choices available to them. It is one thing to make choices that one will regret, another to be devoid of acceptable alternatives; but perhaps most tragic of all is to be prevented from seeing that right before one is an alternative that might provide a way out of the impasse. Circumstances always constrain, of course, as well as afford opportunities. This leads to a more tragic version of the failure of self-fulfillment, in that an observer constantly has the impression that the solution to her friend's problem is right before her eyes. Like a spectator of classic tragedy, one is moved to shout warnings and advice, but the actor is behind a fourth wall and cannot hear us in her rush to perdition.

A surprising amount is becoming known, for example, about the path from genes through neurotransmitters to the temperamental dispositions measured by the five "dimensions" of personality theory: extraversion, conscientiousness, neuroticism, openness, and agreeableness. As noted in a recent issue of *New Scientist*, each of these five independent dimensions of personality varies along a continuum, so that together they generate a vast five-dimensional space, an array of points each of which is highly predictive of the probable responses of persons at each point in that space. But none of these predictions is ever likely to amount to more than a statistical probability.

The very same thing is true if we entirely discard the notion of character. Consider the provocative claims made by Doris (2002) on the basis of such research as Milgram's obedience experiments or the "good Samaritan" experiment (Darley and Batson 1973). These are adduced as evidence for the claim that circumstances, not character, determine responses. But in both cases what is shown is not that there is no variance, but that one prediction is a better bet than another. That leaves, in the Milgram experiment, over 30% of subjects who did *not* conform to the situationist prediction, and at least 10% of subjects whose behavior could not be explained by their situation in the Darley and Batson experiment. The right conclusion, we should perhaps infer, is not that there is no such thing as character, but that character is *rare*. But we knew that, come to think of it, without benefit of psychology or neuroscience. And we have already seen that character is in the same boat: only probabilities are warranted, not certain predictions.

Should we then claim, like modern "soft determinists" and Lucretius before them, that the leeway allowed by those statistical generalizations constitutes the interstices of determinism, the narrow space within which free will benefits from indeterminism? I do not believe it for a moment: for like Hume I believe that the space left open by determinism is merely that of randomness or chance, and therefore wholly unhelpful to the seeker of a home for free will.

And yet, I still think that the "merely statistical" character of the predictability afforded by social science does make room for the spirit of existentialism. This is because it is *predictability* and not *determinism* that is relevant to the Sartrean paradox that we are "condemned to be free." In the absence of ironclad predictability, we have no recourse but to decide, and we have no way of approaching decision other than by deliberating. Deliberation involves *thinking through consequences*, which in turn consists in imagining and reasoning about outcomes. As Daniel Gilbert rightly says in his recent book, the distinguishing essence of the human species is its capacity to *think about the future*. That, in normal circumstances, is done communally, by debating, disputing, arguing, and confronting one's individual emotional responses to those of our fellow humans. And that, as I have suggested, is what has allowed us to escape from the nightmare of Eden, and become human; but we need to concede that we have not all escaped, and that none of us have escaped entirely. Not everyone can be an existentialist. Bob was lucky to be more fully one than most. Lucky, too, were those who both chanced to meet him and enjoyed just the right temperament to benefit from his teaching and example.

# References

Darley, J.M., and C. Batson. 1973. From Jerusalem to Jericho: A study of situational and dispositional variables in helping behavior. *Journal of Personality and Social Psychology* 27: 100–108.

Dennett, D.C. 2006. *Breaking the spell: Religion as a natural phenomenon*. London/New York: Allen Lane/Viking.

Doris, J.M. 2002. *Lack of character: Personality and moral behavior*. Cambridge/New York: Cambridge University Press.

Gilbert, D.T. 2006. *Stumbling on happiness*. New York: Knopf.

Lutz, C. 1988. *Unnatural emotions*. Chicago: University of Chicago Press.

Roskies, A. 2006. A case study of neuroethics: The nature of moral judgment. In *Neuroethics: Defining the issues in theory, practice, and policy*, ed. J. Illes, 17–32. New York: Oxford University Press.

Solomon, R.C. 1973. Emotion and choice. *The Review of Metaphysics* 17: 20–41.

Solomon, R.C. (ed.). 2003. *What is an emotion? Classic and contemporary readings*, 2nd ed. New York: Oxford University Press.

Solomon, R.C., and C. Calhoun (eds.). 1984. *What is an emotion? Classic readings in philosophical psychology*. New York: Oxford University Press.

Stanovich, K. 2004. *The robot's rebellion: Finding meaning in the age of Darwin*. Chicago: Chicago University Press.

Velleman, D. 2001. The genesis of shame. *Philosophy & Public Affairs* 30(1): 27–52.

Wieseltier, L. 2006. The God genome. *New York Times*, 19 Feb 2006.

# Chapter 3
# Between Existentialism and the Human Sciences: Solomon's Cognitive Theory of the Emotions

David Sherman

**Abstract** This paper critically articulates the evolution of Solomon's claim that we choose our emotions and are responsible for them, which was one of the principal ideas in his thought. Solomon's early existential account of the emotions held this view in an unqualified manner, and in this way it went beyond even Sartre's view of the emotions, despite the latter's notorious commitment to the idea of absolute freedom and responsibility. It is argued that, as with Sartre's position, Solomon's early position suffered from an indeterminacy problem. As his thought evolved, Solomon interrogated his earlier position in terms of the work that was being done in biological psychology and anthropology, and the latter in particular prompted him to modify it. Thus, he began to privilege the idea of emotional integrity, which subsumed his freedom and responsibility claim. It is argued that with this move, Solomon adopted a form of social constructivism that was not sufficiently critical in nature. Yet, it is ultimately argued, Solomon's work is best understood as emphasizing the imperatives of the practical standpoint, which necessarily presupposes both freedom and responsibility, and that his work constitutes a warning to a culture that is in the process of falsifying both.

Robert Solomon was a gifted philosopher and a remarkable human being. There are, no doubt, other philosophers about whom this could be said, but what made Solomon particularly unique was the way in which his philosophical approach and his personal character mutually informed one another. Born with a severely defective heart that threatened to end his life at virtually any time (and ultimately did), he not only refused to let this illness define him but also (with the possible exception of minimal prudence) refused to capitulate to it in any way. Such a position, in the face of the dismal prognosis that the medical sciences were offering, dovetails nicely with

D. Sherman (✉)
Department of Philosophy, The University of Montana, Missoula, MT, 59812-5780, USA
e-mail: david.sherman@umontana.edu

the existentialist tenets that he embraced, and these tenets, in turn, constituted the underpinnings of his so-called cognitive approach to the philosophy of emotion, which in the early 1970s was nothing short of groundbreaking. As is well known, it was Solomon's early view that we choose our emotions and are responsible for them; and, although he later hedged his bets by virtue of the latest findings in biological psychology and cultural anthropology, it was a view from which he never retreated. For more than 30 years, some variation on the idea that we are responsible for our emotions was one of the principal ideas in his thought.

Although, broadly speaking, I agree with Solomon's account of the emotions, namely, that they are a cognitive, evaluative, and intentional phenomenon for which we are responsible, I do not buy into it unreservedly. In particular, I have certain concerns relating to the foundations of his claim that we are responsible for our emotions (the "responsibility thesis"). I shall proceed by tracking the movement of Solomon's thought in terms of his commitment to the responsibility thesis, and in the process I shall address certain problems that the particulars of his account raise. Along the way, I also intend to consider a few other problems in the philosophy of emotion that have a direct bearing on his account, and I hope to address these problems in a manner that is reasonably consistent with the spirit (if not always the letter) of it.

To understand Solomon's account of the emotions it is necessary to begin with its existentialist underpinnings. Two of Sartre's works in particular, *The Emotions: Outline of a Theory* and *Being and Nothingness*, clearly had a powerful impact on Solomon's thought. A third work, Heidegger's *Being and Time*, also played an important, although less obvious, role, for aside from Heidegger's influence on Sartre, in one important respect Solomon implicitly does an end run on Sartre to draw on Heidegger more directly.

In *The Emotions*, Sartre attacks the psychological theories of James, Janet, and Freud, and mostly for the same reason: James' physiological view that emotions are only the feelings experienced by virtue of certain changes in one's bodily state, Janet's behavioral view that emotions are to be understood in terms of organized (although inferior) behaviors adopted in response to setbacks, and Freud's psychoanalytic view that emotions result from repressed drives (what Solomon calls "the hydraulic model"), all assume a third-person, scientific standpoint that views emotions in causal terms. For Sartre they all fail to address what an emotion means *for* consciousness, and therefore fail to capture the essence of the phenomenon. Equipped with Husserl's phenomenology (albeit while rejecting certain crucial Husserlian commitments, such as the concept of the transcendental ego), Sartre maintains that emotions are not passively undergone but are conscious, intentional, meaningful acts that are meant to bring about specific ends. Crucially, Sartre makes abundantly clear, as does Solomon later on, that emotions usually start as unreflective acts of consciousness and that they usually do not leave the unreflective plane. Neither the "I" (empirical ego) that constitutes the emotion nor the intentional object that is the occasion for the emotion is explicitly thematized: to be unreflective is to be conscious "non-thetically," a position that Sartre will subsequently flesh out in *Being and Nothingness*. Thus, contrary to the charge that is often brought against cognitive approaches to the emotions, an emotion need not be propositional in nature (although, as an evaluative judgment, it will have an underlying propositional content).

Despite these breakthroughs, Solomon thinks that Sartre does not go far enough in *The Emotions*. In particular, he rejects Sartre's claim that emotions are "magical transformations of the world," which means that they are ways of coping with the world when the ends that one wants to bring about cannot be realized in an instrumentally rational fashion. When confronted with a recalcitrant world, consciousness "magically" transforms itself and the world to relieve the stress of unfulfilled desires. According to Solomon, however, emotions are not merely degraded ways of interacting with the world that result from reconstituting it when the chips are down: among other things, they are qualitatively broader in scope and they are world constituting as an initial matter. Solomon's move here, as I shall discuss momentarily, is made possible by Heidegger's account of moods, as Solomon himself will acknowledge.

In the meantime, however, there is another important point to be made: in *The Emotions*, Sartre's description of the emotions consistently includes a bodily component. He says that "consciousness, plunged into this magical world, draws the body along with it, insofar as the body is belief," and that "in emotion it is the body which, directed by consciousness, changes its relations with the world in order that the world may change its qualities" (Sartre 1976: 86, 61). Accordingly, in his analyses of particular emotions, such as fear and sadness (and, indeed, the phenomenon of "sour grapes"), he invariably offers rich phenomenological descriptions of the various bodily changes that take place with the onset of the emotion. Sartre's rejection of Descartes's substance dualism is already clearly in evidence, and he seems to think that there is an inextricable relationship between the kinds of intentional, evaluative judgments that constitute the emotions and bodily feelings, which is a relationship that, at least early on, Solomon clearly rejects. I shall consider this shortly, but Solomon is surely right to reject the overly rationalistic premise that underlies Sartre's account of the emotions here, namely, the idea that emotions distort our perception of the way the world actually is, which suggests that it can otherwise be objectively perceived in its brute, mind-independent givenness. Although Sartre will more or less reject this position in *Being and Nothingness*, it is not clear to me that his masterwork will have all that much of an impact on his understanding of the emotions themselves.

Unlike Sartre, whose account of the emotions is limited in scope and suggests that emotions are degraded cognitive forms that reconstitute an otherwise objectively perceivable world to resolve psychic tensions, Heidegger's account of moods appears to accord with two of Solomon's own deeply held commitments: they are broader in scope (indeed, they are universal inasmuch as all individuals, or, as Heidegger puts it, *Dasein,* are in some mood or other) and they do not reflect a deviation from a more objective way of perceiving the world but are the condition of cognitively opening up the world to us as an initial matter. Even pure scientific inquiry, which presupposes the independent existence of the objects to be investigated, depends on a prior mood that attunes us to the world in this particular way.

However, given Solomon's commitments, Heidegger's account of moods falls short in at least two respects. First, unlike emotions, moods do not have a particular object, but are generalized ways in which the world is apprehended. Depending on the mood, the world itself can appear fearsome, hostile, or rich with possibilities. Second, by virtue of Heidegger's virulently anti-subjectivist orientation, moods are not private, inner mental states or feelings but are public in nature: the mood of the collective (crudely, what Heidegger calls *das Man*) is the primary phenomenon, and an individual's mood more or less directly derives from it, albeit perhaps with certain peculiar variations by virtue of one's particular social role or personal experiences. This account, notwithstanding its promise in certain respects, leaves little room for the robust account of the emotions that Solomon pursues, since one's emotions would appear to be little more than a function of the public mood, and the public mood, in turn, is something for which no one in particular is responsible. Still, what is crucial about Heidegger's conception of moods is that it opens the door to Solomon's contention that emotions are world constituting in nature, as Solomon himself subsequently acknowledges: "In *The Passions*, I... developed a (quasi-Heideggerian) notion of what I call surreality" (Solomon 2003: 20).

Now, more than any other single work, it is Sartre's *Being and Nothingness*, with its unrelenting commitment to absolute freedom and responsibility, that is the source from which Solomon takes his early cues. In *Being and Nothingness*, Sartre offers a phenomenologically driven ontology to ground this commitment, but the book raises a number of questions for Solomon's thesis, two of which I shall discuss here. First, *Being and Nothingness* mentions the emotions only once, and it does not carefully consider them at all. Roughly speaking, Sartre offers an expansive conception of the Self that implicitly includes but substantially transcends the emotional consciousness with which he had previously dealt. If I understand his position correctly, Solomon views some subset of the myriad commitments that constitute the self—commitments that go to what we love, hate, or envy, or what angers, embarrasses, shames or depresses us—as emotions, and they are emotions whether or not we have particular bodily feelings with respect to them at any particular moment. I shall suggest that Solomon does not need to uncouple bodily feelings from the emotion to make good the commitment that ultimately motivates him here. Second, and more importantly, I shall argue that the conception of the self that Sartre provides raises serious problems for Solomon's responsibility thesis, or at least to the extent it draws on *Being and Nothingness*. And, to the extent it does not, Solomon is still left with the problem of explaining the basis on which he attributes Sartrean-like responsibility for our emotions.

What Solomon rightly finds so troubling about James's feelings-based theory of the emotions is that it loses the intentional, evaluative character of the emotion. According to James, "I am sad because I cry," but, as most philosophers who work in this field are now inclined to say, I am sad not because I cry but because I find some state of affairs in the world saddening (irrespective of whether they are saddening because I find them sad, as Solomon contends, or I am sad because they are saddening, which, as I understand it, is Ronald de Sousa's position). Indeed, I might well be sad about this state of affairs without crying at all. My sadness might be reflected in an entirely different set of underlying biological changes, which do not give rise to tears but to a different set of bodily feelings, and, at least in terms of the way in which we conventionally use the term, I might be sad without any perceivable changes in my underlying biological state at all. Without perceivable changes, I do not have feelings, and therefore on a feelings-based account I do not have an emotion. This is the position that Solomon rejects. Crucially, however, this position, depending on how it is pitched, does not have to be understood in James's terms. It surely is not inconsistent to claim that an evaluative judgment with respect to a state of affairs in the world and a consequent set of bodily feelings are both necessary conditions of an emotion. Understood in this way, an emotion comes about with bodily feelings that arose from evaluative judgments of a certain type. This seems to be Sartre's position in *The Emotions*, and, albeit with refinements, it is a position that can be maintained without too much damage to Solomon's account.

Solomon's rejection of the idea that emotions essentially include feelings seems to be motivated by his view that the necessary preconditions for emotions so understood are thereby given short shrift, and in this respect I think that he is right. Those philosophers who identify emotions with feelings but recognize that there is more to the story than James allows frequently lump together the necessary conditions for the feeling under the label "disposition," but this does not capture the importance of these so-called dispositions or their relationship to what is deemed the emotion proper. Thus, Solomon says that it is strange to argue that love is not really an emotion, but rather only a disposition to have emotions, because there are no peculiarly short-term physiological responses that correspond to it. "Many emotions are enduring processes," and one is not in an ongoing state of arousal throughout these processes: "Long-term love, 'simmering' resentment, and 'cold,' vengeful anger seem to me to be cases in which the presumption that all emotions are episodic is extremely doubtful." To say that these are only dispositions, Solomon holds, "is outrageous to common sense and trivializes the role of human emotions in human psychology, motivation, and life… Many of the emotions, especially the more morally interesting ones, are processes… and they are processes within which we make various choices and thus have considerable control" (Solomon 2003: 202–203). This captures the crux of Solomon's complaint, and as against those philosophers who view everything prior to the actual feeling (and therefore emotion) as a mere prelude, he has a good point.

But it seems to me that the nub of the problem here is that we have an impoverished language for characterizing the diverse phenomena that are potentially subsumable under the term "emotion," which is stretched too thin in its conventional usage and is compressed too much even by those philosophers who equate an emotion with a feeling but will grant that evaluative judgments are dispositions that constitute a necessary precondition for the feeling. From a phenomenological standpoint, neither one of these positions will do. On the one hand, subsuming "cold, vengeful anger" and hot, blood-boiling, head-pounding anger under "emotion" (or perhaps even "anger") does not sufficiently capture the palpable differences between these two phenomena; on the other hand, depicting bodily feelings as the essence of an emotion with little more than a perfunctory nod in the direction of so-called dispositions does not sufficiently capture the way in which these phenomena are unified.

To use Solomon's phrase, an emotion (however it is ultimately defined) ought to be understood in terms of an "enduring process," and resolving the question of what an "emotion" is or at what point in this process we ought to slap on this label should be deemed less important than offering a highly nuanced analysis that both differentiates and unifies the various stages that go into constituting it. Under these circumstances, the cost to Solomon's account of viewing an emotion strictly in terms of bodily feelings that arise from evaluative judgments may be little more than a terminological one, since a proper understanding of the world-constituting, world-orienting, meaning-conferring nature of those phenomena that do not rise to feelings but that Solomon and folk psychology were only too willing to call an emotion will have been achieved. It seems to me, moreover, that such a move actually supports Solomon's later moves.

During his last years, Solomon entertained the possibility that emotions might necessarily include certain feelings (see Solomon 2007: 232–244). Indeed, in "What is a 'Cognitive Theory' of the Emotions, and Does it Neglect Affectivity?," he acknowledges that "there are feelings, 'affects' if you like, critical to emotion, [b]ut they are not distinct from cognition or judgment, and they are not mere 'readouts' of processes going on in the body" (Solomon 2003: 192). With this statement, Solomon brings feelings into his account of the emotions without compromising his cognitive position. However, if he does not make the kinds of fine-grained distinctions to which I have referred (i.e., distinguishing the various stages that go into forming an emotion even if the emotion itself only arises with the feeling), then his commitment to the longer term aspects of the process could well get lost in the shuffle. To the extent that Solomon understands emotions in terms of "enduring processes," one can love, hate, or resent someone or something over a prolonged period of time without having this love, hate, or resentment manifest itself in an ongoing feeling, but if feelings are tethered to emotions, then the sorts of long term "emotions" (by whatever name) to which he is committed would tend to fall out of the story for the very reasons that motivate his attack on those who speak of these processes as mere dispositions.

The theoretical commitments that underlie Solomon's account of the emotions, and thus furnish the basis for his responsibility thesis, are themselves explained by the way in which he demarcates the relationship between the emotions and the Self. For Solomon, the emotions constitute neither irruptions into the Self nor even accretions to the Self; more fundamentally, the emotions are in large part the building blocks of the Self. As he says in *The Passions*: "The Self of concern is something more than [the facts used to describe it]; it, too, is *surreal*, constituted by us according to our values and interests... Every emotion is an act of self-creation, and the nature of emotion will remain incomprehensible without a theory of Self as background" (Solomon 1976: 84). As is the case with Sartre, while Solomon will have no truck with Heidegger's anti-subjectivist bent, his theory of the Self is nevertheless indebted to Heidegger to the extent that the substantive characteristics of the Self (as for Heidegger's *Dasein*) are drawn wholly from one's world and it is the emotionally valenced Self (like Heidegger's moods) that orients one to the world as an initial matter. The Self, in other words, is the most basic organizing principle: it structures one's perceptual field and it provides the reasons that prompt reflection. This is why Solomon speaks in terms of the *surreality* of the Self, which implies that the Self performs the same function for both him and for Sartre as (public) moods performed for Heidegger. In one vital respect, however, Solomon seems to side with Heidegger over Sartre: while Sartre, still committed to some variation of Husserl's phenomenological reduction, retains a standpoint from which to bracket the Self, Solomon does not. And while Sartre is unable to offer an adequate account of how this is done, which raises serious problems for his theory of the Self and, finally, his absolute freedom and responsibility thesis, his failure is instructive for making sense of the problems confronting Solomon's own responsibility thesis.

In *The Emotions*, Sartre says that there are only two ways in which consciousness can disengage itself from an emotion: "Freedom has to come from a purifying reflection or a total disappearance of the affecting situation" (Sartre 1976: 79). In terms of the question of agency, it is only the first that is germane, and as to it he further states: "The purifying reflection of the phenomenological reduction can perceive the emotion insofar as it constitutes the world in a magical form," although "ordinarily, we direct upon the emotive consciousness an accessory reflection which certainly perceives consciousness as consciousness, but insofar as it is motivated by the object" (Sartre 1976: 91).

Just as Sartre applies the distinction between a purifying reflection and an accessory reflection to the emotions in *The Emotions*, he applies this distinction to the Self in *Being and Nothingness*. Crucially, however, despite the fact that the Self is the emotional consciousness's putative successor, there is a basic structural difference: while an emotional consciousness is a corrupted form of consciousness, which implies there is a standpoint for the kind of (purifying) reflection that would enable consciousness to unshackle itself, the Self (like a mood, although originating with the individual) is omnipresent and a fundamental structure of our being. Thus, it is by no means clear from what standpoint a (purifying) reflection can get the traction to enable consciousness to call the Self that fundamentally orients it to the world into question. When he was confronted with this problem, Sartre acknowledged it and provided nothing more by way of clarification ("Is it possible to pass from an immediate consciousness to pure reflection? I know nothing about it..." (Sartre 1967: 142)).

Furthermore, on Sartre's theory, the Self, which is chosen early in one's life, is the result of an "initial choice," and this choice of oneself structures the field in which one's secondary and tertiary projects arise. Now, crucially, Sartre claims that this choice of oneself, as well as any subsequent choice of oneself that would supplant it (as a result of the inexplicable purifying reflection) is not based on reasons but on a spontaneous choice of oneself that is free precisely because it is made without reasons. This spontaneous choice is the ground not only of the Self but also, derivatively, every choice that follows from it, which is to say every choice that a person makes. With this theory of the Self, the absolute freedom and responsibility thesis remains ungrounded: we are free and responsible because of a spontaneous choice of one's Self for which the Self itself cannot be held responsible precisely it is what gives rise to the Self as an initial matter. In sum, then, all reflection would seem to be accessory, which means that all reflection is instrumental because it is trapped within the hierarchy of the Self's purposes, and to the extent a choice of one's Self is possible, the choice is made spontaneously and for no reason, which is exactly why it is deemed free. The basis for the kind of meaningful self-determination that the idea of absolute freedom and responsibility implies is nowhere to be found.

Now, Solomon's theory of the Self includes neither the concept of a purifying reflection nor the concept of an initial choice, and, given the problems that these concepts present, this is all to the good. Nevertheless, these concepts, even though they fail, reflect Sartre's attempt to furnish the basis for his absolute freedom and responsibility thesis and for a supporting theory of the Self. If Solomon's responsibility thesis is to be properly grounded, as the passage previously quoted from *The Passions* indicates it must ("every emotion is an act of self-creation, and the nature of emotion will remain incomprehensible without a theory of Self as background"), it is necessary for him to articulate such a theory, and on this count he seems to be of two minds: Earlier in *The Passions*, on the heels of his claim that a theory of the Self is required, Solomon emphasizes the fact that the Self is intersubjectively constituted, which, although largely true, does little to make sense of his robust responsibility thesis (see Solomon 1976: 83–107). For Heidegger and Sartre, in fact, this is the basis for the existential problem to which only the hazy concept of authenticity is the solution. Alternatively, in the final chapter of *The Passions*, "Self-Overcoming," Solomon emphasizes the demands of the practical standpoint, which I think is a more promising approach because it indicates why we must see ourselves as responsible for our emotions (i.e., why the vocabulary that goes along with the concept of emotional responsibility is not an optional one). Yet, this cannot ground the concept of emotional responsibility either, for it only enjoins us to act "as if," and even this injunction ultimately refers back to the society that would enable one to explicate it in these terms. And, finally, even if Solomon could offer some functional equivalent of the purifying reflection and a supporting theory of the Self, the problem that plagued Sartre's theory, that there are no reasons for the ultimate choice to which all other choices refer (i.e., the choice of the Self), would still remain. Under these circumstances, any meaningful sense of personal responsibility (emotional or otherwise) goes by the wayside, which reflects the limitations of a theory of the emotions that would ground itself *exclusively* in the existentialist approach.

During the 1980s and 1990s, Solomon further developed his existential theory of the emotions by considering its relationship to the latest research findings in cultural anthropology and biology (neurobiology and evolutionary biology), which led him to modify his theory with some degree of frequency. As early as 1980, he acknowledges that he had spoken "far too little about the sociocultural determinations of emotions" (Solomon 2003: 22); and, later on, he cautions that although the new research in neurobiology sacrifices the humanistic perspective with which his own approach to the emotions is concerned, this does not "mean that we can or should ignore the insights that this new research can provide to our understanding" (Solomon 2007: 5).

Although mediating his existential theory of the emotions by sociocultural and biological considerations forced Solomon to temper his responsibility thesis, I would argue that it was beneficial for two reasons: First, it prompts him to move beyond the indeterminacy problem that, at least implicitly, had plagued his earlier view. Biological and sociocultural determinations would now furnish the stuff that would help to make explainable whatever it is that we might mean by the idea of choosing one's Self. Second, and far more importantly, any viable account of freedom (not to mention any account that we would want to adopt in order to make sense of self-determination) cannot understand freedom in terms of "no reasons at all," even if this means that existentialism's conception of freedom must be deflated. This seems to me to be fairly close to self-evident. The genuine problem is not maintaining an untrammeled account of freedom in the face of these sociocultural and biological determinations, but rather retaining any reasonably robust account of freedom at all, which many philosophers who take their cues from natural scientists and social scientists are inclined to bury in any form. To retain some qualified version of the responsibility thesis, Solomon would have to navigate between the Scylla of existentialism and the Charybdis of the human sciences (whether in the form of psychobiological reductionism or social constructivism).

With respect to his account of the relationship between biology (neurobiology and evolutionary psychology) and his existential theory of the emotions, I think that Solomon mainly got it right. Biologically-based arguments concerning the emotions have frequently arisen within the context of the claim that there are universal emotions and that from this it follows there are basic (i.e., innate) emotions. But, as Solomon indicates, proponents of this view glide too quickly over the fact that these characterizations do not amount to the same thing: even if an emotion could be shown to be universal, it does not follow that it is basic, since it might arise due to the common conditions and circumstances of human life. (Conversely, even if there are basic emotions, it does not follow that they are also universal, since they might not be reflected in every culture by virtue of the particularities of its form of life.) Yet, more fundamentally, Solomon attacks evolutionary and neurological accounts because, as he puts it, both tend toward a "debilitating reductionism" that obfuscates the complex nature of the emotions: "An emotion is a holistic phenomenon, and any exclusive emphasis on one aspect or another tends to distort the phenomena under investigation. This is what reductionism tends to do, cognitive reductionism as well as biological reductionism" (Solomon 2003: 131–32).

As to those who offer an evolutionary account of the emotions, Solomon rightly asserts that the evidence they ordinarily adduce in support of their claim that emotions are the result of adaption is not conclusive, given that this evidence is generally consistent with other types of explanation. Thus, even if evolutionary psychology is somehow able to show that different cultures really do have the same emotion despite superficial differences, which is initially required to make good the universality condition, it is still ordinarily not in a position to juggle out all explanations that might be, at least in part, cultural in nature. There are always competing cultural narratives that would call into question the claim that certain emotions are genetically wired, which means that even if an emotion has evolved over time, it could be due to cultural selection rather than natural selection. (Aside from being an object lesson on "morality," I think that Nietzsche's account of "the last man" in *Thus Spoke Zarathustra* is designed to poke fun at this confusion, for it would seem that nature selects for thoroughgoing mediocrity: not too smart, not too passionate, not too courageous, not too adventurous, and a blinkered moderation in all things but moderation itself.) Finally, even if in theory the claim that certain basic emotions are the result of adaption is right, there is still the epistemic question of how one could identify such emotions, for "we have never met a raw, unembellished, basic emotion, one not covered over with the trappings of culture and experience" (Solomon 2003: 118).

This epistemic question applies equally to those who would offer a neurobiological account of the emotions, which contends that basic emotions are in some sense "prewired" in all human beings (thus meeting the universality requirement). Accordingly, Solomon references with approval those philosophers who emphasize the brain's plasticity, for even conceptually this calls into question the possibility of neatly separating the neurological and cultural contributions to an emotion. While clearly acknowledging that biology makes a crucial contribution to the emotions, Solomon rejects the "avocado-pear" model of emotion, which holds that all emotions include a basic neurological core plus some cognition. Changing the direction of a question that was once asked by James to accent the fundamental role of affect in emotion, he asks: "Once you subtract cognition and culture from an emotion, what is left?," and to this he responds "the answer is *nothing*, or at any rate nothing that would be identifiable as an emotion" (Solomon 2003: 133).

Solomon rightly rejects biological reductionism, but, at least with respect to the question of basic emotions, it seems to me (and I might well be wrong here) that he equivocates as to whether *any* scientific inquiries along these lines are useful. On the one hand, he asserts that "the notion of 'basic emotions' is neither meaningless nor so straightforward as its critics and defenders respectively argue, but it is historical and culturally situated and serves very different purposes in different contexts, including different research contexts"; on the other hand, he asserts that "the question is not only whether there are any such basic building blocks of emotion but also whether the search for them distorts rather than furthers our understanding of the emotions" (Solomon 2003: 123, 118).

I wholeheartedly agree with Solomon's first claim. All inquiries into basic emotions are socioculturally mediated, and, moreover, the different perspectives from which such inquiries are undertaken have different purposes that must be kept straight. (When these purposes are not kept straight difficulties can arise, such as occurred with the reception of E. O. Wilson's early work in sociobiology.) It is Solomon's second claim, which I think builds from the first, that concerns me. The fact of sociocultural mediation undoubtedly complicates matters, but in spite of the epistemic challenges this fact creates, challenges that are surely not limited to this area, the search for basic emotions, properly qualified, cannot help but further our understanding of the emotions. More importantly, like Solomon, my concern is mainly with "basic emotions as a moral category," and I think that scientific inquiries into basic emotions are important even in this regard. Solomon acknowledges that there are some experiential phenomena, such as panic, rage, and the startle response, that are "hardwired," but he refuses to call these emotions, and appropriately so. However, as I indicated earlier when discussing whether feelings should be considered an essential part of an emotion, I think that what is involved here is a terminological difference that needs to be transcended by a more nuanced analysis. Even if panic, rage, and the startle response do not rise to the level of an "emotion" strictly defined, they are arguably the forerunners of the emotions, and as such are not without their ethical implications; indeed, while the argument is a tricky one, and surely not one that I want to attempt here, I would suggest that because these forerunners of the emotions seem to be not only basic but also universal, they might get a kind of normative traction that full blown emotions, by virtue of their seeming cultural relativity, do not. For this reason, I disagree with Solomon's claim that basic emotions should be viewed only as those emotions that are basic to a particular culture due to the role they play in it (see Solomon 2003: 138–141).

This claim would seem to crack, if not altogether open, the door to social constructivism, which is clearly a temptation for cognitivist accounts of the emotions in particular. There might still be some wiggle room, however, for (as suggested earlier) even if basic emotions are only relative to a particular culture, it does not necessarily follow that there are no universal emotions, given that the particulars of "the human condition" might call forth a certain set of emotions in all cultures. Understood in this way, certain emotions might constitute something approaching what Heidegger referred to as an "existential." Now, Solomon does weigh in against social constructivism, or at least social constructivism in its more unalloyed forms, but he does so by asserting that "the idea that emotions are either *just* biological or *just* cultural is… unsustainable" (Solomon 2007: 261). Thus, while he agrees with social constructivism insofar as it contends that "every culture creates a language and a vocabulary for talking about emotion according to its needs and contingencies," he pulls back from social constructivism when he goes on to say that "it is not as if every culture creates its own emotions" (Solomon 2007: 261–262). Yet, crucially, I do not think that Solomon has a basis for circumventing social constructivism on biological grounds, for anything that would go beyond a fairly innocuous claim (e.g., our neurological or genetic structures are what give rise to the capacity to have an emotion) would appear to threaten the longstanding commitments that underlie his existential theory of the emotions. I shall not further pursue this argument here, but I shall consider, in concluding, the way in which his embrace of cultural determinations bears on his responsibility thesis.

Although Solomon retains his commitment to the responsibility thesis in his later works, he both grounds this commitment in a different fashion and rolls it into a somewhat more comprehensive one, a commitment to what he calls "emotional integrity." In "On the Passivity of the Passions," Solomon acknowledges that "the heavily existentialist notion of choice too readily suggests a problematic conception of freedom and responsibility," and in place of this "mysterious notion of agency" usually associated with the Kantian tradition (or at least certain interpretations of it), he argues for conceptions of freedom and responsibility that are understood in terms of "the 'fit' between an action (or an emotion) and the rest of a person's character, circumstances, and culture, including his or her reflection on these" (Solomon 2003:

204). Aiming to transcend the troubling notion that freedom and responsibility require an action or decision to be "the cause of itself," which is a variation of what I called the indeterminacy problem in his earlier account (as well as in Sartre's account of freedom and responsibility in *Being and Nothingness*), he now contends that "choice" is not "necessarily the best way to capture this sense of agency," but, rather, that "appropriateness is the truth of emotions"; and "appropriateness," in turn, refers back not only to "one's whole life and character," as Solomon reveals, but also to one's culture, as his approving reference to Aristotle's notion of "second nature" further attests (Solomon 2003: 205). In this way, cultural determinations become not only the stuff from which the Self is constituted but also, at least implicitly, the yardstick against which the Self (i.e., one's "character") and the probity of its actions (including its "mental acts") are measured.

I am not unsympathetic to Solomon's embrace of a neo-Aristotelian conception of ethics, which is concerned with "the cultivation of good character, including the 'right' emotions" (Solomon 2003: 196), but I do have certain reservations. For Aristotle, of course, the cultivation of good character (and therefore the "right" emotions) is contingent on having been brought up in a good *polis*, and a *polis* is good because it engenders the virtues, which are grounded in a biologically rooted account of human flourishing. Although, as history evidences, embracing a biologically grounded account of values is fraught with dangers, I think that there is something to Aristotle's naturalism, even if only viewed in a limiting fashion: within some unspecifiable range of less than optimal social arrangements, human beings are still able to adapt (though not without psychological and physiological costs), but at some point it becomes clear that a culture, along with the emotions that it venerates, is off the beam.

Yet, any standpoint from which even this minimal assessment might be made falls out of the picture on Solomon's neo-Aristotelian account, for as his analysis of the concept of basic emotions suggests, he is unwilling to ground his theory of character and emotion in a biological story. This position is reasonable enough, but by reinterpreting the concept of basic emotions in terms of those emotions that assume a basic role within a particular culture, he evidences a tendency to move in the direction of an anthropologically-oriented social constructivism, which tends to be relativistic in nature. This conclusion is supported by the fact that Solomon does not furnish the criteria by which one could judge a *polis* once the biological component of Aristotle's account is discarded. In some sense, then, while Solomon's theory of the emotions now accounts for the sociocultural determinations that are required to explain the choice of the Self and its emotions, it does not seek to account for a normative standpoint from which the culture, and therefore the Self and its emotions, can be called into question. Instead, the normative standpoint (or the "standpoint of critique") would seem to be coterminous with the concept of emotional integrity itself, which, as was the case with the purely existential approach (albeit for different reasons), tends to narrow the scope of inquiry to the individual himself.

In the concluding pages of *True to our Feelings*, Solomon elaborates on his concept of emotional integrity, and in my view it supports this conclusion. After stressing the importance of reflection for our emotional lives, as well as the important fact that reflection and emotion do not constitute two different levels but are dialectically related, he says that emotional integrity refers to the unity of one's emotional life; and this unity, he contends, does not relate to "consistency" (the ambition of all fundamentalisms) but to "the wise management of emotional conflicts in conjunction with one's heartfelt values" (Solomon 2007: 268). Crucially, according to Solomon, "this concept of emotional integrity is a version of the existentialist concept of *authenticity*," but it "does not have the individualistic implications of authenticity and has built into it the idea of social virtue as well as existential individuality" (Solomon 2007: 268). Solomon's objective here, to mediate the social and the existential, is a commitment that motivates a good deal of my own work, but, as I suggested above, I think that his notion of social virtue remains unmotivated normatively. For this reason, emotional integrity, as authenticity's successor, suffers from what I take to be its predecessor's most basic flaw, namely, some variation of what was called "the authentic torturer" problem, since "the wise management of emotional conflicts in conjunction with one's heartfelt values" also implicitly brackets the substance of one's emotional conflicts and, ultimately, one's heartfelt values.

In my opinion, the social moment requires a critical component, which is best evidenced by the early work of the Frankfurt School (through, roughly, Habermas's *Knowledge and Human Interests*). If sociocultural determinations are the stuff that constitutes the Self and its emotions, then the capacity to call into question, at least in some fashion, these sociocultural determinants is a necessary condition for any meaningful conception of emotional integrity, and, ultimately, any meaningful conception of emotional responsibility. To understand this problem, one need not get into some elaborate story about ideology and false consciousness here (although I believe this story is worth telling, notwithstanding the fact that it has been shunt aside by Habermas and his followers since Critical Theory's linguistic turn): simply asking whether most people would adopt their emotional conflicts, their heartfelt values, and ultimately the social virtues that inform them if they knew the sociocultural story about how they came to be suffices to make the point.

To be fair, however, I think that Solomon is less concerned with providing the proper grounding for his conception of emotional integrity and, ultimately, emotional responsibility then he is with sounding the warning bell for a culture that appears to be in the process of falsifying both. As he emphasizes in the conclusion to "On the Passivity of the Passions," although "one can look at the emotions from several different perspectives," he is content to "rest [his] case on practical and moral considerations," and in particular his belief that "theses about emotions tend to be self-confirming" (Solomon 2003: 232). This goes to the heart of the practical standpoint, and it is a standpoint whose non-negotiability Solomon is absolutely right to insist on. As he rightly contends in "The Politics of Emotion," "personal responsibility is an important piece of the emotions story, and any theory that does not face up to this is itself political" (Solomon 2003: 157). Even taking into account the sociocultural determinations that seem not only to inform but to overdetermine our emotional lives, it is still incumbent upon us to determine what our next move will be, and if we understand ourselves as responsible for what this move will be, then this understanding itself will have substantive (political) reverberations (see Williams 1995: 133). It is for this reason that the existentialist standpoint not only cannot but also should not be juggled out of the emotions story. Near the end of his career, well after his engagement with Marxism and the publication of *The Critique of Dialectical Reason*, Sartre made a remark in an interview titled "The Itinerary of a Thought" that well captures the long term movement of Solomon's thought no less than Sartre's own:

> For the idea which I have never ceased to develop is that in the end one is always responsible for what is made of one. Even if one can do nothing else besides assume this responsibility. For I believe that a man can always make something out of what is made of him. This is the limit I would today accord freedom: the small movement which makes of a totally conditioned social being someone who does not render back completely what his conditioning has given him. (Sartre 1979: 34–35)

**Acknowledgment** This paper constitutes a substantial rewrite of an earlier paper I gave at both the American Philosophical Association and the University of Auckland. The earlier paper, which was much shorter, was also more personal and less critical, which is to say it was much truer than this paper in terms of the way in which I actually thought about Bob Solomon. Because I would feel bad if I did not say something more personal in this paper, even if only in an endnote, I hope that the reader will indulge me. Aside from being a great guy, a fact to which everyone who is writing for this collection could amply attest, Bob was an incredibly important influence in my own life. To put it in terms that I hope he would appreciate, having had Bob as a teacher and, even more, a friend is surely among the things for which I am most grateful.

# References

Heidegger, Martin. 1962. *Being and time*. New York: Harper and Row.
Sartre, Jean-Paul. 1956. *Being and nothingness*. New York: Washington Square Press.
Sartre, Jean-Paul. 1967. Consciousness of self and knowledge of self. In *Readings in existential phenomenology*, ed. N. Lawrence and D. O'Connor. Englewood Cliffs: Prentice Hall.
Sartre, Jean-Paul. 1976. *The emotions: Outline of a theory*. New York: Citadel.
Sartre, Jean-Paul. 1979. *Between existentialism and Marxism*. New York: Morrow Quill.
Sherman, David. 2007. *Sartre and Adorno: The dialectics of subjectivity*. Albany: SUNY Press.
Solomon, Robert C. 1976. *The passions*. New York: Doubleday.
Solomon, Robert C. 2003. *Not passion's slave*. New York: Oxford University Press.
Solomon, Robert C. 2007. *True to our feelings*. New York: Oxford University Press.
Williams, Bernard. 1995. *Making sense of humanity*. New York: Cambridge University Press.

# Chapter 4
# A Critique of Pure Revenge

Arindam Chakrabarti

**Abstract**  When it comes to evaluating the primordial human emotion of vengeance, moral philosophers, ancient and modern, Indian and Western, are divided into two groups: revenge-approvers and revenge-denouncers. Socrates, for example, decries revenge but Aristotle extols it as a virtue. Using the works of Nietzsche and Nozick, insights from the *Mahābhārata*, and Euripedes' *Orestes*, this paper distinguishes between revenge and retribution, and goes on to expose the misleading metaphors behind revenge-abetting phrases such as "teaching a lesson" or "getting even". An elementary mistake of confusing the dictum "Do to others what you want to be done to yourself" with the totally different dictum: "Do to others what they do to you" seems to lie behind the vague concept of "reciprocity" which is invoked by contemporary pro-revenge moral philosophers. Robert Solomon's subtle defense of revenge-fulness as an ineliminably human emotional motivation for justly angry actions is critiqued as slipping into a logical mistake. Finally, the paper proposes a moral psychological explanation of why revenge-spirals unstoppably escalate by the in-built discontent and self-contradiction in the motivational structure of the avenger's principle: "He should never have done that to me, therefore I shall now do exactly the same thing to him!" Any act of revenge is doomed to self-frustration, because it mimics and repeats a wrongdoing in the name of resisting and deterring it, it does the same in the name of doing the opposite, expecting emotional closure and non-closure at the same time.

Do not inflict on others what is hurtful to yourself. This, briefly, is *dharma,* and it takes a course other than what we desire (*Mahābhārata*, Parvan: XIII 139, author's translation).

And virtue will never be guilty of simulating vice in the act of repressing it (Seneca 1928–1935: 179).

---

A. Chakrabarti (✉)
Department of Philosophy, University of Hawai'i at Manoa, 2530 Dole Street,
Honolulu, HI 96822, USA
e-mail: uharindam@gmail.com

K. Higgins and D. Sherman (eds.), *Passion, Death, and Spirituality,*
Sophia Studies in Cross-cultural Philosophy of Traditions and Cultures 1,
DOI 10.1007/978-94-007-4650-3_4, © Springer Science+Business Media Dordrecht 2012

## The Controversy

The air reeks of revenge right now. Not just in Israel and Kashmir, in Iraq and in Taliban hideouts in the hills of Pakistan. Even large number of "world-peace-seeking" American Christians and "non-violent" South Asian Hindus and Buddhists are relishing that stench of reactive violence, albeit from a safe distance. In war, commerce, and war-like commerce, as cool advertisers would put it, "revenge rocks!"

Is desire for revenge a noble feeling or an abject one? Is resentment turning into resolve to retaliate a laudable emotional disposition that we need to cultivate as part of a fearlessly heroic righteous individual (and national?) character, or is it a common human frailty that we need to watch out against and never base our collective actions on? This question divides philosophers into two groups: the *revenge-approvers* and the *revenge-denouncers*. Socrates, though once a good warrior, was a revenge-denouncer. Aristotle, whose military record one has never heard of, appears to be a revenge-approver, though with his routine warning against excess. Carlyle, an armchair hero-worshipper, calls revenge "ever more intrinsically a correct, and even a divine feeling in the mind of every man" (Carlyle, cited in Barton 1999: 29). Jonathan Glover decries it by noticing that "hatred and pleasure ... combine unpleasantly in revenge" (Glover 1970: 145). Robert Solomon (1990), though not a clear revenge-approver, wanted to accord vengeance a central place in any theory of justice, not because he thought it is a rational or non-nasty emotion, but because "it is an undeniable aspect of the way we react to the world ... and as such a basic part of our ... moral sense of ourselves ... in that sense, unavoidable" (Solomon 2007: 113).

Pre-philosophical intuitions are typically indecisive on the question and would perhaps answer it with irritating caution: "It depends on the context." This paper is an attempt, first, to pierce the veil of some confusing metaphors through which we may think approvingly of revenge. It then argues for the position that, unlike some emotions, which can be correct or incorrect, sometimes truth-yielding, sometimes erroneous, vengeance is always befuddled and self-deceptive. It harbors a self-defeating mistake in its basic phenomenological structure. It tries to one-up the *bad* while wearing the mask of the *good* and in the process ends up looking *ugly*. Perhaps, if it is tempered with a heavy dose of sympathy for the unforgivable wrongdoer, genuine distaste for violence, desire for closure, and extreme restraint with regard to proportionality, the feeling of righteous retributive anger—and it is possible for sympathy and anger to co-exist—it can find a place in a balanced set of virtuous emotions. But pure unmixed vengeance remains a vice, an emotional error.

Both Socrates and the *Mahābhārata* reject retaliation as ethically unvirtuous. They do it by the same simple argument: If harming others is evil, then it is evil even to harm the harm-doer. Yet, both ancient Greek and ancient Indian societies—from which their moral sentiments arise and the milieu in which they teach—not only recognize revenge as an ineliminable part of the human motivational structure; the epic narratives of these societies are nothing but valorized sagas of individual and collective revenge.

Although Yudhisthira, the heroic sufferer of many of the moral dilemmas of the *Mahābhārata*, is somewhat like Gandhi (albeit with a passion for gambling), he takes a lot of flack from his fiery wife Draupadi for his conscientious rejection of retaliation. Draupadi rebukes her pacifist husband for his lack of manly rage. The wrath of Draupadi, whom the lewd Kaurava brothers had once tried to strip in public, brings down the ruin of the entire Kaurava clan. The author of the *Mahābhārata*, after describing, in literally gory detail, this fateful tale of collective iterated revenge, ends the book with a lament. He confesses that he has been crying out loud with raised hands that *dharma,* if practiced with proper patience, will eventually lead to pleasure and prosperity as well, but that no one is listening to him.

No one indeed listens. Even Socrates must have known that he was going against average Greek ethos when he was arguing that we should never return wrong for wrong (Plato 1997: 48b–c). His teaching in this regard fell flat on his pupil's pupil. Aristotle (1941) remarked: "It is noble to avenge oneself on one's enemies ... For requital is just, and the just is noble" (*Rhetoric* 1367a). Of course, Aristotle's views about the place of righteous anger in the exemplary virtuous character or about the exact relation between punishment (*kolasis*), return-action (*anti-poiontes*) and revenge (*timoria*) are more complex and I suspect ambivalent, if not incoherent (see *Rhetoric* 1369b and 1378b–1379a).

The *Mahābhārata* recognizes full well that personal rage can hardly wait for legal, cosmic or Karmic justice. It is natural, in one sense, for a human a victim of violence and humiliation to want swift and sure personal revenge. But the great ethical epic still characterizes *resisting* the revenge-impulse as a unique "human" excellence (in this, humans are better than the gods):

> When I am cursed by anyone, I do not curse them back.
> Such self-control I know to be the door of deathlessness.
> Let me tell you this, which is a sacred secret:
> There is nothing loftier than being human. (Mahābhārata XII 299, 20)

In recent Western ethics, moral and legal psychology, vengeance is enjoying a better press than ever before. A passionate resentment ripening into desire for revenge *is* and should be basic to our concern for legal justice, Robert Solomon has argued. This argument is part of Solomon's larger "concern with the expression and satisfaction of emotion in law". Pleading for victim's participation in criminal justice and rejecting the myth of the non-emotional third-party as the best judge, Charles K.B. Barton has made a very convincing case for making revenge central to penal justice (1999). In a paper called "Restitution and Revenge" (1999), David Hershenov has argued that revenge is a form of atonement or debt-payment on the part of the criminal and that vindictive satisfaction from avenging a wrongful aggression should serve as the proper moral motive for restorative justice. Finally, Peter French, who had earlier written a book called *Cowboy Metaphysics* (1997), has published an entire book, *The Virtues of Vengeance* (2001), arguing that, under certain circumstances, the angry avenger is the ideal moral agent, and vengeance is not just permissible but an essential moral quality. Quite openly relying more upon Clint Eastwood's moral intuitions than upon Kant's or even Aristotle's, French interprets the Indian Karma theory of moral desert as basically a cosmic or divine revenge-idea, and he takes ordinary Judeo-Christian or liberal morality's condemnation of vengeance as an inauthentic denial of its own psychological origins.

One of the two main purposes of this paper is to rebut the central arguments offered by these contemporary revenge-approvers and by Solomon, who wishes to heed the voice of vengeance in determining justice. The common human passion of vindictive rage has always rationalized itself in terms of "justice," "duty," and "honor," even "self-defense" and religious "solidarity". But especially in the current international religious-political climate, I think, it would be pernicious to let these philosophical legitimations of individual or collective revenge go unexamined. After all, in more than one sense, *an examined revenge is never worth taking*.

The other purpose of this paper is to offer a phenomenological explanation of violence-escalation in the process of contemplating and executing an act or a series of acts of revenge.

However, in this paper I do not wish to analyze or recommend that complex and controversial quality called "forgiveness" which is sometimes mistakenly thought to be the only alternative to revenge. My critique of revenge is not meant as a plea for non-violence or loving one's enemy. Besides, I shall try to clearly distinguish between retributive punishment and revenge because I don't think revenge can be justified in terms of retributive justice, nor the retributive theory of punishment rejected because it is based on the desire for revenge, because it is not. "Forget and forgive," is by no means going to be my favorite slogan. If I were forced to adopt a motto, "Remember and resist" would be more like it.

## Two Misleading Metaphors

Two or three major metaphors are used in English to talk approvingly and motivatingly of revenge. I would like to argue that each of them misrepresents the moral psychology of revenge. The first is a *pedagogical metaphor*. To take revenge is to teach the first-hitter a lesson. In extreme cases when revenge involves killing the first-hitter, such a metaphor would be sadly inappropriate. Even the hardest taskmaster does not plan to kill off his student as a means of educating him. But nonlethal vengeance too is never motivated by desire to educate. Indeed, if any teaching at all is involved, it seems to happen in the other direction. When Tom calls Dick "a fool" and a humiliated Dick retaliates verbally, either unimaginatively by repeating that same insult or by hurling it back with an added alliterative expletive, Dick as the avenger is taking a lesson from Tom, getting the idea from his initial attack, using him as a role-model, rather than teaching *him* something.

True, there is a method of correcting a pupil's errors by repeating an absurdly exaggerated version of that same error, hoping he will see the silly mistake for himself. This idea is captured by Hobbes' approving definition of revenge: "desire by doing hurt to another to make him condemn some fact of his own" (Hobbes 1994, I: ch. 6). But that is not at all what goes on in a typical case of what I call pure revenge. When I take pure revenge I mimic the wrong of the first hitter with a secret desire to advertise that I could have done it first if I had wanted, with no pedagogical intention whatsoever. The first-hitter's promise not to repeat the mistake in the future would do nothing to alleviate the retro-focused resentment of the avenger. Quite to the contrary, revenge comes often with the abetment to the first hitter to do it again so that next time the avenger, a fast learner, can take a swifter and sweeter revenge. The Hindu zealots who demolished the fifteenth-century Mosque in North-India, in retaliation of the Mughal Rulers' past destruction of Hindu temples, or the American fanatics who supported the Afghanistan war as a response to the 9/11 attacks, were expecting a repetition of Muslim communal violence or another Al Qaida attack on America in response to their patriotic acts of vengeance. They were avowedly learning from the vandals and the suicide-bombers, not teaching them anything.

Then there is the metaphor of *balance-restoration* or *getting even*. Originally there is some default position of equality. The first-hitter disrupts that by declaring himself superior, thereby unduly lowering the status and wellbeing of the victim. The victim's need to personally punish the wrongdoer and to see him suffer springs from the legitimate desire to restore equality, by raising himself and lowering the wrongdoer. The popularity of this metaphor clearly brings out one feature of revenge: *that it has little to do with suffering-alleviation or the self-defense of the victim and everything to do with honor-protection.* Jon Elster has skillfully demonstrated that honor is a triadic rather than a dyadic relation: *A gains honor by humiliating B in the presence of C* (Elster 1990). But by the same token, the metaphor of Restoring Equality turns out to be self-deceptive when used as an excuse for revenge. Even Peter French, who makes the strongest ethical case *for* vengeance, denies that the purpose of revenge is to diminish the worth of the offender. According to the avenger, the offender's moral worth has already been diminished by his heinous first attack (French 2002: 193). As an innocent victim, the avenger is at a moral advantage even before he starts to take revenge.

And even if the victimized has been humbled by the initial attack, how is a counter-humiliation going to take away that suffering and help restore balance unless the victim, not by comparisons of wellbeing, but by arbitrary social norms that measure honor in terms of revenge-dexterity, hopes to get richer again and regain his status? Even by the standards of a honor-shame score-keeping society driven by what Elster calls the "norms of revenge" (Elster 1990), the avenger does not wish to end up equal to the offender, whom he really hates. He wishes to come out superior to the first-hitter in power as well as moral merit. So the rhetoric of equalizing or evening out that is used to make revenge look like justice crumbles under examination.

Hershenov, who takes this leveling out metaphor very seriously, has argued that since the victim feels a warm satisfaction when he exacts his revenge, it makes the impoverished victim actually *"wealthier."* Equality is established "not just by lowering the wellbeing of the offender but by raising that of the victim back to or near the status he enjoyed prior to being victimized" (1999: 87). This is why he thinks it is an atonement, a compensation, a paying back of a debt. Such a "persuasive definition" of the "virtue" of vengeance at best tells us that vengeance is the attempt to buy equality of insult at the cost of equality of crime. Apart from the tragic self-mockery of such an agenda, the idiom of owing and repaying a debt that it naturally slips into springs from another seductive but deeply flawed idea, the idea that the desire for revenge is a sort of negative gratitude. As a hero in a Western film is prone to saying: "I owe him a debt of death."

## Revenge and Gratitude

As we shall see shortly, contrary to some popular representations, Nietzsche is not a revenge-approver. He does not say that we ought to be revengeful towards our aggressors just as we ought to be grateful to our benefactors. But he does make the converse claim that gratitude is a mild form of revenge. He even invokes Jonathan Swift in support of this cynical comparison: "If he did not have the compensation of gratitude, the man of power would have appeared unpowerful ... Swift suggested that men are grateful in the same degree as they are revengeful" (Nietzsche 1986 I, §44: 36.).

This thought encourages the debt-payment metaphor for revenge. In some upper-class circles of conceited conspicuous consumers, norms of gift-giving or party-throwing may resemble the code of tit-for-tat. If one regards receiving a gift as an honor-diminishing injury, then, of course, a return gift would count as a form of sweet revenge for the original humiliation of having to accept a gift. But all of this sounds pretty perverse to me. Here are four reasons why the psychology and norms of revenge and gratitude could never be on a par:

(a) If you repay a good deed by another good deed, then there is no paradox of repeating the allegedly reprehensible action—the paradox that haunts the retaliator. To call an act good is to recognize it to be worthy of redoing. To call it bad or wrong is to commit oneself to the belief that it should not have been done in the first place and once done, should never be repeated. "That was wonderful. Let's do it again. This time I shall do it" makes perfect sense. But "That was terrible. Let's do it again. This time I shall do it" makes much less sense. When resenting someone's wronging me makes me wrong him in return, I violate my own commitment to this meaning of "wrongness." There is no such violation in emulating the benefactor. Hence the two kinds of "return actions" have totally opposed logical structures.

(b) A grateful person does his own duty by reciprocating a good act. A vengeful person B tries to extort a duty (the duty of knowing-by-undergoing exactly how B suffered in A's hands) out of the original wrongdoer A by forcing him to suffer as B himself had suffered. B can thereby try (unsuccessfully) to feel not like a victim but a morally superior person who does a favor to A by "giving it back to him", almost like helping him perform an expiatory penance. There is a certain other-regarding paternalism about the avenger's warning, "You ought to suffer for doing what you did." If such a spiteful message accompanies an act of return generosity or gift, such a "Here, you take back what you gave me" gesture does not merit the name "gratefulness."

(c) A benefit received is naturally regarded as a debt. But it is a sick rhetoric to speak of one's indebtedness to someone on account of a harm or insult. Since I did not get any richer by the initial attack on me, there is no question of my giving back what I borrowed. The aggressor did not offer the harm to me as a loan expecting to get it back, unless one takes all attacks as masochistic provocations for counter-attacks. A *reductio ad absurdum* of the debt-payment model of vengeance would be to imagine, as a logical consequence, institutions of violence-enhancing investment-banking systems whereby one starts with a minor abuse and waits for years patiently to get back a gruesome murder as compounded interest-income.

(d) In revenge we try, albeit in an utterly futile fashion, to wipe out the memory of the original act of aggression, torture or injustice. In gratefulness we try to remember and acknowledge the original good act. We never wish to "undo" the first nice gesture by our return gesture, or try to look for ways in which we can equalize it, as if it did not happen in the first place. It follows from this that we do not aspire to pay back our debts of gratitude without any residue and are often happy to acknowledge that our reciprocation did not quite match up to the original kindness shown to us. With revenge the opposite is the case. The avenger does try to eliminate, equalize, and one-up the initial act of aggression.

## Instinctive Self-Defense and Revenge

There is one kind of defensive counter-blow that people instinctively deliver even towards inanimate objects with anger and annoyance. Let us call it DC, short for "defensive counter-blow". This has to be distinguished from the dish of maliciously relished calculated revenge that is best served cold. Nietzsche in a remarkably insightful piece called "Elements of Revenge" (1986 II/2 §33: 316–318) draws some of these distinctions.

First, DC is instantaneous and immediately follows upon the first attack. It is usually uncalculated and unstoppable. Revenge, on the contrary, takes time to brew and usually takes a lot of clandestine planning. Herbert Spencer even defined revenge as a postponed retaliation (Spencer 1978: II:V).

Second, DC is totally self-centered. Even when a defensive counterattack is against a human enemy, "self-preservation alone has here set the clock-work of reason in motion." But the revenge-taker is totally absorbed in returning harm to the other: "to secure himself against further harm is here so far from the mind of the revenger that he almost always brings further harm upon himself and very often cold-bloodedly anticipates it" (Nietzsche 1986 II/2 §33: 317). A heroic avenger is typically ready to die for sake of revenge. One usually is not ready to die for the sake of self-preservation.

Third, DC is driven by the fear of a future blow, which it tries to prevent. Revenge is driven by the memory of the past blow and a desire to prove that one is not afraid.

Finally, DC has to do with some expected benefit or at least prevention of a loss to the organism that practices it. Revenge has no concern for the avenger's benefit. It is consumed with the desire for saving honor—as in a duel—and restitution.

While Nietzsche observes that a revenger is often confused between these two utterly different motives and starts off reacting with DC but later on construes that as pure revenge, he still maintains, like Aristotle, that honor-preserving revenge is *nobler* than life-saving DC. This is where much of Western ethics of emotions is still in the grips of the heroism of the Elizabethan revenge tragedies. Any refusal to play the revenge game is always suspected as betraying cowardice and weakness. Nietzsche however does suggest three very interesting psychological conditions under which a person will not wish to take revenge. If I either have no imagination to understand or care about what the enemy is thinking, if I despise the wrongdoer so deeply that I do not wish to receive any honor from him, and if I am hopelessly in love with the enemy, then revenge will not be taken. When powerful people or nations spend enormous amounts of energy and take huge risks to avenge an attack, it proves that they do not despise the enemy enough; indeed they wish to look good in his eyes, hence, secretly admire him.

But what if I am simply demanding the punishment that the enemy deserves. Isn't that going to be society's revenge on him? In the next section we argue for a firmly negative answer to this question.

## Revenge and Retribution Distinguished

The distinctions between revenge and retributive punishment tend to be overlooked by both friends and foes of revenge. The hackneyed allusion is to the Old Testament dictum: *an eye for an eye*, etc. But as Gregory Vlastos has shown in his masterly article called "Socrates' Rejection of Retaliation," that famous formulation of the *lex talionis* "aims to put a lid on the extravagance of revengeful passion by stipulating that for any given harm, no greater may be inflicted in return … If someone has knocked out one of your eyes you might well feel like knocking out both of his—or more if he had more. The rule says: Only ONE" (Vlastos 1991: 182). So it is retribution, a curbing of revenge, and that too belongs only to God, not to the victim. Assurance of divine punishment is a way of controlling the natural human hankering for revenge.

Robert Nozick has drawn the following distinctions between these two concepts so often confused even now by sharp philosophers:

| Pure Revenge | Retributive Justice |
|---|---|
| 1. Personal, Private, often Secretly conducted (Note Tyndareus's speech quoted as epigraph) | Public, Open, Impersonal |
| 2. Emotional, sadistic | Rational, not primarily emotional; definitely not delighting in the criminal's suffering |
| 3. Returns wrong for wrong (e.g. rape for rape), imitative | Punishes wrong with suffering and humiliation (never rape with rape) |
| 4. The angry avenger may insult, kill or injure someone else knowing that he is not the original agent of the misdeed. | Legal retribution cannot be unfocused, e.g. arrange for the rape of the sister of the rapist. |
| 5. Lawless, non-universalizable (two acts of revenge for the same crime on two occasions may be utterly unequal in intensity) | Universalizable, law governed. |
| 6. Tends to escalate and spiral on, not seriously intended to lay violence to rest | Proportionate, finite, and intended to end |

Why does it always tend to go on and on, rather than be put to rest after one round? I try to give an explanation in the last section.

## Confusions About Reciprocity

Charles K. B. Barton recognizes that punishment and revenge cannot be equated, because there could be consequentialist (deterrent or reformative) punishment or symbolic punishment, which is not like revenge in structure, and also personal maverick forms of revenge, which are not retributive in nature. But he still insists that revenge is a form of retributive punishment, namely non-institutionalized, personal, retributive punishment. Revenge is a virtuous passion because it is based on the fundamental principles of negative desert and victim-empowerment. "It is a morally motivated desire for equity and justice retributively conceived as *reciprocity*" (Barton 1999: 10). Without engaging with Barton's meticulous analysis, let me quickly expose the fundamental error of this appeal to *reciprocity*. By reciprocity we could mean any one of the following principles:

 I.  Do not do unto others what is hurtful to yourself (the *Mahābhārata* formula).
 II. Do unto others what you want to be done to yourself (the positive golden rule).
 III. Do unto others what they have done to you (the tit-for-tat principle).

Now, although these principles sound somewhat similar, they are wide apart in their logical implications. Especially the first and the third principles are in direct mutual conflict. This becomes apparent if, in the tit-for-tat principle, we replace the phrase "what they have done to you" with "what is hurtful to yourself," which is exactly what the avenger docs in the name of personal retribution. From III, we derive:
"Do unto others what is hurtful to yourself" which is a direct contradictory of the *Mahābhārata* principle. So, an honor-obsessed avenger can somehow reconcile principles II and III by saying: "Yes, I want to retaliate and if I ever insult or injure someone wrongly, I want to be attacked in revenge by them as well." But there is no way in which he can reconcile the first and the third meanings of reciprocity in the case of a hurtful treatment by another. Yet, the average avenger appeals simultaneously to both of these meanings in order to dress up his irrational rage as a commitment to justice. The escape route that co-referential expressions are not substitutable under the intentional context "Do unto others ..." is not available to the revenge-planner. It is not just what is referred to by the phrase "what was hurtful to me" that he wants to hurl back to the other—in fact it has to be something extensionally distinct, since an act-token is unrepeatable—but another act which fits the description "what is hurtful to me" and for the reason that it was so hurtful. So the substitution is intention-preserving. He both appeals to as well as violates the genuine reciprocity principle, which is the *Mahābhārata* rule. This is why even Solomon admits, "Self-deception plays a far larger and more dangerous role in resentment than is usually admitted" (Solomon 1999: 125). Actually, reciprocity is a terribly loose concept. Each of the following questions raises a distinct problem about a separately discussable case of reciprocity: Should we be intolerant towards intolerant

communities and religions? Should we be uncaring towards our uncaring friends? Should we reciprocate cruelty with cruelty, shyness with shyness, mendacity with mendacity, bigotry with bigotry, tactlessness with tactlessness? These are not easy questions to answer. Any formulaic appeal to the concept of reciprocity as justice would be a bogus ground for any uniform set of answers.

## Solomon's Passionate Justice Argument and Its Fallacy

Robert Solomon is sensitive to all the above distinctions. So he does not wish to *reduce* revenge to punishment or punishment to revenge. But, as an institution, retributive punishment, he holds, is an *expression* of hatred, resentment and that passionate desire to witness the suffering of the aggressor that the victim craves, just as Picasso's *Guernica* is an *expression* of outrage, indignation, horror and despair, although there is much more to that painting than those emotions. I think Solomon gets carried away with his vindication of vengeance, though, and slips into comments like: "to revenge oneself against evil—that seems to lie at the very foundation of our sense of justice, indeed, of our very sense of ourselves" (Solomon 2007: 111). I think the opposite is true: as long as the avenger feels the need to strike back, he is not himself, he is an unhappy consciousness, simulating the role of the aggressor.

Why does Solomon say that vengeance must be central to criminal law? I agree with him that the idea that the neutral judge should be free from all emotions needs to be questioned. Emotional culture and empathic ability to feel from the point of view of both victim and the criminal and other affected parties adds essential clarity of vision to legal judgment. But it is incredible that Solomon is thinking of putting vengeance back into the justice system on the basis of the following argument:

> Emotions must have a place in law, because totally dispassionate law tends to be inhuman.
> Vengeance is an emotion.
> Vengeance must have a place in law.

Even for such a radical champion of so-called negative emotions, the first premise is not universally quantified: All emotions must have a place in law! Religious fanaticism, homophobia, or disgust at communists, or personal jealousies are also strong emotions. Must they therefore have a place in law? They actually, often, do drive court decisions, sadly. But those are precisely the cases where the justice system fails us, not because emotions have come to play a role in the verdict, but because the wrong emotions have.

Then Solomon proceeds to give an argument that sounds like the following:

> We punish because we resent the crime.
> We wish to avenge because we resent the crime.
> Therefore, punishing is an institutionalized controlled form of avenging.

Compare this argument with the following:

> People want a higher salary because they hate to be poor.
> People want to rob a bank because they hate to be poor.
> Therefore, wanting a higher salary is a controlled form of wanting to rob a bank.

The non sequitur here is too glaring! But then this is perhaps not a fair comparison. Let us listen to some of the deeper details of Solomon's reasoning in favor of the "just" spirit of gloating at the victim-inflicted injury suffered by the aggressor in return for his initial act of aggression.

In the process of developing his theory of revenge, Solomon says many surprising things. For example, to give a face-lift to revenge he remarks, "The satisfaction of vengeance … has not so much to do with the actual punishment as it does with *reconciliation,* which might not involve punishment at all"(Solomon 2007: 142, emphasis added). But then he would blur the distinction between retributive punishment and victim's vengeance. Apart from the theoretical vacillation, this is surely changing the meaning of "revenge," though I can imagine a tribal society where harm is inflicted precisely so that one's friend can show his manliness by rising to the occasion and gallantly flinging a counter-harm. If he does not do that, the first attacker may feel insulted because he is not taken seriously. In that case, I can imagine the victim retaliating in the spirit of reconciliation or of honoring the attacker. In this sense, in some recent literature, revenge has been spoken of as a natural human "communicative action" between humans competing for a kill or an honor or booty. But, I thought we had left behind such honor societies where people enjoy and "demand" counter-violence, like "gallant" moves in a blood sport! Unless I hate the attacker, I would not take revenge. And as long as I hate the attacker, why should I want to reconcile?

Now, people have used the word "revenge" with all sorts of interesting twists. If we start calling any form that resentment or anger takes, any counteraction or reaction to a grievous harm done to oneself, "revenge," then of course, even without desire to make the attacker suffer, one can be having one's revenge. Needless to say, that won't be pure revenge, of which I aim here to expose the futility. Here is one such extended use of the term "punishment" that as an alternative to pure revenge, I find a really attractive idea:

> You stupid man, who believes in laws that punish murder by murder, you have no power of vengeance except in calumny and defamation. When you find a woman who knows how to live without you, your vain power turns into fury. Your fury shall be punished by a smile, by an adieu, and by lifelong unconcern—George Sand, Fiancé of Chopin (quoted in Jacoby 1983: 182)

## My Moral Psychology of Revenge and its Iterative Escalation

Suppose aggressor A has done harm H to me. When planning to take revenge, my own emotional rationalization roughly takes the following route:

*A has done this nasty undeserved harm H to me. I cannot rest in peace until I do H\* to A, and pay him back in his own coins. Normally I would not do H\* to anyone because it would be as wrong as H. But since H has been wrongly inflicted on me by A, doing H\* to him would be not only permissible, but obligatory on my part. But while I am planning H\* as an equal return-action, there are three crucial respects in which H\* falls short of—and indeed is known to be—unequal to H.*

*First, H, the first attacker's original act was unprovoked, whereas my H\* would be*
*provoked. In the scale of intensity of harms or wrongs or acts of violence, ceteris*
*paribus, the provoked and expected is milder than the unprovoked unexpected. H*
*was, by my own standards, undeserved, unjust, and wrong, whereas H\*would be,*
*just by the norms of revenge, well-deserved by A and the right thing for me to do.*
*Once again, H\* being justified as a "right" act, does not have that edge of evil,*
*that bite of badness that H had. Finally H was fresh and the first hit. Even if I am*
*a creative revenge-artist and H\* has some creative additional cruelty to it, it will*
*essentially remain a stale second hit and an act of copying.*

*However, an objector could say here, it is not at all obvious that H and H\* are really*
*intended to be tokens of the same act-type since there are true descriptions of H\**
*that are not true descriptions of H. (Compare two shootings: one an unprovoked*
*murder and the other a justified act of capital punishment.) But the revenge taker*
*cannot say this with a straight face, because he also claims that the two acts are*
*tokens of the same act-type, because, unlike the retributionist, he appeals to*
*"paying back in the same coin" or doing to the perpetrator exactly what was*
*done by him. So the contradiction is not at the level of wanting H\* to be consid-*
*ered just while recognizing H to be unjust, but wanting H and H\* to be actions*
*of the same type while also wanting them not to be actions of the same type.*

*Of course the only important respect in which the avenger wants them not to be*
*actions of the same type is that his action is "just because it is provoked," and*
*that would be no argument in defense of his incoherent double description since*
*the defense was supposed to answer that very question: "Can a harm-doing be*
*just simply because it is provoked?" or the question "Was it just to be provoked*
*on this occasion?" In response, to say "It was just because it was provoked"*
*would at best beg the question and would do nothing to mitigate the*
*incoherence.*

*Now, how am I ever going to get the satisfaction of hurting A **just as he hurt me**, the*
*vindictive pleasure of doing the same thing to him, by doing something so different*
*and—in the scale of harms so deficient?*

Plagued by the fundamental contradiction of repeating what one resented just by
exchanging places, as the victim-avenger, I am, at this point, caught between hating
the first hitter and envying him, between wanting to do what the first-hitter did and
thinking that I myself would never do it to anyone, between trying to let the world
know that I can be violent just like the wrongdoer and be as " bad" as him and proving that I am a good right-doer unlike him, the wrongdoer.

Anger is not by itself necessarily an enemy of clarity of self-vision. In some critical
moments anger can even make things suddenly clearer. I have nothing against anger
per se as an emotion. But when it is fed by this inherently inconsistent agenda and
self-image, the only way in which I can overcome or try to overcome this sense of
qualitative inadequacy of H\* in the face of H is by intensifying the quantity or
harshness of the harm. Retaliations thus are planned to be greater harms, given a
chance, than what they are retaliations of. Now, let us call this margin of violence:
$M = H\*-H$. By the norms of revenge, A deserved equal suffering or harm but not this

margin of violence. So now, A feels that he has a right to take revenge for M, and for the same reasons as above inflicts M\*, which again tends to be harsher than M. To M\*- M, I should feel an equal urge to retaliate. And so the vendetta-spiral goes on, exposing the insincerity of the hope of closure with which the first revenge was contemplated. Incidentally, this analysis exposes the collective bad faith with which civilized nations speak of counterterrorism for the sake of ending terrorism.

This explanation of the escalation may be too idealized. But it has the advantage of capturing the built-in discontent that comes with not only the victim's need to make sure that the offender suffers, but the blood-boiling need to bring that suffering upon the offender oneself, to see him suffer and to derive gloating pleasure out of the sight.

A charge of incoherence could be raised against my account here. I have repeatedly said that there is no inherent proportionality or calibration involved in pure revenge, that even when it is cold, it is wild and rule-less. Yet, am I not ascribing to the avenger a keen desire to do exactly the same amount of harm to the harm-doer, in my own story of how it escalates?

I may concede part of this objection. Maybe the escalation into a vendetta-spiral does not have to happen in every case of revenge simply because there are not any measuring norms for revenge. But actually this objection draws our attention to the same erratic, confused mindset of the typical avenger. It does and does not appeal to proportionality or getting even. And because of this indecisive swing between hit-because-he-made-me-mad and hit-because-I must-get-even, there is always a sense of inadequacy and non-closure in such past-directed and proudly unprincipled methods of "remedy".

In American English, one synonym for angry is "mad." But that may be because in the culture there is an underlying celebration and denigration (and celebration because of denigration) of wild anger as irrational in the sense of out-of-control. What if collective or individual revengeful wrath were made rational by introducing elements of prudence into revenge? Revenge can thus be future-directed and involve a deterrence factor: part of the lesson that the revenger wants to teach the wrongdoer (and others) is the expectable cost to them of doing such wrongs next time. This deterrence feature can then set "extrinsic" proportionality constraints upon the severity of the revenge taken: in many circumstances too harsh a revenge may well be likely to lead to an escalation that is unprofitable for all involved. Thus self-interested or utilitarian revengers will often be in a situation of having to play an iterated series of zero-sum games where the best strategy is demonstrably going to be "tit-for-tat," allowing an equilibrium to evolve. Hence even if there are no intrinsic proportionality restrictions on revenge, there may be "extrinsic" restrictions that lead the prudentially rational revenger to eschew escalation.

Let me conclude by responding to this very sensible objection:

Pure revenge is exclusively past oriented. The "prudentially rational revenger" is an oxymoron. You may control and limit the passion of vengeance—which is not non-cognitive but has an incoherent and erroneous cognitive content—with extra-retaliative, coherent thoughts of future benefits, humaneness or reasonableness, but revenge by itself does not care what happens in the future as a consequence of the act of revenge. That is why, like a dutiful but greedy debt-repayer's afterthought that a good repayment record will facilitate future loans, the revenge taker's desire to deter or prevent future attacks are strictly outside the "deontological" motive of repaying because one must, and not part of the revenge-contemplation. "Just revenge" made to look lovelier by the support of extrinsic utilitarian considerations is never *just* revenge or sheer revenge.

## Macho-morality and The Secret Charm of the Violent Harm-Doer

As I get overpowered, wounded and defeated, I am usually also profoundly impressed by my attacker. The stunning anger felt at that time of humiliation and loss is, somewhat self-deceptively, a "mixed feeling." It makes me hate the attacker so much that I wish to be like him. The sheer force of shameless aggression—bodily or verbal, short-term or sustained—at once embitters, brands, and fascinates me. The more unforgettably it hurts, the more I am seduced by its cruel charisma. Through my hatred, I start making the monster my model. How hurt ferments into envy and how malice then matures into emulation is one of the mysteries of cognitive-emotional psychology that I would have liked to explore jointly with Robert Solomon (had death not disrupted our immensely enjoyable philosophical sparring on this issue).

This ambivalence at the heart of vengeance should not be taken as a deviant emotional kink, like secretly enjoying being tortured by the first attacker and there-fore returning the favor in a friendly spirit. (I have rejected the gratefulness analogy with much fanfare earlier.) There is no kinky addiction to suffering or self-torture here. But revenge is also not taken for the sake of lessening anyone's suffering in the future or increasing happiness. There is simply an awe at the (apparent) power of violence. Until Gandhi and Hannah Arendt (from very different starting points) arrived at the clear realization that violence is not power, that it is a symptom of insecure fear of loss of power, the equation of power with violence has been more or less entrenched in the human mind. George Bush's initial military strategy in Iraq was called "Shock and Awe." Destructiveness, cruelty, unrepentant wrongdoing have their own awe-inspiring impact on their victim. The "How could you?" of incredulous outrage turns into the irresistible "Why can't I?" of emulation.

It is this secret admiration, this aggression-envy, which wins over the simultaneous moral sentiment of total condemnation, the deep disdain of such a pattern of action, which should come in the form of the feeling: "I would never do such a horrible thing to anyone," without which the condemnation cannot merit the name of a "moral outrage" at all. Genuine *outrage* should use the rage to get me out of the situation, whereas revengeful rage has the opposite tendency to drag me back into it. But when the secret admiration and "vying for worse violence" takes over, it is easy to feel the drive to imitate, to do what has been done to me, and to treat such duplication of injustice as justice. In fact, as John Elster shows in his "Norms of Revenge," to the extent that revenge is about regaining "honor" in front of a society of on-lookers, whether the return-violence is proportionate or done back to the original perpetrator sometimes becomes irrelevant (1990). Whether the diminished victim can raise his status in the eyes of the honor-monitoring society by performing an equally violent act is all that matters. Such acts of defiance are actually acts of diffidence, springing from some primitive code that equates terror with triumph, violence with victory and being cruel with being "cool". This, then, is self-deceptively dressed up with the rationalization of retributive punishment, which is what we have shown revenge is not.

Neither Solomon nor I are talking about loving one's enemy or forgetting the harm people have done to us instead. Solomon is afraid that those who abstract from particular feelings of strong resentment and admonish us to think of the *universal abominability* of the initial act of violence, would tend to be heartless and insensitive to the passionate nature of our *particular personal situational moral sentiments*. But I am optimistic that one could be passionate about the *universal* as well, that it should be possible—hard and unusual, but emotionally feasible—to transform the affective energy of the initial hate and outrage into a deepened resolution **not** to repeat this act, not to waste one's energy playing the game one was unwillingly dragged into, and as far as possible prevent it from being done to anyone, even to one who did such a thing, who should be punished in some other way.[1]

A merely intellectual and rational understanding of my "error-theory of vengeance" is not going to be motivationally powerful enough to curb the revenge-addiction already ingrained in the average human psyche (and even the psyches of other animals, especially apes). It has to be boosted up with its own counter-rhetoric, such as "Prove your strength by refusing to copy that lowly attacker"; "Aggression is not power, it is weakness, and counter-aggression is doubly feeble"; "Remember and Resist." As long as one's community with its valorized identity-forming narratives cheerleads counterviolence, praises the befuddlement of rage-rush or cold scheming of calculated retaliation as emotional heroism or manliness, this weaning away from the misperception of vengeance as honorable cannot succeed.

Perhaps Bob was right: revenge is humanly unavoidable. There is an incurable revenge-addict in each of us. For us verbally combative philosophers, this addiction shows up in our public refutations of each other. But when Bob responded to my fairly trenchant "attacks" on him about this very issue at the Eastern Division American Philosophical Association meeting a couple of days before his death,

---

[1] Over the years, after Solomon's tragic untimely death, I have begun to understand Solomon's position better and I see that we have a deep base of agreement on emotions having satisfaction-conditions, analogous to but not reducible to beliefs' having truth-conditions. But the justification of revenge in the sophisticated version of "honor society" that we still live in could not be endorsed simply because it is widespread and natural to act out of vengeance. I distance myself from the strong "naturalism" implicit in such an ethical stance. Even in the *Mahābhārata*'s warlike honor society, it may be politically and *reputationally* heroic to avenge a harm done to you with matching violence, but being able to resist the revenge-impulse is regarded as morally heroic. Refusing to engage in the game that the first attacker starts puts the attacker, especially in an honor society, eventually to more shame if there are other ways of showing that one could have retaliated, but chose to ignore the insult or injury.

warmly, firmly, passionately but without any touch of counter-attack, showing how we differed but also showing that he understood where I was coming from, he somehow strengthened my faith that perhaps someday some superior human beings, feeling all the nuances of normal human resentment and anger, would refuse to mimic bad behavior in the act of correcting or disciplining it. And others may start mimicking *those* uncommon non-retaliation-artists rather than the common violence-artists.

> Tyndareus: *This*, Agamemnon's son, this *thing*? …
> What should he have done? When his father died
> Killed, I admit, by my own daughter's hand,
> An atrocious crime which I do not condone—
> And never shall—he should have hauled his mother
> Into court, charged her formally with murder …
> Legal action, not murder. That was the course to take.
> Under the circumstances, a hard choice, true
> But the course of self-control and due respect for law …
> But as things stand now, what is the difference
> Between him and his mother?
> No, vicious as she was, if anything
> The evil he has done by killing her
> Has far surpassed her crime. Think again
> Suppose a wife murders her husband.
> Her son then follows suit by killing her,
> And his son then must have his murder too and so on.
> Where, I want to know, can this chain of murders end?

(Euripides 1959 l. 495–510: 39–40)

# References

Aristotle. 1941. Rhetorica (Rhetoric). In *The basic works of Aristotle*, ed. Richard McKeon, 1317–1451 (trans: W. Rhys Robert). New York: Random House.

Barton, Charles K.B. 1999. *Getting even: Revenge as a form of justice*. Chicago: Open Court.

Elster, Jon. 1990. Norms of revenge. *Ethics* 100: 862–885.

Euripides. 1959. Orestes. In *Euripides III: Orestes, Iphigenia in Aulis, Electra, The Phoenician women, The Bacchae*, ed. David Grene, 3–105 (trans: Richmond Alexander Lattimore). Chicago: University of Chicago Press, New York.

French, Peter. 1997. *Cowboy metaphysics: Ethics and death in westerns*. Lanham: Rowman and Littlefield.

French, Peter. 2001. *The virtues of vengeance*. Lawrence: University Press of Kansas.

Glover, Jonathan. 1970. *Responsibility*. New York: Humanities Press.

Hershenov, David B. 1999. Restitution and revenge. *The Journal of Philosophy* 96: 79–94.

Hobbes, Thomas. 1994 [1651]. *Leviathan*, ed. Edwin Curly. Indianapolis: Hackett.

Jacoby, Susan. 1983. *Wild justice: The evolution of revenge*. New York: Harper & Row.

Nietzsche, Friedrich. 1986 [1886]. *Human, all too human: A book for free spirits* (trans: R.J. Hollingdale). Cambridge: Cambridge University Press.

Plato. 1997. Crito. In *Plato: Complete works*, ed. John M. Cooper and D.S. Hutchinson, 37–48 (trans: G.M.A. Grube). Indianapolis: Hackett

Seneca [Lucius Annasus]. 1928–1935. On anger. In *Seneca's essays, I: Moral essays*, 106–355 (trans: John W. Basore). London: W. Heinemann/The Loeb Classical Library.

Solomon, Robert C. 1990. *A passion for justice: Emotions and the origins of the social contract.* Reading: Addison-Wesley.

Solomon, Robert C. 1999. Justice v. vengeance: On law and the satisfaction of emotion. In *The passions of law*, ed. Susan A. Bandes, 123–148. New York: New York University Press.

Solomon, Robert C. 2007. *True to our feelings: What our emotions are really telling us.* New York: Oxford University Press.

Spencer, Herbert. 1978 [1893]. *The principles of ethics*, vol. 2. Indianapolis: Liberty.

Vlastos, Gregory. 1991. Socrates' rejection of retaliation. In *Socrates: Ironist and moral philosopher*, ed. Gregory Vlastos, 179–199. Ithaca: Cornell University Press.

# Chapter 5
# Chakrabarti's 'A Critique of Pure Revenge': A Response

Robert C. Solomon[†]

**Abstract** Vengeance is sometimes justified, contrary to what Arindam Chakrabarti argues. The legitimacy of vengeance depends very much on the culture in which it is embedded. In "honor" cultures (as opposed to "institutional" ones), vengeance is typically prima facie legitimate and justifiable (if not necessarily justified). Even in institutional societies, many contexts are still bound up with honor, and vengeance still plays a role (if not a violent one) in these contexts. Chakrabarti stresses the opposition between "revenge approvers" and "revenge denouncers," but there is a vast area between these extreme positions. Accordingly, when one is motivated by revenge, one has other options besides seeking vengeance and being merciful. One, termed here "righteous *Schadenfreude*," is taking satisfaction when harm occurs to someone who has offended one, directly or indirectly. Righteous *Schadenfreude* is much more common than vengeance as such, and it is innocent of the most serious charges brought against vengeance (both in terms of deontology and in terms of bad consequences).

To start, let me express my thanks to Arindam Chakrabarti and point out the extent to which, despite his provocative thesis, we are on the same side.[1] His thesis is that I am a defender of vengeance, while he is opposed to it. But we agree that vengeance, which is rarely taken seriously by moral philosophers, is indeed a serious moral concern. We also agree that vengeance involves emotions that have substantial

---

[Editors' note:] This response was presented on December 29, 2006, only a few days before Bob's death. What we present here is an edited version of the commentary he sent to Arindam Chakrabarti as a "very rough draft," not to be "taken as gospel."

[1] My thanks to Arindam Chakrabarti and Tamler Sommers for their contributions to my thinking.

[†] R.C. Solomon
(Deceased)

K. Higgins and D. Sherman (eds.), *Passion, Death, and Spirituality*,  55
Sophia Studies in Cross-cultural Philosophy of Traditions and Cultures 1,
DOI 10.1007/978-94-007-4650-3_5, © Springer Science+Business Media Dordrecht 2012

cognitive and evaluative content, what these days might be called "emotional intelligence," even if I have a lot more respect for that intelligence than Arindam does. We also agree that vengeance has a phenomenology, that it is a way of being in the world and a way of interpreting what happens to us in the world and what we should do about it, and we both "recognize [that] revenge [is] an ineliminable part of the of the human motivational structure." We also agree that an admirable but rare alternative to vengeance is the "above all, do no harm" response advocated by several of the "wisdom traditions" both west and east—in Plato, for example, and in the *Mahābhārata*, which urges us to "resist the revenge-impulse." This is, I agree, "a unique 'human' excellence" and we do not disagree about what is admirable or virtuous.

The pressing question that separates Arindam and me is whether vengeance is ever legitimate or justified. (These are quite different, the first political, the second moral or prudential.) My answer is yes, it is. Arindam's answer is, no. (He tells us, "Pure, unmixed vengeance remains a vice, an emotional error.") So it looks as though we have a real disagreement. But that is not the whole of it.

In this brief comment, I want to restrict myself to two points. The first is that the legitimacy of vengeance depends very much on the culture in which it is embedded. The second is that there is a variation on the vengeance theme that is much more common than vengeance as such, which is innocent of the most serious charges against vengeance (both in terms of deontology and in terms of bad consequences), and has been virtually ignored in the philosophical literature. I don't have a proper name for it yet, but "righteous *Schadenfreude*" will do as a placeholder.

## Two Sorts of Societies

One can find situations in which vengeance is legitimate, politically and morally, but in which, for various reasons, it might still be a very poor strategy. It might have disastrous consequences and might even include one's own demise. (The Chinese have a saying, "If you seek revenge, dig two graves.") There are, of course, various schema for deciding whether vengeance should be pursued, whether or not it is warranted, and what "warrant" amounts to. We can raise the deontological question of whether vengeance is ever justified, that is, whether it can be justified according to a rational moral principle. (Kant insists that punishment—retribution—is a rational duty, but he thinks that vengeance is at best amoral if not immoral because it is an inclination, so he is a problematic guide on this issue.) We can consider the utilitarian question of whether vengeance as pursued in this or that particular case is best for all concerned. (Rule-utilitarians might ask whether vengeance could be defended as a general rule, but this has always struck me as contrary to the particularist spirit of utilitarian philosophy.) And then we might raise what these days would be called the virtue ethical question, although, as Arindam nicely illustrates with his references to Plato and the *Mahābhārata*, this is in fact a very ancient line of inquiry.

Arindam seems to choose virtue ethics in his plan of attack ("Is desire for revenge a noble feeling or an abject one?"), despite the fact that his aim is to defend, on deontological grounds, the thesis that vengeance is never justified. I think that this is the right way to discuss the question of vengeance, but I have doubts about Arindam's conclusion. (We seem to agree that utilitarian arguments alone do not capture either what is wrong or what is right about vengeance.)

My main objection to Arindam's plan of attack is that it oddly ignores the social-cultural-institutional context of vengeance. It is, I think, hopelessly individualistic. This is odd because Arindam of all people is exquisitely sensitive to social-cultural concerns. Virtue ethics, too, tends to be sensitive to social-cultural context, the idea being that what counts as a virtue is largely determined by its appropriateness to context. As Plato famously argues, it is wrong to give back weapons owed to a madman. But perhaps there are cultures in which pursuing vengeance is a virtue rather than a vice. Indeed, Plato was responding to one, the Homeric warrior culture. (Of course, in order to count as a virtue the effort must be successful and carried out well. Usually this would mean getting one's revenge on the battlefield. It would be both vicious and cowardly to merely stab your enemy in the back.) It is exemplary that both Plato and the Vedic literature challenge the on-going culture, but it is significant that they both hold onto a metaphysical anchor beyond the culture. In the *Mahābhārata,* Yudhisthira appeals to *dharma* despite the fact that his unmanly virtue fails to satisfy either the local culture or his wife's expectations. Plato, of course, has the World of Being to appeal to. Nevertheless, it seems to me that one cannot easily override the local culture, and although one might heroically appeal to super-human *eidé* or *dharma*, the question of the legitimacy and justification of vengeance is first of all a cultural question.

My objection to Arindam's general argument turns on one particular social-cultural concern. It makes a huge difference whether one is arguing within a social context that one might describe as "honor-defined" (or simply as "an honor society") and another that might be described as "institutional." (I confess that I have not made this distinction clear enough in my several essays on the subject of vengeance, and I owe a considerable debt to Tamler Sommers for clarifying it for me and spurring my interest (Sommers 2009).) Honor societies tend to be closely focused on families, groups, communities, and "tribes," although one should be careful not to assume that they are therefore more primitive than other societies. (Ancient Athens was an example of such a society, and so would be modern Japan.) Institutional societies are those in which the civil law trumps such loyalties.

It should be obvious that the two models overlap and are not usually or easily distinguished. One might have an honor society (or lots of honor societies) within the confines of a legal framework, and one can develop all sorts of legal institutions within an honor society. Boy Scout troops, the Marine Corps, sororities and fraternities, the American Philosophical Association, scientific societies, and clubs for sports fans might be considered honor societies, but in my country they are governed by the laws of the United States. (It is not irrelevant to the argument that our Founding Fathers described the political structure that they instituted as "a government of laws, not men.") The legal framework puts certain constraints on such organizations, but within those restrictions, they are free to defend their "honor" (whatever that might mean in their very different contexts) as they choose.

On the other hand, legal institutions can (and usually do) develop *within* honor societies. Looking outside the United States, the legal institutions of modern Japan, by any measure a model of modern civilized society, can be shown to have developed within a traditional honor society. Honor and shame are still the most salient categories in Japanese ethics, while "legal" and "illegal" tend to be subsidiary notions (it is shameful to break the law). In the United States, by contrast, shame and honor are taken to be rather quaint notions, especially where the legal system is concerned. (How many CEOs of corrupt, lawbreaking companies in the United States resign in shame, as would almost any Japanese CEO in a similar position? Conversely, how often do we hear in defense of truly shameful behavior, "well, there was nothing *illegal* about it," as if that alone were the last word?)

My suggestion, following Sommers, is that in honor societies vengeance tends to be prima facie legitimate and justifiable, governed by the particular culture and the circumstances. This is not to imply that such vengeance is *justified*, needless to say; that depends on the merits of the particular case. But the notion of justifiable revenge is not to be simply dismissed on a priori grounds. Indeed, in honor societies vengeance may even be obligatory and, therefore, by cultural standards, virtuous.

In institutional societies, by contrast, there is an a priori and general argument to the effect that vengeance is not legitimate, at least when it conflicts with legal process. Vengeance is personal, but justice is not. (The blindfold on the statue of Justice represents the irrelevance of the personal.) Punishment must be sanctioned by law. Thus lynch mobs and vigilante groups, even if their actions were defensible on the basis of incontestable facts, are illegitimate. Capital punishment is the exclusive province of the state. So, too, only the state can put criminals in prison. No matter what the grounds, private citizens are not allowed to imprison others. Military tribunals, we are now coming to realize, must be carried out with the same legal protections that prevail in the civilian judiciary system. Personal vendettas, even if they would be legitimate and justified within the context of one or another honor society, are permissible only with the sanction of the state in institutional societies. Civil law suits may explicitly be acts of vengeance. (The second O.J. Simpson trial, it was widely commented, obtained vengeance for the family of Nicole Simpson, bankrupting the [allegedly] murderous husband, even when the usual form of legal punishment, a jail sentence or the death penalty, had been denied. People often sue for damages—as well as "for pain and suffering"—explicitly as a way of "getting even," even when it is transparent that nothing of the sort is achieved.) However, in the context of such vindictive suits, the coercive transfer of money (whether by way of compensation or for punitive damages) is legitimate only because it is ordered by the Court. (Of course, such transfers may take place by mutual consent without the intermediary of the law, but that is usually in anticipation of what the law might command.)

In the case of legal punishment in criminal cases, it is an open question whether and to what extent a desire for revenge on the part of the aggrieved (the surviving victims of a crime) should enter into or be considered by the courts, judges, and juries.

Not long ago, it was argued that there should be no such considerations; vengeance is personal and not part of the law. More recently, "victims rights" organizations have argued, among other things, that the desire for vengeance ought to be taken into account both with regard to the guilt of the accused and sentencing. This is what I argue in the essays cited by Arindam.

But Arindam's argument, while he focuses on my contribution to a book on law and emotion (Solomon 1999), is a much broader campaign against vengeance. He takes the pursuit of vengeance to be a personal vice. And this is true whether or not it is pursued within an institutional society or any legal context. Vengeance need not preempt the law to be illegitimate. It is the motive itself that is vicious. Within the legal frameworks of states and counties in the United States, many circumstances involve some kinds of personal transgression and/or some kind of revenge. The law may provide limits and constraints on our behavior (for instance, it forbids our killing people), but it does not speak to the legitimacy or justifiability of acts of vengeance within the bounds of law. (Here is one source of the distinction between legitimacy and justification.) A professor may well respond to a flagrant public insult by an academic colleague by humiliating him in public, thus getting his revenge, but the question of whether this is wise or warranted is not settled by any institutional considerations, including the rules and policies of academic institutions. In a United States court case several years ago, the court decided that the law provided no protection for a controversial professor who had been publically criticized—but not in legal terms "harassed"—by his colleagues. Arindam would condemn such behavior and the mindset that motivated it. I would say, at least in some cases, "well-done and much-deserved." (Does that make me a bad person?)

If we are looking at what I am calling honor societies, we need to take a very different perspective. Mediterranean honor cultures, for instance, also have legal institutions and frameworks, and these often come into conflict with traditional expectations and customs regarding honor and vengeance. "Honor killings" are illegal in most of these societies, but this legal prohibition does not seem to be very effective in preventing them. In the *Mahābhārata*, the least of Yudhisthira's worries should be his wife's dissatisfactions. He is required by *dharma* to seek revenge. A man who does not avenge the rape of his sister or the murder of his brother does not dare show his face in society. Tamler Sommers quotes a Corsican,

> Whoever hesitates to revenge himself, said Gregorovius in 1854, is the target of the whisperings of his relatives and the insults of strangers, who reproach him publicly for his cowardice. In Corsica, the man who has not avenged his father, an assassinated relative or a deceived daughter can no longer appear in public. Nobody speaks to him; he has to remain silent (Busquet 1920: 357–358).

Now one might well argue, despite my previous warning, that such societies are "primitive" and therefore not to be taken seriously as models of morality. And in some cases, I would endorse such a view, not because of the practice of vengeance as such but because of a more general lawlessness, or because of the societies' intolerance and their crude attitudes towards women and children. However, I also think that some of the ingredients that motivate revenge and define honor societies are in dangerous decline in institutional societies: honor and shame, most obviously, but also a broad range of moral emotions, such as a sense of human dignity and what we might describe as "the feeling that one matters." It is for that reason that I want to give vengeance its due. I would not defend lynch mobs and vigilante groups, to be sure, but I do believe that institutions flourish only insofar as they incorporate and to some extent satisfy personal emotions. And I think that vengeance, whether or not it is ever legitimate in itself and whether or not there are other, better ways of satisfying the emotions that drive it, represents a conception of justice (yes, justice) that cannot and should not be dismissed, as Arindam seems to insist upon.

Vengeance, whatever else it might be, is an expression of human dignity (family honor, personal pride) and an affirmation of "the feeling that one matters." Many people report a sense of immense satisfaction when they have gotten revenge (assuming, as Aristotle rightly demands, that vengeance is warranted, measured, and appropriate). Most people get some satisfaction, although at one removed, when someone else avenges a wrong committed against them, a friend or a relative or sometimes even a stranger. So there is a very real psychological question—and it is a psychological more than a philosophical question—of whether that same sense of satisfaction can be brought about when it is the impersonal "machinery of the law" that applies the relevant punishment, quite independently of any personal feelings or desires. A partial answer to this question is a philosophical answer: punishment will not be personally satisfying (and here we are not just talking about the feeling of satisfaction) if the victim and his or her distress are explicitly excluded from the proceedings.

It is not my intent to celebrate honor societies, much less the barbaric codes of conduct that accompany the sense of honor in certain parts of the world. My argument is geared more towards such sophisticated cultures as ancient Athens, ancient India, and modern Japan. But the existence of more primitive honor societies is instructive. One might think of them as more "distilled" or "pure" instances of a form in which shame and honor, and consequently vengeance, play a central role in the structure of a society not served or not served well enough by the legal institutions that relegate such emotions and behavior to secondary status in institutional societies.

One might also note that when institutional societies break down, they often revert to a vengeance paradigm. One thinks today of Iraq after the American "liberation," or the city of New Orleans after Hurricane Katrina and the ensuing flood destroyed all vestiges of legal authority along with so much else. Such situations are usually described as "utter chaos," but this is sociologically obtuse. In the absence of any legitimate legal institutions, the social world shrinks to the size of one's immediate family and neighborhood or, in the cases of Iraq and New Orleans, one's sect or gang. The violence was and is not "indiscriminate" (despite the impossibility of predicting the damage caused by improvised bombs or the "collateral damage" caused by inexpert use of automatic weapons). Such violence is, at least by intention, directed, by way of revenge, at precisely those who have wronged you.

So too in times of war, in the absence of authority or in the midst of urgent life-and-death situations, justice tends to be immediate and without principle. Reprisals tend to be the coinage of justice in war. (The terrific Australian movie *Breaker*

*Morant* shows an excellent understanding of the dilemma of soldiers in such a situation.) Vengeance is often a product of impatience or despair when there is no effective higher power. People who believe in a just and ultimately rewarding and punishing God encourage one another to abstain from vengeful behavior, but perhaps only for the reason that wrongs will surely be avenged in the future. When government has broken down or become so weak or corrupted that the law is no longer a dependable dispenser of justice, vengeful behavior (and vigilante groups) are likely to proliferate. In such circumstances as in honor societies, vengeance may not only seem legitimate and justifiable, but *obligatory*. Arindam will certainly disagree with this. I, too, find such phenomena extremely disturbing, but I am more willing, perhaps, to say "this is how people behave in such circumstances," so we should try as hard as we can, through good government, to avoid bringing such situations about.

The idea that vengeance might not only be legitimate and justifiable, but *obligatory* receives support from a most unexpected source, Immanuel Kant. Kant expresses the point in a problematic way, since he rather rigidly separates reason and duty from the inclinations (of which the desire for vengeance would be a prime example). Nevertheless, he famously writes,

> But whoever has committed murder, must die. There is, in this case, no juridical substitute or surrogate that can be given or taken for the satisfaction of justice… Even if a civil society resolved to dissolve itself with the consent of all its members—as might be supposed in the case of a people inhabiting an island resolving to separate and scatter themselves throughout the whole world—the last murderer lying in prison ought to be executed before the resolution was carried out. This ought to be done in order that everyone may realize the desert of his deeds, and that blood-guiltiness may not remain upon the people; for otherwise they might all be regarded as participators in the murder as a public violation of justice (Kant 1996: 158).

To be sure, Kant would turn in his grave at the thought that he is capturing something important about the sociology of vengeance, but I think that he is right to insist that vengeance may, in certain extreme circumstances, become a moral duty and obligatory. Most readers of this passage recoil in horror at the extremity of Kant's position, as they might also recoil in horror at the defense of such behavior in the name of reason. But if I am right about this, what Kant sees is how vengeance might become a moral duty in circumstances in which legal institutions and much of what we call reason has broken down.

I will now proceed through the several sections of Arindam's presentation. The contours of my argument are already apparent. Culture makes a difference. There may be very few "pure" honor societies (and they might well fill us with horror), but *within* these societies vengeance may be both legitimate and justifiable. But there are also cultures defined by legal institutions in which the role of vengeance is not so clear. I argue that vengeance still has a role to play. (I have not argued here what I have argued extensively elsewhere—since Arindam seems to be in agreement with it—that vengeance is something of a "natural" moral response to intentional harm, granting that this claim requires serious qualification). It is admirable that both Plato and the *Mahābhārata* (and now Arindam as well) take on the whole of society insofar as society embraces rather than rejects vengeance. I think Arindam is also correct in his diagnosis of a great deal of current thinking, that vengeance is tempered by forgiveness. But one can reject the former without embracing the latter.

We do not live in an honor society, to be sure, so I think that Arindam is correct to insist that the warrant and justification of legal punishment should not be construed solely as an expression of vengeance. (He attributes some terrible arguments to me in this regard.) However, we live in a society in which many contexts are bound up with honor, both group honor and personal honor, and the legitimacy and justification of vengeance in such contexts is by no means to be glibly dismissed. Arindam argues that it is a serious flaw in one's character to give in to the desire for vengeance, admitting that such desires exist and leaving open the question of whether the desires themselves are ever justifiable; but I think that this is a topic for serious debate. Insofar as the law's imposition of punishment on those who have offended us give expression to personal desires for vengeance, a serious question can be raised about the extent (if any) to which these desires should influence the law's decision to punish. If the law acts as agent for the aggrieved, then this would be so. But typically, a crime against an individual is tried as "The State v. [the criminal]." Nowhere is the identity of the victim even relevant. (Thus the nature of the crime is *breaking the law*, not inflicting harm on the victim.)

In his analysis of revenge, I think Arindam dwells too much on the extreme and violent forms of vengeance, the sort that is emphasized in the Old Testament: "an eye for an eye, a tooth for a tooth…"(Ex. 21:23–25), and ultimately, a life for a life. As I have already suggested, there are all sorts of more or less civilized examples of vengeance that do not involve violence and are clearly within the constraints of the law, humiliating an obnoxious colleague being one of them. Sorority sisters snub one another in return for a prior snub, refuse to invite each other to parties in return for not being invited to a previous party, spread nasty rumors about one another in return for some other slight or humiliation. (When Tony Bennett sings, "Revenge is sweet," he is presumably not praising murder.)

Vengeance is bound to seem barbaric to us if we focus only on brutality and violence. But it takes on a much more human and civilized face when we focus on everyday tit-for-tat responses. (Indeed, such acts are only comprehensible within a well-defined civilized culture.) Not that such human, all too human responses are therefore justifiable, needless to say, for we may well judge such behavior as petty, mean-spirited, and detrimental to the very relationships that are supposedly at stake. Vengeance might be condemned, at least in such cases, as betraying poor character, bringing the focus back to virtue ethical considerations. (The utilitarian consequences of such behavior, by contrast, will typically be insignificant.) The pettiness of these quotidian acts of vengeance perhaps explains the attraction of the more dramatic life-for-a-life type cases that usually populate discussions of vengeance (as well as the more global and literally earth-shattering cases such as depicted in the—surprisingly good—film *V for Vendetta*). No one can simply dismiss the vengeful responses of someone whose life has been destroyed by an evil dictator, though one might well ask to what extent our favorable reactions to such vengeance are driven by our repulsion to evil and dictatorships, and not instances of approving of vengeance itself.

## Righteous *Schadenfreude*: An Alternative to Revenge and Forgiveness

I hope I have already laid the basis for insisting that the real debate about vengeance is not a contest between "vengeance approvers" and "vengeance denouncers." There may well be people who would approve of certain acts of vengeance, but I doubt if anyone would insist that, across the board, getting revenge is a good thing. Even those who applaud certain acts of vengeance might well concede that vengeance, even when justified, is the wrong thing to do. Most of us, I think, are of the opinion "yes, but…," opening up a rich territory of reasons, justifications, and excuses that lie between approval and denunciation.

I gather that Arindam considers himself to be among the vengeance denouncers. This position is just what I want to question—not whether such a stance is intelligible (it obviously is), but whether it is defensibly human, as opposed to saintly. One can refrain from getting revenge, even when it is at hand, and one can do so, as Arindam has argued, without advocating forgiveness. I think that this is a good point, although Arindam does somewhat overstate my own defense of revenge as a "natural" response to offense and harm. But I think that Arindam leaves something out, as does most of the literature on revenge.

To put the point simply, the perspective almost always taken up—whether by way of attack or defense—is what I would call the *heroic* perspective (borrowed from the classic literature—Greek, Indic, Norse—in which revenge plays such a central role). The key to the *heroic* perspective is that the hero (or in any case, the offended agent) *takes* revenge, he or she does the vengeful deed. Indeed, the very meaning of the word "revenge" might be argued to demand such action. One might *avenge* someone else (for example, someone who is the now deceased victim of wrongdoing), and similarly one might *be avenged* by another (a "hero," as I am using that term here, not sympathetically). (One may or may not be knowledgeable about or party to the avenging, but insofar as one is involved, it probably counts as revenge). The basic idea is that revenge is an action, something one *does* (or "takes"), in return for some slight or offense.

The alternative, as it is usually stated, is some variation of mercy (having the right to revenge but not taking it), forgiveness (having the right to revenge but in some sense canceling out the offense while nevertheless regarding it as serious), or forgetting (whether dismissing the offense as unimportant or just letting it slip one's mind). But there is another possibility, probably much more common and much less commented upon. It is the joy or satisfaction one gets from seeing (or hearing of) harm that has been done or has happened to some one who has offended you, whether directly or indirectly. One feels even better if there is some "poetic" element, some fittingness to the resultant harm. The important point is that there must be a direct link between the joy and the offense, although one has no hand in the subsequent harm, which would clearly be revenge if one had perpetrated it. How should we judge this? We might well agree that returning evil for evil is in every case wrong, if not because it is on the face of it another instance of wrongdoing, then because of the consequences (deontological and utilitarian objections respectively). But suppose one had no hand in causing the harm. The offender just happens to be crushed by a falling building (best, it is the building he contracted with rigged contracts and shoddy construction) or gets killed in the very trap he had set up for the intended victim (a favorite in film noir movies, for example, *The Big Sleep*).

Thus the Ella Fitzgerald's revenge love song, "Goody Goody," revels in the fact that the beloved who dumped her has gotten dumped in turn. Notice that this is not exactly revenge, and it is in the nature of the case that the wounded victim does nothing but watch bitterly from the sidelines. What is this phenomenon? And how do we evaluate it? Since there is no action and no agency, there is no blame, in the usual sense. But from another point of view, the virtuous point of view, feeling joy or satisfaction in such circumstances, enjoying the harm or hurt of another person, would seem to count heavily against one's virtue. No doubt a saint would feel no such emotion. But we (most of us anyway) are not saints. Is it legitimate or justified to feel such emotions? Here, I think, is where Arindam's view and mine come to virtual blows, not with respect to what is ideal or what would make a person saintly, but regarding what would be normal and acceptable, even if "human, all too human."

Here is where the distinction between righteous and ordinary *Schadenfreude* comes into play. Ordinary *Schadenfreude* is typically rather grubby, petty, and mean-spirited, as when the prettiest girl in the class gets hit in the face by an icy snowball or the smartest student gets an "F" for bad paper formatting. The harms in question cannot be construed as appropriate to anything that can justifiably be cited as a wrong or an offense on the part of the person harmed. Glee over these misfortunes might stem from a general bitterness—some people enjoy *Schadenfreude* as their primary form of entertainment. Or it might be a result of a general dislike of the victim, or the dislike of a whole group to which the victim belongs. Righteous *Schadenfreude*, however, like legitimate retribution (which is sharply distinguished from vengeance by many authors), presumes a more objective point of view. The difference between retribution and vengeance, I would argue, is not that the former is institutional and the latter merely emotional, but rather that retribution involves the social confirmation of a personal emotion. The one is an embellishment and enrichment of the other, not its antithesis.

Legal institutions and rules of punishment provide the most obvious examples of social confirmation of vindictive emotion, but honor societies have their own extra-legal forms of social confirmation that pay more attention to local mores. Thus we might say that righteous *Schadenfreude* differs from ordinary *Schadenfreude* in involving fitting comeuppance both from the offended party's point of view and from some larger social point of view. The scope of the "social" needs to be further clarified, for this confirmation will be only virtual in most cases. One great advantage of righteous *Schadenfreude* over vengeance is that *Schadenfreude* need not involve any public declaration or display. The vengeful victor, Achilles may roar in glory over Hector's dead body—indeed, his vengeance would not be complete without doing this (or overdoing it, as it turns out), but someone can enjoy his or her *Schadenfreude* utterly in private, betrayed, perhaps, only by a sly smile at an inopportune moment. *Righteous Schadenfreude* is distinguished, at least in theory, by the fact that it can (or could) objectively be defended by the same sort of argument that we employ in justifying any sort of punishment or vengeance, namely, "he got what he deserved."

I would only add that this raises some interesting questions about the satisfaction of emotions. I would not argue that all emotions have conditions of satisfaction, but surely some do. Anger is one of them. We speak quite easily of satisfying one's anger (as of satisfying one's "thirst for revenge"). The linkage between emotion and desire is an intimate one. However, I do not think that the satisfaction of an emotion is the same thing as the satisfaction of a component desire. But let me leave this tantalizing topic for another occasion.

# References

Busquet, J. 1920. *Le droit de vendetta et les pacii corse*. Paris: Pedone.
Kant, Immanuel. 1996 [1797]. *The metaphysics of morals*, trans. and ed. Mary Gregor. Cambridge: Cambridge University Press.
Solomon, Robert C. 1999. Justice v. vengeance: On law and the satisfaction of emotion. In *The passions of law*, ed. Susan A. Bandes, 123–148. New York: New York University Press.
Sommers, Tamler. 2009. The two faces of revenge: Moral responsibility and the culture of honor. *Biology and Philosophy* 24: 35–50.

# Chapter 6
# Sentimentality in Life and Literature

Jenefer Robinson

**Abstract** In his paper "In Defense of Sentimentality" in the book of the same name, Robert Solomon aims to rehabilitate the concept of sentimentality both in life and in literature, and to defend it against its many critics. He argues that the root sense of "sentimentality" is simply "an expression of and appeal to the tender emotions" and that the most common criticisms of sentimentality as a kind of emotional affectation, falsity, or self-indulgence fail. In this paper I argue that the critics are right to say that sentimentality in *real life* can be ethically problematic, but that Solomon is right to say that sentimental responses to sentimental *literature* are (usually) ethically harmless. It's true that sentimental literature is not usually "great literature." Its goal is usually pleasure rather than increasing our moral understanding, and partly for this reason it may not be as aesthetically valuable as the great realist novels of George Eliot, Henry James and company. On the other hand, Solomon is quite right to argue that sentimental novels serve an important ethical function in promoting what literary scholar Robyn Warhol calls the "effeminate" virtues of tenderness and compassion.

## Introduction

In his paper "In Defense of Sentimentality" in the book of the same name, Robert Solomon mounts an attempt to rehabilitate the concept of sentimentality, both in life and in literature, and to defend it against its many critics. He argues that the root

J. Robinson (✉)
Department of Philosophy, University of Cincinnati, Cincinnati, OH, USA
e-mail: Jenefer.Robinson@uc.edu

K. Higgins and D. Sherman (eds.), *Passion, Death, and Spirituality*,
Sophia Studies in Cross-cultural Philosophy of Traditions and Cultures 1,
DOI 10.1007/978-94-007-4650-3_6, © Springer Science+Business Media Dordrecht 2012

sense of "sentimentality" is simply "an expression of and appeal to the tender emotions" and that the most common criticisms of sentimentality as a kind of emotional affectation or self-indulgence fail (Solomon 2004a).

In this essay I will argue that with respect to situations in *life*, Solomon overstates his case: the term 'sentimentality' does have the positive meaning Solomon ascribes to it, but it is also correctly used in a negative sense. I will suggest that the negative meaning or meanings of 'sentimentality' correspond to ethical flaws to which the tender emotions are particularly susceptible, although sentimentality in the negative sense is not confined to the tender emotions. However, when we turn to literature the situation is very different. When Solomon argues there's "nothing wrong" with sentimentality in *literature* and that the tender emotions evoked by sentimental literature can be a force for good, I believe he is largely right. For most people in most situations, sentimental literature is ethically harmless and may even be ethically positive. But, although ethically respectable, sentimental literature is not the highest form of literature from an *aesthetic* point of view. The greatest works of realist literature avoid the simplistic stereotypes that sentimental literature characteristically employs. Nevertheless, given their much wider currency, sentimental novels may be a more powerful force for good than more aesthetically valuable novels. Moreover, sentimental novels and films typically endorse what Robyn Warhol calls "effeminate" values of tenderness and hopefulness that may be "mythologies" but are nonetheless ethically valuable. Like Warhol, Solomon advocates for these values and is to be applauded for doing so.

## Defending the Tender Emotions

As Solomon rightly notes, the word "sentiment" has a noble heritage in the moral sentiment theory that flourished in the eighteenth century with Hume, Hutcheson, Burke, Adam Smith and others, and was taken up by thinkers of the French Enlightenment such as Rousseau. "A man of sentiment" was a man of fine feeling, and this was a good thing to be. This positive sense of "sentimental" is still current.[1] Thus we might say of a person that she is *more sentimental* than her sister because she, unlike the sister, is more emotionally sensitive and empathetic. Perhaps, for example, she has more tender memories of their less than ideal father, sympathizes with him, tends his grave, and speaks of him with affection and respect. Similarly, Marcia Eaton imagines a television anchorman tearing up on screen after a particularly affecting story and excusing himself by saying he is "sentimental," meaning simply that he is emotionally sensitive and has tender feelings (see Eaton 1989: 270).

---

[1] Thanks to Kathleen Higgins for insisting on this point in her comments on an earlier version of this paper, read at the American Society for Aesthetics Pacific Division meeting, April 2008. I am very grateful to Professor Higgins's insightful comments, which led me to make extensive revisions to my paper.

But the term "sentimental" is often also used as a term of abuse. In this sense sentimentality is "the name of a deficiency or a weakness," a defect in moral character (Solomon 2004a: 4). Marcia Eaton documents "the earliest undisputed use of 'sentimental'" in a 1749 letter from Mrs. Balfour (Lady Bradshagel) to Samuel Richardson, where the term clearly has positive connotations, comprehending "everything clever and agreeable" (Eaton 1989: 270. See Sprague 1933). But Eaton notes that already by 1785 the term is used in a derogatory sense by Henry Mackenzie in *The Lounger*, where "refined sentimentalists" are described as "content with talking of virtues which they never practice, who pay in words what they owe in actions" (p. 270).[2]

So how are we to define sentimentality, as a virtue or as a vice? In line with the eighteenth century moral sentiment theorists, Solomon defines the 'core' or 'minimal' sense of sentimentality as "an expression of and appeal to the tender emotions," such as "pity, sympathy, fondness, adoration, compassion" (2004a: 9). But he acknowledges the existence of other more negative definitions, the "loaded" definition in terms of "emotional weakness or 'excessive' emotion," the "diagnostic" definition "in terms of emotional self-indulgence," and the "epistemological" definition in terms of 'false or 'fake' emotions" (p. 8). These conceptions of sentimentality correspond to some of the leading arguments of its critics, that sentimental emotions are excessive or self-indulgent, and that they are false in some way.[3]

Solomon argues that these criticisms of sentimentality are criticisms of the tender emotions themselves, indeed indirectly of *emotions* themselves. It is after all a common belief in our culture that emotions – as opposed to reason – are signs of weakness or excess, self-indulgence and error. According to this mythology, whereas reason is strong and masculine and authoritative, emotion is weak, self-indulgent, and error-prone, like the female of the species (see, e.g., Lutz 1998, ch. 1). Solomon argues that by focusing on sentimentality in a pejorative sense, critics have brought the tender emotions into disrepute.

Underlying Solomon's argument is a passionate defense of the value of the emotions in general and, in particular, the virtues of tenderness, compassion, sympathy, fondness, affection and so on, which he thinks are undervalued in our culture. Solomon claims that when sentimentality is attacked, "what is being criticized… is all too often neither an excess of emotion nor a lack of hard-headed rationality, but the very evidence of emotion as such" (2004a: ix). Again: "Our disdain for sentimentality is the rationalist's discomfort with any display of emotion, warranted as well as unwarranted, appropriate as well as inappropriate" (p. 4). And he retorts that "if the tender emotions … are thought to be not only ethically irrelevant but also ethically undesirable, then it is not sentimentality that should be called into question

---

[2] As she notes, this remark anticipates Oscar Wilde's widely quoted description of sentimentality as "[having] the luxury of an emotion without paying for it." See also footnote 11.

[3] Newman (2008) has criticized Solomon's definition of sentimentality on the grounds that it fails to explain how the positive concept of sentimentality relates to these other more negative concepts. But, as I will argue shortly, Solomon could respond that sentimental emotions in the bad sense are tender (or other) emotions that are evoked in inappropriate circumstances of certain kinds.

but the conception of ethics that would dictate such an inhuman response" (p. 9).[4]
He also defends sentimentality in literature and the other arts: there is nothing wrong
with arousing emotions, including the tender emotions, and nothing wrong with a
"good cry" over a sentimental novel or film. Indeed, there is something badly wrong
with artworks that *fail* to touch our emotions, however skillfully crafted they may be
or however cleverly they deconstruct themselves.

Now, emotions are not in general either good or bad in themselves. As Aristotle
said long ago, the virtuous person is one who feels the right emotion in the right
degree for the right object for the right reason. Some emotions might seem to be
always vices, such as envy, hatred, or anger, but admiring envy can be a spur to
virtue, while hatred of the genuinely hateful and anger at what is genuinely offensive
are reasonable and just. Even compassion can be excessive or misplaced. On the
other hand, it is the tender emotions that come closest to being virtues. Even when
compassion, love or sympathy *is* excessive or misplaced, it is usually harmless. If I feel
excessive compassion for my car that has to drive me around for such long hours on
very bumpy roads, this might be foolish but in itself it is hardly unethical.

Solomon seems to agree with Aristotle when he admits that he doesn't "want to
argue that sentimentality (or emotions in general [sic]) is 'good in itself'" (2004a: 11),
because "whether a particular emotion is 'appropriate' depends upon the situation,
including the object and nature of the emotion in question, the identity and character
of the person having the emotion, and the overall social context" (p. 11). But he is
also very insistent that there is basically "*nothing* wrong with sentimentality," (p. 4)
which seems to imply that the tender emotions are in normal cases ethically positive, or at worst neutral. He argues that "though one can manipulate and abuse such
feelings (including one's own), and though they can on occasion be misdirected or
excessive, there is nothing wrong with them as such..." (p. 4). Or again: "We can
agree that certain sentiments and sentimentality can be inappropriate and excessive
without granting that sentiments and sentimentality are immoral or pathological as
such..." (p. 7). But no emotions are "immoral or pathological as such," and all emotions can be "inappropriate and excessive" at times.

Solomon is quite right to praise the tender emotions as essential to a healthy
emotional and ethical life. And he is probably right that most of the time "there is
nothing wrong with sentimentality," defined as "an appeal to tender feelings." What
I want to deny is that there is "nothing wrong" with sentimentality even when it is
defined pejoratively. Solomon argues that the so-called ethical flaws, such as "falsity"
and "self-indulgence," of which the tender emotions have been accused, are not
flaws after all. But, as I will show, when we are talking about real life (as opposed
to sentimental literature) sentimentality does refer to certain ethical flaws, flaws to
which the tender emotions are especially prone. It is comforting to see the world
through rose-colored glasses, i.e., to distort or falsify the way the world appears in
order to feel tender about it. This is the accusation that the tender emotions have a
false or distorted object. Because the tender emotions are usually virtuous, they

---

[4] Solomon blames Immanuel Kant for the anti-emotion stance in ethics.

make us feel good and they make us feel good about ourselves. Hence it is easy to indulge them just because they make us feel good. This is the accusation of self-indulgence. And because it is so much more pleasant to feel tender and to feel good about oneself for feeling tender than it is to actually *do* anything, there is less motivation to actually perform any tender actions. This is the accusation of failing to make one's actions fit one's feelings. In short, I suggest that the tender emotions are peculiarly susceptible to certain flaws, which critics of sentimentality have rightly identified.

When Solomon argues that there is "nothing wrong" with sentimentality, he is largely right if by 'sentimentality' he means an appeal to the tender emotions when they have the right object for the right reason in the right degree. But when he argues that there is nothing wrong with the distortion, failure to act, and self-indulgence that are the flaws to which the tender emotions are prone, he is going too far.

Interestingly, most of the examples Solomon presents to rebut the case against sentimentality draw upon examples from sentimentality in *literature* and the sentimental responses that sentimental plots and characters aim to evoke, rather than from sentimentality in life situations. I think this is highly significant. As we will see, many of the arguments against sentimentality in real life have little force against sentimentality in literature and film.

## The Ethics of Sentimentality in Real Life

Solomon argues that the accusations against the tender emotions on which the various pejorative senses of 'sentimentality" are based are in fact unjustified: (1) *All* emotions "falsify" or "distort" in a certain sense, so there is nothing wrong with the tender emotions that is not just as much of a problem for every other emotion. (2) There is nothing wrong with the so-called "self-indulgence" of tender emotions. (3) And although sentimental people may, as Michael Tanner argues, "avoid following up their responses with appropriate actions" (Tanner 1976–1977: 140, emphasis removed), *all* emotions are subject to similar "hypocrisy, self-deception, and incontinence" (Solomon 2004a: 13). In short, Solomon argues that *either* there is "nothing wrong" with sentimentality as a moral trait, *or*, if there *is* something wrong, it is nothing that other emotions don't suffer from as well.

(1) **Falsity**. Solomon says that "[t]he most common charge against sentimentality is that it involves false emotion" (2004a: 14). Mark Jefferson, for example, criticizes sentimentality as "[involving] attachment to a distorted series of beliefs" (Jefferson 1983: 526). The "fictions that sustain sentimentality" emphasize "such things as the sweetness, dearness, littleness, blamelessness, and vulnerability of the emotions' objects" (pp. 526–527). He claims that "[t]he simplistic appraisal necessary to sentimentality is also a direct impairment to the moral vision taken of its objects" (p. 527), and while this may sometimes be "harmless," the danger is that sentimentality, once allowed, will "naturally [extend] itself elsewhere" and affect "one's

moral vision" of other things too (p. 527). There are two objections to this dire view of the matter. First, on the face of it, there seems little wrong with emphasizing the sweet, the blameless and the vulnerable, and second, there is no reason to think that sentimentality is a kind of virus that infects *all* one's emotions even when they have nothing to do with the sweet and the blameless.

Solomon has a different argument. He objects that even if it is true that sentimentality "distorts" the world in the sense that it focuses only on the sweet, the innocent, the vulnerable, etc., in this respect it is like every other emotion, since *all* emotions take a partial viewpoint on the world: "anger only looks at the offense and fails to take account of the virtue of the antagonist; jealousy is aware only of the threat and not of the wit and charms of the rival..." (Solomon 2004a: 16). What Jefferson calls the "distorted" view of reality we get from sentimental emotions is really a "'focus' or 'concern,'" and all emotions focus on one aspect of a situation rather than another. As Solomon says: "All emotions construct a perspective of reality that is specifically suited to their natures" (p. 16). Thus the tender emotions are "specifically suited" to the sweet, the dear, the little, the blameless, and the vulnerable. We naturally feel tender towards babies and innocent children, towards small cuddly (non-threatening) animals and the dear old folks at home.

But this benign picture is oversimplified. In particular, it fails to note that the "falsification" in which sentimentality (in a negative sense) traffics is not just a focus of attention on certain ways of seeing the world rather than others. Some ways of seeing the world are probing and thoughtful; others are simply the result of accepting common stereotypes. A tender emotion that is sentimentalized in the negative sense views real children as pure, innocent, and vulnerable regardless of what they are like as individuals. Solomon is right to argue against Jefferson that all emotions focus attention on the world as viewed from a particular perspective, rather than from the balanced all-things-considered viewpoint demanded by rationality and objectivity. But what he ignores is that a sentimental viewpoint 'falsifies' its objects insofar as it is based on viewing the world in terms of stereotypes.

It may be morally harmless, of course, to view little children as innocent and vulnerable, but sometimes tender emotions take an inappropriate object, as when an old soldier feels nostalgic for war: he remembers the camaraderie but forgets the deaths and the killing.[5] Moreover, such falsifications are usually the result of an unworthy *motivation*, namely a desire for self-gratification. This is the accusation of self-indulgence.

(2) **Self-Indulgence**. Anthony Savile agrees with Jefferson that when I "sentimentalize" an object, "something in my thought about it will be false or evidentially unjustified," but he thinks that these faults "do not capture [the] essence" of sentimentality (Savile 1982/2008: 337).[6] After all, he argues, the sentimentalist will cling to the thought on

---

[5] Solomon says that such cases – which I would say are of tender emotions with inappropriate objects – do not constitute an indictment of the tender emotions *in themselves*, but, as we have seen, he also agrees with Aristotle that there are no emotions that are good or bad *in themselves*.

[6] In his essay Solomon does not cite Savile, but he is to my mind the most sophisticated of the critics of sentimentality.

which the emotion rests, even when shown its falsity or lack of evidentiary support, because "what holds the thought in place is not a desire for truth and knowledge" but "a desire that can be satisfied by seeing the object in a false light" (p. 338), namely a desire for some enjoyable emotion. "Where the object itself does not properly support the thought" on which the emotion should be grounded, the sentimentalist resorts to "projection" (p. 338). Savile has a nice example: "I may sentimentalize the duckling I am about to eat "by falsely representing it to myself as eagerly waiting for the pot" (p. 338), thereby enabling me to feel pleasant feelings of benevolence and gratitude to the duckling. Here my tender feelings are inappropriate and rest on a "falsification" of the duckling and its "feelings." Or I may sentimentalize children or pets by "projecting onto them an exaggerated vulnerability and innocence," solely in order to be able to view myself as a person of "gentleness and fine feeling" (p. 338). Mary Midgley agrees: "Being sentimental is misrepresenting the world in order to indulge our feelings" (Midgley 1979: 385).

As Savile points out, many emotions (he thinks *all* emotions) can be "sentimentalized" in this way, not just the tender emotions that Solomon emphasizes. Savile claims that what "sentimentality" refers to is not a particular kind of feeling, but "a *mode* of feeling or thought" (Savile 2008: 337. As he says, it is not only emotions that "we experience with pleasure" (p. 338) that can be sentimentalized; a man can be "sentimentally angry or indignant" if feeling these emotions "works to enable him to take a gratifying view of his own character," and one can even imagine sentimental jealousy or hatred if, say, "my jealousy [supports] a pleasing view of myself as a man of grand passion" or "my hatred for some luckless neighbour [serves] to endow me with a gratifying heroism that otherwise I would not take myself to possess." (p. 339). In short, the sentimentalist "achieves a certain kind of gratification by false-colouring an object in his thought" (p. 339). The peculiar kind of gratification involved in a "sentimental fantasy" is the result of a "tendency to idealize its objects, to present them as pure, noble, heroic, vulnerable, innocent, etc." In summary, for Savile "a sentimental mode of thought is typically one that idealizes its object under the guidance of a desire for gratification and reassurance" (p. 340).

I am not sure that "idealize" is quite the right word here. Phidias and Michelangelo *idealize* the gods and heroes they represent, but their sculptures are far from sentimental. Jefferson's diagnosis of "what's wrong with sentimentality" points in the right direction: as we saw, he claims that when tender feelings are sentimental, it is because they are focused on the sweet, the dear, the blameless, and the vulnerable, in other words, on *stereotypes* of the proper objects of tenderness, such as angelic little girls, cuddly small animals, and the old folks at home. Given that *any* emotion can be "sentimentalized," the stereotypes will vary depending upon the emotion in question. The man who is sentimentally indignant sees himself as embodying the stereotype of a man of fine feeling who stands up for justice at any cost. The man who is sentimentally jealous sees himself as embodying the stereotype of "a man of grand passion."

According to this view, sentimentality is not so obviously ethically positive or neutral. If the (or a) reason one feels tender feelings towards one's aged parents is that it gives one a gratifying sense that one is a model of filial piety, this is not ethically praiseworthy. Similarly, if the (or a) reason for one's moral indignation is that it allows one to feel self-righteously pleased with oneself for having such fine feelings, this does not seem very virtuous either. Sentimentality in the negative sense so well analyzed by Savile is a form of emotional dishonesty or hypocrisy.[7]

In his own discussion of the accusation of self-indulgence, Solomon focuses on a remark by Milan Kundera in *The Unbearable Lightness of Being*. Kundera characterizes kitsch – or sentimentality – as causing "two tears to flow in quick succession. The first tear says: how nice to see children running on the grass! The second tear says: How nice to be moved, together with all mankind, by children running on the grass! It is the second tear that makes kitsch kitsch" (Kundera 1984: 251). In Kundera's example, we perceive "children running on the grass" as stereotypes of children as pure, innocent, and vulnerable and we respond to them with tender feelings: "how nice to see children running on the grass!" We then reflect on these feelings in a self-gratifying way: "How nice to be moved, together with all mankind, by children running on the grass!" We get pleasure out of feeling these tender emotions (or, in other cases, indignant or jealous emotions) solely or mainly because it enhances our self-esteem. The children are not the real object of the emotion; they are just the occasion for feelings of self-satisfaction.

Solomon tries to rebut the accusation of self-indulgence by arguing that there is nothing wrong with either Kundera's first or second tears: "we feel good about ourselves when we experience the tender emotions, and we feel even better when, reflectively, we perceive ourselves as the sort of people who feel such feelings" (Solomon 2004a: 11–12). Kundera's attack fails because *reflection* on the tender emotions is not wrong at all. On the contrary, such reflection is good, and there is no reason why it shouldn't be accompanied by a tear.[8] What this argument ignores, however, is that it is not the *fact* of reflection that makes Kundera's example sentimental. It is the *nature* of the reflection. I am congratulating myself on my sensitivity, when all I have actually achieved is a "cheap" apprehension of the innocence and vulnerability of childhood, or something of that sort. Children running on the grass may indeed be innocent and vulnerable (although maybe not), but we know nothing in detail about these children, nothing to warrant musings about their vulnerability or innocence.

The focus of a sentimental emotion, whether love or compassion or indignation, is the self and its self-congratulation, and there *is* something wrong with this. And if, further, the chief *reason* for having the emotion is not to focus on innocent little children (or whatever), but to achieve a flattering sense of oneself, then this simply compounds the wrong. In consequentialist terms, perhaps, this kind of self-congratulation may have no ill effects on other people (although it is not helpful to them either), but it is certainly a character flaw.

---

[7] It probably often involves self-deception.

[8] Solomon also says (2004a: 11–12) that similar reflection about one's anger or fear would not be regarded as sentimental, but this is wrong, as we have seen from Savile's discussion.

In short, while it is surely good practice to reflect upon one's emotional responses to situations and events, and especially to reflect on their ethical implications, sentimental reflections of the sort identified by Kundera are not good training for morality, as Solomon claims, because the reflection is not honest or careful or indeed genuine *reflection* at all. The so-called "reflection" is "shallow" and "unearned:" a gratifying thought about how sensitive or morally virtuous one is without any real thought about the actual object of the emotion, the vulnerability or innocence of childhood.[9]

(3) **The absence of appropriate action**. The sentimentalizing stereotyping of the object of one's emotion is responsible for the "falsity" of a sentimental emotion; the feeling of gratification one gets from having the emotion is responsible for the "self-indulgence" of the sentimental emotion. And because, as Savile says, it is much "harder [for me] to be a man of fine feeling by proper response to the objects around me" than "to fabricate such a characterization of myself by some factitious projection," self-indulgence often goes together with a lack of appropriate response: "provided that the feeling I generate is one that does underpin the character I want, sentimentality may offer me the added advantage that I may not need to go on and actually do anything about it" (Savile 2008: 338). This complaint about sentimentality is echoed by Michael Tanner who characterizes as sentimental "that range of feelings which help to increase one's sense of one's own superiority so long as no activity is required" (Tanner 1976–1977: 139–140), for example, "righteous indignation, on the basis of which no action can be taken" (ibid.: 139). He notes *inter alia* that one mark of sentimental people is that they "avoid following up their responses with *appropriate* actions; or if they do follow them up appropriately, it is adventitious" (Tanner 1976–1977: 140). So, for example, one feels tender feelings towards one's aged parents after they have died, although while they were alive one made their lives a misery. Here the tender feelings occur only after tender actions are no longer possible.[10] Now, in this particular example such thoughts do no damage to the deceased parents, because they are deceased, but it is a strong indication of a character flaw, namely, a certain sort of emotional dishonesty and self-flattery.[11]

Solomon's response to this accusation is oblique. He claims that "there is always room for hypocrisy, self-deception, and incontinence," but he asks rhetorically "is there any greater danger here than elsewhere in the realm of human behavior?" (2004a: 13). He seems to be saying that the accusation is not something peculiar to

---

[9] Both Oscar Wilde and Michael Tanner have stressed that the sentimental emotion is "unearned" and "shallow." See Tanner (1976–1977). Savile's account of sentimentality explains in what sense this is right.

[10] One can also sentimentalize the deaths themselves, thinking to oneself (as one pockets one's inheritance) how lucky it is that they both died at the same time and how comforting it will be for them to arrive in heaven together.

[11] This accusation about sentimentality was articulated memorably by Oscar Wilde in a letter from prison to Lord Alfred Douglas: "[A] sentimentalist is simply one who desires to have the luxury of an emotion without paying for it. ... Even the finest and most self-sacrificing emotions have to be paid for. Strangely enough, that is what makes them fine." Quoted in Tanner (1976–1977: 127).

sentimentality, presumably in the sense of "the tender emotions," and, as we have seen, this is quite true: *any* emotions can be "sentimentalized." Moreover, beliefs and desires are also subject to hypocrisy and self-deception. But this argument does not show that the particular hypocrisy under discussion here is not unethical. On the contrary: Solomon seems to grant that it is indeed ethically problematic.[12]

It seems to me that Savile and others have conclusively shown that sentimentality in the negative sense is an "ethical flaw" and not "an ethical virtue" (Solomon 2004a: 9). True, there is nothing wrong with "the tender emotions" when experienced for the right objects, in the right degree and for the right reasons, but they are peculiarly susceptible to being "sentimentalized." Moreover, *all* emotions are open to this kind of hypocrisy and self-indulgence, and it is not ethically praiseworthy.

The case is very different, however, when we turn to sentimental literature and film.[13] Here the accusations against sentimentality do not have the same bite. As I remarked at the end of the previous section, it is significant that most of Solomon's examples when he is defending sentimentality are taken not from life, but from literature.

## The Ethics of Sentimentality in Literature

Solomon makes large claims for the importance of literature that evokes the tender emotions in its readers. A "good cry" over Little Nell (in Dickens' *Old Curiosity Shop*) or Little Eva (in *Uncle Tom's Cabin*) "stimulates and exercises our sympathies without straining or exhausting them" (Solomon 2004a: 19). It gives us practice in feeling the tender emotions, and that is a good thing: "sentimentality in literature might best be defended as the cultivation and 'practice' of our moral-emotional faculties" (p. 9). Moreover, even if it is granted that we *enjoy* feeling tender over Little Nell or Little Eva, there is nothing wrong with such enjoyment. Indeed it is good to enjoy feeling the tender emotions. When, over and over again Solomon insists that there is "*nothing wrong*" with sentimentality, I suspect he has mainly in mind sentimental novels (and other artworks) and readers' sentimental responses to them rather than sentimentality in real life.

The case against sentimentality in literature and our responses to literature is similar in some ways, but not all, to the case against sentimentality in life. (1) When it comes to matching one's emotional responses to appropriate actions, it would seem that there are *no* appropriate actions to be taken in response to sentimentally described characters and situations in literature, unlike sentimentally conceived

---

[12] I suspect that the real reason why Solomon's argument here is weak is that most of his examples focus on sentimentality in *literature* where, as we shall see shortly, this particular criticism of sentimentality does not apply.

[13] There is also sentimental *painting* such as the Bouguereau painting that Solomon discusses in Solomon (2004b): 235–254, but I don't have space to discuss it here.

people and situations in real life. But (2) with respect to both life and literature, one's emotional responses can be "distorted" in a similar way and (3) can be subject to the same sort of "self-indulgence." Finally, (4) Solomon discusses a criticism of sentimental responses to literature that has no counterpart in the critique of sentimentality in real life: sentimental novels and films *manipulate* our emotions, whereas sentimental responses in real life are typically the result of our own psychological manipulations – often unconscious – rather than anyone else's. I will briefly discuss each of these criticisms in turn.

(1) **The absence of appropriate action**. As Solomon points out, when we read in a novel about the death of Little Nell or Little Eva there is nothing we are called upon to *do*, since nothing we are able to do will alter the fate of these fictional little girls. So the accusation that sentimentalists do not match their actions to their feelings is inappropriate when we are talking about feelings for fictions.[14]

But what is so interesting about these and similar cases is that, as Solomon points out, sentimental novels have often been a powerful force for social change. Dickens laid bare the appalling conditions in which the urban poor lived during the Industrial Revolution and was partly responsible for a number of important social reforms. *Uncle Tom's Cabin* was very influential in the eventual abolition of slavery. So we cannot criticize sentimental responses to literature as ethically flawed on the grounds that they never result in appropriate action. Quite the contrary. *Uncle Tom's Cabin* in particular was overtly a work of propaganda: Harriet Beecher Stowe explicitly writes that she has tried to demonstrate as vividly as possible the "heartbreak" and the "horrors" of slavery. And she succeeded: the book evoked powerful emotions in its readers that had real positive ethical consequences in the actual world.

(2) **Falsity**. Solomon criticizes the idea that sentimental emotional responses to literature are "distorted" or "false" in some way. He cites Midgley as arguing that Little Nell, for example, is a "false" character, in the sense that she is not "true to life" and that our feelings for her are therefore "distorted" (see Midgley 1979: 385–386). Little Nell – "dear, gentle, patient, noble Nell" – is an impossibly angelic little girl, who never has an unkind thought or performs a malicious act, and who has spent her whole young life looking after her grandfather. As we saw earlier, Solomon claims that what Midgley and Jefferson call "distortion" is better thought of as 'focus' or 'concern:' the focus of the novel is on Little Nell's purity, selflessness, gentleness, and goodness, and, he asks rhetorically, what is wrong with that? Far from being ethically problematic, responding to scenes such as Little Nell's death encourages us to feel the tender emotions, which are so essential to our moral life. One might reply that there is nothing to be morally proud of in responding tenderly to Little Nell, but, nevertheless, Solomon is quite right that it isn't ethically harmful either.

(3) **Self-Indulgence**. According to Savile, the main problem with sentimentality is that it 'distorts' or 'falsifies' "under the guidance of a desire for gratification and

---

[14] I suppose we could revile the authors for killing off these angelic little girls, but this would hardly make us any less sentimental in our response to these novels.

reassurance" (Savile 2008: 340). Readers enjoy weeping over the death of Little Nell partly because it induces in them tender feelings that are enjoyable to experience and gratifying to reflect on: feeling tender about Little Nell is evidence that one is capable of feeling the tender feelings, and that makes us feel good about ourselves.[15] But unlike in real life, there isn't anything ethically wrong with this: because Little Nell is fictional, we are not morally compelled to see her death as a terrible tragedy, as it would be in real life. Deep grief for Little Nell would be inappropriate. If we respond emotionally in a "self-indulgent" way to a sentimental novel, this is a harmless way of getting "gratification and reassurance," which, after all, we all need and seek in our lives. We know that Dickens's description of Little Nell's death is tendentious, but we get pleasure from accepting the rose-colored view of the world that is presented to us. This is, after all, a form of "escapist" literature. So for normal readers in normal circumstances, it is hard to find anything ethically harmful about weeping "self-indulgently" for Little Nell, nor does it seem to be a sign of a defective moral character. Solomon seems to be quite right that there is "nothing wrong" with indulging one's tender feelings by reading sentimental novels and he may also be right to suggest that indulging one's tender feelings for the fictional Little Nell can encourage us to react tenderly to her real-life counterparts.

(4) **Authorial Manipulation**. This final argument is restricted to literature and has no apparent relevance to real life. Solomon addresses the argument that what is wrong with sentimentality in literature is that it involves the *manipulation* of the reader's emotions. This supposedly results in both a "moral flaw," namely, the reader's "failure to control and contain these emotions," and an aesthetic flaw, namely interference with the reader's "autonomy and aesthetic appreciation." According to this view, although "any normal reader" will probably feel some emotion in reading a novel, "this is as irrelevant to good literature as it is to doing the right thing in ethics" (Solomon 2004a: 9).

Solomon thinks that this line of attack is nothing less than an attack on the emotions themselves: "It is emotional engagement as such that is alien to the properly rational and ideally detached self" (Solomon 2004a: 10). As he quite rightly points out, *all* authors "manipulate" the emotions of their readers in the sense that authors always and inevitably describe characters, events and situations from a particular perspective, often an emotional perspective, and (almost always) encourage their readers to adopt this perspective. In this way literary works invariably influence how we see the world and react to it. Indeed, this is one of the reasons why we praise novels: they get us to see the world in new ways so that we may experience emotional responses different from those which we normally have and thereby expand our emotional repertoire (see Robinson 2005).

What Solomon ignores or downplays, however, is that authors "manipulate" their readers in very different ways. The authors of sentimental novels write in such a way that they strongly encourage the reader to adopt certain emotions without inviting

---

[15] Solomon says in his comments on Kundera, "we feel good about ourselves when we experience the tender emotions, and we feel even better when, reflectively, we perceive ourselves as the sort of people who feel such feelings," Solomon, op cit pp.11–12.

much reflection about whether these emotions are appropriate or not. Dickens, for example, clearly wants us to think of Little Nell as a perfect little child and to think of her death as peaceful and angelic, just like she is herself, so he says nothing about any pain or suffering or bodily decay (see Eaton 1989: 276). Little Nell is pictured as happily and uncomplainingly ascending into Heaven, where all the other little angels are, and readers are encouraged to feel both pity and pleasure at the scene, rather than reflecting on the state of medical care in Victorian England or whether Little Nell is realistically drawn.

Nevertheless, once again Solomon is right to say that there is nothing ethically wrong with this kind of manipulation by a sentimental novel. Although the sentimental author manipulates the readers' emotions and discourages deep reflection about them, and although there is something self-indulgent in enjoying the tender feelings the author has aroused – and enjoying one's self-image as a tender-hearted person – nevertheless, such sentimental responses to literary and other fictions seem to be ethically harmless. The death of a young child in real life is tragic and there is nothing pleasurable about it. If the child is angelic, that may simply make the tragedy more poignant. If one's tears at the death of a real child, however angelic, are accompanied by gratification at how tenderly one is responding, that would be morally appalling. But where the response is to a sentimental fiction, there is no such moral stigma. One is, after all, supposed to *enjoy* reading such fictions.

All in all, Solomon's case is far stronger for sentimental responses to literature than for sentimental responses in life. Indeed he seems to be right that there is nothing wrong with "a good cry" over the death of a fictional little girl, even if it is accompanied by a pleasantly self-indulgent frisson. And if the little girl is an outspoken advocate for the abolition of slavery, then the tenderness we feel for her may translate into virtuous action: we may join the ranks of abolitionists. Yet Solomon's defense of sentimental responses to literature may nevertheless make us uneasy. Even though he is right to argue that there is no serious ethical deficiency in the sentimental novel, his defense of the sentimental novel downplays the limitations of the genre from an *aesthetic* point of view.

## The Sentimental Novel as a Literary Genre

As we saw earlier, the concept of "sentimentality" originated in the eighteenth century with the moral sentiment ethical theorists. Sentimental literature was born at around the same time. Famous examples of eighteenth century sentimental literature include Samuel Richardson's *Clarissa* and *Pamela* (satirized by Henry Fielding in *Shamela*), in which pure, innocent young girls resist rich and evil seducers.[16] Such classics were followed by "thousands of widely read potboilers and romances,

---

[16] Laurence Sterne's *A Sentimental Journey through France and Italy* (1768) seems to be exploiting the tradition of sentimental literature while simultaneously poking fun at it. Jane Austen's *Sense and Sensibility* also mocks the tradition: Marianne Dashwood has too much "sensibility" and too little of her sister Eleanor's rational "sense."

turned out by "a flood of popular women writers" (Solomon 2004a: 6). As has been widely documented, the novel was a genre designed to satisfy the new middle classes of Europe and North America, and in particular middle class women, and within the genre of the novel, the *sentimental* novel became a popular sub-genre, an early example of art for the masses.

Noël Carroll has described mass art as "designed to gravitate in its structural choices to those choices that promise accessibility with minimum effort" (Carroll 1998: 196), a description which admirably fits the sentimental novel, which makes few intellectual demands on its readers, and which powerfully encourages readers to feel certain fairly specific emotions. Carroll describes how different popular genres of film and literature are designed to arouse emotions that are "criterially pre-focused," by which he means that "the descriptions and depiction of the object of our attention in the text will activate our subsumption of the relevant characters and events under the categories that are criterially apposite to the emotional state in question" (Carroll 1999: 30). Thus, *horror movies* typically feature loathsome monsters that are "criterially apposite" objects of fear and disgust, *suspense movies* are suspenseful and typically evoke suspense, and *melodramas* typically evoke *hatred* or *contempt* for the evil villain and *pity* for the misfortunes of the virtuous, attractive, and long-suffering heroine (or hero) as well as *admiration* for her (or his) courage and endurance. Sentimental novels are a species of melodrama, with the focus not so much on an evil oppressor as on the pure and innocent victim.[17] The "criterially pre-focused" emotions we feel for these victims include the "tender emotions" of sympathy, pity, and affection.[18]

The function of all mass art genres is ultimately *pleasure*. Popular genres such as melodrama, suspense, and horror are all genres of "entertainment," which are designed primarily to entertain, i.e., to bring *pleasure* to readers and viewers. Sometimes a member of one of these genres will rise "above" the genre, and adopt "higher" cognitive and/or aesthetic goals, but popular culture is by definition designed to appeal to and to delight the populace, not to preach to them or talk over their heads or make them work too hard to understand what is going on.[19] The different popular genres Carroll discusses give pleasure in different ways, through the evocation of different "criterially pre-focused" emotions.

---

[17] The movie *Brief Encounter*, a paradigmatic sentimental movie or "weepie," lacks any villain and focuses throughout on the pitiable fate of the heroine (and to a lesser extent, the hero) and her moral courage in accepting it, and invites us to feel *compassion* for her situation and *admiration* for her fortitude.

[18] I do not have space here to give a more detailed account of melodrama, or to justify my examples as belonging to the genre of sentimental melodrama. Most of my examples are of sentimental scenes or sentimentalized characters in larger works which may not always be sentimental as a whole. For example, while Dickens' novels almost always have sentimental elements and can legitimately be classified as melodramas, his greatest masterpieces such as *Our Mutual Friend* and *Bleak House* are far more complex than most melodramas and include elements of social criticism and satire as well as sentimentality.

[19] Of course, classics of our day may have started off as popular works only to find themselves canonized in later life.

Interestingly, all three of the genres that Carroll identifies essentially require the evocation of emotions that would normally be characterized as negative: hatred for the villain and sorrow for the pure innocent victim are deliberately invoked by melodrama, fear and disgust by horror movies and novels, and anxiety and suspense by suspense movies and novels. Some viewers and readers may avoid these genres precisely because they do not want to experience these negative emotions, but each of these genres has avid fans, and for these folk the pleasure clearly outweighs or defeats any negative emotions that might also be experienced. I will not speculate here on how this works with respect to horror or suspense, but in the case of the sentimental novel or film, the pleasure clearly *depends upon* the prior evocation of the negative emotions in question.

Consider again the death of Little Nell. I have said that it induces tender feelings in readers, which are pleasurable to experience, as well as a pleasurable (albeit "self-indulgent") sense that one is a good person for feeling such tender feelings. But how does the novel succeed in giving us so much pleasure when it also works so hard to get us to feel sorrow, which is a negative emotion, and compassion, which seems to depend upon feeling sorrow? One way the novel achieves this goal is by emphasizing not the unpleasant aspects of Nell's death but the fact that she has been taken directly to Heaven, that her virtue has been unpolluted (something difficult to maintain in a longer life), and that because of this she has triumphed over death. As Robyn Warhol points out in *Having a Good Cry*, her study of sentimental narratives in literature, film, and television, "having a good cry" at a sentimental novel or film is not (or not just) a symptom of sorrow but a deeply satisfying experience: 'good cry' films "almost always end 'happily,' steeped in [a] sense of triumphant relief." (Warhol 2003: 47). In Little Nell's death scene goodness and purity triumph over evil,[20] and the reader's tender compassion and sympathetic feelings of relief triumph over sorrow.

In this example we see exemplified many of the characteristic features of sentimental novels which are responsible for their characteristic emotional effects and the type of pleasure characteristic of the genre. These characteristic features include *character*, *plot*, *tone* and *theme*. (1) We have already seen that the main *characters* in sentimental novels or films are stereotypes of some sort: pure, innocent, virtuous little girls who are victimized by fate or an evil oppressor, or the impossibly virtuous, noble, self-sacrificing hero, such as the hero in the movie *Brief Encounter*. (2) The *plots* of sentimental novels and films typically concern the triumph of the innocent and courageous but long-suffering heroine/hero over an inexorable fate or an evil oppressor. In a melodrama good almost always triumphs and evil is punished. The trajectory of a typical plot is such as to invite such tender emotions as sorrow, compassion and affection for the innocent victim as well as fear for her fate, and ultimately pleasurable feelings of relief when (s)he triumphs over fate and/or oppression. Indeed the pleasure we feel clearly *depends upon* the prior evocation of negative

---

[20] The evil Quilp cannot triumph over Little Nell. He is thwarted by her death.

emotions such as sorrow and fear, and the greater the sorrow and fear we are induced to feel, the more exultant and relieved we are likely to feel at the ultimate triumph.

Now, it might seem as if the examples I have relied upon do not exemplify this pattern: after all, Little Nell, Little Eva and Uncle Tom all die. But, on the contrary, all three are described as triumphant in death; the way these deaths are described is designed to make us feel joy and hope in the midst of sorrow. The death of Little Nell is portrayed as a victory for goodness and innocence, and readers are encouraged to rejoice even as they weep: this is a paradigm of "the good cry." The death of Uncle Tom in *Uncle Tom's Cabin* is cruel and ignominious, but Stowe does not describe the details of his torture but instead portrays his death as the triumph of virtue. Like Little Nell, he is going straight to heaven to get his just reward. The novel ends on a note of uplift, of hope for Eliza and her newly reunited family in their new life in Liberia,[21] as well as hope that slavery itself will be abolished if Christians in both North and South would only understand the horrors of slavery and come to realize how very unchristian the institution of slavery is. When the death of a "good" character is treated as a spiritual and moral triumph, the sadness and distress we feel at the death makes the joy at the triumph of goodness not only more poignant but also more powerful.

(3) The *tone* of a sentimental novel reflects this mix of joy and sorrow. It is typically an elegiac or bittersweet tone, but the balance is on the sweet rather than the bitter: the bitter is sweetened but the sweet is not embittered. We feel joy at the triumph of goodness and purity over evil, the timelessness of virtue as opposed to the transience of evil and misfortune. The death of an innocent is an occasion for pathos rather than grief. This is in stark contrast to the genre of tragedy, where pleasure as an aesthetic goal is subservient to revealing the tragic truth about the human condition. The blinding of Oedipus and the death of Cordelia are not "sweetened" in any way and are among the most painful events in literature.[22]

(4) Finally, the *themes* of sentimental novels and films are one of the most important sources of the pleasure they provide. In general, the characteristic themes of sentimental novels typically exemplify "mythologies" that we would dearly like to believe rather than the more unsettling truths we find in tragedy: after discussion of such novels and films as *Little Women, An Affair to Remember, Sleepless in Seattle* and *Uncle Tom's Cabin*, Warhol suggests the following as typical sentimental themes: "family affection does transcend death; sisters are friends forever; true love will prevail; courage will be rewarded; [and] affectionate domestic relationships will put an end to racist oppression" (Warhol 2003: 50). Just as the characters of the sentimental novel or film tend to be oversimplified stereotypes, so too the themes of sentimental novels and films are heartwarming but oversimplified, ideals that we would love to accept as universal truths but which in our more skeptical moments

---

[21] Stowe (like her father, who preached that liberated slaves should move to Liberia) seems to have thought that this is a good outcome for Eliza. Other more "radical" voices at the time disagreed.

[22] In his account of tragedy, Aaron Ridley stresses the big difference between the appropriate response to tragedy as compared to the appropriate response to horror movies (Ridley 2003).

we recognize as at best only sometimes or rarely true. But for those who enjoy engaging with sentimental fictions, it is deeply pleasurable to find these ideals, naïve though they be, affirmed and exemplified in the story.

So far I have given broad characterizations of the typical plots, characters, tone and themes of sentimental novels and films. Warhol has some more specific suggestions about the "familiar and highly formulaic narrative practices" – the "technologies of affect" (Warhol 2003: 41) – which sentimental novels and films employ in order to induce a 'good cry.' For example, she thinks that tear-inducing scenes in sentimental novels are often presented from the point of view of a victim or someone who has triumphed over oppression or "sympathetic intermediary figures who are not, themselves, directly oppressed" (p. 45), such as Eva in *Uncle Tom's Cabin*. On other occasions the narrators of sentimental novels use "earnest, direct address to a narratee, calling upon him or her to recognize parallels between lived experience and the situations represented in the fiction" (p. 46). And she suggests that sentimental novels typically make use of "heightened" or flowery language. ("Even so, beloved Eva!... Thou art passing away...") All these "technologies of affect" are designed to deepen our emotional engagement in the sentimental narrative and to induce the mixture of sorrow and joy that is the characteristic emotional effect at which such narratives typically aim.

If this brief and oversimplified account of the sentimental novel is roughly right, it follows that authorial "manipulations" and "distortions" are part and parcel of the genre itself, and the evocation of "self-indulgent" bittersweet emotions is the means by which the sentimental novel achieves the kind of pleasure that it is explicitly designed to provide. None of this seems ethically problematic. The pleasure that sentimental novels provide is merely a harmless diversion or escape from the more complex realities of real life. It seems like mere priggishness to object that sentimental literature and film should not be enjoyed, and that feeling tender emotions for innocent and virtuous little girls is somehow wrong.

For most of us, who are aware of the way the world really is as well as the way it is portrayed in sentimental fictional works, this is all true. For such folk it is a welcome relief to visit for a while a world in which true love prevails, virtue triumphs, and the death of a child signifies another little angel in heaven. Indeed, for those who live in dangerous or difficult circumstances, it may well be psychologically important to ignore the way the world is and enjoy instead a fictional world where things are more hopeful.[23] But while for most of us sentimental reactions to sentimental novels and films are harmless, for certain groups of people such reactions may have potential moral pitfalls. Thus ignorant teenage girls in the West who buy into the myths and stereotypes of sentimental fiction may choose unworthy or

---

[23] In the literature on coping strategies associated with negative emotions such as sadness, fear, anger and anxiety, one mode of coping with negative emotions is precisely to engage in *denial* of the circumstances that generate the emotion. See, in particular, Lazarus (1991). A classic case of such denial is to deny the reality of the death of a young child or to cope with grief by denying that the death is altogether bad: if the young child has gone straight to heaven, then in addition to sorrow one can also feel a sense of joy and relief at the triumph of innocence and goodness.

unrealistic life goals. Such girls may become dissatisfied, disillusioned, and cynical when they discover that true love does not always prevail, courage is not always rewarded, and sisters are not always friends forever. It is potentially morally dangerous to accept the characteristic themes of sentimental fiction as truths about the actual world, and to respond to a work that belongs to the genre of *sentimental* novels or films as if it were a *realistic* novel or film giving a realistic picture of life. However priggish this may sound, it is ultimately better to learn the way the world is rather than the way we would like it to be.[24] On the other hand, for those of us who are skeptical about the myths underlying the sentimental work, it is true that there is usually "nothing wrong" in embracing those myths for a time as we escape into the world of the fiction.[25]

The proper way to appreciate a sentimental novel or film is to allow oneself to be *manipulated* by the fiction, to *indulge* one's emotions in order to get the pleasure the novel or film is designed to induce, and to accept the *distortions* of reality that are part and parcel of the sentimental genre. If we do this, we can experience the pleasure that well written and well-structured sentimental fictions can impart. And sometimes, under the influence of a sentimental "mythology," we may be moved by the fiction to change our actual behavior so that, for example, we are motivated to work to change the conditions in which some oppressed group now lives. But although sentimental novels seem to be ethically harmless for most of us, and sometimes a force for positive good, they suffer *aesthetically* by comparison with the greatest realist novels of the Western tradition, as we will see in the final section.

## The Aesthetics of the Sentimental Novel

Solomon argues that the attack on sentimentality is nothing more nor less than an attack on the emotions themselves. But what are generally agreed to be the greatest realist novels ever written – the best works of Tolstoy, George Eliot, Henry James,

---

[24] In his discussion and defense of sentimentality Ira Newman considers the idea that sentimental works "encourage audiences to acquire oversimplified beliefs and to act on these oversimplifications" (Newman 2008: 345), and he maintains that audiences have to take responsibility for their reactions to artworks, including sentimental artworks, and that people should simply "strengthen" their background knowledge so that they can appreciate a work "from a more balanced perspective" (p. 346). What this response ignores or underemphasizes is that the myths promoted by sentimental novels are very powerful and emotionally seductive, especially to the ignorant and unsophisticated. Mature audiences can deliberately decide to read a mawkish novel because they want to be entertained. Few of us, after all, want a "steady diet" of nothing but the classics. But naïve readers may not know or recognize the conventions of sentimental melodrama, and may take melodramas as realistic and as setting out realistic ideals for life.

[25] Not that the *world of the novel* is necessarily pleasanter than the real world. The worlds of Dickens novels and *Uncle Tom's Cabin* are harsh indeed.

for example – all appeal to the reader's emotions. The big difference between sentimental novels and the greatest works of realist literary art is not that the one evokes emotions and the other does not. Rather, sentimental novels manipulate their readers' emotions mainly in order to provide pleasure, whereas the best novels in the realist tradition arouse emotions in their readers in order to encourage them to reflect upon and learn from the emotions thus aroused.[26]

Compare, for example, the pity we are invited to feel for Little Nell with the pity that George Eliot encourages us to feel for Bulstrode, one of the lesser characters in her great novel *Middlemarch*. As we have seen, pity for Little Nell involves, among other things, focusing on the goodness and innocence of the little girl, who is described as a paradigm object for the reader's tender emotions. Pity for Bulstrode, on the other hand, involves focusing on his moral flaws, his narrow, unforgiving, puritanical conception of morality, his desire to be seen as upright by his neighbors even as he conceals his checkered past, and his hypocritical claims to be acting out of the highest scruples while in fact driven by the desire to save face. Bulstrode does not seem to be very pitiable, but George Eliot manages not only to make us understand him, but also to pity him. We see that he does recognize what he has done and its unpleasant implications for his wife as well as himself, and we understand that his downfall comes in a peculiarly painful way to one who has so courted public opinion. We also see that he has genuine affection for his wife and she for him. In feeling this way, we come to understand that pity can be more appropriate to sinners than to saints. In short, unlike Little Nell, Bulstrode is not at all an obvious candidate for the tender emotions to respond to, but Eliot nevertheless gets us to pity him. The pity we feel is unsentimental and "hard-earned," in the sense that we pity him despite all the evidence Eliot has given us for despising him and enjoying his downfall. This, I would argue, is a genuine exercise in morality, played out in the emotional realm. Eliot gets us to learn something about the morality of pity.

In general, great realist novels not only arouse our emotions, but try to teach us the nuances of those emotions and how and why these emotions are aroused. Compare our reactions to stereotypical villains such as Richardson's Lovelace and Dickens's Quilp with our reactions to the villains in Henry James. Gilbert Osmond and Madame Merle in *Portrait of a Lady* are evil, and they "oppress" the pure and innocent Isobel Archer, but our responses to the characters are far subtler than our response to the death of Little Nell. Readers are emotionally involved and fearful for Isobel as they might be for a sentimental heroine, but they are also interested in the

---

[26] Cf. R. G. Collingwood, who distinguishes sharply between what he calls "pseudo art," which aims simply to amuse or entertain by deliberately arousing what Carroll would call "criterially pre-focused emotions," with "art proper" in which the artist sets out to discover (bring to awareness) his own emotions by articulating them in works of art. Collingwood emphasizes the *cognitive* value of art and in particular the value of art in encouraging the author – and the audience who wants to understand his work – to explore his or her emotions so as to get clear about what they are. Works of "art proper" not only sincerely express an artist's genuine emotions but also encourage reflection about those emotions. See Collingwood 1938. See also Robinson 2005.

details of her psychology and her social situation and *how* and *why* she came to be in thrall to her "oppressors." The villains too have complex psychologies and we come to have a certain pity for Madame Merle. Moreover, the outcome of the story is not "triumphant" as in most sentimental novels, but realistically downbeat: the villains' machinations are not triumphantly defeated; Isobel Archer is permanently damaged by them. This is tragedy (of a domestic sort), rather than sentimentality. The pleasure we get from reading the novel is partly a matter of enjoying the subtlety of James's conception, as expressed in his subtle language use, and partly a matter of enjoying reading about important issues in human life treated with subtlety and penetration (cf. Ridley 2003).

Today many of us defend the importance of the cognitive values of art, including the ability of the great realist novels to express truths about human nature and how the world works. But perhaps in the wake of postmodernism this stance is simply old-fashioned. Ira Newman, for example, in his discussion of sentimentality, claims that "truth" in novels and other literary works is often overridden by other values such as "audience pleasure… and escapism" (p. 344).[27] This is surely right, but the question is whether the aesthetic value of a work lies primarily in its cognitive value or in the degree of escapist pleasure it provides. The eighteenth century mainly emphasized pleasure, although in Hume and Kant the notion of aesthetic pleasure is certainly not "escapist." Today, many theorists follow R. G. Collingwood (1938) in emphasizing cognitive values as important *aesthetic* values. Thus Matthew Kieran dismisses a "sentimental" painting by Norman Rockwell (one of the *Four Freedoms* series) because "the visual interest is in the service of morally good sentiments which are cheaply won…There is nothing of interest to be won or learnt from looking at this kind of morally sound painting" (Kieran 2005: 184). In short, despite its pleasing and skillful design, its lack of cognitive interest condemns it aesthetically. I too believe that cognitive value contributes importantly to aesthetic value, but I will end this essay with a brief plea in defense of Solomon and Warhol that there is also value in expressing "mythologies," which are not truths but which express important values, especially values that may have been marginalized by the culture.

Warhol is interested in the way that sentimental artworks and responses to artworks are gendered as "feminine" and, like Solomon, points out that according to the stereotype, sentimental novels and films are primarily designed for heterosexual women. As a token of resistance to this oversimplified picture of gendered emotions, she uses the term "effeminate" as a technical term for emotions that are usually associated with feeble females – and that have been stigmatized as a result – and insists that "effeminate affect" is available to women of any sexual orientation and to gay and straight men as well. Very much in the spirit of Solomon, she says that she wants to "[rehabilitate] 'effeminacy' from the pejorative status it currently holds" and "to mount a defense of 'effeminate feelings' in the name of anti-essentialist

---

[27] Newman actually says that such values "often override the commitment to present the w*hole* truth" [emphasis mine], but no novel or other literary work can "present the whole truth." See, e.g., Goodman (1978).

feminism" (Warhol 2003: 10) As Warhol says, sentimental stories "draw upon effeminate culture's store of cherished beliefs – and contrary to the perhaps painful evidence of readers' own live experience – make those beliefs seem to come true" (p. 50).

One of the "technologies of affect" that Warhol identifies is the frequent use in sentimental novels of climactic scenes in which stereotypical characters act contrary to type.[28] For example, when the exceedingly shy Beth March in *Little Women* goes to thank the "respectable, emotionally repressed, publicly powerful middle-class patriarch" (p. 48), Mr. Laurence, for his gift of a piano, she overcomes her shyness and kisses him, and Mr. Laurence is so surprised and delighted that "… he just set her on his knee, and laid his wrinkled cheek against her rosy one, feeling as if he had got his own little granddaughter back again" (quoted in Warhol 2003: 49). Such scenes serve to reinforce the 'mythologies' underlying "effeminate culture":

> When in *Little Women* Mr. Laurence's dead granddaughter seems to have returned to him in the form of Beth, when Meg and Jo are reconciled after a long period of bickering, when their father returns from the war just in time for Christmas; or – in *Uncle Tom's Cabin* – when Eliza and George are reunited at the Quaker settlement on their journey to Canada, when the bigoted Vermonter Ophelia realizes she loves the slave Topsy, when Eva or Uncle Tom dies with the most confident expectation of going to heaven,… the weeping reader… is 'having a good cry,' an affirmation of the mythology being represented in the text: family affection does transcend death; sisters are friends forever; true love will prevail; courage will be rewarded; affectionate domestic relationships will put an end to racist oppression – oh, it is a wonderful life!" (Warhol 2003: 50).

This last reference is of course to the Jimmy Stewart movie. Warhol recalls the episode of *Cheers!*, in which the gang at the bar makes fun of this movie and then while watching it find themselves with tears streaming down their faces. She comments that "the legacy of modernist (not to mention postmodernist) irony makes it impossible" to endorse the message of *It's a Wonderful Life* "without being sarcastic":

> The association of exalted, ecstatic, or optimistic feelings with the darker undersides of bourgeois mythologies (with racism, classism, homophobia, and nationalism especially) makes them suspect, false, 'sentimental' in the most pejorative sense of the word (Warhol 2003: 51).

The reader who weeps at a sentimental novel or show is affirming "the mythology being represented in the text" in a way that our present-day cynical culture can only mock. Like Solomon, Warhol is nostalgic for a time when such sentimental feelings could be endorsed rather than criticized. What's good about the 'good cry'? Her answer is that

> The ideals of sentimental culture – the affirmation of community, the persistence of hopefulness and of willingness, the belief that everyone matters, the sense that life has a purpose that can be traced to the links of affection between and among persons – are good ideals (Warhol 2003: 55–56).

---

[28] This is connected to another of her "technologies," namely the frequency in sentimental novels of "close calls and last-minute reversals" (Warhol 2003: 47).

We should not be embarrassed if we enjoy a good cry at sentimental works: it is an affirmation of effeminate community and can serve to undermine the myths of macho culture. Similarly, Solomon argues that "the usual attack on sentimentality is… too often an attack on innocence" (Solomon 2004a: 19).

Solomon and Warhol in their very different ways both offer ringing endorsements of sentimentality in novels and films. Both claim that in weeping at sentimental novels and films, we affirm important ethical ideals. Solomon suggests that sentimental fictions can function as a sort of "spiritual exercise" (Solomon 2004a: 19) to make us more alert to objects of compassion and tender feeling, and to prod us to act so as to alleviate hardship and injustice. What Warhol adds to his case is the idea that sentimental novels also affirm the "effeminate values" of marginalized members of society such as gays and women. In summary: we have no need to feel guilty if we weep at a "mawkish novel." There is nothing wrong with it and much that is right. Sentimental fictions are not the greatest fictions ever written; they do not explore emotions in the subtle way that George Eliot or Henry James do and they do not teach us much about the emotions they evoke. But they nevertheless serve an important function in validating the "effeminate" and tender feelings and ideals that are so important to our ethical life.

# References

Carroll, Noël. 1998. *A philosophy of mass art*. Oxford: Clarendon.
Carroll, Noël. 1999. Film, emotion and genre. In *Passionate views: Film, cognition and emotion*, ed. Carl Plantinga and Greg M. Smith, 21–47. Baltimore: John Hopkins University Press.
Collingwood, R.G. 1938. *The principles of art*. Oxford: Clarendon.
Eaton, Marcia. 1989. Laughing at the death of little Nell: Sentimental art and sentimental people. *American Philosophical Quarterly* 26: 269–282.
Goodman, Nelson. 1978. *Ways of worldmaking*. Indianapolis: Hackett.
Jefferson, Mark. 1983. What is wrong with sentimentality? *Mind* 92: 519–529.
Kieran, Matthew. 2005. *Revealing art*. London: Routledge.
Kundera, Milan. 1984. *The unbearable lightness of being* (trans: Michael Henry Heim). New York: Harper & Row.
Lazarus, Richard. 1991. *Emotion and adaptation*. New York: Oxford University Press.
Lutz, Catherine. 1998. *Unnatural emotions: Everyday sentiments on a Micronesian atoll and their challenge to western theory*. Chicago: University of Chicago Press.
Midgley, Mary. 1979. Brutality and sentimentality. *Philosophy* 54: 385–389.
Newman, Ira. 2008. The alleged unwholesomeness of sentimentality. In *Arguing about art*, 3rd ed, ed. Alex Neill and Aaron Ridley, 342–353. London: Routledge.
Ridley, Aaron. 2003. Tragedy. In *The Oxford handbook of aesthetics*, ed. Jerrold Levinson, 408–420. Oxford: Oxford University Press.
Robinson, Jenefer. 2005. *Deeper than reason: Emotion and its role in literature, music, and art*. Oxford: Oxford University Press.
Savile, Anthony. 1982. Sentimentality. In *The test of time: An essay in philosophical aesthetics*. Reprinted in *Arguing about art*, 3rd ed, ed. Alex Neill and Aaron Ridley, 337–341. London: Routledge 2008.
Solomon, Robert C. 2004a. In defense of sentimentality. In *In defense of sentimentality*, ed. Robert C. Solomon. New York: Oxford University Press.

Solomon, Robert C. 2004b. On kitsch and sentimentality. In *In defense of sentimentality*, ed. Robert C. Solomon. New York: Oxford University Press.

Sprague, Allen B. 1933. The date of 'sentimental' and its derivatives. *Proceedings of the Modern Language Association (PMLA)* 48: 303–307.

Sterne, Laurence. 2006 [1768]. *A sentimental journey through France and Italy*. Indianapolis: Hackett.

Tanner, Michael. 1976–1977. Sentimentality. *Proceedings of the Aristotelian Society* 77: 127–147.

Warhol, Robyn. 2003. *Having a good cry: Effeminate feelings and pop-culture forms*. Columbus: The Ohio State University Press.

# Part II
# Ethics

# Chapter 7
# Robert Solomon's Contribution to Business Ethics: Emotional Agency

Patricia H. Werhane and David Bevan

**Abstract** In this chapter we will focus on strands of two of the distinctive contribution that forms part of Robert Solomon's legacy. The first speaks directly and explicitly to the field of business and business ethics. The second, perhaps Solomon's most substantial and lasting potential contribution to applied ethics, arises from his work on a cognitive theory of emotions, or as some call it a cognitive *structure* of emotions (Ortony AG et al. (eds), The cognitive structure of emotions. Oxford University Press, New York, 1988), and his more contentious argument that "we are (at least sometimes, to some extent) responsible or our emotions and our emotional responses" (Solomon RC, Not passion's slave. Oxford University Press, New York, 2003: vii). We will suggest that there is much to be learned in applied or business ethics from Solomon's work on the emotions, because through this theorization the emotions become potentially instrumental or agentic in changing our mental models: in affecting the mind sets through which we each frame, focus, evaluate, and judge our experiences. In acknowledging the potential of this theorization we become more responsible for our actions as inspired by our emotions.

Robert Solomon made multiple contributions to the possible ways of interpreting and understanding or thinking about the emotions. Through an extensive, recursive and analytic intellectual project, lasting more than 30 years, he examined and re-examined emotions (Solomon 1973, 1976, 1984, 1988, 1992c, 1998, 2003, 2004), a field which he considered to have been unduly neglected by philosophy. His work establishes what is generally termed a cognitive theory of emotions, which he, and others, regarded as

P.H. Werhane (✉)
Institute for Business & Professional Ethics, De Paul University,
1 East Jackson, Suite 7013, Chicago, IL 60604, USA
e-mail: pwerhane@depaul.edu

D. Bevan
Centre for Leadership and Responsibility, CEI BS, Shanghai, PRC

K. Higgins and D. Sherman (eds.), *Passion, Death, and Spirituality*,
Sophia Studies in Cross-cultural Philosophy of Traditions and Cultures 1,
DOI 10.1007/978-94-007-4650-3_7, © Springer Science+Business Media Dordrecht 2012

the touchstone for all philosophical theorizing around the subject (Solomon 2002b). Normatively, Solomon exhorts us—as adults—to wish to take responsibility for what we do and what we feel (Solomon 2002a). In this appreciation we will focus on strands of two of the distinctive contribution that forms part of his legacy. The first speaks directly and explicitly to the field of business and business ethics. The second, perhaps his most substantial and potentially lasting contribution to applied ethics arises from his work on a cognitive theory of emotions, or as some call it a cognitive *structure* of emotions (Ortony et al. 1988), and his more contentious argument that "we are (at least sometimes, to some extent) responsible for our emotions and our emotional responses." (Solomon 2003: vii) We will suggest that there is much to be learned in applied or business ethics from Solomon's work on the emotions, because through this theorization the emotions become potentially instrumental or agentic in changing our mental models: in affecting the mindsets through which we each frame, focus, evaluate, and judge our experiences. In acknowledging the potential of this theorization, we become more responsible for our actions as inspired by our emotions.

First, let us reconsider Solomon's contributions to business ethics and business practice. Solomon's seminal work in business ethics is his book, *Ethics and Excellence* (1992), which at one point draws our attention to the problem of 'cowboy capitalism' (Freeman 1988). As Solomon (1992) outlines, most applied ethics, and thus business ethics, has been derivative of traditional ethical theories, most often drawing on what are held by many to be the two great pillars of ethical theory: deontology and utilitarianism. These two approaches seem to be deployed in an array of specific ethical issues, familiar to us all. For any particular issue one view will be juxtaposed against the other as though they are distinctly alternate decision-making models. Consequentialist and non-consequentialist positions are dichotomized, perhaps crudely, in a digital either/or relation as though they may be opposing, or even mutually irreconcilable. Further, "such theorizing is … irrelevant to the workaday world of business and utterly inaccessible to the people for whom business ethics is not merely a subject of study, but is (or will be) a way of life" (Solomon 1992: 99).

At a first reading of *Ethics and Excellence*, it might appear that Solomon has taken the same approach, this time appealing to Aristotle's virtue theory as a theoretical arbitrator. Thus applied, ethics is simply the working out of applications of ethical theories, in this case by bringing the logic of Aristotle to moderate practical problems in commerce. If we seek to resolve practical ethical dilemmas with this sort of methodology, as Norman Daniels suggests, then "we solve practical problems in ethics by supplying a description of a particular situation that allows us to subsume it under a relevant moral principle" (Daniels 1996: 11). Thus we merely selectively and partially direct the problem to a set of principles most likely to lead us to a resolution that is essentially pre-conceived.

But *Ethics and Excellence* proposes something far more significant than the mere application of some Aristotelian rhetoric and logic to ethical issues in business: the impact is at least two-fold. Part of its import is to succinctly repudiate the myth of cowboy capitalism (Solomon 1992) that pervades much of management thinking. Solomon achieves this not merely by attacking ethical egoism, the common whipping boy for many philosophers (Bevan 2008). Rather he adduces the alleged father of *laissez-faire* capitalism, Adam Smith, and shows that even in the *Wealth Of Nations* (1976), Smith was not an egoist; that according to Smith greed was never good; and that self-interest is not by any means the same as selfishness. Rather, in commerce it is self-interest as the virtue that makes possible cooperative ventures and fair competition, Smith argued, which are bases for and driving force of free enterprise. We might add in parenthesis that Smith did not invent the term laissez-faire; indeed he was critical of such a concept. Nor did he employ the term capitalism anywhere in this work (Werhane 1989).

Further and more audaciously, Solomon presents another vision of capitalism—another mindset regarding how free enterprise in general, and corporations in particular, could operate. Arguing from the position that business is an intrinsically social activity, he proposes that the Aristotelian virtues are applicable both to managerial and corporate behavior, and that indeed, that way of thinking about commerce would have lasting value-added both to shareholders and to communities. As he writes at the end of the book,

> … as the first full century of corporate business comes to a close one would like to think that there is at least as much hope as there is cause for despair, that in the competition for corporate survival that will rock many industries in the next few years one of the most important constant ingredients for success as well as survival will be the Aristotelian virtues—a sense of community and cooperation … the importance of integrity both for the individual and the company … Ethics and excellence, community and integrity, are not mere means to efficiency and effectiveness. They are the ends without which the corporation will have lost its soul (Solomon 1992: 266).

This is neither a description nor a prescription but Solomon's individual, normative vision: his belief in the positive power of emotions, translated to the practice of contemporary management as an ethics of practice. He offers us a new and positive way of thinking about commerce, through a mindset that is not antithetical to profitability but rather integrates an emancipatory goal of broader human flourishing. This is truly an innovative mental model for commerce that is now being adapted and taught, albeit gradually, in leading business schools and exemplified in the practices we can identify in at least some companies today.

Let us now turn to the second theme: one of Solomon's best known contributions to philosophical thinking, his lifelong work on the emotions and their overlap with cognition. We will not reiterate the various versions of his theory(ies). Rather, focusing on his personally revised collection of essays, published as *Not Passion's Slave* (Solomon 2003), we will apply a social constructivist reading of these ideas. Such a reading may suggest why Solomon's seminal book on business ethics is a mind-altering work—in terms of presenting a new, socially-constructed view of commerce in which managers and executives are responsible. Whether Solomon would agree with this interpretation must remain unresolved.

We begin by outlining (without fully developing the arguments) Solomon's cognitive theory of the emotions. According to Solomon, "emotions are 'cognitive' in nature, which means that they are something more than mere feelings or sensations and something more than physiological reactions." (Solomon 2003: vii) Indeed, according to Solomon, "emotions are construed primarily as evaluative judgments"

(Solomon 2003 book jacket). Secondly, as we noted earlier, Solomon argues that we are by and large responsible for our emotions, and that there is a sense in which one can say that we choose them.

According to Solomon, emotions have five dimensions and it is a mistake to reduce the concept of emotion to just one of these. Emotions display themselves through behavioral and verbal expressions, they are physiological, phenomenological, they exist in social contexts both as interpersonal relationships and as part of one's culture (thus there are cultural differences in emotions), and they are cognitive, that is, they are evaluative, judgmental, and reflective. (Solomon 2003: 131)

There is no direct reference to this list of traits as being derived from Sartre, although certainly, and elsewhere, Solomon's sense of integrity relies heavily on the notion of good (and bad) faith (Sartre 1958), even if Solomon frequently exemplifies integrity by reference to Sartre's fiction. Here, we suggest that the affective structure of emotions outlined in *"The Existence of Others"* (Sartre 1958) may be relevant and informative as a support for Solomon's theoretical work. In Sartre's discussion of the *Cogito* he speaks of the subject mediating all objects as necessarily for-the-subject-itself: "this ontological structure is *mine*; it is in relation to myself as subject that I am concerned about myself, and yet this concern (for-myself) reveals to me a being which is *my* being without being-for-me." For Sartre this structure is a "non-positional self-consciousness .../... accessible to reflection" (245) which puts me "in the position of passing judgment on myself as an object" (245–246).

Concerning emotions as judgments, Solomon's argument is that every emotion is judgmental, that is, it emotionally evaluates an event, an experience, a friendship, a policy, a historical moment. Solomon thinks of judgments as constitutive of emotions, and he claims, "[a]n emotion is rather a complex of judgments and, sometimes, quite sophisticated judgments, such as judgments of responsibility (in shame, anger or embarrassment) or judgments of comparative status (as in contempt or resentment [or even love.])" (Solomon 2003: 188) We can also study and evaluate our emotions, just as they themselves are evaluative. This does not lead to the conclusion that emotions are always conscious or deliberate, although they can be. But they often just happen involuntarily without conscious intervention.

Does this lead to the conclusion that emotions are passive and out of our control? Solomon thinks not. Many of our emotions arise from our subconscious, many are physiologically connected, and a number of them appear to be out of our control. But others can be produced deliberately. We can elicit, control and change our emotions, even those that arise passively. Just as we can change our habitual behavior, and just as we are responsible for our habits, even those that seemingly operate unconsciously, so too, Solomon argues, we are responsible for our emotions. Through reflection we can come to understand and change our emotions. So there is a sense in which we choose them. They are ours. While he moderates this conclusion by admitting that not all our emotions are under our control or revisable, still, it would be irresponsible to deny that we can control and alter at least some of our emotions. As Solomon concludes, "…we are adults. We must take responsibility for what we do and what we feel, and in our taking responsibility we learn to recognize the responsibilities we have, including responsibility for our own emotions."

(Solomon 2003: 232) Otherwise we are falling into the role of the passive victim to our emotions and ignoring the responsibilities that they bring to our attention.

At the end of *Not Passion's Slave* Solomon concludes that "how we think about our emotions—as something we suffer or as something we "do"—will deeply affect both our behavior and our understanding of our behavior. In other words, theses about emotions tend to be self-confirming." (Solomon 2003: 232) We would suggest that this is a form of social construction, that is, that one can create mindsets that affect how one envisions oneself and how we act. Is Solomon a social constructivist?

The origins of social constructivism may be traced to Immanuel Kant's critique of a *tabula rasa* construct of the mind, which he in turn attributes to one of his predecessors, David Hume. Kant's thesis is that our minds do not mirror experience. Rather, our minds project, constitute and/or reconstitute phenomena, the raw data of all experiences, into structured, ordered coherence and thus to knowable experiences. Kant concluded that all human beings order and organize their experiences through an identical set of formal concepts. While the content of our experiences may be quite different for each of us, the ways in which we structure and order these experiences is the same, universally for all human beings. In this chapter we will not elaborate on that view, which we assume is well known to the reader, regardless of whether or not you agree with Kant or his conclusions.

Today, we tend to challenge both whether, and how, minds are hard-wired as proposed by Kant. What remains, however, within a social constructivist perspective, is the idea that each of us perceives, frames, orders and organizes the data of our experiences through a lens, from a point of view or with set of frames, each of which, contra Kant, are socially acquired and developed. These lenses, perspectives and frames are conceptual schemes or mental models that serve as selective organizing, filtering, and focusing *technologies,* by the use of which we "construct" meaning. In the social constructivist paradigm such mental models frame all our experiences. They focus, schematize, and otherwise technologically facilitate and guide the ways in which we recognize, react, and organize the world. How we define the world is entirely dependent on such schemes, and thus all realities are subjectively structured. In the socially constructed paradigm the multivariate conceptual scheme is the means and mode through which we (re)constitute our experiences. Because these schemes are socially learned, fragile, transient and changeable, each is always incomplete or unfinished, such that one never gets a totally holistic worldview (Gorman 1992; Senge 2006; Werhane 1999).

Reflecting this thinking, many philosophers argue that conceptual schemes are semantically based (e.g. Anscombe 1976; Johnson 1993; Putnam 1990; Rorty 1993; Wittgenstein 1953). Whether human beings conceptualize or deal with the world non-linguistically is not a topic for this essay, but as Hilary Putnam and Richard Rorty argue, "*[E]lements of what we call 'language' or 'mind' penetrate so deeply into what we call 'reality' that the very project of representing ourselves as being 'mappers' of something 'language-independent' is fatally compromised from the start*" (Putnam 1990: 28; cited with approval in Rorty 1993: 443; emphasis Rorty's). Language shapes our perspectives in such profound ways that it is difficult to imagine how we would conceptualize or frame experience purely non-linguistically, because the very act of describing and explaining such concepts and frames employs language. This leads Rorty to conclude that the notion of reality as "something outside all schemes" or observers makes no sense. (Rorty 1993: 443)

Nevertheless, there is a difference between claiming that one cannot get at reality, or the world, or even experience except through some conceptual scheme, and concluding that reality or experience is itself merely created or solely socially constructed. Arguing that the incomplete and disparate ways in which we present and distill experiences are socially constructed is different from arguing that experience or reality itself is socially created. We argue here that how we conceive the world is conceptually dependent, that is, "[e]ssence is *expressed* by grammar" (Wittgenstein 1953: 371, our italics). But as G.E.M. Anscombe has pointed out, this is quite different from concluding that "essence is *created* by grammar" (Anscombe 1976: 188). When essence is merely *created* by the use of grammar, we may call it lying, fantasy, storytelling, or mythmaking. Within any belief system we are generally concerned to distinguish fantasy and myth from "the real," "the true," or "the facts," even though each may be socially structured.

Donald Davidson describes conceptual schemes as follows: "conceptual schemes, we are told, are ways or organizing experience; they are systems of categories that give form to the data of sensation; they are points of view from which individuals, [institutions], cultures, or [historical] periods survey the passing scene" (Davidson 1974: 5). Davidson's critique engages with commensurable distinctiveness between conceptual schemes. If they are not commensurate, as he suggests, then they must be philosophically uninteresting. He concludes, "[w]e have found no intelligible basis on which it can be said that schemes are different [even though] it would be equally wrong to announce…that all speakers of language, at least, share a common scheme and ontology" (Davidson 1974: 20). But not all versions of social constructivism are to be equated with conceptual relativism, a conclusion we read Davidson as reaching. One can distinguish what Davidson calls a "common coordinate system," (Davidson 1974: 6) or the essence that is expressed through grammar, from what others call conceptual schemes or mental models, which are partial schemata through which we frame our experiences. This idea of a conceptual scheme, when not confused with a common underlying coordinate system, helps to examine the notion of differing belief systems or worldviews, because it is not inconceivable that there are, or have been, more than one belief system or worldview. The idea of a common underlying coordinate system also becomes an explanatory notion to account for our being able to identify if not accommodate what appear to be logically incommensurable conceptual schemes (Werhane 1999).

Because all mental models or mindsets are incomplete, they are learned, fragile and changeable schemata. Moreover, we can engage in second-order studies, evaluations, judgments and assessments about our own, and other operative mental models just as, to quote Solomon, we can engage in "reflective recognition that we can change or intensify our emotions." (Solomon 2003: 208) Of course this is highly complex since the act of reflection is itself a technology of framing or reframing and not, to invoke Thomas Nagel, a view from nowhere. What we are unable to do is to escape from any frame to an idealistic objective view from nowhere. For us this is analogous with Heisenberg's realization that in science one cannot eliminate the observer from her effects on the observed; the mere act of observing affects the object observed (Heisenberg 1959). Returning to our question, is it plausible to consider Robert Solomon as a social constructivist? We suggest that as an admirer of Nietzsche (1997, 2003), he was at least skeptical of positivist claims to absolute truth and thus likely to be inclined to a socially constructed ontology. We can also trace some nuances of Nietzsche and *will* in Solomon's emotional agency. In some places Solomon speaks of "basic emotions" that we all share. It may be that what we share as human beings is that we are each emotional as well as cognitively capable individuals. At one point he writes, "Basic emotions are those *considered to be important in some particular society.*" (Solomon 2003: 139) But elsewhere he asserts that, "it does not follow that the emotions are irreducibly cultural, depending on the values and goals of a particular society. It may well be that the basic emotions, so construed, are those which are essential to the human condition and thus pan cultural." (Solomon 2003: 138) He writes, "a basic emotion (as an affect program) is universal; emotions that involve cognition and complex appraisals, by contrast, might be 'socially constructed'" (Solomon 2003: 138). We would like to propose that if he were able to respond, he would inject both a disclaimer and another, clearer, explanation we have not yet considered.

Still, a social constructivist perspective on emotions is not without merit although perhaps in a more complex construct than we have delivered here. R. M. Dancy pointed out that the early Greeks used color words not merely to refer to a hue, but each word was connected with a family of associations some of which are not ordinarily connected with that particular color in English. "For example the word [for] green of Euripides' blood carries with it [for the Greeks] associations with moisture, fresh vegetation and youth, and even fear" (Dancy 1983: 285). Of course this is true for English color words as well, e.g., "blue," which may or may not have all the same connotations in Greek. The point is that these are emotionally laden words, words whose emotional content is culturally learned, thus socially constructed, by particular language forms and cultures. Moreover, like mental models, words can *affect* the emotions of others when they are uttered. Indeed, and this would be a longer argument, we suggest that many words act as evaluative judgments. For instance, it was common after Enron to depict all managers and CEOs as 'scumbags' (to employ a contemporary term of art), an emotionally judgmental term; since 2008 we have refocused our odium on bankers. But what if we were to reframe our commentary to concentrate on the virtues and good deeds that some managers and companies actually exhibit as suggested in some recent continental literature (Aasland 2008)? This approach, suggested by Solomon, might change mindsets and assist managers to actively reconfigure their corporate goals and their performance as a matter of personal responsibility inspired by their newly adopted emotion(s) as virtuous managers.

An emotional constituent can also be, or have, political agency (Solomon 1998). Allegedly cognitive, cold-blooded accounts of emotion and passion may also affect the mindsets and the emotional reactions of an audience, or other participants: this much we agree to be obvious. It implies, moreover, that we professors, scientists, managers, CEOs, social workers, philanthropists, consumers, politicians, parents and children may need to think about not merely the facts—because these are always socially constructed from a partial perspective—but also the emotional-cognitive dimensions according to which we might be affecting the mindsets of others. Let us present an empirical example from commerce, which was covered by NBC's *Dateline*.

H. B. Fuller is a large chemicals manufacturer located in Minneapolis, Minnesota, U.S.A. The company has a reputation in that community for philanthropy, good treatment of employees, and a concern for customers, etc.; that is to say, according to mainstream business ethics, we would consider it to be a socially responsible company. In the 1990s in an effort to reduce costs, better serve local customers, and provide jobs in a blighted community, it opened a glue factory in Honduras. This glue, Resistol, is used by shoemakers, particularly in developing countries, to make shoes. The company has a clean factory, protects its workers against the fumes from the glue, pays a living wage, charges a reasonable price for the glue, and its managers, mostly Honduran, work with the local communities on poverty reduction initiatives. However Fuller discovered that local distributors of its glue were repackaging it in small plastic bags and selling it to homeless street children who sniffed it. Inhaling the solvent vapor creates a sedative effect and also alleviates the pangs of hunger. The children became known as *Resistoleros*, even when the glue they sniffed was not sourced from Fuller (Bowie and Lenway 1993).

If, as teachers, we were to present a written up version of this case to a group of M.B.A. students in a business ethics class, the informal, crowd-source (Brabham 2008) consensus of the class, most typically would be that while the solvent sniffing is undesirable and perhaps even a tragedy, this is not morally attributable to, nor the responsibility of, the manufacturer. Indeed, Fuller is being a responsible employer and manufacturer, doing what it can by providing good jobs and making profit for shareholders—the abuse of its product is an unintended consequence arising from improper use and conditions which it does not condone. But if we then use different media and present a news media/documentary video that shows the lives of these children and the devastating results of glue sniffing (the glue eventually affects their brain functions!), the class becomes at least split in its conclusions about Fuller and its moral agency and responsibilities. The sight of street children sniffing glue has a strong emotional and cognitive effect that the written case does not convey. By adding explicit emotional content—specifically the faces and lives of those involved— the video literally reconfigures the mindsets of many of the students watching it.

Our assertion here is that *Ethics and Excellence* has a similarly transformative affect. It works to reconfigure our mindsets about commerce, about ethics, and about creating value and contributing to a flourishing economy. Solomon deconstructs the term "value-added," often implicitly read as "economic value-added" or "profitability." By reinterpreting that mental model of profitability with the same terminology, "value added," Solomon's work forces us to think beyond bottom-line considerations to different mindsets that redefine value creation as human flourishing for all those affected by free enterprise. This shift enables companies and critics to evaluate many dimensions of value-creating or destructive behaviors. Global companies and their individual managers are thus challenged to take emotionally inspired action, to do better all the way around. Interestingly, after the Dateline coverage H. B. Fuller reevaluated its Honduran operations and glue manufacture. It has been able to find an additive to its glue that makes it repellent to the human sense of smell and it can no longer be tolerated by sniffers. The problem of child poverty is not easily eradicated or resolved, but one (more), accidentally toxic route to escape has consequently been closed off. Now it is for others to see perhaps how their emotional reaction to such examples of global blight can lead to further remedial action.

We have discussed in some detail two strands of Solomon's contribution to business ethics and we consider these to be highly normative. The first serves as a persistent reminder that managers may not plausibly invoke the morally vacuous claim that business is conveniently or otherwise amoral. The second, an awareness of the cognitive analysis of emotion along with its proposed agency—a practice of reaction and action—offers us, as individual teachers or managers, a means of translating our emotions into more thoughtful management relationships for which we are all responsible.[1]

## References

Aasland, D.G. 2008. *Ethics and economy: After Levinas*. London: MayFlyBooks.

Anscombe, G.E.M. 1976. The question of linguistic idealism. In *Essays on Wittgenstein in honour of G. H. Von Wright*, ed. Jaakko Hintikka et al., 181–215. Amsterdam: Acta Philosophica Fennica, North Holland Publishing.

Bevan, David. 2008. Continental philosophy: A grounded theory approach and the emergence of convenient and inconvenient ethics. In *Cutting-edge issues in business ethics: Continental challenges to tradition and practice*, ed. Mollie Painter-Morland and Patricia Werhane, 131–152. New York: Springer.

Bowie, Norman and Stephanie, Lenway. 1993. H. B. Fuller in Honduras: street children and substance abuse, In *Ethical issues in business*, 4th ed, ed. Thomas Donaldson and Patricia H. Werhane. Englewood Cliffs NJ: Prentice-Hall.

Brabham, Daren C. 2008. Crowdsourcing as a model for problem solving: an introduction and cases. *Convergence: The International Journal of Research into New Media Technologies* 14: 75–90.

Dancy, R.M. 1983. Alien concepts. *Synthese* 56: 283–300.

Daniels, Norman. 1996. *Justice and justification*. New York: Cambridge University Press.

Davidson, Donald. 1974. On the very idea of a conceptual scheme. *Proceedings and Addresses of the American Philosophical Association* 47: 5–20.

Freeman, R.Edward. 1988. The myth of cowboy capitalism. *The Darden Report* 14: 28–32.

Gorman, Michael. 1992. *Stimulating science*. Bloomington: Indiana University Press.

Heisenberg, Werner. 1959. *Physics and philosophy*. London: George Allen & Unwin, Ltd.

Johnson, Mark. 1993. *Moral imagination*. Chicago: University of Chicago Press.

---

[1] Some ideas considered in this essay have previously appeared in *Moral Imagination and Management Decision-Making* (Werhane 1999). Reprinted here by permission of the Patricia Werhane who holds the copyright for this book.

Nietzsche, Friedrich. 1997[1886]. *Beyond good and evil*. Mineola: Dover Thrift Editions.
Nietzsche, Friedrich. 2003[1887]. *The genealogy of morals*. Mineola: Dover.
Ortony, Anthony G., Gerald L. Clore, and Allan Collins (eds.). 1988. *The cognitive structure of emotions*. New York: Oxford University Press.
Putnam, Hillary. 1990. *Realism with a human face*. Cambridge, MA: Harvard University Press.
Rorty, Richard. 1993. Putnam and the relativist menace. *The Journal of Philosophy* 90: 443–561.
Sartre, Jean-Paul. 1958. *Being and nothingness*. Abingdon: Routledge.
Senge, Peter M. 2006. *The fifth discipline*. New York: Random House.
Smith, Adam. 1976 [1776]. *The wealth of nations*. Chicago: University of Chicago.
Solomon, Robert C. 1973. Emotion and choice. *The Review of Metaphysics* 17: 20–41.
Solomon, Robert C. 1976. *The passions*. New York: Doubleday.
Solomon, Robert C. 1984. Getting angry: The Jamesian theory of emotion in anthropology. In *Culture theory*, ed. R.A. LeVine and Richard Schweder, 238–254. Cambridge: Cambridge University Press.
Solomon, Robert C. 1988. On emotions as judgements. *American Philosophical Quarterly* 25: 183–191.
Solomon, Robert C. 1992. *Ethics and excellence*. New York: Oxford University Press.
Solomon, Robert C. 1998. The politics of emotion. In *Midwest studies in philosophy*, 22nd ed, ed. Peter French, 1–20. Notre Dame: University of Notre Dame Press.
Solomon, Robert C. 2002a. On the passivity of the passions. In *Feelings and emotion*, ed. Anthony S.R. Manstead and Agneta Fischer, 1–29. Cambridge: Cambridge University Press.
Solomon, Robert C. 2002b. Thoughts and feelings: What is a 'cognitive theory' of the emotions, and does it neglect affectivity? In *The philosophy of emotions*, ed. Anthony Hatzimoysis, 1–18. Cambridge: Cambridge University Press.
Solomon, Robert C. 2003. *Not passion's slave*. New York: Oxford University Press.
Solomon, Robert C. 2004. *Thinking about feeling: Contemporary philosophers on emotions*. New York: Oxford University Press.
Werhane, Patricia. 1989. *Adam Smith and his legacy for modern capitalism*. New York: Oxford University Press.
Werhane, Patricia. 1999. *Moral imagination and management decision-making*. New York: Oxford University Press.
Wittgenstein, Ludwig. 1953. *Philosophical investigations* (trans: G.E.M. Anscombe). New York: Macmillan.

# Chapter 8
# Virtues, Concepts, and Rules in Business Ethics: Reflections on the Contributions of Robert C. Solomon

Robert Audi

**Abstract** This essay is an exploration of some major elements in the ethical theory and moral psychology of Robert C. Solomon. The main context for the discussion is business ethics, an area in which Solomon was a major and frequent contributor for some three decades. Special attention is given to his construction of his own version of Aristotelian virtue ethics. In building his virtue-ethical position, he gave a major place to the psychological aspects of virtue. In particular, he brought out the ethical importance of emotions as at once cognitive and affective and as major elements in both the constitution of virtue and the sustenance of ethical conduct in day-to-day life. The essay explores his treatment of certain virtues, his view of the character traits particularly important for business ethics, and the perennial question whether any virtue ethics is normatively complete.

Both virtue ethics and moral psychology have been prominent and growing subfields in the past quarter of a century. Few have been substantial contributors in both areas. In my view, Robert C. Solomon achieved a unique combination of breadth in both areas and brought virtue ethics vividly to life in relation to business practice as no one else did. He also gave a special vitality to discussions of business ethics itself. He was a creative moral psychologist himself, with a knowledge of psychological, philosophical, and other literature that enriched his discussions of such topics as emotion, human motivation, self-deception, weakness of will, intention and practical reasoning, and moral responsibility. Here, and in his writings on ethics and on such philosophical figures as Nietzsche and Sartre, we have seen more than a powerful

R. Audi (✉)
Department of Philosophy, University of Notre Dame,
100 Malloy Hall, Notre Dame, IN 46556, USA
e-mail: Raudi@nd.edu

K. Higgins and D. Sherman (eds.), *Passion, Death, and Spirituality*,
Sophia Studies in Cross-cultural Philosophy of Traditions and Cultures 1,
DOI 10.1007/978-94-007-4650-3_8, © Springer Science+Business Media Dordrecht 2012

intellect. We have also seen a raconteur. As a writer, he had imagination, insight, intellectual versatility, humor, and fine literary style. As a person, he exemplified the kinds of virtues he wrote about. In this short study, I can consider only some broad elements in his virtue ethical approach and some of his portraits of concepts important both for business ethics and for other major domains of applied ethics.

## Solomon's Approach to Virtue Ethics

In *Ethics and Excellence* (which I view as one of his major books, at least in business ethics), Solomon tells us that he is providing "an Aristotelian approach to business ethics," (Solomon 1992b: 7) and (here as elsewhere) he certainly does. He describes many dimensions of an Aristotelian virtue ethics and many aspects of business ethics on which virtues of character particularly bear. The basic business virtues he explicates and illustrates are honesty, fairness, trust, and toughness. (I refer here just to that work; other virtues he discusses will be noted below.) It will be instructive to review some of his points and bring out their significance and, in some cases, a different emphasis. In this section, I will concentrate—briefly and very selectively— on some representative concepts Solomon treats in detail in more than one of his writings.

### *Honesty*

In characterizing honesty, Solomon says much that is significant, but what I find most noteworthy is that he introduces self-deception as a liability (Solomon 1992b: 212). For most writers on honesty, self-deception would not be a serious focus, but it is surely a liability in the social contexts that call for honesty and not, as the name might suggest, just a self-focused deficiency. The notion is elusive (as I have noted myself—see, e.g., Audi (1989) and Audi (2006)), and the phenomenon is among the more subtle lapses of honesty whose moral evaluation is complicated by the unconscious elements that, typically, cause or sustain the condition. Among the major questions connecting self-deception with the understanding of honesty are these: Do self-deceivers lie to others or only to themselves? Can they help lying, if the self-deception is a defense mechanism important in their psychic economy? Whatever the answers to these questions, Solomon's writings, in this book and elsewhere, indicate that moral responsibility is not necessarily undermined where a statement or deed arises from self-deception. Indeed, one of his aims as a moral psychologist was to enhance self-understanding in a way that both contributes to our theoretical appreciation of the scope of responsibility and enhances our capacity to live up to it.

## *Trust*

As to trust—which is virtually universally agreed to be pivotal for the existence of business—Solomon distinguishes it both from naivete on one side and from prudence on the other. He says that trust is "not a principle"; it is "an attitude, a working pre-supposition… It is trust that makes the system work" (Solomon 1992b: 213). He says a great deal both about what trust is and about how it is to be earned and maintained. He includes *systemic trust*, as we might call it—the kind an economy needs to sustain flourishing businesses—and *interpersonal trust*, the kind familiar in relations between or among individual persons. It is regarding interpersonal trust that I want to question one view he proposes: that "trust is an affective attitude, an emotion" (see Solomon and Flores 1996).[1] I accept a negative point underlying this view: the point that "Trust is not a set of beliefs or expectations" (p. 60). Even if trusting someone entails having these, weakness of will can prevent a person with the appropriate beliefs or expectations from behaving as trust requires. If you trust someone, you will take certain risks on the strength of the person's word; but where taking a risk is fearsome or otherwise aversive, one might fail to do the relevant deed not from lost or flagging trust, but because one lacks the will power to overcome the obstacle. I can also accept the point that trust implies a tendency to feel betrayed if the trusted person fails to do what one counts on in virtue of the trust. But this feeling—which is emotional—is not a requirement of trust itself, which of course is not always betrayed.

Perhaps Solomon would split the difference with me here, noting that an affective attitude need not be an emotion or—perhaps—that an emotion need not be *felt*, at least in the way in which "core" emotions like fear, anger, and jealousy are. He does, after all, speak in the same essay of "the exaggerated distinction between emotions, articulate expectations and strategies"[2] (p. 69). What is uncontroversial regarding this essay is that it connects trust with related phenomena, rejects reduction of trust either to purely cognitive elements or to purely emotional elements, and raises fruitful questions about just how cognitive, attitudinal, emotional, and, in a broad sense, strategic trust is.

## *Toughness*

Toughness is another business virtue that most other writers in the virtue-ethical tradition would overlook or underemphasize—if only because the term suggests an element of ruthlessness or at least aggression. But toughness, as Solomon portrays

---

[1] There is far more to discuss in this wide-ranging essay.

[2] That the concept of emotion is vague and that expectations of the kind that express ardent desire have an emotional character are important points, but why strategies come in here I am not sure. Both emotions and trust can figure in strategies; but they do not seem difficult to distinguish from those. In any case, that Solomon might split the difference with me is not a mere conjecture. In a later work (referred to in note 7) he says, of both trust and empathy, that "neither one seems to be an emotion *as such*" (p. 20).

it, is "not simply self-interested, but neither can it be considered an altruistic or self-sacrificing trait of character" (Solomon 1992a: 328). Nor is toughness equivalent to fortitude, a cousin in the traditional pantheon of virtues. Fortitude is less active, whereas toughness includes both bearing up under stress and even surviving serious failures. Solomon's suggestion seems to be that, at least in business, the tough exhibit their toughness in what they *do*; our fortitude, by contrast, is exhibited primarily in what we *bear*. Toughness even has what he called "an ethically painful element," as where a manager has to release loyal competent employees to save the company (1992b: 214). In my view, what Solomon calls toughness is much like what is sometimes called *moral courage*. In any case, it may be fruitfully compared with that virtue.

## Fairness

I have not yet described fairness, which Solomon rightly associates closely with justice. Here he provides an excellent elaboration of one dimension of fairness that is crucial for ethical business: recognition of merit in remuneration. He describes the elements of remunerative fairness in terms of equality (roughly, paying people equally in relation to comparable contributions to the business organization in question); two kinds of day-to-day merit workers can have (achieving results and expending effort); ability; need; rights (as where there is an agreement, such as a contract, regarding remuneration); the public good (which may be a factor in what some employers can or should pay); duties and responsibilities (which some workers fulfill better than others); market value (which we know "merits" attention in business and elsewhere); bearing risk and uncertainty (which can call for monetary compensation); seniority; loyalty (which merits financial recognition in some cases); moral virtue; and tradition ('precedent' would be another term for what he has in mind under tradition—Solomon 1992b: 238–239).

## Sympathy and Empathy

These notions have been much discussed both in ethical literature and in moral psychology. In his wide-ranging "Free Enterprise, Sympathy and Virtue" (Solomon 2006),[3] Solomon locates these three elements historically, with attention to Hume, Adam Smith, and others, provides accounts of their nature and difference, and contrasts their place in virtue ethics with their standing in the Kantian tradition that (for a time, at least) spawned "the exile of the kind sentiments and the 'inclinations'

---

[3] A chapter that is part of a collection posted on the SSRN website in the Economics Research Network at http://papers/ssrn/abstract=927482

in general from moral philosophy" (p. 5). Given that Solomon was a defender of the cognitivity of the emotions—and indeed even of a judgmental theory of emotion (see, e.g., Solomon 1993)—it is noteworthy that, concerning sympathy, empathy, and many other emotional elements, he was opposed to intellectualist reduction. He says, for instance, that "we err when we turn either sympathy or empathy into something essentially projective and contemplative, a product of thought rather than shared feeling in a shared relationship" (p. 20). One may object that in special cases sympathy and perhaps even empathy do not require any connection between persons deserving the term 'relationship', but that is perhaps a minor point. They are social even if not necessarily anchored in "relationships." What emerges clearly in Solomon's work is that such cognitive elements as belief and knowledge are not sufficient for the understanding of either emotions or the virtues.

## Altruism

Altruism is often misunderstood because it is assumed to be the polar opposite of egoism, rather than a psychologically realistic contrast with it. Here it is noteworthy that Solomon opposes the common view apparently based on this assumption (still far too widely accepted, I believe) of altruism as entailing self-sacrifice.[4] He speaks, for instance, of the false antagonism between 'selfishness' on the one hand and what is called 'altruism' or 'selflessness' on the other…altruism isn't self-sacrifice' (Solomon 1992b: 22). He might have added that, just as egoistic behavior need gain nothing for the egoist, one need not lose anything in altruistically doing something for the sake of someone else, even entirely for such a reason. An altruistic action can be both enjoyable and beneficial—nor does that fact entail that one's *motive* must have been to derive pleasure and benefit: one might not even suspect that one would—or, for that matter, have any expectation of unpleasant consequences or feelings of guilt if one does not. Solomon also clarifies and makes use of an Aristotelian conception of altruism: "it's just a more reasonable conception of self, as tied up intimately with community, with friends and family who may, indeed, count (even to us) more than we do" (p. 22). Here one is reminded of Aristotle's view of friendship in the *Nicomachean Ethics,* a view on which our conception of our good may essentially include a concern with the well-being of those we love.

More broadly, Solomon sees altruism and indeed other desirable elements in character, as crucially connected with community, in a sense of the term wide enough to include business organizations. He says at one point, for example, "To call the approach 'Aristotelian' is to emphasize the importance of community as such (I want to consider corporations as, first of all, communities)" (Solomon 2004: 1023). As I understand him, he does not take individuals to be merely social constructs (even if their

---

[4] Ayn Rand is a source, or anyway an influential proponent, of this view. Critical discussion of her treatment of altruism is provided (Audi 2009).

individuality is "socially constituted"),[5] but rather to be, in a far-reaching way socially engaged—at least if they are virtuous members of a community. The statement just quoted is followed by the qualification: "This emphasis on community should not, however, be taken to eclipse the importance of the individual and individual responsibility [but] … it is only within the community that individuality is developed and defined" (p. 1023). Developing the idea further, he says that "A virtue has a place in a social context, a human practice" (p. 1025). This may seem to imply that apart from social relations there would be no virtues, but it does not. One could have certain "individual" virtues, such as imaginativeness and self-discipline without *exercising* them in social contexts. This does not entail that they are not *relevant* to social relations; the point is that even if every virtue corresponds to one or more human practices, not all virtues, like honesty and fidelity, must be manifested in social contexts.

## Ethical Styles

The insightfulness in moral psychology that I have already mentioned carries over to Solomon's sense of ethical *styles*, roughly the manner in which virtues and other moral characteristics manifest themselves in conduct, by contrast with the specific deeds performed. He was sensitive to what, in my terms, is the distinction between obligations of *matter*, which are to do things of specific act-types—say, to furlough an employee—and obligations of *manner*, which are ("adverbial") obligations to do what one must in a morally appropriate *way*, say sympathetically rather than summarily or dryly.

*Ethics and Excellence* describes seven styles in ethics: the rule-governed style, understood deontologically; the utilitarian, conceived (as I interpret it) in relation to various kinds of maximization efforts; the loyalist, which stresses obligations of fidelity to persons or institutions; the prudential, in which long-term self-interest is central; the virtuous, in which actions are judged in relation to one's character; the intuitive, in which people tend to follow their conscience; and the empathetic, in which feelings of sympathy and compassion are central (Solomon 1992b: 255–256). These styles are clarified by noting degenerate cases of their use as well as their more normal employment. The styles encompass obligations of manner as well as those of matter, and the former obligations seem to be at least implicitly covered particularly in relation to the empathic style. An empathic person, for instance, who must be tough in criticizing a junior member of the team, does it in a *manner* that takes account of how it is felt and not just of how it is understood cognitively.

---

[5] As he suggests in Solomon (1992a) in which he says this and that individuality is also "socially situated" (p. 326).

The ethical styles Solomon speaks of are connected with what he called "The Six Dimensions of Virtue Ethics" (see Solomon 1992a: 326–330). These are community, excellence, role identity, integrity, judgment, and holism. I have already emphasized the communitarian element in his virtue ethics; a central point here is that ethical individuals must be capable of proper functioning as moral agents in a community. Excellence is of course the qualitative dimension of virtue crucial for understanding the proper exercise of any particular virtue. Success in a range of activities is its crucial mark. The notion of role identity is one that Solomon connects with business practice in particular, but he also accommodates the range of roles that mark other domains of human activity. Regarding integrity, that virtually all-time favorite in business ethics, he says, "integrity represents the integration of one's roles and responsibilities and the virtues defined by them" (p. 328). This emphasis on integration, which captures a core element in the concept of integrity, is especially welcome given how often 'integrity' is used to refer simply to a single virtue, especially honesty.[6]

The fifth and sixth dimensions of virtue ethics need only brief mention here. Judgment, which Solomon identifies with *phronesis* (roughly, Aristotelian practical wisdom), is essential for the possession and exercise of any virtue; and holism, like integrity, concerns the kind and degree of unity in a life. The virtuous life exhibits interconnected capacities and practices; it is not a mere compilation of desirable ones. Ethical style in a person is a matter of the distinctive way these six dimensions of virtue are realized in the person's life. In people of integrity, there will be no radical break between conduct in business settings and conduct in other social contexts. Implicit in what Solomon is saying is that people of integrity neither have two faces nor lead double lives.

In later work, on which Solomon drew in his contributions to the highly comprehensive reader, *Honest Work* (Solomon et al. 2007), he incorporates his virtue-ethical approach in a strategic planning section. Here he poses a series of 12 questions. In line with his emphasis on the social character of virtue, he calls on those doing life-planning or career-planning to ask what kind of people they like to spend their time with and whom they want to please. These are crucial questions for guiding ethical life of any kind. In elaborating on the last question, he shows his humor, an element sprinkled throughout many of his works. He writes: "'Yourself' is the fashionable but usually false answer. 'My mother' and 'my father' are a bit overworked, thanks to Freud. Try again." (Solomon 2007: 107).

## Some Limitations of Virtue-Ethics

Solomon was both ecumenical and judicious, and I cannot tell whether he thought that the Aristotelian virtue-ethical approach is normatively self-sufficient, that is (roughly), adequate to deal with questions of what we are obligated to do and

---

[6] For an account of integrity as figuring in business ethics—including some discussion of some of Solomon's views on the topic, see Audi and Murphy (2006).

(related to this) of what is and is not intrinsically good. The question is not easy to answer because there are such rich resources in Aristotle—and certainly in Solomon, who generally sought to theorize in a broad way that enabled him to take on board the best elements even in theories that, overall, he rejected. But in an essay of this character, I should in any case say something substantive about the relation between my views and Solomon's, so let me simply comment on that question as I see it.

On my view (argued in, among other writings, Audi 1994), the *deontic* concepts—notably those of right and wrong and of moral obligation—are not derivable from *aretaic* (virtue-theoretic) concepts, such as being honest, being fair, and being loyal. This is not to deny that if someone *has* the latter concepts (the aretaic ones), the person could, or even would, *thereby* have the former (the deontic ones). We cannot have the concept of a library without having that of a book, but the concept of a book is still the prior one.

But how far should we take the library analogy? Should we say that the deontic concepts are really prior and that virtues are something like internalizations of moral principles? I am not claiming that, though the position is arguable. It is certainly true that what constitutes a virtuous person can be understood at least in part in terms of internalized standards of obligation. My point here is more modest: it is that what constitutes, say, obligatory action cannot be *basically* understood in terms of what virtuous persons characteristically do. But this can be so even if the deontic concepts are not prior to the aretaic notions. Some third set of concepts, say axiological ones, could be prior to *both*. I suspect Solomon would have argued that there is a false contrast here; as some of the above indicates, he was constantly denying dichotomies and questioning established distinctions. He certainly would not accept my point at face value.

Suppose I am mainly right on the question of conceptual priority. This does not imply that no one should teach business ethics in terms of a virtue emphasis above all. My own view is that in teaching ethics we should use every approach we can to clarify moral matters and to help students and businesspeople make ethically better decisions and live up to them. Moreover, I have long held that if aretaic concepts are not conceptually basic in ethics—or *more* basic than deontic notions—they *are* essential in the theory of moral worth. Aristotle in effect distinguished between actions that express virtue—roughly are motivationally grounded in virtue—and those merely in conformity with it, just as Kant distinguished actions from duty and those merely in conformity with it. (The similarity between Kant and Aristotle here is in my judgment too little noted.) The latter two kinds of action—those just of the right behavioral type—are not morally *creditworthy*. A business traveler's turning in only expenses the job required is the right thing to do, but doing it is not morally creditworthy if it is motivated only by a desire to avoid punishment.

Ethics calls on us not just to do the right thing but to do it for the right reason. If we do not cultivate the elements of character that make doing the right thing for the right reason natural, we are unlikely to be reliable in doing the right thing at all.

Solomon saw this, and his writings provide vivid and multifarious routes to the ethical cultivation that is essential in business ethics. They are a unique and lasting contribution to our literature in both that field and in moral psychology.[7]

# References

Audi, Robert. 1989. Self-deception and practical reasoning. *Canadian Journal of Philosophy* 19: 246–266.

Audi, Robert. 1994. Acting from virtue. *Mind* 104: 449–471.

Audi, Robert. 2006. *Practical reasoning and ethical decision*. London/New York: Routledge.

Audi, Robert. 2009. Objectivity without egoism: Toward balance in business ethics. *The Academy of Management Learning and Education* 8: 263–274.

Audi, Robert, and Patrick E. Murphy. 2006. The many faces of integrity. *Business Ethics Quarterly* 16: 3–21.

Solomon, Robert C. 1992a. Corporate roles, personal virtues: An Aristotelian approach to business ethics. *Business Ethics Quarterly* 2: 317–330.

Solomon, Robert C. 1992b. *Ethics and excellence*. New York: Oxford University Press.

Solomon, Robert C. 1993. *The passions: Emotions and the meaning of life*. Indianapolis: Hackett.

Solomon, Robert C. 2004. Aristotle, ethics and business organizations. *Organization Studies* 25: 1021–1043.

Solomon, Robert C. 2006. Free enterprise, sympathy, and virtue. In *Moral markets: The critical role of values in the economy*, ed. Paul J. Zak, 16–41. Princeton: Princeton University Press.

Solomon, Robert C. 2007. Strategic planning – For the good life. In *Honest work*, ed. Robert C. Solomon, Joanne Ciulla, and Clancy Martin, 106–107. Oxford: Oxford University Press.

Solomon, Robert C., and Fernando L. Flores. 1996. Rethinking trust. *Business and Professional Ethics Journal* 16: 47–76.

Solomon, Robert C., Joanne Ciulla, and Clancy Martin (eds.). 2007. *Honest work: A business ethics reader*. Oxford: Oxford University Press.

---

[7] This essay is dedicated to the memory of Robert C. Solomon. Bob was a friend of mine at the time we were graduate students at the University of Michigan, and we kept in touch through the decades that followed. I recall many discussions during our year of overlap at the University of Texas in the early 1970s, a joint session on emotion at a conference later in the 1970s after I went to the University of Nebraska, at least one visit of Bob's to Nebraska in the 1980s on which he gave us a essay and lecture in philosophical psychology, another such visit in the 1990s when his topic was medical humanities, and still another when he and Kathy were together and visited in our home. There were also several occasions in the past 20 years or so when I gave essays at the University of Texas, and there Bob was always both an instructive respondent and a lively conversationalist over dinner. We met regularly at meetings of the American Philosophical Association as well as at the Society for Business Ethics, and I was looking forward to closer ties through our increasingly overlapping work in business ethics. I had wanted him to speak at Notre Dame.

# Chapter 9
# Robert Solomon's Aristotelian Nietzsche

Christine Swanton

**Abstract** In taking seriously Nietzsche as a moral philosopher Robert Solomon situates Nietzsche in the Aristotelian virtue ethical tradition. This is broadly understood as teleological and "self realizationist". Accordingly it is reasonable to conceive of both as subscribing to the following constraint on virtue:

(C1) A trait cannot be a virtue if it characteristically impairs or undermines the growth and development of its possessor.

Three difficulties for this reading are addressed and overcome:
(a) Nietzsche's concept of will to power as a central value is incompatible with virtue in any normal sense.
(b) Nietzsche does not believe in universal virtue, and is only concerned with the life affirmation (self realization) of the higher types, for it is on this that cultural enhancement in Europe depends.
(c) For Nietzsche, Solomon claims, all morality is perspectival, and as a consequence for him there are no moral truths. If this is so, Nietzsche cannot endorse (C1) as a truth of virtue.

## How to Read Nietzsche

In his *Living With Nietzsche: What The Great "Immoralist" Has to Teach Us*, Robert Solomon states that

> In this book, I suggest that we read [Nietzsche] from an existential point of view, as a provocative writer who means to transform the way we view our lives (as he attempts to transform his own). In other words, we should take Nietzsche *personally* (Solomon 2003: 12).

C. Swanton (✉)
Department of Philosophy, University of Auckland, Auckland, New Zealand
e-mail: c.swanton@auckland.ac.nz

K. Higgins and D. Sherman (eds.), *Passion, Death, and Spirituality*,
Sophia Studies in Cross-cultural Philosophy of Traditions and Cultures 1,
DOI 10.1007/978-94-007-4650-3_9, © Springer Science+Business Media Dordrecht 2012

I agree. However, as Solomon also suggests, taking Nietzsche personally is worthwhile only to the extent that he has something good to say. Indeed, Solomon continues:

> ...the existential approach I take here is by no means to be taken as a substitute for serious analysis and scholarship, for close textual and intimate biographical study (Solomon 2003: 12).

Understanding Nietzsche from both these points of view, I, and Solomon, take him as a philosopher who has something good to say about ethics, where this is understood as philosophical enquiry into what it takes to lead a good life. This in fact is the moral theoretical perspective of virtue ethics. A virtue ethical approach can thus harmonize both points of view, assuming that serious analysis can place Nietzsche in the virtue ethical tradition, and that leading a good life is a serious *personal* concern. Solomon's "Aristotelian Nietzsche" is in fact within that tradition, and has that concern. From my perspective, furthermore, and I believe to some extent from Solomon's, taking Nietzsche personally requires a theoretical perspective on the virtues and virtue ethics. So I need to say something about reading Nietzsche from that theoretical perspective.

Solomon (2003) maps Nietzsche onto Aristotle in fundamental respects. He begins by agreeing with Julius Moravscik's claim that Aristotle and Nietzsche were 'two of a kind... both functionalists, both naturalists, both "teleologists," standing very much opposed to the utilitarians and Kantians' (p. 129). In fact, Solomon claims, 'Nietzsche's ethics, like Aristotle's can best be classified in introductory ethics readers as an ethics of "self realization" (p. 129). Accordingly, 'what is essential to this view of ethics... an ethics of virtue, aretaic ethics – is that the emphasis is wholly on excellence, a teleological conception' (p. 131).

Understanding the nature of this 'teleological conception', purportedly common to Nietzsche and Aristotle, requires a foray into the theoretical base for virtue ethics within which both Aristotle and Nietzsche can be situated. Accordingly, in the following section, I give an account of what one might call the "meta-ethics" of Aristotelian virtue ethics. Here I suggest that on one reading of Aristotle, we can reasonably ascribe such a meta-ethics to Nietzsche. I then consider three difficulties for an Aristotelian picture of Nietzsche. These are Nietzsche's conception of will to power (the third section), his apparent view that virtues are not universal and that self realization is only for the higher type (the fourth section ), and his view that objectivity is not constructed from the point of view of the virtuous agent (the final section).

## The Meta-Ethics of Aristotelian Virtue Ethics

Virtue ethics in the Aristotelian tradition can be defined by one central meta-ethical claim. All evaluation presupposes evaluation of items as good of a kind, or as relative to a purpose. If I say 'It's a good thing that it's raining' for example, I am saying implicitly that it is good relative to my interests as a gardener, or the interests of the drought stricken Northland farmers and so on. Evaluations of items as being good of a kind will differ fundamentally according to whether the items evaluated are artefacts or organisms (including respectively their purposes, and their actions, reactions and behaviours). The former presuppose a purpose or function relative to the aims of those for whom the artefact is useful or serves a purpose. Evaluation of the latter does not presuppose this. Rather, for Aristotle, good of a kind evaluation for organisms is relative to their '*ergon*' or characteristic activity, and an understanding of that in turn requires an understanding of their nature as organisms of a certain natural kind. At this point an important move is made by Aristotle. Strictly speaking, good of a kind evaluation is evaluation as good *qua* F – good as an F. However, for Aristotle, in the case of organisms what makes something good *qua* F is what is good *for* F.

Now the question arises: given that what is good for an organism can be assessed as relative to many different roles that organism may occupy, what is the most fundamental form of evaluation as being good of a kind? For Aristotle, what is good for human beings is determined by a hierarchical approach to goodness, with the hierarchy terminating in what is good for a human being *as a human being*. How can this be? Organisms are items that have a *telos*, a characteristic growth and development; and it is good for an organism as that type of organism, that it exhibit that characteristic growth and development, albeit shaped by its environment, culture, history, and so on. But culture and environment themselves can be critically assessed in terms of their impairment or otherwise of the growth and development of the organism as a type. Certainly Nietzsche's attack on European culture took exactly this form.

Finally Aristotle made one extra move: the evaluative hierarchy terminates in *eudaimonia*, which is not just good for humans in general but is good for each individual human. So we move from the good *qua* human, to the good *for* human, to the good for humans *qua human*, to the good for humans *qua* human being *eudaimonia*, which in turn is good for each individual human being. On this view too, it is a necessary condition of *eudaimonia* that one have and exercise the virtues, so it is a necessary condition of being a virtue that it characteristically be good for its possessor.

How do we understand what is good for a person as a constraint on virtue? In a virtue ethics of self realization, it is natural to understand the 'good for' in terms of self realization, so that such a virtue ethics accepts as a constraint on virtue the following:

(C1) A trait cannot be a virtue if it characteristically impairs or undermines the growth and development of its possessor.
(C1), it should be noted, does not entail the following constraint accepted by neo-Aristotelians:
(C2) It is a necessary condition of a trait being a virtue that it characteristically *benefit* its possessor.

It is possible for traits to be risky bets for agent benefit in a normal welfarist sense without those traits undermining personal development; for example great devotion to very unpopular but worthwhile causes, great courage in dangerous times, passionate, driven, artistic creativity. Indeed this is one of Nietzsche's foremost assumptions underlying his attacks on eudaimonistic ethics as he understands it. For the purposes of this paper I shall read Aristotle as endorsing (C1), and leave open the question of his espousal of (C2) and the sense of 'benefit' involved in any such espousal. Although Solomon's "Aristotelian Nietzsche" certainly has him subscribing to a healthy list of Aristotle's virtues, he does not saddle Nietzsche with belief in (C2). Nonetheless if we interpret Aristotle in terms of the "self realizationist" thesis (C1), I think ascribing to Nietzsche an Aristotelian meta-ethics is reasonable.

However there is a difficulty in ascribing (C1) to Nietzsche. To understand this difficulty we need to clarify the relation between virtue and (C1). To say that (C1) is a constraint on virtue is not to say that (C1) is the focus or point of the virtue. (C1) for example does not imply that all virtues have as their targets or aims the growth and development of their possessors, or that a virtuous agent has that in mind when she is exercising a virtue. Virtues of love or friendship are focussed on others, not on the agent, and people exercising those virtues are themselves focussed in that way. The question then arises: what is the connection between not undermining the growth and development of human beings *qua* human, and realizing the point or target of the virtues, which may not be focussed on that good? Given that the growth and development of the possessor of a virtue is not the point of all the virtues, or even of most of them, is it possible that successfully meeting or realizing a virtue's aim, its target, may characteristically undermine the growth or development of its possessor? If this is so, then there are problems for Solomon's "Aristotelian Nietzsche" understood as a Nietzsche concerned with self realization.

To address this problem, we need a schematic definition of a virtue namely:

> A *virtue* is a good quality of character, more specifically a disposition to respond to or acknowledge items within its field or fields in an excellent or good enough way (Swanton 2003: 19).

The target or aim of a virtue is, schematically, to respond well to items in its field in a manner characteristic of the virtue. What counts as such responsiveness will vary according to the field of the virtue, and the normatively salient features of that field to which an agent is to be responsive, and which is the focus of the virtue in question. To have a conception of how virtue secures a normative grasp on the world (the various fields of the virtues with their normatively salient features) we need an account of those features – what I have elsewhere (Swanton 2003) called the bases of moral acknowledgement. Here I shall focus on just one, value, for that is a central notion in Nietzsche, and well illustrates the possible tension between a virtue not undermining the personal development or growth of its possessor, and realizing the point or aim of that virtue. Values should be understood as properties of items: they are not things. According to the basic conception of 'value', valuable items are worthy of preservation, maintenance, enhancement, creation and so on. There are many things that are valuable besides the good of individual human beings, let alone the agent. Hence the normative pull of the world on the virtuous, expressed in value-talk, may be in tension with the idea that virtues do not undermine the growth and development of their possessors.

If however there is no real tension, three apparent difficulties would need to be overcome:

(a) Nietzsche's concept of will to power as a central value is incompatible with virtue in any normal sense, including the schematic definition given above.

(b) Nietzsche does not believe in universal virtue, and is only concerned with the life affirmation (self realization) of the higher types, for it is on this that cultural enhancement in Europe depends.

(c) For Nietzsche, Solomon claims (2003: 47–48), all morality is perspectival, and as a consequence for him there are no moral truths. If this is so, how can we claim that Nietzsche endorses (C1) as a truth of virtue, which any good moral theory should recognize?

Each of these difficulties is addressed in turn in the following three sections.


## Virtue and Will to Power

We turn now to the first difficulty: Nietzsche's conception of will to power.

Solomon, unlike myself, does not take Nietzsche's conception of will to power very seriously as a notion important for Nietzsche. Solomon relegates the notion of will to power in Nietzsche to the status of serving as a reminder that we are not motivated solely by pleasure, but also by desires for status, for control, and so on (Solomon 2003: 85). I by contrast think the notion is central, indeed fundamental to understanding the difference between virtue and vice as Nietzsche sees it, for it plays a powerful theoretical explanatory role in that understanding. In particular, not only is Nietzsche's notion of will to power compatible with virtue in any normal sense, it gives content to (C1). Accordingly a huge amount of his philosophy gives an account of the varieties of distorted 'will to power' which underlie various vices. Distorted will to power appears precisely in forms which express impoverished personal development or undermine growth and creativity.

The notion of 'will to power' thus plays a central role in Nietzsche's view that psychology should be reinstated as the 'queen of the sciences' (Nietzsche 1973 §23: 54) for that science can uncover the 'depths' of our being, unlike traditional moral philosophy which he describes as superficial and timid. ('All moral philosophy hitherto has been boring and a soporific') (Nietzsche 1973 §228: 157). Nietzsche himself described his psychology as '*the development-theory of the will to power*' (Nietzsche 1973 §23: 53; see Lehrer 1999). Nietzsche claims (rightly in my view) that this development theory provides, in his hands, a deeper account of the nature of virtue and vice than that supplied hitherto. As he says: 'thanks to another self examination and deepening on the part of man' we reject that idea [that virtue, what is of value, lies in intention] as superficial: we come to believe that 'the decisive value of an action resides in precisely that which is *not intentional* in it.' (Nietzsche 1973 §32: 63).

Given that a virtue is a disposition of excellent or good responsiveness to items in its domain (such as threatening or dangerous situations, pleasure, friends or potential friends), a virtue ethics based on the idea of will to power will require that an agent express or enhance not her will to power as such, but her undistorted will to power. But what does that mean? First, what is meant by will to power? Will to power as a genus must be distinguished from its various species. As a genus, it is a highly general idea, applicable to all life forms:

> A living thing desires above all to vent its strength - life as such is will to power... (Nietzsche 1973 §13: 44).

As applied to humans, the need to 'vent one's strength', expand, is connected essentially with their nature as active, growing, developing beings, rather than mere receptacles of pleasure or welfare. It is important to realize that for Nietzsche the 'will to power' should not be conceived as consisting of something called the will, which is a will to a single thing, power. This is a mistake on two fronts. First the idea of a mental entity, "free will" which is the operation of an 'indifferent substratum' existing 'behind' the action, and which can either switch on its "will" or not, is a metaphysical fiction (Nietzsche 1996 I §13: 29). Rather as Nietzsche says in real life it is only a matter of *strong* and *weak* wills' (Nietzsche 1973 §21: 51), or rather, there are strong and weak individuals "willing" in a way which expresses their strength or expresses their weakness.

The expressive character of our action as strong or weak enables us to make sense of Nietzsche's denial that our actions are unegoistic:

> 'Unegoistic!' – this one is hollow and wants to be full, that one is overfull and wants to be emptied – both go in search of an individual who will serve their purpose. And this process, understood in its highest sense, is in both cases called by the same word: love – what? is love supposed to be something unegoistic? (Nietzsche 1982 §145: 91–2).

Nietzsche's claim here is that love is expressive of neediness: the only issue is whether the neediness is healthy or strong, or weak; whether the loving behaviour expresses valuable or disvaluable states in the individual. The 'intention' to act for the sake of another is, for Nietzsche, superficial. If that intention is expressive of being 'overfull' and a need to bestow, then it is "egoistic" in a valuable sense. Such a person gives from a position of psychological strength as opposed to a self sacrificial giving borne of inner weakness. The latter giver, who is empty and needs to be filled, is not affirming or enhancing her own life, but is rather externalizing self contempt by loving for and through others.

Once it is understood that 'will to power' is not a type of act or motive that presupposes the fiction of free will, but is expressive, we can unmask the second mistake: that the will to power is a will *to* a *single* thing: power. If everything is 'will to power' why does Nietzsche speak so often of other apparent "wills", such as the will to memory of the sovereign individual, and the will to truth of the ascetic philosopher? Will to power is not a will to a single thing, power, but in seeking truth, seeking justice, using one's memory, for example, one can exhibit various kinds of weaknesses (or strengths) in that seeking or deployment. Thus Nietzsche frequently speaks of forms of the will to truth and the will to memory that exhibit distortion (such as the 'unconditional will to truth'). The will to truth of the ascetic philosopher is *in him* an expression of a 'domineering spiritualization', the will to memory of the sovereign individual is 'protracted' and relentless. There is no single thing "power" which Nietzsche's various types seek. Rather they more or less powerfully aim to develop, grow, expand, vent their strength, and some of these ways of expressing strength are, for Nietzsche, distorted.

Many kinds of distorted will to power such as resentment, cruelty turned inward, resignation, various forms of escape from self, underlie vice, whereas virtue is marked by an absence of such distortion. Pity as a vice can thereby be distinguished from virtuous altruism which Nietzsche frequently calls 'overflowing'; laziness as a vice can be distinguished from virtuous "letting things be"; resignation or "willess-ness" distinguished from sublimation, and (virtuous) solitariness; and anxiety ridden fear from proper prudence.[1]

To conclude: Nietzsche's notion of will to power, far from being a "value" incompatible with virtue at all, actually underwrites the conception of virtue which subscribes to (C1). However this notion, far from underwriting (C2), may even be incompatible with it.

## Virtue and Types of Human Being

I turn now to the second of the difficulty (b) on page 117. This is the thought that Nietzsche denies the existence of universal virtue and that it is only the self realization of the few with which Nietzsche is concerned.[2] I shall argue that though Nietzsche relativizes at least some virtues to types of human being, this is compatible with a view which I believe he holds: there are many important universal virtues, and (C1) can reasonably be seen as applicable to all. Indeed Nietzsche and Aristotle are in the same camp in this respect. For Aristotle some virtues are able to be possessed only by subclasses of human, notably magnificence and *megalopsychia* (great souledness), but these are "differentiated" forms of a universal virtue. What is interesting here is that Aristotle does not rely for example simply on talk of a single universal virtue denoting an excellence of character in relation to the field of getting and spending money, and on the idea of *phronesis* (practical wisdom) determining how this single virtue is to be expressed in various circumstances. Rather he thinks that the one "basic" virtue (an excellence of character in regard to the field of getting and spending money), is able to be differentiated into two virtues: liberality and magnificence. (We might wish to add a third, thrift). The differentiated virtues are salient and conceptually useful to the point that we have names for them, but not for the undifferentiated basic form. The same general point

---

[1] For more on the distinction between virtue and vice in Nietzsche see Swanton (2011).

[2] I cannot here fully address the second of these issues, concentrating mainly on the first. (But see Swanton 2006).

applies to *megalopsychia*. The *megalopsychos*, properly understood, is a type to be admired, for he is worthy of great things and has an accurate conception of his worth. He is thus to be distinguished from the merely modest – he who is not worthy of great things and who also has an accurate conception of his worth. The general basic virtue concerns excellence in the field of one's attitude to one's worth or achievement, but again, the basic virtue appears to have no name.

Nietzsche is Aristotelian in that he too relativises some virtues to types of being, as Solomon recognizes. However I have two points of possible difference with Solomon. First Solomon appears to accuse Nietzsche in this respect of 'elitism', a pejorative term, whereas both Aristotle and Nietzsche are emphasising various respects in which we are unequal, and some of these inequalities need to be recognized in differentiated virtue. Secondly, unlike Solomon, I do not believe that, for Nietzsche, all the differentiated virtues are of the "overflowing" passional type. In this regard my Nietzsche may well be more Aristotelian than Solomon's.

I turn now to the problematic area of the relativization of virtue to types of human being. A major area of controversy, as far as Nietzsche is concerned, are the virtues proper to *types* of 'man', particularly those of the herd or of the higher type such as the 'free spirit' of *Beyond Good and Evil*. It may be thought that his views commit him to a kind of relativism described by Leiter (2002: 44) as 'the view that judgments are only "valid" relative to a "framework" or "perspective," so that conflicting judgments can, in principle, both be true', as opposed to what Leiter calls relationalism: the idea for example that something may be good for one type of thing but bad for another – a view that is of course compatible with objectivity. I want to show that the relationality of Nietzsche's virtues is compatible with the idea of there being universal virtue for Nietzsche, and if that is so, any move from relationality to relativism is to some extent undercut. Nietzsche can be read as a someone who accepts universal virtues based on universal facts about human nature, while making room for the idea of virtue differentiated in various ways; not only by cultural variation, or roles, but most importantly for him, by types of human being. Accordingly we can speak of the virtues of the herd, for example, or the role virtues of a business person or a lawyer. For example, claims Nietzsche, 'the virtues of the common man would perhaps indicate vice and weakness in a philosopher' (Nietzsche 1973 §30: 61). Hence compatible with talk of universal virtues of generosity and creativity for example, are the specific forms of generosity proper to, or not proper to, business executives; the specific form of discipline proper to the creative talented artist, and so on.

Let us focus on the difficult area of the "virtues of the herd". Here is Nietzsche:

> On the other hand, the herd-man of Europe today makes himself out to be the only permissible type of man and glorifies their qualities through which he is tame, peaceable and useful to the herd as the real human virtues: namely public spirit, benevolence, consideration, industriousness, moderation, modesty, forbearance, pity (Nietzsche 1973 §199:121).

First, are the so-called herd virtues itemized here really virtues for Nietzsche? To answer this question we need to distinguish the herd from the sick. Although Nietzsche frequently exhibits contempt for the herd, that contempt is based on the idea that they are by and large sick, as well as herd-like, for they are characteristically resentment-filled, and as such drag society into mediocrity. A symptom of this sickness is valorizing the "herd virtues" as the real virtues that *all* should aspire to. But *that* reason for Nietzsche's contempt of the herd is compatible with the idea that there are indeed virtues proper to a *healthy* herd, which are differentiated forms of genuine basic virtues. Patience, consideration, forbearance, industriousness, public spiritedness, *are* virtues for all, but will take different forms in different types of human being, including the herd. For example, consideration in the higher type will manifest as politeness towards the herd, but consideration in the herd will be the common or garden form of the virtue.

Public spiritedness in the higher type will take the form of leadership, and benevolence the form of tenderness and patience towards one's inferiors:

> Zarathustra is gentle with the sick. Verily, he is not angry with their kinds of comfort and ingratitude (Nietzsche 1954 I: 145).

In *Beyond Good and Evil* Nietzsche claims:

> Few are made for independence – it is a privilege of the strong. And who attempts it, having the completest right to it but without being *compelled* to, thereby proves that he is probably not only strong but also daring to the point of recklessness. (Nietzsche 1973 §29: 60).

Nietzsche is not claiming here that independence in some form or other is not a universal virtue; he is merely claiming that only in the strong should it take the form of 'recklessness'. For 'what serves the higher type as food or refreshment must to a very different and inferior type be almost poison' (1973 §30: 61). Here as elsewhere Nietzsche is subscribing to a relational but not necessarily relativistic view, but one that I think is also compatible with the idea of universal virtue. In types who should not venture into labyrinths multiplying 'by a thousand the dangers which life as such already brings with it' (p. 61), independence (as normally understood) can still be a virtue, but it will take the form of, for example, non-parasitism. Independence can thus be seen as a universal virtue at the basic level.

This point is important for an understanding of virtue in Nietzsche. For many, what would be naturally called 'virtue to excess' is genuine virtue for Nietzsche. Hence the virtues are described as 'overflowing', have extreme enthusiasm and passion at their core, and practical wisdom is nowhere or hardly to be seen. This appears to be Solomon's view. However I do not believe that even Nietzsche would believe that all the differentiated virtues are of the "overflowing" passional type. A kind of unwise 'overflowing' may be appropriate to the particularly creative higher type, but for ordinary people occupying needed ordinary roles, judiciousness in e.g. one's role as a judge or a mother, is surely required. As the above passage about independence shows, Nietzsche does not advocate independence to the point of daring and recklessness for everyone. Overflowing, "unwise" courage, creativity, generosity, is toxic to many personalities, and not only bad for them but also bad for society. I do not think therefore that the metaphor of overflowing and a denial of Aristotelian *phronesis* necessarily applies to all forms of courage as a virtue for Nietzsche, as Solomon thinks (Solomon 2003: 149).

Not only do virtues take forms appropriate for the "herd" that are different from those appropriate for the strong; virtue for the herd should be distinguished from vices, such as pity, which are standardly exhibited by the herd. Pity is not a herd virtue as Nietzsche understands it: rather it is not a virtue at all, since it is a trait of the sick. The admission that there are virtues for the (healthy) herd, however, does not entail that the herd should universalize them *in their differentiated form*. On the contrary, to do so is the road to mediocrity, for it is destructive of "man's lucky hits": the creative experimenter, the free spirit, the talented artist, who signal and promote society's progress, and higher culture. Healthy herd types would not do this, but would rather concentrate on their own roles in a well functioning society.

Herd virtues then are differentiated forms of basic virtues, some or many of which are universal as basic virtues. They should be distinguished from traits of the sick, from which even the herd should free itself:

> May they [the herd-like sick] become convalescents, men of overcoming, and create a higher body for themselves! (Nietzsche 1883–1954 I: 145).

To be a 'man of overcoming' is not necessarily to turn oneself into a cultural leader: one may instead become a healthy member of the herd, and thereby play one's part in halting the slide into mediocrity.

It is not always easy, however, to distinguish traits which are not virtues at all, from traits which are virtues for the herd but are not virtues for the higher type, and traits which are virtues in the convalescent, but not virtues for the higher type. Consider the distinction made by Nietzsche between cynicism and honesty in *Beyond Good and Evil*:

> Cynicism is the only form in which common souls come close to honesty; and the higher man must prick up his ears at every cynicism, whether course or refined, and congratulate himself whenever a buffoon without shame or a scientific satyr speaks out in his presence (Nietzsche 1973 §26: 58).

Nietzsche's point is that cynicism is at least better than the wilful ignorance of him who makes 'everything around us bright and free and easy and simple', of him who employs language which 'cannot get over its coarseness and continues to speak of antitheses where there are only degrees and many subtleties of gradation...'(Nietzsche 1973 §24: 55). But it is unclear whether cynicism is a virtue of the 'convalescent' who is on his way to genuine honesty, or whether society needs the cynics, where cynicism is a genuine herd virtue. I suspect that there is a sense in which both claims are true: let him who is capable of strength overcome cynicism, but cynicism can be seen as a herd-role virtue (if not taken to excess) of, for example, journalists.

To show that there are universal virtues which are differentiated according to types of human being is not to show that for Nietzsche, the virtues of the herd satisfy Constraint (C1) of virtue. It is not to show that herd virtues are not inimical to the self realization of members of the herd, as opposed to conducing to the culture of "European Man". That is a task which cannot be completed here, but as we have seen, Nietzsche does suggest that the virtuous herd is a healthy herd, and members of a healthy herd are 'men of overcoming'. They too must overcome distorted will to power.

## Virtue, Objectivity and Truth

In his *Nicomachean Ethics* Aristotle claims:

> To arrive at the truth is indeed the function of intellect in any aspect, but the function of practical intellect is to arrive at the truth that corresponds to right appetition (Aristotle 1976: l. 1139a16-b2).

The aim of *virtue* is to arrive at practical truth understood in terms of hitting the mean ('virtue aims to hit the mean,' 1106b16-24). Yet Solomon's "Aristotelian Nietzsche" seems to reject the very idea of practical truth, for it is apparently incompatible with his moral perspectivism. According to Solomon, Nietzsche 'denies that there are any "moral facts"' (Solomon 2003: 47), because (for Nietzsche) forms of morality are perspectival. This has the following implications for Solomon:

(a)   There is more than one perspective of morality.
(b)   The truth of (a) 'tends to neutralize the claim of any one perspective of morality to be the "right" one' (Solomon 2003: 48).

It is true that Nietzsche believes (a): slave and master morality are moral perspectives. However, on my view, (b) is false. Furthermore, even if there is no single right moral perspective there can be wrong ones. Indeed Nietzsche makes it quite clear that he thinks there are. He claims:

> Against this theologians' instinct I wage war: I have found its traces everywhere... This faulty perspective on all things is elevated into a morality, a virtue, a holiness: ...and no *other* perspective is conceded any further value once one's own has been made sacrosanct with the names of "God", "redemption", and "eternity". I have dug up the theologians' instinct everywhere: it is the most widespread, really *subterranean*, form of falsehood found on earth (Nietzsche 1954 §9: 575–6).

Since slave morality is thoroughly imbued with the 'theologians' instinct' it is quite simply, false. The putative "moral facts" touted by slave morality are not facts at all. Of course they are interpretations: Nietzsche makes it clear that moral facts are all interpretations, but some interpretations are better than others. Some are 'superficial', as Nietzsche claims of moralities that rely on the value of surface intentions, and some are pernicious: wrong in a serious way which is deeply distorting for the whole of culture. Such is true of slave morality. It is true that, as Solomon claims, Nietzsche is opposed to a Kantian model of truth understood from outside all perspective. But that is not to say that he could not have a model of practical truth closely allied to virtue, as does Aristotle.

However this will all seem pie in the sky if we cannot move from Nietzsche's perspectivism to a notion of objectivity which enables us to judge that some perspectives are better than others. What Nietzsche would object to is a rather bloodless "hyperobjective" notion of objectivity (Swanton 2003) such as the impartial spectator, detachment, and a perspectiveless point of view (the "view from nowhere"). Can another, more virtue-centred notion be found?

In his *Genealogy of Morals* Nietzsche provides a notion of objectivity which can be understood as a target of a personal virtue of objectivity, yet there is no clear picture of a qualified judge such as a virtuous agent, or an authoritative moral sentiment, in terms of which objectivity is to be defined. Rather for Nietzsche, knowledge is necessarily perspectival for that is part and parcel of human cognition. That is, one person cannot have the definitively objective perspective. This is not *ipso facto* to claim that objectivity is impossible. Objectivity may simply require a set of dispositions (virtues) which are appropriate for dealing with the necessarily perspectival nature of human knowledge. Specifically it involves recognizing and dealing appropriately with multiple perspectives, and the necessarily limited perspective of any human agent, including the virtuous.

To say *merely* that knowledge is perspectival is to fail to contrast objectivity as a state reached through the exercise of a range of *virtues*, with the disposition of *inter alia*, thinking, acting, and feeling as if one's own perspective (even if virtuous) alone generates knowledge. On the other hand to say that knowledge is perspectival is not to imply that 'Human knowledge distorts or falsifies reality' (Clark 1990: 127). For that would be to suppose that ("true") objectivity should be understood in terms of some non-perspectival fiction.

How then are we to understand a Nietzschean virtue of objectivity? Nietzsche provides a clue about how objectivity is compatible with the perspectival nature of knowledge in the following well known passage.

> Perspectival seeing is the *only* kind of seeing there is, perspectival knowing the *only* kind of knowing and the *more* feelings about a matter which we allow to come to expression, the *more* eyes, different eyes through which we able to view this same matter, the more complete our 'conception' of it, our 'objectivity' will be. (Nietzsche 1996 III §12: 98)

The passage claims both that knowledge is perspectival and that we can become objective or more objective by allowing 'to come to expression' as many perspectives as possible. The question arises: is Nietzsche's conception of objectivity compatible with the following central claim of virtue ethics?

> (S) Some perspectives are superior to others, and in particular virtuous persons have a perspective superior to those of vicious persons, at least characteristically.

Certainly the above quoted passage implies that one is not objective just by having a superior perspective; perhaps even the best perspective (that of a virtuous agent). Indeed having a superior perspective on an issue may not even be necessary for objectivity. For Nietzsche claims not that *superior* perspectives yield objectivity, but that

> (M) The more perspectives one brings to bear on an issue the more objective one is.

(M) is compatible with (S) because even superior perspectives have to be subjected to the points of view of multiple perspectives. It may be objected: why would one bother with a lot of inferior perspectives when one's own is superior? "More eyes" may contaminate and corrupt a superior vision. To answer this objection we note the following points.

(a) Even if one's perspective is superior, one needs an attitude of appropriate epistemic humility towards one's own perspective. That is a moral and intellectual virtue which is part of practical wisdom demanding consideration of other perspectives.

(b) Even if the perspective of the virtuous is by and large superior, inferior perspectives overall may have something to offer, just as overall inferior theories may contain grains of truth which should be preserved.

(c) Even the virtuous have limited perspectives, lacking expertise in many areas, and inevitably limited by their historical and cultural location, and other factors. It is not the case then, that having the best perspective (if such exists) is sufficient for objectivity, and nor is it the case that being objective entails that one has the best perspective.

(d) To avoid "more (and inferior) eyes" contaminating superior perspectives, or those superior in certain respects, we need certain dialogical and epistemic virtues. These virtues are not merely intellectual but also have a "moral" dimension including epistemic humility, courage, perseverance, appropriate frankness, openness, open-mindedness, and kinds of strength.

Virtue notions are central in this picture of objectivity, for objectivity requires the expression of a range of virtues, whose target is the appropriate integration of different perspectives. This of course is a far cry from saying that each perspective is equally worthy, or even that all have some worth. Nonetheless on this view one will not say that objectivity is constituted by the perspective of single virtuous agents. For even the perspectives of non virtuous agents may have something to offer and will need to be appropriately integrated for objective points of view to be attained. What counts as integrating perspectives and how this is done cannot be discussed here. (See Swanton 2003).

At any rate the Aristotelian conception of virtue in its form (C1) can be reinstated as a moral truth underpinning the claim which I believe Nietzsche endorses: slave morality with its "life denying" "theological instincts" is a perspective that is both false and pernicious.

# References

Aristotle. 1976. *The Nicomachean ethics* (trans: Thomson, J. A. K., rev. H). Tredennick. Harmondsworth: Penguin.

Clark, Maudemarie. 1990. *Nietzsche on truth and philosophy*. New York: Cambridge University Press.

Lehrer, Ronald. 1999. Adler and Nietzsche. In *Nietzsche and depth psychology*, ed. Jacob Golomb, Weaver Santaniello, and Ronald Lehrer, 229–245. New York: State University of New York Press.

Leiter, Brian. 2002. *Nietzsche on morality*. London: Routledge.

Nietzsche, Friedrich. 1954 [1883–1885]. *Thus spoke Zarathustra* (trans: Kaufmann, Walter). In *The portable Nietzsche*, ed. Walter Kaufmann, 103–439. New York: Penguin Books.

Nietzsche, Friedrich. 1954 [1888]. The antichrist (trans: Kaufmann, Walter). In *The portable Nietzsche*, ed. Walter Kaufmann, 565–656. New York: Viking/Penguin.

Nietzsche, Friedrich. 1973 [1886]. *Beyond good and evil*. (trans: Hollingdale, R.J.) London: Penguin Books.

Nietzsche, Friedrich. 1982 [1880]. *Daybreak: Thoughts on the prejudices of morality* (trans: Hollingdale, R.J.). Cambridge: Cambridge University Press.

Nietzsche, Friedrich. 1996 [1887]. *On the genealogy of morals*. (trans: Smith, Douglas). Oxford: Oxford University Press.

Solomon, Robert C. 2003. *Living with Nietzsche: What the great "immoralist" has to teach us*. Oxford: Oxford University Press.

Swanton, Christine. 2003. *Virtue ethics: A pluralistic view*. Oxford: Oxford University Press.

Swanton, Christine. 2006. Can Nietzsche be both an existentialist and a virtue ethicist? In *Values and virtues*, ed. Timothy Chappell, 171–188. Oxford: Clarendon.

Swanton, Christine. 2011. Nietzsche and the virtues of mature egoism. In *Cambridge critical guide to Nietzsche's On the genealogy of morality*, ed. Simon May, 285–308. Cambridge: Cambridge University Press.

# Chapter 10
# Robert Solomon and the Ethics of Grief and Gratitude: Toward a Politics of Love

Kelly Oliver

**Abstract** Robert Solomon's work suggests that the moral dimensions of grief and gratitude may obligate us to change social mores for ones more consistent with what we learn from rational reflection on the essential characteristics of emotions. His work brings with it a faith that philosophical reflection can change attitudes and behaviors, not only to make us better people, but also to make the world a better place. In this chapter, I argue that for Solomon, grief is a continuation of love and both emotions can take one out of one's self. Both are in an important sense morally obligatory. And, moreover, both the ethics of love and the ethics of grief have significant consequences for thinking about politics.

In a chapter from *In Defense of Sentimentality* entitled "On Grief and Gratitude," Robert Solomon says "grief…is not just a form of suffering nor merely a response to a devastating loss. Grief is a moral emotion… grief is not only expected, as the appropriate response to the loss of a loved one, but also in a strong sense is obligatory…" (Solomon 2004: 75). In what sense, as Solomon claims, is grief "morally obligatory" (p. 78, 97)? In this essay, I would like to explore the ethics of grief as developed in some of Solomon's writings; and in the spirit of his work, extend his analysis of grief and gratitude to what might be called a politics of grief and gratitude.

Solomon argues that both grief and gratitude are moral emotions because they "involve… an admission of our vulnerability and our dependence on other people" (Solomon 2004: 76). Solomon delineates some of the essential characteristics of grief such as: putting us in touch with our mortality, putting us in closer touch with love, opening our imaginations to lost possibilities, loss of part of one's self and of personal identity, and a longing for what one can no longer have. He suggests that grief may seem to lead to inactivity and withdrawal from the world and others, but

K. Oliver (✉)
Department of Philosophy, Vanderbilt University, Nashville, TN, USA
e-mail: kelly.oliver@vanderbilt.edu

K. Higgins and D. Sherman (eds.), *Passion, Death, and Spirituality*,
Sophia Studies in Cross-cultural Philosophy of Traditions and Cultures 1,
DOI 10.1007/978-94-007-4650-3_10, © Springer Science+Business Media Dordrecht 2012

the purpose of that withdrawal is perhaps the most important activity for creating a meaningful life, the activity of reflection (p. 92). Grief can also lead to more obviously *active* sorts of activities like commemorating and honoring the lost person, dedicating activities to him, in his memory and in the spirit of his life. Solomon says that the process of grief itself—and he insists that it is a process, even a project— "could be construed as dedicated to the lost loved one" (p. 92). He argues that

> grief has positive value in that it gives us good cause for reflection and a new sense of what needs to be done, not for ourselves but for the memory of those we have lost. The loss suffered in grief may be enormous and irredeemable, but the further loss suffered by ignoring or denying the importance of the grieving process only amplifies, it does not erase, the suffering (p. 101).

Ultimately, Solomon says that grief is a "kind of relationship" between the griever and the lost person (Solomon 2004: 87). Moreover, grief is the result of a particular kind of relationship; had it not existed "the other person would not have been even a candidate for grief" (p. 88). The relationship in question is one of love; "grief is the continuation of love" and "the obligations of grief are the obligations of love" (p. 90). The denial of grief, then, is the denial of love. And to understand the moral obligation to grieve, we must understand the ethics of love.

Solomon has written volumes on love. Indeed, in one way or another love comes up in almost every book Solomon wrote. One of the primary characteristics of love that makes it ethical, perhaps even a moral obligation, and certainly definitive of humanity, is an "experience of expansion of ourselves," an "overflowing" that takes us out of ourselves and toward others and the world (Solomon 2002: 34). This moving beyond self is not an abandonment of self, but rather a transformation of self that Solomon associates with what he calls "naturalized spirituality" (p. 6). In *Spirituality for the Skeptic*, he says "when I have to summarize naturalized spirituality in a single phrase, it is this: the thoughtful love of life" (Solomon 2002: 6). Love is a passion that we can live in relation to other people, animals, the world, and life itself. Solomon explains his notion of spirituality as including "a generalized erotic love of other people, a love that has learned to appreciate their depth and mystery, a love that has learned to listen, probe, and share" (p. 38).

Following Nietzsche, Solomon insists that in an important sense, "love, too, has to be learned" (Solomon 2002: vi). It is a way of seeing the world and others that "improves and intensifies... our perceptions" (p. 36). It is a choice to see the world as beautiful and sublime. In this regard, we are responsible for loving just as we are responsible for all of our passions. Indeed, we could say that we are obligated to love insofar as ethics or ethos is about relationships with others that allow us to share the world and a sense of community or solidarity. We are obligated to learn to love our neighbors by teaching ourselves "to look at others from an enchanted perspective, enjoying... the richness of human intimacy"; we must learn "to view the world... as an object of love and fascination" (p. 36).

Are we also obligated to love people we don't know, those with whom we will never be intimate, perhaps even our enemies? If love is a social passion, is it also a political passion? bell hooks claims that there is no political passion without love; and that the problem of the left in this country is that there is no longer room for love in politics. She says, "without an ethic of love shaping the direction of our political vision and our radical aspiration, we are often seduced, in one way or the other, into continued allegiance to systems of domination—imperialism, sexism, racism, classism" (hooks 1994: 243). Love is the ethical agency that can motivate an attempt to understand others, across differences, beyond familiar or personal intimacy or neighborly proximity to strangers and those unfamiliar. Love can motivate us to move beyond self-interested political action toward compassions for others not like ourselves. hooks argues that in order to see beyond our ethical and political blind spots, the blind spots that perpetuate oppression, we need to consciously and decisively adopt an ethic of love. She concludes, "the ability to acknowledge blind spots can emerge only as we expand our concern about politics of domination and our capacity to care about the oppression and exploitation of others. A love ethic makes this expansion possible" (p. 244). Seeing our own blind-spots requires an ethics of love that is not itself blind. It is not a-critical love. Rather, hooks comments on the importance of critical reflection in her own experience of love:

> When I look at my life, searching it for a blueprint that aided me in the process of decolonization, of personal and political self-recovery, I know that it was learning the truth about how systems of domination operate that helped, learning to look both inward and outward with a critical eye. Awareness is as central to the process of love as the practice of freedom (hooks 1994, 248).

The loving eye, then, is also a critical eye; loving perception is the result of reflection. And, I would add, learning "the truth" is an on-going process that must be undertaken continually and vigilantly in order to love. Moreover, self-awareness as self-recovery of this sort demands self-transformation that continually acknowledges our indebtedness and dependence on others, even those whom we do not know.

bell hooks associates the testimony of love, with the practice of freedom. She says, "the moment we choose to love we begin to move against domination, against oppression. The moment we choose to love we begin to move towards freedom, to act in ways that liberate ourselves and others. That action is the testimony of love as the practice of freedom" (hooks 1994: 250). Like Solomon, hooks emphasizes that love is a choice; it is a willful decision. We can choose to love or we can choose not to love. In this regard, love is an attitude that we willingly cultivate toward others. We can choose to close ourselves off to others or we can choose to *try* to open ourselves towards others. But only through critical reflection on our own performance of that opening can we hope to maintain this loving attitude. Love is not something we choose once and for all. Rather, it is a decision that must be constantly reaffirmed through the vigilance of "self-reflection."

hooks cites Martin Luther King's proclamation "I have decided to love" (hooks 1994: 247). She argues that the civil rights movement had the power to move the masses because it was rooted in this love ethic; and King was a charismatic leader because he called for love. hooks suggests that any progressive movement that compels the masses must do so by compelling the hearts and souls through the promise and proclamation of love. Opening a public space of love and generosity is crucial to opening a space for transformative politics. Yet, only by maintaining the critical capacity of the loving eye do we resist the temptation to unquestioningly "kneel and pray," so-to-speak, at the altar of love.

If love is divine, it is not because it is otherworldly or disembodied. Rather, as Solomon suggests in *Spirituality for the Skeptic*, love is essential to a naturalized spirituality. The ethics of love, born from critical reflection, is the affirmation of our relationship to the other people, the world, and life itself. Relations with others do not have to be hostile alien encounters. Instead, they can become loving adventures, the advent of something new. Difference does not have to be threatening; it can be exciting, even the source of the meaning of life. In the thrilling adventure of love, the unknown and incomprehensible compel rather than threaten. Falling in love, the mystery of the other person is the greatest joy; and vulnerability in an encounter with another is a sweet surrender, a gift rather than a sacrifice. The other person's potential to make me better than I am is the transformative power of love.

Love's transformative power, the power of loving eyes to see the world and others from a perspective of gratitude, rather than a judgmental perspective of superiority or resentment, makes it not only an essentially moral emotion but also necessary for any truly transformative politics. Differences and the unfamiliar can be seen as awesome or inviting mysteries or they can be seen as incomprehensible or hostile threats, depending on one's attitude toward life. We can try to understand and appreciate what at first seems unrecognizable—even if in the end we do not embrace it—or we can lash-out and try to extinguish anything we do not call our own.

In *In Defense of Sentimentality*, Solomon says "being capable of and expressing gratitude is not only a virtue but also part and parcel of the good life. It is not just an acknowledgment of debt and an expression of humility but a way to improve one's life" (Solomon 2004: 104–105). He concludes the chapter "On Grief and Gratitude": "Those who feel gratitude are less likely to be vengeful, and vice versa. Thus gratitude and forgiveness are also related, and give the existential choice between living a life based on gratitude and forgiveness and living a life based on resentment and vengeance, the choice to be made should be obvious" (p. 107). In this chapter, the discussion of grief leads to a discussion of gratitude because the reflective attitude produced by the process of grieving leads to gratitude, for the life of the beloved as well as the life of the bereft, and most especially for the relationship of love shared by them. Solomon begins the chapter with the following epigraph from a character in a Philip K Dick novel: "Grief is the most powerful emotion a man or child or animal can feel…. Grief causes you to leave yourself. You step outside your narrow little pelt. And you can't feel grief unless you've had love before it—grief is the final outcome of love . . ." (p. 75).

Grief is a continuation of love and both emotions can take one out of one's self. Both are in an important sense morally obligatory. And, moreover, both the ethics of love and the ethics of grief have significant consequences for thinking about politics. Consider again the passage from Dick's novel; the protagonist suggests that even animals feel grief and that grief takes us out of our "narrow little pelt," suggesting that we are like animals with pelts. Yet, is it socially acceptable to grieve for animals? Solomon mentions that in our culture you might get a couple of days to mourn for your beloved and then you have to go back to work. But, what if your lost beloved is a dog or a cat?

Although to my knowledge—and I have to admit that I haven't read the entire library that is Solomon's work—Solomon has not developed a theory of animal emotions, unlike most moral theorists (outside of those explicitly debating animal rights), he consistently allows a place for animals in his accounts of grief, gratitude and love. Even while emphasizing the connections between emotions and reason, Solomon makes space for animals; for example, discussing the reflective quality of grief, Solomon qualifies his remarks: "this is not to say that dogs, whales and elephants cannot grieve, but the notion of 'reflection' would have to be understood quite broadly" (Solomon: 2004: 99). He brings animals into his account of gratitude, too, pointing out that gratitude is not only essential to human beings but may be significant among social animals as well (p. 102). And, again considering the role of self-reflection and the virtues of the "examined life," Solomon opens the space for animal spirituality:

> I do not want to deny that animals, perhaps elephants, apes, whales and some of our favorite pets might have some such awareness, of death, of tragedy, of self. But at the very least, their awareness seems to be more limited and less articulate than ours. This is not the place for species chauvinism, however; on the contrary, if spirituality means anything, it certainly includes a certain kindred spirit with our animal colleagues in life, whether or not they have the same awareness or anything like the sense of spirituality that we do (Solomon 2002: 10).

It would be interesting to consider how Solomon's theory of the morally obligatory nature of emotions might apply to animals. Does their ability to feel emotions obligate them? Does it obligate us? Certainly it seems that his theory suggests that the emotions of animals, and moreover our relationships to them, and dependence on them, should affect the ways in which we value both their lives and their deaths.

Solomon's work not only includes a phenomenology of grief, but also considerations of the social customs that determine what are the appropriate practices of grief and mourning in various cultures. How would our culture and our conceptions of ourselves and of the life that surround us, of the earth that sustains us, change if it was not only socially acceptable but morally expected to grieve for animals? This question points out the central connection between grief and love insofar as imagining grieving for animals requires imagining loving them.

Solomon's work is not just descriptive but also suggests that the moral dimensions of grief and gratitude may obligate us to change social mores for ones more consistent with what we learn from rational reflection on the essential characteristics of emotions. His work brings with it a faith that philosophical reflection can change attitudes and behaviors, not only to make us better people, but also to make the world a better place. Perhaps opening the possibility of grieving, even the obligation to grieve, nonhuman life would be such a change.

Before we move to animals, however, we might consider all of the human lives that we do not, and given our prejudices, cannot mourn. Solomon says that some people are candidates for grief while others are not. But, if as Solomon suggests, grief is the continuation of love, and love can be extended to the world or to the whole of humanity, shouldn't the same be said of grief? If love has to be learned, then aren't we ethically required to teach ourselves to grieve, too, even for those with whom we are not intimate, perhaps even for our enemies? If love is necessary for a transformative politics, then what about grief?

These questions are especially relevant currently in light of the U.S. invasion of Iraq, where hundreds of thousands of Iraqi civilians have died as a result. One estimate is that 600,000 Iraqis have died since the first bombings in March of 2003 (Altman and Oppel 2008). Do we grieve for them? Or does vengeance still drive us into war? Within days of the terror attacks in 2001, U.S. sentiment quickly turned from grief to vengeance, as if killing others would bring back our own dead or quell our sorrow and fear. Just 10 days after the attack, President Bush opened a speech by proclaiming that "our grief has turned to anger and anger to resolution" (Bush 2001). How might our attitudes change toward our enemies and our concern for people dying from famine and war across the globe, if we believed that we have an obligation to grieve for all life lost? Indeed, our willingness to grieve certain lives and not others is a test of whose lives we value and whose we do not, whose lives are worth mourning and whose are not.

In *Precarious Life: The Powers of Mourning and Violence*, feminist philosopher Judith Butler discusses the ways in which some lives are valued and therefore grievable while others are not. Most obviously, we mourn our own dead soldiers but we do not mourn our dead "enemies." Butler also points out that few lives lost to AIDS are publicly grieved because the lives of homosexuals and drug users are not valued. So too, she says, "the extensive deaths now taking place in Africa are also, in the media, for the most part unmarkable and ungrievable" (Butler 2004: 35). Her argument is not just that these lives are seen as undesirable and therefore not worth mourning, but rather that they are not seen at all. There are some lives that are devalued to the point of not being considered lives. For example, dehumanization is often a tactic in narratives justifying torture and slavery. People are reduced to "animals" or "rags" (as they were in the Nazi concentration camps), which makes it easier to justify abusing them. They are not seen as people, let alone as lives worthy of love, respect and gratitude. Butler mentions the case of obituaries for Palestinian families rejected by the *San Francisco Chronicle* for fear of "offending" their readership. Why are we prohibited from publicly mourning these deaths? Is it because they are not considered real deaths? Or, because they are causalities of war? Or, more particularly because they are on one side of a war and not on the other? Is it because their lives are not valuable *to us*? Certainly their lives are valuable to their families and loved ones.

Suggesting that another dimension of the ungrievability of these lives is our disavowal of our own violence that lead to their deaths, Butler asks, "What is the relation between the violence by which these ungrievable lives were lost and the prohibition on their public grievability?" (Butler 2004: 35–36). Do we refuse to mourn certain lives because we do not want to accept responsibility for our part in their deaths? Is it because we refuse to acknowledge our own investment in the violence that caused them? As I argue in *Women as Weapons of War*, we deny our own investment in violence in order to continue to put "us" against "them," to continue to devalue some lives for the sake of others (Oliver 2005). This again raises the question of what lives are worthy of grief because they are worthy of love and gratitude.

Can we mourn people (or other creatures) whom we have never met? And isn't the gratitude for life, all of life, that Solomon endorses, necessary to begin to overcome the worst violence that we inflict on each other and on other creatures?

As Solomon points out, the loss of friends and family results in grief as a desperate longing for the presence of the beloved and for the relationship and experiences shared with them. Obviously, the deaths of strangers cannot result in this kind of loss. But, can it—or should it—obligate us to the aspect of grief that Solomon finds *morally* compelling, which is to say, reflection on life, more specifically reflection on the meaning or value of life? It may be a moral obligation to grieve for lost loved ones because grief is a continuation of love and a way of honoring the beloved. But, much more problematic is grieving for the unfamiliar; it is more difficult to grieve for a life that challenges the very idea of shared experiences, a life that calls into question what counts as virtuous or valuable. Butler points out that in grieving for familiars or intimates,

> I am not disturbed by the proximity of the unfamiliar, the proximity of difference that makes me work to forge new ties of identification and to reimagine what it is to belong to a human community in which common epistemological and cultural grounds cannot always be assumed…But at what cost do I establish the familiar as the criterion by which a human life is grievable? (Butler 2004: 38)

I would extend Butler's questions to all of life. As she points out, we consider some human life valuable and therefore worthy of grief if lost, but what of animal life? What of the life of the planet? Of course, in these times of war and continued genocide the question of human life does, and perhaps should, take precedence. As I have argued elsewhere, however, we cannot disassociate the ways in which we value other forms of life, particularly animal life, from the way that we value human life (Oliver 2009). Even Kant with his hierarchy of species and preference for reason over emotion argued that we learn how to treat people based on how we treat animals. If we allow that animal lives are worthy of love and of grief, we are left with the question of the possibility of loving or grieving the lives of those who are not our familiars, whether they are other people or other creatures with whom we share the earth. And yet, following Solomon, it seems that until we can learn to both love and grieve those whom we do not know, those who are not our familiars, until we can learn gratitude for life itself in all its forms, we cannot stop killing ourselves either through war and genocide or through the destruction of the earth.

Solomon suggests that while grief and love may be values in themselves, they are also essential to what he calls "the thoughtful love of life" that is naturalized spirituality. And, he says that this spirituality "is ultimately social and global, a sense of ourselves identified with others and the world" (Solomon 2002: 6). One of the important lessons that we can learn from the loss of our loved one is the value of life itself, of every human life, perhaps every sentient life, not only because of the devastating effects of grief on those close to them, but also because of their potential for love and relationships. If the lessons of love and grief, insofar as they translate into the transformative power of thoughtful reflection on life, are social and global, then they seem to bring with them obligations to others across this shared earth.

Whatever the problems with Immanuel Kant's moral justifications for republican federalism, it is instructive that he founds the connection between morality and politics on the limited surface of the earth. In his essay "Perpetual Peace," in the section on universal hospitality, he says,

> The stranger cannot claim the right of a guest to be entertained, for this would require a special friendly agreement whereby he might become a member of the native household for a certain time. He may only claim of right of resort, for all men are entitled to present themselves in the society of others by virtue of their right to communal possession of the earth's surface. Since the earth is a globe, they cannot disperse over an infinite area, but must necessarily tolerate one another's company (Kant 1970: 106).

Kant imagines a "cosmopolitan constitution" of continents engaged in peaceful mutual relations that bring the entire human race under the same universal laws of hospitality. He contrasts this ideal to the "inhospitable conduct of the civilized states" "especially the commercial states, the injustice of which they display in *visiting* foreign countries and peoples (which in their case is the same as *conquering* them) seems appallingly great" (Kant 1970: 106). Kant's 1795 description of European interests in the Caribbean is chilling in light of current U.S. interests in the Middle East and our economic woes. Kant says:

> The worst (or from the point of view of moral judgments, the best) thing about all this is that the commercial states do not benefit by their violence, for all their trading companies are on the point of collapse. The Sugar Islands, that stronghold of the cruelest and most calculated slavery, do not yield any real profit; they serve only the indirect (and not entirely laudable) purpose of training sailors for warships, thereby aiding the prosecution of wars in Europe. And all this is the work of powers who make endless ado about their piety, and who wish to be considered as chosen believers while they live on the fruits of iniquity (Kant 1970: 107).

Kant's condemnation of piety and religion as justifications for war speaks to both sides in the so-called war on terror. Hyperbolic rhetoric on both sides clouds material and economic issues with self-righteous attributions of Good and Evil, the Faithful and the Infidels, the Godly and the Damned. Solomon's warning that "the notion of spirituality…has been hijacked by organized religion," the history of which is the "history of intolerance, persecutions, and massacres" must be taken to heart if we are to understand the role of religion in contemporary politics and public life (Solomon 2002: xiii). The intolerant notion of spirituality embraced by fundamentalist religions goes against the spirit of spirituality, especially the naturalized spirituality that Solomon describes.

In fact, we could say that spirituality is precisely what these fundamentalisms lack. Insofar as spirituality is reflective and thoughtful, it must challenge any form of fundamentalism. For, fundamentalism asks for thoughtless, mindless, unquestioning belief in principles that, in practice, at least, seem to demand the sacrifice of one group of "believers" by another. They are modes of "belonging" at the expense of others; they are defensive ways of identifying with a group that excludes and abjects anyone who doesn't belong; they are born out of Nietzschean resentment that can define itself only through its hate of another. These types of religious beliefs are, in Solomon's words, "more like club passwords or code words than propositions that can be explicated or defended," or, I would add, that can be questioned or opened to the kind of philosophical reflection essential to naturalized spirituality (2002: 13). Unexamined principles are not only empty, but also dangerous, even deadly.

In a speech before UNESCO in 2002, French philosopher Julia Kristeva described what she takes to be Kant's two pillars of peace: "first, that of universality—*all men are equal* and all must be saved. Second is the principle of *protection of human life*, sustained by the love of the life of each" (Kristeva 2005: 424). She insists that although we are far from achieving economic justice for all, it is the second pillar and not the first that is in the most danger today. She says, "the efforts for realizing social, economic, and political justice have never in the history of humanity been as considerable and widespread. But it is the second pillar of the imaginary of peace that seems to me today to suffer most gravely: The love of life eludes us; there is no longer a discourse for it" (pp. 424–425). It is not just economic, racial and religious inequalities that prevent peace — although these are immense — but also the lack of a discourse of the love of life.

Perhaps more than any other contemporary philosopher, Robert Solomon has given us a philosophy of love that provides such a discourse. His writings on love, grief, and gratitude suggest the need for learning how to live together by learning how to value all of life. As he says, this is a pedagogical process that requires attention and reflection, not just the penetrating gaze of an objective observer, but rather the loving—even passionate—caress, whether literal or metaphorical, of embodied beings sharing a life. Across his vast writings, and in various ways, he consistently develops a discourse of the thoughtful love of life as a way to give meaning to our existence. Perhaps Solomon's writings on love can help provide the most precarious pillar of peace, namely, learning the love of life.

# References

Altman, Lawrence and Richard Oppel. 2008. W.H.O. says Iraq civilian death toll higher than cited. *New York Times*, 10 Jan 2008.

Bush, George W. 2001. President Bush's address on terrorism before a joint meeting of Congress. *New York Times*, September 21, B4.

Butler, Judith. 2004. *Precarious life: The powers of mourning and violence*. New York: Verso.

hooks, bell. 1994. *Outlaw culture, resisting representations*. New York: Routledge.

Kant, Immanuel. 1970. Perpetual peace. In *Kant's political writings*, ed. Hans Reiss (trans: Nisbet, H.B). Cambridge: Cambridge University Press.

Kristeva, Julia. 2005. Peut-on faire la paix? In *La haine et le pardon*. Fayard: Paris; in English translation as Can we make peace?: for Teresa Brennan. In *Living attention: On Teresa Brennan*, ed. Alice Jardine, Shannon Lundeen, and Kelly Oliver, 117–126 (trans: Hoff, Shannon). Albany: State University of New York Press, 2006.

Oliver, Kelly. 2005. *Women as weapons of war: Iraq, sex, and the media*. New York: Columbia University Press.

Oliver, Kelly. 2009. *Animal lessons: How they teach us to be human*. New York: Columbia.

Solomon, Robert. 2002. *Spirituality for the skeptic. The thoughtful love of life*. New York: Oxford University Press.

Solomon, Robert. 2004. *In defense of sentimentality*. New York: Oxford University Press.

# Part III
# Comparative Philosophy

# Chapter 11
# Grief and the Mnemonics of Place: A Thank You Note

Janet McCracken

**Abstract** This chapter brings together several themes evoked by memories of Robert C. Solomon: domestic animals, especially dogs, because Bob loved dogs; grief, because Bob really liked a paper by the author on that topic; and Persian philosophy, because the author's two book chapters on that topic were written for anthologies that Bob co-edited. These themes intertwine in a discussion of how we mark places in rituals of mourning, in order to help us remember those we have lost. The focus in this chapter is particularly on the Funeral Games in Book 23 of *The Iliad* (Homer 1990) and the ancient Zoroastrian ritual of the Sag-deed, or "look of the dog." The former assists memory by marking the ground, and so is associated with place and material existence. The latter assists memory by looking and moving on, and so is associated is carrying the spirit on in memory. Both are necessary in the dialectic of mourning.

I write this chapter to honor Bob. Preparing for it, I thought about a paper of mine to which Bob did great honor in his book, *In Defense of Sentimentality*, the very chapter that Kelly Oliver cited in her chapter (also in Chap. 10) (Solomon 2004: 139–156). That paper claimed that grief was essentially dedicatory, directing us to think about and honor those we loved, now lost (McCracken 2005). It was meant, and is still meant, to be a companion piece to one as yet unwritten, about mourning, where mourning is to actually do the honor toward which grief calls us. This talk cannot lay claim to being the intended companion piece on mourning, but once I was asked to present a paper to the University of Texas conference in his honor, it had to become a sort of middle-play of what would thus become a trilogy. It became a paper for Bob, a demonstration of the grief that, without occasions to reflect, it is hard to feel enough.

J. McCracken (✉)
Department of Philosophy, Lake Forest College, 555 N.
Sheridan Road, 60045 Lake Forest, IL, USA
e-mail: mccracken@mx.lakeforest.edu

K. Higgins and D. Sherman (eds.), *Passion, Death, and Spirituality*,      139
Sophia Studies in Cross-cultural Philosophy of Traditions and Cultures 1,
DOI 10.1007/978-94-007-4650-3_11, © Springer Science+Business Media Dordrecht 2012

One faces life with a rather paradoxical set of presuppositions. The first is that life is fleeting, that mortality is the very core of life—and so, that life must include loss and grief. The second is that life is ruled by responsibility or obligation, in other words, that one must live one's life obligated to continue one's life into the future, with others who will also continue. My particular interest in these paradoxes links to my interest in domestic animals—and Bob's interest in them. This, in turn, links to the firmness of my belief that people should live with pets, which—except for parrots, which I don't understand very well—have a much shorter lifespan than most people, so that to commit to a pet is to commit to grieve for it.

I am interested in domestic life, lived with domestic animals; I am interested in grief and mourning; I am interested in teaching and writing and the responsibility involved in these professions. The obviousness of Bob's influence on these interests is overwhelming and, I think, must be acknowledged, for several reasons. One, Bob's championship of my paper on grief, which was the height of Bob's championship of my career in philosophy, the most important to me of the many extremely generous gestures on Bob's part. Two, I would like to address Bob's interest in world philosophy. This was based on my experience writing on Persian philosophy for two anthologies at Bob and Kathy's request (Solomon and Higgins 2003, 1994). Three, in my investigation of Persian thought, I came across the ritual of the "sag-deed," the Zoroastrian funerary ritual in which a yellow dog with spots above its eyes must look at each corpse before it is left to be eaten by birds and other scavengers. The ritual of the sag-deed has really stuck with me. Four, I always think of Bob and Kathy to some degree when I think about Nietzsche, and I tend to think of Nietzsche to some degree when I think about Zoroastrianism.

Lastly, then, when I think about grief, mourning, and dogs, I think of a question that has been informing my thinking for some time. "Why, in *Iliad* 23, does Achilles commemorate Patroclus' death with a set of athletic competitions? What is the deal with the funeral games?" Homer, I know, is trying to tell us something about doing honor. In this chapter, then, I want to do honor to Bob's memory, by thinking about doing honor, marking places, and dogs.

## What's the Deal with the Funeral Games?

Patroclus, Achilles' "dearest friend in arms" (*Iliad* 17: 475), died trying to fulfill Achilles' obligations to fight for the Achaeans. Until this experience with grief, Achilles was a pouty jerk willing to let his countrymen fight and die without his divinely-mandated help, because Agamemnon, another pouty jerk, stole his lady. Patroclus went to battle for Achilles, was killed by Hector, and was fought over by the Achaeans and Trojans. At that moment, Homer stopped the action to say: "Achilles' horses wept… staunch as a pillar planted tall above a barrow, standing sentry over some lord or lady's grave-site, so they stood,… the horses mourned" (17:490–510). Here, domestic animals, chariot racing horses, are likened to a gravestone, dedicating their tears to their lost driver, marking the spot as if with a libation. Their gesture is their very stillness, the stony eternality of their stance. I want to investigate here these still, everlasting, tears of Achilles' horses, tears which, like the pouring of a libation or the construction of a mausoleum, mark a place to mourn.

Patroclus' death finally called Achilles to his duty, as Achilles and all the Achaens sought vengeance for it. Vengeance—an emotion which Bob calls "that passion which alone would seem to give some fuel to the notion of punishment" (Solomon 2004: 39), is, for Bob, part and parcel of the underlying rationality of justice. "Vengeance," he states, "is not the antagonist to rationality but its natural manifestation" (p. 39). Bob links this comment to Nietzsche's definition of humanity as a kind of domestic animal, an animal bred with "the right to make promises." (Nietzsche 1969 [1887], II/2: 29).

Achilles' grief is irremediably infused with a desire for revenge and with the guilt of causing Patroclus' death. "Let me die at once," he says to his mother Thetis, "since it was not my fate to save my dearest comrade from his death…" (*Iliad* 18: 110–120). Thus, Homer intimates very early that vengeance, grief, justice and reason are inseparable, and he implies that these linked feelings occur because *we* are domestic animals. Like the stony horses who wept for Patroclus in the previous book of the *Iliad*, Achilles mourned by trying to return his own body to the soil: "Both hands clawing the ground for soot and filth, fouled his handsome face… sprawled in the dust, Achilles lay there, fallen…" (18: 20–30). This gesture is quite similar to the funerary ritual in Book 23: "They covered [Patroclus'] body deep with locks of hair they cut and cast upon him…" (23: 150–260). Here, on this spot, marked with tears, wine, and blood—here, we mourned Patroclus.

Patroclus' cremation was accomplished, his urn buried and marked— "Around the pyre they planted a ring of stone revetments… and… turned to leave" (*Iliad* 23: 280–90). But the ritual was incomplete. Achilles stopped the proceedings—not only the exit of the troops, but apparently the entire waging of the war. "Now for the funeral games," he stated (23: 298–300), listing at length the prizes for each competition, and adding that neither he, Achilles, nor his horses, would participate in the contests, because they were stony-still and dragged to the ground in grief (23: 320–330). And then, for 500 lines, Homer describes the games. And with the athletics came all the trimmings: spectator commentary (23: 500–520), betting (23: 525–555), an argument with the umpire (23: 580–660), an old-timer's trophy (23: 680–690), and good-natured cheating (23: 850–880). Immediately following the games Achilles had an audience with Priam, who released Hector's body for burial. In other words, having avenged, burned, and buried Patroclus—and having held a day of athletic competition—justice was served and resolution achieved. Achilles pitied Priam for his loss, his vengeance waned, his grief continued unmixed with the desire for revenge, and it indeed became a vehicle to justice.

Why the games? Why did Achilles hold everything up for them? The funeral is over. His obligations to the gods are met. Why the games? The answer to this question, I think, lies in the profound similarity of structure and presentation between this second-to-last book of the *Iliad* and its second book, "The Great Gathering of Armies," in which Homer gave us the much more commonly referenced "catalogue of ships." These two penultimate books, perhaps better book-ends than the first and last, are occupied with etching the ground, marking the ground, as with tears, or wine, or blood—only in these cases, with names. Like gravestones and libations, like the stony statues of athletes that lined the entrance to the Olympian stadium and the path to the Oracle at Delphi, the funeral games and the catalogue of ships are what in the fund-raising world are called, "naming opportunities." To etch your name in stone is a kind of libation, a kind of mourning, not so much of a person as of her or his having taken up *space*, having been *here*. In Book 2 as in Book 23, there's comic relief, Odysseus dressing down a coward, Nestor trying to tell more stories than anyone wants to hear. The Boeotians… the Hyrians—sent 50 ships each, the Aspledons sent 30, the Phocians sent 40, and on and on and on.

It's not a very profound idea, maybe: these places existed, these men lived and died; this battle occurred, these men were victorious, these men lost their lives. Homer prayed to the Muses that they let him record the names: "Who were the captains of Achaea?" he sang, "Who were the kings? The mass of troops I could never tally, never name, not even if I had ten tongues and ten mouths, a tireless voice and the heart inside me bronze…" (*Iliad* 2:570–590). Homer gave us no similar evaluation of the funeral games, only telling us that they honored Patroclus. Still, I read them in light of Homer's explanation in Book Two—in this place, on this occasion, some people did impressive things, enjoying the fact that they had strong bodies and cunning minds: here, right here—look at the ground on which they walked. Stop here a moment and take note. Stop and read this name. Taking note, recording a name on a piece of rock, this is, as Diotima says in Plato's *Symposium*, "an immortal thing for a mortal creature to do" (206 c). As mortal creatures, even if we had ten tongues, ten mouths, ten minds—we couldn't remember everyone who has lived and died before us. So we do things like gather at conferences, read our papers: like weeping horses, we lived and died and honored Bob. In the act of marking, somehow, our desire for vengeance against the gods wanes, we do some small justice to Bob, and we are able to move on in our own inadequate, mortal, lives. This is one way to deal with the inadequacy of memory, which is perhaps the motivating force of grief.

## The Sag-Deed

In his "'What Is Philosophy? The Status of World Philosophy in the Profession" Bob lamented, "Philosophy is in a crisis… We should [not] look at excessive romanticism and analytic philosophy as poison and antidote, respectively… They are two parts of a dialectic that, at its worst, causes mutual defensiveness, self-righteousness, and mutual assured misunderstanding." (Solomon 2001: 103). In the same context he remarks, "[It] becomes evident [in view of its history and the cultural conditions of its development] that philosophy has a great deal in common with religion" (Solomon 2001: 101).

In this spirit, I now move from the ancient Greeks—who got to be a part of the Western dialectic of philosophy—to their noble opponents, the ancient Persians— who have been omitted from the Western dialectic. I also move closer and closer to practiced religion. In the *Iliad*, Homer *represented* a possibly true funerary ritual, in order, I have argued, to reflect upon the meaning of funerary rituals as marking a spot of ground lest we forget. The ancient Persians, on the other hand, had actual funerary rituals that, I believe, demonstrate the faith that we *will not* forget—more like, or with, dogs. These "mainstream" and "alternative" reflective themes were tied together long ago by Hegel.

In paragraphs 444–483 of the *Phenomenology,* Hegel considers the development of consciousness reflected in funerary rituals, wills, mourning, and other social activities dedicated to the dead. These activities are linked to the consciousness of the family, a sort of naturalistic prelude to full ethical or social consciousness, in which the notion of one's familial ties leads one to the recognition of a community greater than oneself. The family is a community to which one automatically belongs by virtue of being born, a community one affirms, but does not really choose. Consciousness of that belonging comes with consciousness of obligation, and hence, becomes ethical. "The duty of the member of the Family is… to add to [nature], in order that the individual's ultimate being, too, shall not belong solely to Nature and remain something irrational, but shall be something *done*, and the right of consciousness to be asserted in it…" (Hegel 1977: 270). The family accomplishes this by burial, or at least by funerals, "keeping away from the dead this dishonoring of him by unconscious appetites and abstract entities…" (p. 271). In a sense, then, burial is a way of filling the inert earth with human meaning. But I think, more even than burial itself, the "right of consciousness is asserted" by *marking the grave* with a stone and a name. The earth is composed of dead things, but only representatives of human consciousness have *names*.

In paragraph 474, Hegel refers explicitly to the ancient Persians, in a discussion of the role of the earth—the land that characterizes and brings together a community, or nation. Here, he represents marking the earth as, essentially, the revenge of the Family against the nation, the way families—the more natural and less social communities—assert themselves in the face of the nation-state that sends their children to war, and worries about the rights of inheritance, and replacing the dead at work, etc. This revenge of the Family is acted out in mourning. Oddly, for Hegel the enemies of displaying mourning by marking the earth are the *Persians*.

> The dead, whose right is denied, knows therefore how to find instruments of vengeance, which are equally effective and powerful as the power which has injured it. These powers are other communities whose altars the dogs and birds defiled with the corpse, which is not raised into unconscious universality by being given back, as is its due, to the elemental individuality—the earth—but remains above ground in the outer reality, and has now acquired as a force of divine law a self-conscious, real universality. (Hegel 1977: 287)

Like Antigone, Hegel believes that the dead have a right to be buried, and that communities who do not mark the ground with the bodies of their dead are the enemies of the dead, letting it be forgotten they lived as individuals. Leaving a corpse to be eaten, digested, and scattered on the ground by dogs and birds—the ritual of these enemy communities, called "defilement" here by Hegel—is the ancient Zoroastrian funerary rite. The ancient Zoroastrians worshipped dogs.

Fargard 13 of the *Vendidad* of the *Zend-Avesta* goes into head-spinning detail about the proper vengeance to be taken on one who smites any one of a variety of types of dog. In chapter eight we learn that "[a dog] has the character of a priest... a warrior... a husbandman... a strolling singer... a thief... a [wild beast]... a courtesan [and]... a child." These characters played by dogs in the *Zend Avesta* are not unreminiscent of Nietzsche's "lion, camel, and child," the famous "Three Metamorphoses" of the spirit that Nietzsche describes in the first chapter of *Thus Spake Zarathustra* (another name for 'Zoroaster'). The repeated epithet of Ahura Mazda, the god worshipped by Zoroastrians, is "Maker of the Material World"; Ahura Mazda's greatest blessing, in other words, is that material things exist, and dogs are the protectors of this blessing. Dogs *protect* the human world *for* us, so that we don't *have* to emblazon it on our memory.

In Fargard Eight, which dictates the funerary rituals to be practiced by Zoroastrians, the faithful are instructed to purify *the places* through which the dead have been carried by "caus[ing] a yellow dog with four eyes [a dog with two spots above the eyes], or a white dog with yellow ears, to go three times through that way" (Fargard 8/III:16). This Sag-deed, or "look of the dog" upon a dead body causes the evil spirits to fly away out of it—"to the regions of the North," i.e., *not* the ground. The dog is supposed to participate in this task willingly. If the dog is unwilling, the ritual must be performed twice as many times. According to Mary Boyce, the four-eyed dog and its place in funerary ritual are reminiscent of the four-eyed dogs of Yama mentioned in the *Rigveda* as guarding the gates of heaven, both of which bear similarities to the Greek Cerberus (Boyce 1998–2011). For Zoroastrians, however, because they practiced exposure of the dead instead of burial or cremation, the dog had the additional purifying power of being able to devour corpses with impunity and *go on*. In this, they save it from the oblivion of sinking into the earth "untreated" or unnoticed. Boyce believes that this responsibility was also given to dogs in part because of their sense of smell, which could discern the sufferer from coma from someone who had really passed away. So, the dog *protects* life, however vegetal, from the oblivion of death. The few Parsis still practicing Zoroastrianism no longer worship dogs. According to Boyce, "all rites in which dogs are concerned have been under attack by reformists since the mid-19th century, and have by now been wholly abandoned by them..." (Boyce 1998–2011). They do, however, still base their creation myth in Ahura Mazda's generous gift of domestic cattle, and they still drink ox urine as a purifying ritual. Drinking the urine of a domestic animal is *playing the role of the earth, marked*, by urine. This act purifies the living for the ancient Persians, where, for the ancient Greeks, libations mark the dead earth with a human stain.

I suppose the Parsis' eschewal of the Sag-deed and other dog-related liturgy is tied up with some modern notions of what is proper and improper to religion. Whatever their reasons, I think they've lost something valuable by no longer worshipping dogs. Dogs are domestic animals, perhaps the most domestic of all, and their glance at the dead may be a key antidote to gravestones, libations, commemorative plaques, the keeping of urns on mantelpieces, and all the other myriad rituals through which *people* mark *places* in memory of their lost companions. The Zoroastrians were an extraordinarily domestic, landed people. According to Boyce in "Priests, Cattle and Men," "the only terms which [Zoroaster] uses for a male lay member of the tribe are *nar* 'man' and *vastrya* '*herdsman*'... every pastoralist was 'at the same time a fighting man, who was ready to defend his property" (Boyce 1987: 511). "The [very] act of creation begins, [according to Zoroastrianism] effectively, with the divine bestowing of cattle on men" (p. 517). This characterizes the Zoroastrian's places as *being marked*, by domestic animals while their caretakers are above ground and alive. Taken in this context, the Sag-deed is as much an acknowledgement of the gift of bodies—a kind of herding of them into heaven—as it is a mark. In death as in life, our domestic animals are at our side and on our side, working for us. Of course this is literally so in those ancient practices where a person's dogs or horses or cattle were actually buried with him or her. In the Sag-deed the guilt, the need for vengeance against the gods and the Trojans, the sense of injustice, that prompted Achilles to sponsor funeral games, is assuaged by funeral, sparing burial. The dead are released from this place and become free. Somehow, this ritual evokes for me the idea that if the dogs know we were here—if the dogs acknowledge that we died—we need not fear death, we need not fear forgetting, we can *move on*.

Human beings, as material creatures, live and die *in particular places*. The more modern, more cerebral, less territorial, less dog-inspired, notion of those we have lost that accompanies current religious and social practices is a notion less domestic, less loyal to place, than its predecessors. Marking the ground, as I read *Iliad* 23, the *Gathas* of the *Zend Avesta*, and dogs, is a desperate, suspicious attempt to remember our lost companions, in the belief that if we don't etch the ground with their names, God won't let us remember them. Dedication by naming, etching, marking, pouring, crying, is symptomatic of the fear that those we love will fade from our memory. Athletic feats and death are among our heaviest, most embodied, acts, the most paradigmatic of our capacities *qua* mortal. It matters where they occurred. Home games pose different challenges from away games. People care where their ashes are scattered. When I am home, I go to visit my parents' graves. It's not that I really believe they are *there*; I don't have any important associations with that cemetery in Ardsley, New York. There is something about sitting there, though, with those bronze markers in the ground, reading their names, that occasions my memory of them, my thoughts about them, that is very different from remembering them in my prayers. That place elicits my gratitude. But the ashes of my dog Emily, next to my bed, live on with me, protecting my memory. They walk with me willingly in some odd way, and so will be able to walk on after I'm gone.

I think this freedom that we see in dogs is because of dogs' deep, abiding loyalty. And I think Bob's capacious writing, his willingness to be named and move on, Bob's graciousness, accompanies a quality of his as yet undiscussed, his dogged loyalty. I believe that loyalty is, in a sense, what *freed* Bob from labels like "existentialist," from attachment to place in a mournful way. Bob's attachment to those he loved went with him everywhere, and this loyalty of his for us allows us to remember him without the need to mark our memories with labels, or for reminders etched in stone.

## What's the Deal with World Philosophy?

I know I'm supposed to be discussing world philosophy. What really interests me about world philosophy in the general sense is less its pluralistic ethics than its acknowledgment of the mysterious effect of place on at least some beliefs. Perhaps place and thinking are always mediated by culture or language; perhaps the kind of thinking that differs from place to place and time to time is less real or less true or less important than the kind of thinking that is eternal and universal. I'm actually inclined to agree with both these claims. Nonetheless, it *matters*, philosophically, where one was born, where one lived, where one died. It matters where one went to school. It matters where one met one's spouse or best friend, where one traveled, where one fought, where one played. In his "On Fate and Fatalism," Bob touches on these facts, quoting Heraclitus' "fate is character." "Fate and fatalism," he states, "focus 'locally' on what is most significant about us, our births, our sweetest romances, our best successes, our worst failures, our calamities, our deaths… Just for completeness, let it be said that families and cultures have character, too… The fate of a nation is just another story we tell" (Solomon 2003: 448). Bob was a cosmopolitan guy, with a deep appreciation for different places.

I would not know about the Sag-deed were it not for Bob. And perhaps it was appropriate that Bob died in an airport. But that's a place too, a very telling place, a place to remember. Like a dog with spots above his eyes, Bob died on the fly, marking the ground and moving on, the happy existentialist, the analytic continental, staying for decades in an office like Grand Central Station welcoming, and letting go, all comers and goers. Bob and his work are being remembered all over the world and will be long into the future: but a memorial conference was held in Austin. Why?

## References

Boyce, Mary. 1987. Priests, cattle and men. *Bulletin of the School of Oriental and African Studies, University of London* 50(3): 508–526.

Boyce, Mary. 1998–2011. The dog in Zoroastrianism. http://www.caissoas.com/CAIS/Animals/dog_zoroastrian.htm. Accessed 28 Dec 2007.

Hegel, G.W.F. 1977 [1807]. *Phenomenology of spirit* (trans: Miller, A.V). New York: Oxford University Press.

Homer. 1990. *The Iliad* (trans: Fagles, Robert). New York: Penguin.

McCracken, Janet. 2005. Falsely, sanely, shallowly: Reflections on the special character of grief. *International Journal of Applied Philosophy* 19: 139–156.

Nietzsche, Friedrich. 1969 [1887]. *On the genealogy of morals* (trans: Kaufmann, Walter). New York: Vintage.

Nietzsche, Friedrich. 1969 [1883–1885]. *Thus spoke Zarathustra* (trans: Hollingdale, R.J). New York: Penguin.

Solomon, Robert C. 2001. What is philosophy?: The status of world philosophy in the profession. *Philosophy East and West* 51: 100–104.

Solomon, Robert C. 2003. On fate and fatalism. *Philosophy East and West* 53(4): 435–454.

Solomon, Robert C. 2004. *In defense of sentimentality*. New York: Oxford University Press.

Solomon, Robert C., and Kathleen M. Higgins (eds.). 1994. *World philosophy: A text with readings*. New York: McGraw-Hill.

Solomon, Robert C., and Kathleen M. Higgins (eds.). 2003. *From Africa to Zen: An invitation to world philosophy*, 2nd ed. Lanham: Rowman and Littlefield.

# Chapter 12
# Of Grief and Mourning: Thinking a Feeling, Back to Robert Solomon

**Purushottama Bilimoria**

**Abstract** The paper considers various ruminations on the aftermath of the death of a close or loved one, and the processes of grieving and mourning. The conceptual examination of how grief impacts on its sufferers, from different cultural perspectives, is followed by an analytical survey of current thinking among psychologists, psychoanalysts and philosophers on the enigma of grief, and on the associated process of mourning. Robert C. Solomon reflected deeply on the 'extreme emotion' of grief in his extensive theorizing on the emotions, particularly in his essay 'On Grief and Gratitude', commenting that grief is 'often described as a very private, personal emotion, characterized by social withdrawal and shutting oneself off from the world' (Solomon RC, On grief and gratitude. In: *In defense of sentimentality*. Oxford University Press, New York, 2004: 73). While dialoguing with the spirit of Solomon by way also of a tribute to his immense insights, the paper engages in critical reflections on recent thinking in this area elsewhere—notably, in Heidegger, Freud, Nussbaum, Casey, Gustafson, and Kristeva—and offers a refreshing critique toward an alternative to the received wisdom.

## Troubled Passions and the Dark Night of Gloom

> *No one ever told me that grief felt so like fear. I am not afraid, but the sensation is like being afraid. The same fluttering in the stomach, the same restlessness, the yawning. I keep swallowing…*(C.S. Lewis 1976: 1–3)

This paper presents a novice's reflections (with a delicate personal touch) on the aftermath of the death of a loved one, discussing the process of grieving and mourning,

P. Bilimoria (✉)
University of California @ Berkeley (Religion & South Asia Studies), California, USA

University of Melbourne (Historical and Philosophical Studies), Melbourne, Australia

Deakin University (Philosophy), Victoria, Australia
e-mail: pbilimoria@berkeley.edu

K. Higgins and D. Sherman (eds.), *Passion, Death, and Spirituality*,      149
Sophia Studies in Cross-cultural Philosophy of Traditions and Cultures 1,
DOI 10.1007/978-94-007-4650-3_12, © Springer Science+Business Media Dordrecht 2012

with a comparative focus, i.e. straddling across continental, cross-cultural and analytical philosophical treatments. I shall also indulge the reader in a couple of anecdotal narratives, personal communications, and poetical musings to illustrate how grief is viewed, and how it affects its sufferers, from somewhat different cultural perspectives. This will be followed with an attempt at an analysis and survey of some current thinking among psychologists, psychoanalysts, and philosophers on the enigma of grief, and on the associated praxis of mourning. Since Robert C. Solomon (beloved Bob) was concerned to make his own reflections on the 'extreme emotion' of grief in his extensive and groundbreaking theorizing on the emotions, particularly in one of his last books, *True to Our Feelings* (2007), and in his chapter 'On Grief and Gratitude' (2004)—close to a period when he has also thinking deeply about death and perhaps his own mortality—I shall be taking this opportunity to dialogue with the spirit of his thinking on this challenging subject-matter. Solomon comments that grief is 'often described as a very private, personal emotion, characterized by social withdrawal and shutting oneself off from the world' (2006: 73). Indeed one's wishes when struck by an experience of death of someone very near and dear are as W. H. Auden (1976) and Smith (2004) describes in his moving poem:

> Stop all the clocks, cut off the telephone.
> Prevent the dog from barking with a juicy bone,
> Silence the pianos and with muffled drum
> Bring out the coffin, let the mourners come.
>
> The stars are not wanted now; put out every one,
> Pack up the moon and dismantle the sun.
> Pour away the ocean and sweep up the wood;
> For nothing now can ever come to any good.

All these things seem unnecessary now; in colloquial terms their 'use-by-date' is over and Nothingness has come to be.

Couldn't the world and speeding motorists just stop for a moment to notice—as the hearse moved towards the crematorium after the last rites—that the cosmos, nay Existence (*sat, ens, esse*) itself, has come to a grinding halt? Its underbelly of the inseparable Non-existence (*asat-ca-sat*) has emerged triumphant against traditional Brahmanic wisdom and promises; perhaps the Buddhists, Jains, and nihilists have it right. It is as one beholds in the *bardo*: existence is just another appearance, an illusion, a mirage, emptiness all around. The Pascalian wager (bet) I had gratefully placed— staked on game-theory determined probability against the nihilationist condition (unclinically termed cancer)—has now been lost; we are returned to the cascaded parade of 'all souls of the faithful departed'. 'Where the hell is God or gods?'(Leonard 2010).

'*So this is the end, my friend, love of my life?*'—the first words that came to my mouth as I had held her still warm-hands minutes after the fatal moment—echoed resoundingly in the defiant darkness that had slowly been enveloping the earthly horizons and the terrestrial realms, and inwardly too (Masel 2011).

> Betake thee (deceased) to the lap of the earth the mother, of earth
> Far-spreading, very kind and gracious.
> Young dame, wool-soft unto the guerdon-giver, may
> She preserve thee from Destruction's (Death's) bosom.
> (*Rig Veda*, X, 18; Funerary Ritual, *antyeshti*, incantation).

*gate gate pāragate pārasaṃgate bodhi svāhā*
(gone, gone beyond the other shore - of suffering - well-gone), (Prajñaparamita mantra, *Heart Sūtra*).

*And when the mind was freed from death*
*it became the moon (candra).*
*So having gone beyond death,*
*the moon now shines up there.* (*Bṛhadāraṇyaka Upaniṣad* 2.5.7, Olivelle 1996)

*Beautiful face, mind heart*
*The dark/Shadow...*
*The wakening in brightness*
(Hutchings, in Charlesworth 2003).

The rituals that many of the ancient (perhaps so-called 'primitive' as well as 'civilized') traditions bring to the last rites, honoring the deceased in a gesture of sending the parting 'soul' onto its yonder journey, tend to ease if not blunt the devastation and the avalanche of sensations and feelings that continue to flood the body and mind—as if for one unending eternity—of the survivors. But this reprieve may not last too long. Associated with the gloom of grief is a series of unsettling sensations and feelings: not least, an arresting sense of hopelessness, loss, fear, anxiety, wrath, if not indignant anger, a 'collapsing of the house of cards', a throbbing of the heart in deep pain, swallowing, tightness in the chest, and perhaps also in the stomach that has all but lost its usual appetite, and insomnia. Because of the intensity and insufferable 'jab of red-hot memory' whence all this "common-sense" vanishes like an ant in the mouth of a furnace (C. S. Lewis 1976), followed by doubts about what one is actually feeling, sometimes denying the obvious only to be hit with wave upon wave of discomfiture, tears and inexplicable sensations in various parts and organs of the body, grief is often said to be the most negative of "negative" emotions—though Solomon seeks to de-emphasize this presumed polarity between positive and negative emotions. His argument "is not that there is no such thing as valence...but rather that there are many such polarities and oppositions" (2007: 171).

(And so in a moment of confessional guilty grief:) *'Why did I not see her pain and agony more consciously? How could I have been, my beloved, so self-possessed? Whose is the blame here?'*

In that vein, taking upon oneself the responsibility for the woeful pain of the other even as the person is passing, C. S. Lewis (1976: 62) perspicuously compares his pain with that of the deceased (in this instance his own dear wife) while she struggled through her illness, being stricken down by cancer. 'It comes in waves... and it goes in waves.' Lewis goes on to describe an experience he later had, as he puts it, inside his mind, and one of immense intensity, but absent of any intentionality or motivation or trigger for action. He valued it not for the probabilistic evidence or any quantification of the lessening pain it might provide, but for its intellectual quality and unemotional character; he notes:

Just the impression of her mind momentarily facing my own. Mind, not 'soul' as we tend to think of soul...just intelligence and attention...Certainly the reverse of what is called 'soulful'. Discounting the presence of any voice, message, re-union...rather 'un-love': 'I had never in any mood imagined the dead as being so –well, so business-like. Yet there was an extreme and cheerful intimacy. An intimacy that had not passed through the sense or the emotions at all' (Lewis 1976: 62).

The chilling idea that emotion could be absent had repelled him; but now he is at peace with it—with the ghost of his own mind as the other mind—his will is back, he is a rational man again. So it might seem.

A harrowing anecdote from my own experience in the last mystifying moments brings out Lewis's reflection here rather poignantly, namely that emotions could be at abeyance momentarily, and one is overpowered by the sense of the sheer intellect of the receding other that does not stop being the strong presence it always has been, as well as continuing the intimacy. When my philosopher colleagues arrived at the hospital to find me tearless and in a frantic state by the bed where my just deceased beloved lay, a calmness and peaceful demeanor shrouded her otherwise long fatal battle with a cancer (of the fiercest endometrial ovarian variety). I was—as described to me later—unselfconsciously *livid*, like Nietzsche's madman (who came down from the mountains with a lit lantern in broad daylight, looking for God upon being given the unexpected news 'God is Dead!') or as if suffering from stage fright, but nonetheless loquacious for that:

> 'We had been talking since this morning, and just moments ago before I left the room we made plans to go abroad again…to India actually, where our to-be-adopted child [from an orphanage in Bangalore] awaited 'the picking' and bringing back home. How could [the] *mind and language* simply vanish: just like that? That's bizarre!…'

(Someone dares to mention on an incoming phone-call:) 'Regarding her *matti* (funeral)…sorry, but we cannot come for it.' 'Whose funeral, baba? Who has died? (Turning toward the nurses:) 'What do you mean, *she has passed*, passed to where?' The nurses seemed terribly anxious to whisper into my ears 'She's gone; she just passed as you walked out the door…there is no pulse…look closer, the eyes are not responding'. 'Hummmm, bloody hell, what has pulse to do with consciousness?… look here, her eyes are focused on me and we are talking as we have been all morning…'

The somber voice of one of my colleagues standing across chipped in: 'Young man, you are asking metaphysical questions'.

> 'Goddamn-it, what else should I be asking…doing? Singing "*Old Aquinas*"?'
> 'You should be crying', another sermonized ever gently.
> 'Crying? I have not known tears in all my life!'
> 'You will…and you will see her.'
> 'Good grief, I see her, there she is, *here*!'

My interlocutor could be said to be anticipating the surge of memories and para-doxical desires verging on an occult aspect, 'as if those memories and details might be used to "conjure up" the lost one, as in a séance or an invocation' (Solomon 2004: 85). In a dream, I hear, 'It is natural (for one) in the physical state to mourn', echoing Krishna's sermon to Arjuna in the *Bhagavad-Gītā* (1985: 2.11): 'but grief (*śocya*, pitiable lamentation) is for oneself not for the departed…have resilience; you have work yet on earth's platform…attending to tasks and bodily health, with diligence and self-love…'

As if prophetically, some weeks later in a dream or two I am reflecting,

'You mean I should be loving myself; a self that is hanging on in threadbare smithereens...a
self negated?'
(Still in the twilight state I hear) Tring-tring tring—the cell phone goes off:
'Honey, remember to bring me organic pasta from the supermarket, the one I like...'
'Okay, I will...but hang on, aren't you supposed not to be...well...alive, no?'

Another night, like the owl of Minerva, the dream-voice whispers Hermes'
message to me:

*'Let us get up and leave the hospital beds now.'*
*'But what will people think, you're supposed to be dead?'*
*'Who cares what people say...I am here with you, am I not? Here take my hand—can't you
feel the warmth?'*

A Buddhist monk and an Indian sadhu may well identify with this sentiment, or
*vedana*, which I go on to briefly discuss. But as I argue shortly, drawing on Solomon,
grief is not all about sentimentality either. It is more a moral episteme entangled with a
deeper emotional response than might be thought. It may even be more, as one moves
to consider variations to this theme cross-culturally and in psychoanalytic wisdom.

The Sanskrit terms *śocya* [pitiable] or *duḥkha* (Pali *dukka*) [suffering] are not
specific enough to cover the deep sense of loss, (*kampāva*) and pain of mind (*sanvē-
gaya*), and sorrow (*kalakirima*) —from *kala* [time] and *kriya* [completed action;
'termination of time', that is death] (Obeyesekere 1985: 144). Here folk psychology
proceeds through legends or parables, a famous one of which is that of the mustard
seed, which goes like this: Kisā Gotamī's first and only child died in infancy.
Distraught with pain and grief, she went from place to place seeking some medicine
to resurrect her child. She eventually came to the Buddha and asked the sage whether
he could revive the dead child. The Buddha said that he could if only she would
bring a mustard seed from a house in which death had not occurred. Elated, Kisā
Gotamī's went from one house to another seeking the impossible mustard seed. She
soon came to the realization that her own personal grief is simply a part of the larger
universal problem of suffering...in this recognition lay her redemption.

In Indian traditions (Jain, Hindu, and Buddhist) the stark reminder that a deceased
person is to be sent onwards to her own journey and that she may be reborn in
another body—even possibly in the same-household—is intended at the same time
to help one to cathartically confront one's grief and be consoled that all is not lost
and that one could, perhaps should in due course, be ready to move on—with life's
sojourn here and its spiritual trajectories being preparation for the eventuality of
one's own demise as well (Gielen 1997: 52–71).

In the Jewish tradition the principal mourners withdraw indoors from public life
for a set number of days, a sharing of the grief of the living, in an observance known
as Shivah. It is obligatory to formally mourn (not necessarily to grieve). There are
prescribed rituals associated with an almost ascetic existence; one refrains from
domestic chores, as well as entertainment, driving, work, and other mundane preoc-
cupations. The recitation of the Mourner's Kaddish, lighting of candles, and sharing of
food brought by family members and other visitors occur as well (Heilman 2001: 21;
Alpert 2010: 25–40).

In some cultures, wailers are paid (indeed handsomely compensated like our professional therapists) not only to join the mourners in expressing their remorse and sorrow, but also to take part in other practices. In the highland village of Kaluli in Papua New Guinea, an elaborate commemorative ritual involves dancing around a bonfire in the middle of the night, ending with the enraged survivors leaping up and stamping a burning torch on the shoulders of the hired dancers. The intensity and scope of the ritual performance permits the mourners or the survivors to let their repressed anger, rage against the gods and righteous indignation at the gratuitous loss to surface from the soul, in all its dark shades, and to be thereby 'cleansed, cleared and purified' (Lutz 1985).

> And there is anger…why did you die on me? Couldn't you have lived on, like everyone else we know? Is that you David? The cats are fine… What is it like being dead? (Stephanie Lewis on David Lewis—2003 conversation in Princeton)

Renato Rosaldo the anthropologist, describes his experience at the site of the fatal accident overlooking the body of his lifeless wife, Michelle Rosaldo, at the bottom of a 65-ft sheer precipice: 'I felt like in a nightmare, the whole world around me expanding and contracting, visually and viscerally heaving.' He found himself embattled by 'rage, born of grief'; and he began to understand the force of anger that is possible in bereavement (2004: 167–8).

Months later, someone whispers… 'You getting over the sorrow ok? Seeing a counselor, getting professional help?' 'You must stop worrying "*Why she die?*" You[r] ki'ney-lever no' functioning well…brain over-working all [the] time. Yu'needa som'acupun'ure' 'Not your fault.' 'Heal yourself.' 'She'be right, mate.' It seemed almost obligatory, a grid-like pattern to follow, set stages one supposedly goes through:

> 'You must be on stage three now…displaced anger, irritability.
> Open to a few possible goals, testosterone count coming up…you must be strong and resilient, my friend, life must go on; you've got responsibilities…'

> 'I'm rather finding it more helpful splitting my time between the streets of the East Village (in New York)—"*going mad in anonymity,*" and mostly solitary in my retreat by beachside Venus Bay (outside Melbourne), as also sequestered stoically in our village home, research enclaves, ashram retreats and Ayurveda clinics by the holy rivers and towns up and down the Indian subcontinent (after the last rites with the sacred ashes got completed). *Sacrifice sacrificing itself to sacrifice.*'

This latter "escape" route is somewhat reminiscent of the 'twice-phoren' sojourn of the uncontrollably cantankerous Indian character in Salman Rushdie's moving novel, *Fury* (Rushdie 2001). One Professor Malik Solanka is the ingenious inventor of masked "dolls" that debate philosophical imponderables and scientific verities and engage in fiendish feuds on multi-mediated web-channels. One fine day, with his immense dividend earnings intact, he stealthily flees his stable suburban home, leaving behind his loving wife and a young son, and a cozy job in Cambridge University. The philosopher, of great esteem to the popular audience in the U.K., decides to "black-out" in New York, "the *seductive* World-City" of expanding and contracting *māyā,* that he much loves and resonates with at some deep level, but is disdainful of for its horrendous pretensions —devoured gullibly by upper-Manhattan's mechanized, rudderless selves—and its scary politics laced with theo-babbling fundamentalism. He is burdened by a double-dose of wrath and indignation in the altered states of America. 'Those whom the gods would destroy they first make mad' (p. 184). The rupture he sought from his now all but buried pasts—erstwhile in Bombay, followed by in the U.K.—drove him toward a schizoid frame of mind, and he struggles to unearth the mysterious forebodings within his soul. Hoping to overcome his faults and foibles and to retreat from his darker, counterfeit self, the self of his dangerous fury, through renunciation, through '*giving up*', he falls into new and more grievous denizens of fury and other demons within.

Or as Rusdhie's narrator exquisitely captures in non-prosaic psychoanalytic flourish the sinews of the catastrophic perturbations gyrating within,

Malik Solanka who had latterly become conscious of the inexplicable within himself, had been firmly of the prosaic party, the party of reason and science in its original and broadest meaning: *scientia*, knowledge. Yet even in these microscopically observed and interminably explicated days, what was bubbling inside him defied all explanations. There is that within us, he was being forced to concede, which is capricious and for which the language of explanation is inappropriate. We are made of shadow as well as light, of heat as well as dust. Naturalism, the philosophy of the visible, cannot capture us, for we exceed. We fear this in ourselves, our boundary-breaking, rule-disproving, shape-shifting, transgressive, trespassing shadow-self, the true ghost in our machine. Not in the afterlife, or in any improbably immortal sphere, but here on earth the spirit escapes the chain of what we know ourselves to be. It may rise in wrath, inflamed by its captivity, and lay reason's world to waste (Ibid 128–9).

We are a sign that is not read
We feel no pain, we almost have
Lost our tongue in foreign lands.
(Friedrich Hölderlin, in Heidegger 1977b: 359)

Fast-forward to a nimble apartment on Rue B in the East Village (when not on the LIRR to Stony Brook): I left behind Melbourne, hounded, mystified, overwhelmed (or rather underwhelmed) and brought 'to the knees', that woefully lonesome wandering and wondering went on intermittently for some good four long years (in between teaching at local universities and wide reading). Whence also I reluctantly submitted to analysis and 'healing' therapies (thanks to recurrent advice). Especially insightful were the regular weekly sessions on the couch, as it were, with an astutely gifted psychiatrically-trained Buddhist psychotherapist on the upper East-side (Manhattan). He had me work through, among various modalities besides 'talk' therapy, Atīśa's 'Seven-Point Mind Training' and Śāntideva's *Bodhicaryā-vatāra*, interspersed with yoga, long hours of meditation, visualization and introspective contemplations. This would be followed by peregrinations, mostly in Central Park, so as to find some 'direction home' or for a little solace and company, taking long strolls along Riverside, by the Hudson, with my friend and erstwhile colleague Hazel Rowley (whose untimely *gate gate pārasaṃgate* in 2011 in New York simply exacerbated the residual grief. Hutchings 2011: 313). Needless to say, of course, much more came up in the sessions than just the numbing melancholia of bereavement, especially, to note a few such tropes, issues of childhood, overbearing parental expectations and their own domestic turmoils, sibling relations and rivalries–hence early-life traumas. Additionally there surfaced signs of mendacity, a plethora of follies, particularly combativeness, self-defensiveness, obsessive compulsive reactions, aggression, bashful hostility, judgmentalism, temperamental moodiness, obfuscations, being strung-out, forgetfulness, impermeability, alleged emotional abuse, and relationship difficulties. Not to mention certain inane suspiciousness, insecurities, lashing out with blaming accusations, criticisms and empty words (even against those who brought care, love and new relationship opportunities). There were also signs of various deficiencies—such as the capacity for compassion, empathy, vulnerability, accountability, gratitude, openness, humility, or being able to be present to the moment. Alongside were symptoms of a dysfunctional mind, embodiment dissonance, sexual disorientation, mild addiction, and the failure to come to grips with my own oblivion to the vanishing present. Every act and gesture of surrounding persons seemed to become calculated occasions for antics and foibles of the petty ego and the confrontational, mystifying intellect, confounded by confusion and baneful unmindfulness, overseas jaunts and long absences in elusive pursuits, especially during the drawn-out process of the other's illness. Nothing was any longer what it appeared to be; and the hitherto buried psychic traces (*saṃskāras,* or *kleśas* [hindrances], those of the sedimented crusts of karma itself) would spill over or become enmeshed in the embodied (or more aptly, disembodied) state one is blindly walking around in, or insufferably clinging onto while and living through day-to-day regularity (rather irregularity).

Why was it necessary in attempting to deal with the present grief to delve so deeply into the inexplicable psyche and early childhood issues? Because, as I came to understand later in dialogue with another psychotherapist: 'Oftentimes when a person suffers a major loss in adulthood, they are unexpectedly confronted with unresolved earlier grief and losses from their childhood. The extent to which they were able, or unable, to fully grieve and process those earlier losses impacts their ability to fully meet, experience, and process the present grief. It is not unusual, therefore, for latent feelings, unresolved emotional traumas, and maladaptive emotional responses and behaviors to surface during periods of extreme loss and grief' (Tinara M. Benson, personal communication).

> *The soul becomes a ball of splashing seaweeds*
> *entangling colors of flora and weeping corals*
> *in the seabed of endless time;*
> *the hour-hand ticking losses.*

## The Work of Mourning and Grieving

> *Grief shows in the face.*
>
> —Wittgenstein

I should now like to offer some theoretical reflections.[1] Following the painful or unacceptable loss of a loved and/or esteemed one, both grief and mourning are undergone. While grief is the more immediate response, an episodic act or experi-

---

[1] Here I have been greatly assisted (indeed guided) by very helpful and poignant responses (virtual summaries) to the read draft version from Edward S. Casey, to whom I am most grateful. Some of the paragraphs in the theoretical reflections are cited verbatim, in places without quotation marks, if in a talking-paper of this nature one can assume and exercise this indiscretion. (See note 2.)

ence, mourning, it is noted, is a state, whether a state of mind or state of collectivity. The feeling of grief is experienced as 'acute emotionality that is insistently conscious; while mourning need not be conscious at all: hence its many vicissitudes, including those of hating the lost one', being angry with them, or identifying with him or her intensely (Casey, personal communication). There may be no conscious recognition of this state as mourning until a close friend or an analyst points this out; thus the variety of ritualistic enactments, almost underscoring the difficulty of mourning—or as Derrida would say, 'the impossible mourning that nonetheless remains at work' (2001: 95), and thus its tendency to be unconscious, which makes way for its public performance with others, or by their intervention in the mourning process.

Often however, the experience of grief—or even the absence of it—is viewed more in pathological terms than as one of the regular everyday emotions because it seems so out of the ordinary. Philosophers have not refrained from asking if 'normal grief is a mental disorder?' (Wilkinson 2000). Solomon nevertheless avers that this is a misguided question: 'If grief were simply a negative reaction to a loss, or even a physical condition that (it has often been pointed out) fits the definition of a mental disorder, a medical illness, this would be incomprehensible.' (2007: 75) On the contrary, like anger, righteous indignation, and wrath, grief is 'a strategy for engaging with the world,' despite the denials and obsequious self-obsessions. A closer survey of the symptoms of grief reinforces Solomon's view. Thus, Eric Lindemann describes the more general symptomology of grief, thus:

> The picture shown by persons in acute grief is remarkably uniform. Common to all is the following syndrome: sensations of somatic distress occurring in waves lasting from 20 minutes to an hour at a time, a feeling of tightness in the throat, choking with shortness of breadth, need for sighting, and an intense subjective distress described as tension of mental pain. The patient soon learns that these waves of discomfort can be precipitated by visits, by mention of the deceased, and by receiving sympathy…Another strong preoccupation is with feelings of guilt. The bereaved searches the time before the death for evidence of failure to do right by the lost one. He accuses himself of negligence and exaggerates minor omissions. In addition, there is often a disconcerting loss of warmth in relationship to other people, a tendency to respond with irritation and anger, a wish not to be bothered by others at a time when friends and relatives make special effort to keep up friendly relationship. These feelings of hostility, surprising and quite inexplicable to the patients, disturbed them and were again often taken as signs of approaching insanity. Great efforts are made to handle them, and the result is often a formalized, stiff manner of social interaction (cited in Lamm 2000: 142–3).

Mourning, although somewhat formalized in modern cultures, nevertheless, seeks to extend the grief to a more shared burden of feeling in the larger community or collectivity; the role of narration in mourning ineluctably takes us into the inter-subjective sphere as well. Hence there are both personal and collective locations, especially of mourning, if not of grief itself. And as Solomon points out, in cultures that are less individualistic and more socially connected, grief is a tightly communal and shared experience. 'The logic of grief is entangled with the social structure of mourning, and the peculiarity of grief as I will describe it is that the mourning is minimal' (2004: 75); although perhaps not so minimal, as the anthropological work of Catherine Lutz (1985) demonstrates.

Psychological anthropologists no longer consider emotions to be mere private, psychobiological phenomena; they are substantially mediated by culture. Jenkins and Karno have argued that a culture provides its members with an available repertoire of affective and behavioral responses to the human condition, including illness. In addition, it offers models of how people should or might feel and act in response to the serious illness of a loved one. This may involve anger and hostility in one context or sadness and sympathy in another (1992: 9–21).

As much as one would like to emphasize the cultural (extra-personal) dimension, the collective repertoire and resources thereof, over the intrapsychic processes, the internal (inward-tending) dimension, that acutely personal festering of the 'dark night', should not be overlooked (as it often is in reductionist and behaviorist psychologies, that overwhelmingly focus on the external symptoms and environmental stimuli or triggers at the expense of the deeper intentionalities, emotional and mental challenges), and for which a more balanced spiritual response may be more apposite. 'Indeed', notes Edward Casey, 'we cannot keep them apart, especially in mourning, given that virtually every state of mourning is at least interpersonal—minimally, between the lost one and the survivor—but also ramifies into larger social and political groupings. An even more concrete transition is made when there are expressive gestures mediated between affect and the law, and the 'empathic projective identification' encircles the outlying world of indefinite pluralities right up to the level of the state or the nation (thus, 'A National Day of Mourning', or a Week or a Month, 'The World Mourns Today').

The quick theoretical reflection here is that there are both cognitive and affective aspects to mourning, just about throughout the process; however, there are differential emphases on the two dimensions in any given or particular case, as the anecdotes also well demonstrate. Thus, when I mourn, I must believe certain minimal things: that someone or something has departed forever, that there is no possible or adequate replacement for this loss; that my life has become that much more empty, etc.' 'By the same token, however', as Casey draws out well the implication here, 'I feel the loss within; I not only notice it, I react to it emotionally.'[2] I will say a little more on the distinguishable but inseparable status of these two dimensions as the epicenters of mourning in the final section. Meanwhile, the appearance of the loaded negativity associated with this emotion may have escaped us. So the question this raises is important to pause for.

## The Analytic of 'Moral Emotion' vis-à-vis 'Grief Pathology'

*I don't mind dying - I just don't want to be there when it happens.*

— Spike Milligan

*We are too late for the gods,*
*And too early for Being.*

— Martin Heidegger

---

[2] The quotations here are the response (plus personal communication of Edward Casey to the first draft of my paper, presented at the Stony Brook-Manhattan conference on 'Living with Grief: Coping with Public Tragedy' in 2003).

Just what happens when one is brushed by death? Heidegger answers that there is a deep anxiety that one is poised to becoming "nothing", the challenge of "nullity" of any and all being, hence being-ness, as one is "thrown-toward-death", which is always a possibility; so too for the other who now fully bears witness to this truth (1977a: 108). There is a practical affirmation of the finitude of one's being, of the inauthenticity of existence, that the illusion of immortality has been totally shattered: what other illusion (read Hindu *māyā*) remains? The metaphysical fear of death that one experiences for the other is also at the same time, and perhaps as for Solomon, the real challenge here (Malpas and Solomon 1998: 17). It is a reminder of one's own, albeit temporarily submerged, fear of dying, and not of the suffering part of it. The first-person fears are inextricably mixed up with the loss felt in the dying of the second-person, whose presumed fears and suffering at the hands of indiscriminate agents of death now become my burden also.

Hauntingly, with the onset of death of another, there is a reminder, impossibly, of one's own death, as if remembering a future memory—as when a 'wake' for my friend with a terminal prognosis, Murray of Venus Bay, is held where each of his 200 friends and family members recalls the good times they have had with him over the decades and what each would miss when Murray finally succumbs to the claws of death. Murray even organized his own funeral with the help of his dear friend, Effie, and narrated in his 'swan song' the choice of the coffin, the location of the burial site, the rites he prefers, the celebrant he has prepared for the sacred occasion, and what brand of beer would be distributed at the reception. (It was not unlike the dream Gabriel Garcia Márquez narrates of organizing his own funeral, 1993) This seemed like a sanguine gesture and an humane acceptance of the inevitable; the difficult and painful thought of the passing of someone so close as Murray is to the village folks (and indeed to me) was made part of everyday reality; sadly, his very close 'mate', Brian, passed on prematurely, and Murray himself breathed his last late 2011. Brian, passed on prematurely in the interim.)

Still, why is it that grief is so often looked upon as a 'negative' and undesirable emotion—even as one of the 'basic' emotions (along with sadness)? Why is it that the color black, darkness, and two-dimensional shades of colorless and timeless surrounds are so overwhelmingly associated with mourning and the funerary rites? The *Mahābhārata's* list of negative emotions includes grief, alongside anger and sorrow (Bilimoria 2003). But why is grief looked upon as suffering in the way that sorrow is? Most approaches in folk psychology are all too readily disposed to deal with grief by healing one speedily of the malaise, 'the shocking blow', the physical pain and mental burden. Often many Westerners who help the bereaved, as Rosenblatt observes, hold to some notion or other of 'grief pathology'—for example, grief that is never expressed; that goes on too intensely for too long; that is delayed; that involves delusions, that involves threats to others, that involves self-injury (Rosenblatt 1997:41). Grief pathologies, like grief, may suggest a human universal, but what is forgotten is that symptoms of grief vary from culture to culture. Thus, Rosenblatt cites three instances that point to the differences: a mother in Cairo suffering from a 7-year depression over the loss of her child is really not perceived in her culture to be behaving pathologically.

A bereaved Balinese who seemingly laughs off a death is also behaving appropriately by the standards of her culture; in another society, a person who is possessed by spirits of the dead may be in line with what is entirely understandable and quite common in bereavement in her own society (Rosenblatt 1997:41).

Yet philosophers have waxed ambivalent on grief's nature and especially its relation to other emotions and affects, and to morality, and indeed to the cooler rationality or *primacy of intellectualization* (rephrasing Stocker 2003: 144). Thus, Robert Solomon, in a paper read in Melbourne, also questions why this paradigm case of emotion is often listed (though typically as sadness) as one of the "basic" emotions and a "negative" and (thus) undesirable one? Instead, he wishes to argue that 'Grief is a moral emotion…It is for this reason that grief is not only expected, as the *appropriate* reaction to the loss of a loved one, but in a strong sense *obligatory*, and much more.'

But grief is not merely "normal" or "natural," for it would pass the test for a "duty" in the Kantian scheme of things. *Some feelings are obligatory*, and this is because they are deeply embedded into the fabric of our moral lives (Solomon 2004: 75–78).

I think that what Solomon wants to underscore here is that grief should not be looked upon as a disease or mental aberration and reduced to the clinical picture of the suffering—or limited to the overly mystical picture of a ghostly presence (as in C. S. Lewis's account above). His basic argument is that there are deep—and deeply felt—moral (hence the dedicatory gesture) and reflective dimensions to grief directed toward the loved one who has been lost. Without love there would be no grief; the greater the love, the greater the grief. The other important distinction Solomon makes 'is that one does not suffer *from* grief, but rather one suffers grief'.

That grief is a painful and undesirable emotion is obvious, but then it is not as if the feelings of grief are themselves painful…It occurs in our lives in unwanted circumstances, and its very presence means that we have suffered a serious loss (Solomon 2004: 80).

But there is a peculiarly unique value to this emotion, which, as I read Solomon and much of the cross-cultural literature—e.g., those in Buddhism, explored by our Melbourne-based Sri Lankan colleague, Padmasiri de Silva—'is not only measured by the circumstances that prompt it, and it might just be that grief is the most desirable and in that sense "positive" emotion in a tragic situation' (cited in Solomon, ibid).

We may press on the notion of moral obligation for a while, inquiring as to its congruency with grief, and ask: whose obligation is it? How far does the circle stretch out, as it were? Shall we assume also that it is a 'right' reciprocally demanded by the deceased, or by the social milieu; but so also in the sense of a 'rite' entailing the entitlement to be able to perform or trump a claim to that privilege? And whose right? Whose grief counts? Why not that of Hamlet's mother, Gertrude, who too made no effort (as did Hamlet) to symbolize the death of her husband? (Shakespeare 1992: *Hamlet* Act I, scene ii.; Solomon 2004: 76–77) Indeed cultures vary as to who has the obligation or right to grieve, 'who is defined as the principal mourner, and who is seen as experiencing the most loss with a given death'. As Rosenblatt (who observed small scale societies reports):

One cannot, for example, assume that a new widow or widower feels the rights, obligations or feelings of a principal mourner for a deceased spouse. One cannot assume that the person wailing most loudly or supported most attentively by others from her or his culture is a close relative of the deceased' (1997: 41).

In one reported incident at a funeral, after a mourner with no apparent relation to or even acquaintance with the family fainted while wailing loudly did it come to light that she was the covert mistress of the suddenly collapsed deceased, whom he had been supporting materially along with a mix of offspring from her previous marriage and possibly their own bigamous de-facto relationship. Her wailing could be interpreted as her bold attempt at seeking attention to her suffering and at the same time staking a claim in the "family loom", which she indeed did in due course of time; whenceforth she won a sizeable share of the deceased's estate.

Likewise, in some cultures, wailers are paid to enact mourning for the immediately affected but somewhat emotionally at-sea family members. As Solomon notes himself, such a position confuses grief with mourning, which is an expression of grief and is often embedded in a complex social structure (as anthropologists have keenly observed everywhere). Where mourning is minimal and institutionalized (i.e., cut short to a few hours and attendance at service that is more or less by 'invitation'), a sense of obligation marks the occasion; but in cultures, such as those of the Maori or Aboriginal Australians, where funerary ceremonies can continue for 3 or more days, mourning is woven into the everyday life as part of the communal affective-fare. Even so, a distinction has to be made between a gesture expected or considered to be *appropriate*, and an act done as a matter of *duty* or out of a sense that it is *obligatory*. The latter might reflect a deeply social genealogy of these emotions, which carry out social mandates as it were (Casey, response, see note 2.).

But let us dwell a little longer on the larger moral claim: the test of "duty" (*Pflicht*) or the categorical imperative. There is lot at stake here: first is the suggestion that grief is not simply a set of primitive physiological sensations, raw feelings, pain; that it is not like anger, sorrow, depression; even that it is not just the 'episodic attack' in the brain (as mental disorders and pathologies are thought to be); instead, it has a different, albeit a propositional structure (that-*p*). This suggestion comes from Don Gustafson's essay, one of the rare few on this subject in analytical philosophy (1989). Gustafson's argument is that grief necessarily includes a desire contrary to the belief that the lost beloved is lost, while sorrow involves only a wishing and not such a desire (Solomon's phrasing).

I wish to draw caution to this position by questioning some of the presuppositions underpinning the premises in respect of their universalism or essentialism/ realism, if not the stultifying aridity, and coherence overall. I will draw instead from psychoanalytical and cross-cultural ruminations for my skepticism. I wish to move the analysis towards the completely affective state, and bring into the picture melancholia, unconscious processes, and bodily impact to draw or trace out the inexpressive a little further.

Bob Solomon was among the early proponents of a Pure Cognitive Theory in which emotions were analyzed solely in terms of beliefs, desires and other intentional states, claiming that emotion is an 'evaluative (or normative) judgment, a judgment about my situation and/or about all other people' (1976: 186). If one interprets 'cognition' or the cognitive as being evaluative, as Solomon did in his early views, then this is what marks the emotion of grief as much as it would other emotions. The intense evaluative judgment or 'appraisal' element here would include increasing references to an agent's desires and goals—or their frustration. Since then philosophers such as William Lycan, William Alston, Roland Alan Nash, and to an extent Martha Nussbaum, among others, have insisted on the bodily disturbances—'unthinking energies'—and perturbations of non-intellectual mentation processes (Nussbaum's 'thought') in the agent so that experiences such as trembling, blushing, perspiring, pangs, throbs, tingles, burning and other sensations, adrenalin secretions, increase in heart and respiratory rates, alterations of blood flow, changes in blood pressure, digestive processes and other neurological symptoms are not excluded: indeed, these would be fundamental structural markers of emotional response. And this is evidenced not just in human beings with their quaint sentimentality, but apparently also in other animate creatures, in animals[3] (and ancient cultures believed this to be the norm among deceased ancestors, angels and gods/goddesses as well). This also gives warrant to the idea that grief involves a much larger tapestry, as it were, in its processing than, say, in the more short-fused emotions such as anger or even moral indignation. Grief is not something that can be 'talked through' and resolved intellectually, as when parties come to understand that the anger and rage, or a flurry of accusations based on jealousy, were actually a result of some gross misreading of signs or cues or earlier interaction between them.

Solomon is right in emphasizing that grief is not a fleeting emotion, and that therefore the phenomenological structure of cognition (the cognitive act) is not expansive enough to contain, so to speak, the protracted space in which grief 'happens' and demands its process. Thus 'the process of grieving is the process of coping with that impossible desire and intolerable loss' (2004: 85). And to that end there is an inexorable reflective, contemplative, introspective, introjective and even deeply meditative structure (if one needs to continue to use the cognitive model) to the process. Solomon is right about the reflective and dedicatory qualities of grief, meaning that the surge of feelings (sensations, emoting) is marked by a deep sense of care, gratitude, reverence, honoring, commemorating, celebrating, and still an unrequited longing, a resilient desire for it to be otherwise than the loss so deeply felt.

Importantly, there is in this expression of grief a moral *reciprocity*, if not also the moral responsibility or blame (hence guilt) one is overcome with, the sense that somehow one was oneself implicated in the cause of the death, which in turn compounds the sentimentality of loss. To have the courage amidst this turmoil to be able to face the issue and stare deeply without even as much as a blink at the fathomless reach of death that has brought about this loss through the imagined (or real at the moment of the death) eyes of the beloved—not unlike the ceaseless gaze into a beloved's living eyes–this courage is considered to be a quasi-virtue (like valor in the face of tragic assault or aggression, in the Aristotelian sense). That is Solomon's point.

I wish to take up each of the stages I discern in the welling-up of this emotion, following Solomon, while drawing from the Indian tradition. Thus, I have argued elsewhere that in Indian theories the body is the *locus classicus* of feelings, sentiments,

---

[3] Witness, for example, self-grieving of dog Devi, and grief on the face of Rasa, baby-dog, and their carers, honored with canine last rites: http://www.youtube.com/watch?v=SGBsWllRep4; http://www.youtube.com/watch?v=5d0iN4COY78; and www.pbilimo.com

and affects (Bilimoria 2003: 214–6). And I illustrate this from the opening scene in the *Bhagavadgītā* (1985), where a despondent Arjuna presents a first-hand report of his state-of-being on the battlefield as he encounters the prospect of the impending death of his kith and kin: his body is overwhelmed with sensations of feelings described as quivering, shivering, giddiness, nervousness, heaviness of breathing, weakness of his limbs, hair standing on end, and swallowing.

Martha Nussbaum, in her essay 'Emotions as Judgments of Value and Importance' (1997),[4] much like the early pre-repentant Solomon and Gustafson, considers the emotion of grief to be a form of judgment—about important things—involving judgments in which we acknowledge our neediness and lack of self-sufficiency or incompleteness before those elements that we do not fully control. And this view by her own account is a modified Stoic or neo-Stoic position, wherein the 'unthinking bodily movements', powerful and constitutive as they are, are not considered sufficient to render them an emotion; this is done by the more intelligent cognitive component. Nussbaum reinscribes judgment into this capitulating state by bringing in features or markers of intentionality (object-directedness with or without a defined causal relation to the unthinking-perturbations), beliefs (ways of "seeing that" or very complex objects), and value (2001: 189). Objects of emotion are valued for their importance, and are items of concern; hence their welfare holds significance—in terms of the agent's flourishing and happiness.

So the *necessary* and *sufficient conditions* for emotion (although not identical) are relevant beliefs (of which there are three, to be indicated below) and perceptions; the rest of the features—the non-belief, non-thinking features, as Nussbaum calls them, or the objectless wandering feelings of pain and/or pleasure, are relegated to the *constitutive* parts— even while she wonders aloud; 'What are they like if they are not about anything?' (The three beliefs are: that the suffering is serious; that the person does not deserve the suffering; and that the possibilities of the person who experiences the emotion are similar to those of the sufferer (Nussbaum 2001: 62)). And so the jab in the stomach and sensations of being ripped by slivers of glass at the news of her mother's impending death—like Arjuna's inner tears—are recastable in plain-language propositional terms:

> My mother has died. It strikes me, it appears to me, that a person of enormous value, who was central to my life, is no longer there. It feels as if a nail has entered my insides; as if life has suddenly a large rip or tear in it, a gaping hole. I see, as well, her wonderful face—both as tremendously loved and as forever lost to me. The appearance [and this is the crux of her argument] in however many ways we picture it, is propositional: it combines the thought of importance with the thought of loss, its content is that this importance is lost. And, as I have

---

[4] See Solomon's comment in his review of Nussbaum (poignant for his critical retraction, siding with the so-called Adversary): '…can you make all of the evaluative judgments that supposedly constitute the emotion and nevertheless not have that emotion? I have come to the conclusion after many years that the Adversary (now reinforced with some powerful studies in neurobiology) must be reckoned with, and that my old, rather ruthless line between those cognitive features of emotion that are essential and those non-cognitive features of emotion that are not essential was (in the context of the time) heuristic and is no longer so. (Nussbaum insists on necessary and sufficient conditions in her study, p. 62.)' (Solomon 2002: 900).

said, it is evaluative: it does not just assert, "Betty Craven is dead". Central to the propositional content is my mother 's enormous importance, both to herself as well as to me as an element in my life (Nussbaum 2001: 197).

According to this view, then, the judgment is the grieving (it does not just precede or follow it): this is the upheaval. Encounters with death and the attachments to the dying or deceased (the intentional objects) come in a variety of forms, differing even in kind —from death of a pet animal, to that of a spouse one identifies strongly with (perhaps more deeply than with a parent), to the passing of bodhisattvas and gods; the rawness and intensity of the responses, the amorphous, involuntary and pre-linguistic sense of lack, the dissonance and ambivalences of the will, indeed vary also in proportion to attachment schemata and one's ill-disposition, or unpre-paredness, or the absence of symbolization in the moment, as the case of Hamlet well illustrates. I think it not unfair to quip that 'if the emotion of grief is judgment-laden, then Nussbaum's account itself is heavily theory-laden.' In other words, the judgment-ladenness of emotions had already figured as fore-structure/fore-grounding in her general theory of emotions, which she imports into her account of grief after the initial shock and the emblematic response to the traumatic news. Hence she is able to set aside all those troubling, disturbing, physiological, neurological, 'the insufferable animal' or demonic bodily sensations and biological symptoms that psychologists, healers, acupuncturists, folk counselors of various persuasions, animal nurses, and *Fürsorgenden* [carers] worry about, particularly if these are not recog-nized and acknowledged for their significance as necessary constituents of the emotion (or whatever category they slot grief into). It is curious that none of them think of treating the symptomology just in terms of beliefs and judgments (as the sufficiency principle). Perhaps the state of being belief-contrary —"I wish she had not died"—is excepted, since it can be a focus of therapy, but it is mainly understood as a disaffective signifier of denial which is also there in melancholy and sorrow. Perhaps too they do think, with Nussbaum's adversaries (*pūrvapakṣins*), that the unthinking markers are indeed the sufficient elements of grief and that the belief-propositional ingredients are constitutive or rather supplementary. The massive ramblings of her tome apart, what Nussbaum has ended up with is rather close to the Hybrid Cognitive Theory that has been around since the late 1980s, in which perception and belief-state still maintain a hegemony or are called the 'paradigm case', but in which nonpropositional contents are not excluded, and these are the 'messier' side of emotion, linked to its own specific evaluative continuum and affec-tive contents. (For example, see the work of Don Gustafson (1989), Ronald Alan Nash (1989), and Dan Moller (2007). The slight exception is the perspicuous under-scoring of resilience and caring by Moller.)

By contrast, a somewhat more sophisticated view is presented in Ronald de Sousa's cognitive alternative account, in which context is given more importance than the contents of emotion, with context weighing heavily on the body's responses in a behavioral (not physiological) mode in a participatory social environment, in which others are co-conspirators in the cultivation of our emotions (see, again, Solomon 2004 and Sousa's chapter in this volume). But where is there the context for cultivation of grief in the cases I have cited and in the numerous folk accounts where people find themselves bowled over by life's movements unannounced, or in a state of utter unpreparedness and confusion by a meteor- or steamroller-like, inexplicable, indeed ineffable, phenomenon?

Occasionally vociferous charges are directed at the pathologically dissociative "cognitive" theory of emotion for excluding affect as an essential element of emotional experience which satisfies grief's conditions of reciprocity, reparation, empathy, compassion, and *Sorge* [care] and is not limited merely to rational or intellectual movement. This charge has been led by Michael Stocker and Peter Goldie, but it has been a central tenet of psychoanalytical theories since Freud. Some argue for the middle way view that cognitive theory can and ought to include affect—not an implausible and unreasonable compromise, but its coherency has yet to be persuasively argued for and tested. This is where Solomon has ended up also, more or less, with his dehistoricized, prudential affective phenomenology of grief. Not much is new here at all. Nevertheless, the battle lines remain drawn along these sharp cleavages, and it is quite plausible that further empirical research—in cross-cultural anthropology, psychology and psychoanalysis, with its forays into the unconscious, an aspect of consciousness not much theorized in analytical philosophy—will veer closer to the so-called adversarial position, or somehow sever this false disjunctive theory-choice. There are some serious reasons for thinking this.

Nevertheless, something in the tussle, as it were, between the emergent 'Evaluative versus Devaluative' divide on the theoretic plane, might be resolved if we condescend to acknowledge that surely grief and mourning involve a quite peculiar sense of evaluation to the extent that the bereaved wishes to honor the missing person by saying, in effect, that the person, now all but lost to their world, is worth this very affective response. This is Casey's concession here, with the qualification that this valuation of 'the degree or kind of worth is here conditioned by circumambient social structures, e.g. family hierarchies and other forms of collective units, including ideologies and entire social imaginaries'. The point is well taken. However, the issue really is whether the evaluation is already part of that emotional response or is it a supplement to it, or indeed a response to this precursive emotion.

Given the current theoretical impasse as described it might be helpful to turn to treatments of empathy in tandem with the Heideggerian concept of *Sorge,* or care (concern and solicitude), where the focus is on the phenomenological structure, i.e., the noematic content, rather than on the cognitive or nomological ramifications of the ego-reified experience: the *that* (*suchness*, in Buddhist terminology) of the experience, rather than the "I am having experience that." (Sharma 1993a, b). Here, comparable to Kant's suggestive notion of the 'sublime', the transcendental of all experiences, as a free-standing aesthetic category (that could be evoked by mystical or occultist encounters as well, including impending death), grief is traced as having the potential of an a priori disposition—albeit, not so much in terms of an abstract conceptual category but more as a soft-wired 'ready-at-heart' physiological response in all those spaces Hume had marked out for the work of sympathy upon the news or first-hand experience of a close-one (or a very significant human figure) passing to the beyond.

## The Sublime Melancholia of Mourning

The Raven[5]

*Ah, distinctly I remember it was in the bleak December,*
*And each separate dying ember wrought its ghost upon the floor. Eagerly I wished the*
*morrow...*

*'Prophet!' said I, 'thing of evil! - prophet still, if bird or devil!*
*By that Heaven that bends above us - by that God we both adore*
*Tell this soul with sorrow laden if, within the distant Aidenn,*
*It shall clasp a sainted maiden whom the angels named Lenore –*
*Clasp a rare and radiant maiden, whom the angels named Lenore?'*
*Quoth the raven, 'Nevermore.'*

*'Be that word our sign of parting, bird or fiend!' I shrieked upstarting -*

*'Get thee back into the tempest and the Night's Plutonian shore!*
*Leave no black plume as a token of that lie thy soul hath spoken!*
*Leave my loneliness unbroken! - quit the bust above my door!*

*Edgar Allen Poe*

In his essay on 'Mourning and Melancholia', Freud (1986: 243) begins by talking about the affect of mourning [and I am here citing Charlie Shepherdson for a more succinct summary]:

'In the face of a death, the work of mourning brings with it a certain affective state. Accordingly, the word for mourning "Trauer," designates not only the activity of the mourner, but also the disposition or grief that accompanies it' (2007: 58).

Freud is really interested in melancholy for which grief serves as a contrasting foil for his theory; and much philosophical and psychoanalytic literature has focused on melancholy as a depressive syndrome (Radden 2000).

In the lover 's mourning, the loss of a loved one results in a loss of the capacity to adopt any new object of love; while in a lover's melancholy (as in the wider range that Shakespeare samples out, rather playfully), the source of the condition eludes the depressive sufferer. In its structural behavioral contexts there is expression of the same elements of guilt, exhaustion, absentee love-object or lack, exhibiting Sartre's nauseating absence, abyss as Nothingness, the Heideggerean "throwness-unto-death" and a kaleidoscopic folding-in of the (Humean) regularity of sight, of time, if not of space also, and all associations, causally marked and free. Indeed, the Cartesian extensions of the senses and of the Nyāya mind (Descartes' 'self' that thinks) recede and become grossly in-tensions, in-turned; there is occlusion of the eyes and vision too, a rather palely hued two-dimensional world-space and a sense of the vaguely meaningless presence of existence hanging over its own frayed or shattered edges and, as it were, lingering on—like an infracted and now dead bit of skin that refuses to fall off the old sore—with no real sense of continuity or futurity. After much that

---

[5] This sorely woody poem (excerpted here) describing Edgar Allen Poe's melancholia at loss of his beloved Lenore, was first published in 1845.

is screened out by this flatness, what hovers around in ghostly perturbations is this uncanny, unmystical irreality, disturbingly so ('Why doesn't the world stop, can't they see my life and vision just have?'). If one has never had a 'mystical experience', this condition would serve as a neat counterfactual: contradict this state and imagine the totally contrary in all possible worlds save this one, and one would sense what the mystic claims to experience as her mind, sense and intellect and 'soul' (which too is bereft in the state in question) soar outwards into seemingly multiple or expanding dimensions.

In melancholy, by contrast, the ego is said to have been split, and there is self-reproach and self-loathing (one part turning on the other), symptoms of neurosis, sometimes over-excitement followed by macabre and chilling withdrawal (the social context of grieving or mourning has been elided), and the agent causally links the source of the debilitating will, the pain and free-floating anxiety, to external conditions of dissatisfactions. There is desire to continue the relationship of love, but the love-object has vanished; in melancholy, again, the relationship so much desired is evasive in the absence of a clear grasp on that desire, let alone the love-object. And this compounds the *duḥkha* as one fails to register what one is attached to; and yet the pervasive sense—the 'feeling'—of attachment has not worked its way through, and even less so when there is a collective melancholia, in which the already detached-attachment is passed on from one generation to another—as in the case of the horrors of the Partition of British India into two nation-states, or the Holocaust.

*The thought of suicide is a great source of comfort: with it a calm passage is to be made across many a bad night.*

—Friedrich Nietzsche

I think it instructive to set out this contrast, but then also to ask at what point grief frays into melancholia, as surely the intentional object of loss, the lack, the absence that makes its presence felt more in dreams and daydream memories, in mirrors of time, gradually vanishes, leaving the unfocussed, restless ego not much to clutch onto but its own dis-esteemed subjectivity. The once reconciliatory voice of the other turns into slashing commands; the persisting amorous phantasies are interrupted by alien/unidentified hosts vying for the agent's love, unleashing symptomatic *jouissance* of pain/pleasure in a sadistic mix (intoxicant addicts will recognize that condition all too well); a hitherto morally neutral disposition turns into moral masochism, self-reproach of a more damaging, even self-castrating or suicidal (*sallekhana*) kind, and so on. Karl Abraham, following Freud's work, concluded that the agent succeeds in establishing the lost loved person in his ego, while the melancholic has failed to do so (Klein 2000: 307), and that the two conditions are not vastly different from each other in kind, even though melancholy—other than perhaps in the scholar, *à la* Shakespeare—is often diagnosed as a pathological condition, and grief not so, or not so frequently, unless it seems excessive (as in the case of the Italian woman returning to the hospital ward where her husband had died, and wailing days-on-end well after the funeral and the wake were held). Melancholy is a paradigm case of an affective state.

*The walls of the ego now melt in naked aloneness*
*as mirrors reflecting back skyloads of pain;*
*the ceiling above pelts down tears of rain,*
*the clouds outside are set ablaze in fire;*
*in these diminished nights of infinite resignations.*

*(www.pbilimo.com)*

I believe, it is also instructive to look closely at the therapeutic situation, what in some cultural contexts would be called the rituals surrounding mourning and healing, to discern the imaginary of grief as affect, for hardly any folk culture is hide-bound by an excessively cognitivist approach to the phenomenon of grief—not even that of behavioral and Skinnerian psychologists. If anything, the complexity of this affect is acknowledged in therapeutic efforts, as well as just how ignorant, occluded human beings in general remain about this most enigmatic and pervasive of emotional experiences. (Unlike love or *Eros* it does not set in at a more or less calculated or expected time-line: it is unanticipated, by and large.)

Some cognitivist work on depression is more likely to shed light on grief than abstract philosophical analysis, it would seem; although called cognitivism, medical psychologists have worked to describe emotions associated with depression following loss. A sequential schema is used, although it is not always causally linear, but more associative. Aaron T. Beck shows that first there is the precipitating event, in some form of "loss" experience; the awareness of this experience causes cognitive states; these states, in turn, effect negative mood states; eventually, physiological reactions ensue. The awareness part is the belief state that initiates the psychological causes of other aspects of depression. Beck differs from philosophical "cognitivists," who posit that the beliefs involved in emotions such as depression are not causes but constituents of those conditions. The adversarial position says that it is affects, not beliefs, that are intrinsic constituents, and these are not just the cause or the consequence of belief-state dissonances experienced by the sufferer. A person's feeling of sadness is not merely *because of,* but also *over or about* his or her loss, they insist. The belief states are intrinsic to the experience of depression, and part of how we identify it as an experience of that kind (Beck 2000: 317–23).

The separation of belief states from affect is a very poignant contention here and one that one must go through if the empirical data Beck draws on and the growing psychoanalytic arguments are anything to go by. To be sure, the belief state and especially the distorted evaluations, overvaluations, hasty and inaccurate conclusions, logical errors, and indeed belief contrary at the onset of grief, etc., are not undermined or marginalized. Denials, negative view about the world, oneself, the future, and a sense of the futility of motivating oneself indeed form the *cognitive triad* (which itself is a way of suggesting that at the theoretical level we need to go beyond the usual dyads or binaries we have become so accustomed to: "Okay, if you are not feeling well and dejected, you must be depressed. Is your blood-pressure alright?"). To that end their causal—trigger—role is underscored and, as it were, moved out of the way just when non-intelligent energies begin to move and swamp the agent's psychic, neurological and physiological constitution. It is hard to see how numbness could possibly embed a belief state, except perhaps in some dormant or distorted sense. Disbelief might be reported, as it often is, but this is mistakenly translated or interpreted by certain cognitivists as belief-contrary states that persist as constituent of grief. "Proposition makes way for affect to do its work" might indeed be a more apt adage.

Following Freud, Julia Kristeva brings out something of this in commenting on the difference between melancholy and mourning, thus:

> If temporary sadness of mourning on the one hand, and melancholy stupor on the other are clinically and nosologically different, they are nevertheless *supported by intolerance for object loss* and *the signifier's failure* to insure a compensating way out of the states of withdrawal in which the subject takes refuge to the point of inaction (pretending to be dead) or even suicide. (1989: 10)

The concealed aggressiveness or anger toward the lost object, revealing the ambivalence with respect to the object of mourning —it rejects, dejects, becomes nothing and in becoming nothing engenders a descent into the wasteland of pathos anguish, violence—these feelings are not reducible to primary intellectual determinants. They are not perceptions or even on a par with perceptions, but rather like drives and desire with which these are metonymically connected as the dis-satisfying conditions; they are better understood as being part of affect rather than read propositionally or rationally. One can do something rationally about weakening of will—correct it or prop it up again, use a walking stick—but that is not invariably available for even mildly depressive states. Imagine a gunshot received by the agent: this will evoke a startling response—a sudden jerk of the body. Amplification of the immediacy of the discrete affects evoked in an encounter with the death of loved one is felt across the body by means of correlated sets of facial-muscle, blood-flow, visceral, respiratory, vocal, and skeletal responses. The immediate behavioral response is also imprinted with this analogue.

Virginia Demos and Samuel Kaplan comment, rightly I believe: 'The biological importance of this amplifying function of affect is to make the organism care about quite different kinds of events in different ways' (1986). The affective resonance in similarly presented stimuli (e.g. memory and items of the object lost around the house) evokes more of the same affect in a feedback loop. Affective resonance is a prominent element in empathy, what Hume called sympathy (the arousal of similar emotive states in one observing signs of sadness or sorrow in another), and what in Buddhism is refined as compassion. In grief, the structuration is expanded somewhat diffusely to encompass a sense of loss (the feeling of shock and horror) with belief contrary or the cognitive trigger, to constitute a rite of reciprocation: an offering, an exchange, a gift, so that the pain of the severance of the agent from the love object is felt, acknowledged and fully experienced while also letting go of the love object in the recognition that its return is impossible, that the loss is forever, and that time which trundles along indiscriminately will both remind one and cover over the dreadful effect. That sort of wisdom underpins the rites and ceremonies. A baby cow-seal sheds a tear when its mother is suddenly trapped and snatched away by New Guinean sea-hunters for their next communal meal. Of course, this is a built-in biological or mammalian code-response in animate creatures as a survival-evolutionary strategy; but it is also an emotional experience, an affect, where its expression comes with certain signifiers, cognitive, bodily, physiological, and unconscious (manifest, at least in us, in dreams and aggressiveness and depression).

A 'soul to soul' eulogy for a couple's 3.5 old son, offered at the funeral by Tinara Benson, brings together some of the elements of grief in a more positive and sagacious light:

> Grief lets us know that we are alive, that we are human, that we have loved. There is an eternal river made up of all the tears that have ever been shed through all the ages. All the grieving mothers and fathers, children, spouses, lovers and friends have all in their time contributed their tears to this river. All of us in our own time are called upon to add our tears to this river. None of us is exempt. It's not fair, and we don't have to like it or want it. What we can do is hope for the grace to add our tears willingly. That when it is our turn and we are called to grief, that we have the courage, the faith, and the support, to stay open to the pain, open to the loss, open to the love, and even grateful for the ability to feel it all (personal communication; cf. Masel 2011; Leonard 2010).

This, it seems, is only part of the story of the enigma, and it embellishes more than clinches anything very novel in the stories we do have in philosophical literature. There is neither any sort of spiritual or philosophical epiphany at the end of this questful inquiry and journey. Philosophers, too, are not immune from the need for therapy at some point or other in their social or worldly life—it catches up with us all. As Socrates reminded Celebes (in *Phaedo* 61), even the wisest are moved to grieve, but philosophers seem less troubled at the prospect of facing their own dying and death if they 'apply themselves in the right way to philosophy', whatever that might be. Then only and truly can one proclaim, 'There shall be no mourning', again, as Lyotard reminded his audience in anticipation of his death, and as Derrida en-acted out this *self* deconstructing affect (akin to the Bodhisattva's no-self statis, as he, I believe, saw it) when he too passed beyond by disallowing the social-collegial (not to say, the State-sponsored, as in Sartre's case) final performative of public mourning. (At least he gestured toward that, for mourning was, silently, rather widespread; see Taylor in *NY Times* 2004). I have not withheld myself in that way because of the different cultural ambience and because of the phenomenological angst toward fathoming the shock, tear- and fear-fully.

## Unconcluding Remarks

This paper, as should be obvious, was evoked by an incident in my personal life for which I was least prepared. As a philosopher I had hardly given any thought to this particular emotional state even while I was writing on the more exotic and aesthetic, if not somewhat less troublesome, plethora of recognized emotions and feelings known in the Indian tradition with Renuka Sharma, whose seminal work on empathy I much admired and learnt from. For this I would also often engage in conversations with Robert (Bob) Solomon, who had a particular interest in cross-cultural critique of the passions and emotions, even as he wrote in the area largely from his more familiar ground of Western philosophy and psychology. But being (as irrepressibly experienced by most dear ones) archetypically a thinking, conceptual, intellectual 't-wit', I entirely lacked any empathic understanding at the subtler level of feeling-states (i.e. paradigmatically emotionally) of what it would be like to be, as it were, struck like a lighting bolt unawares by the more enigmatic of what otherwise is seen as a "negative" emotion, or a hard one at least. Philosophical literature disappointingly yielded very little to go by, especially in the analytical tradition, which perhaps suggests that philosophers don't always think about everything that may be of significance, or as deeply and unprejudicially as would be their calling toward such troubling human predicaments. I had to turn to psychology, psychoanalysis and cross-cultural anthropology, not to speak of poetry and certain mystical and spiritual writings as well.

In the space I allowed myself for this paper, I have done little more than present vignettes of different perspectives and reflections that have emerged across the board. Of course there is a considerable amount of literature in the therapeutic and healing-hand areas, but apart from their phenomenological and often anecdotal value, it proved too difficult to extract a decent and consistent theoretical hermeneutic from this area. The field is still fraught with uncertainties and mysteries yet to be fathomed.

Once again I was guided by the insights of Bob Solomon. However, Solomon continued to look at all emotions from within the framework he had established and was comfortable working within, namely the pure cognitive model—from which he nevertheless got to *affect*, while my thinking went from affect to the cognitive, and back. (Hence the sub-adage in the title: 'Thinking back to Robert Solomon'.) Of course, Solomon toned down the excessive requirements of the cognitive model in which belief and evaluative judgment, along with intentionality, would play a defining role, and he did not see grief in the same way as the other greater advocate of the propositional character of grief, namely Martha Nussbaum. Instead, Solomon chose to emphasize the quasi-Kantian *obligatoriness* of grief. But this too may be a perspective from within the Western culture, informed by quasi-Enlightenment philosophy (despite his own Nietzschean predilections). Again, this began to sound rather too categorical, for taking on something as one's (surprisingly sudden) duty requires an element of calculative thought and deliberations about utility, consequences, the force of the authority, even the rights of the subject toward whom the emotion is directed.

As Hamlet's father's ghost pointed out, it is unbecoming for someone to feel empathy and grieving for another to be a mere obligatory act, though obligation might apply to certain forms of public mourning, as I explain. The evidence from the ground, as it were, discloses a process much more impromptu, and even to an extent spontaneous, in its response, unself-consciously proceeding without much awareness or sign of it being a cognitive act, or even that it is as clearly intentional. I veer towards alternative theories that underscore "unthinking energetics" of feeling-states, that accord a minimalist intellectual content and allow the analogues from experiences of the aesthetic and erotic sublimes to find commonalities here. In constructing this argument to the best explanation I found myself drawing liberally from psychoanalysis, feminist continental thinkers, and Indian philosophy of aesthetics.

And yet as I moved contingently towards the end of this inquiry, I could only confess that much conceptual work still remains to be done on grief, and to a lesser extent on mourning.

*Syllogistic sūtra for a requiem*[6]

Love of Life
Death of Love
Life in Death

— (San Anselmo, CA/Venus Bay, Vic., May-July 2011)[7]

# References

Alpert, Rebecca. 2010. Grief and the rituals surrounding death: A Jewish approach. In *Religion, death and dying*, Bereavement and death ritual, vol. 3, ed. Lucy Bregman, 25–40. Santa Barbara/Denver/Oxford: Praeger.

Auden, W.H. 1976 [1936]. Stop all the clocks [Funeral blues]. In *Collected poems*, vol. 120, ed. Edward Mendelson. New York: Random House.

---

[6] This śloka summarizes the contour of this inquiry.

[7] This essay had its genesis in a spiel I was asked to present by Bob Solomon at the launch of the volume *Thinking About Feeling*, in the University of Texas, Austin; I was to speak on my chapter 'Perturbations of Desire' in the collection (Solomon 2003). This was circa December 2002, shortly after a personal tragedy that engaged me intensely in this hermeneutic of the raw feelings I was undergoing, which also had me re-think the hitherto abstract theorizing on the emotions. I learnt a lot discussing this essay as it evolved, with Bob Solomon and Kathleen Higgins; I am grateful to Kathleen for including it in a publication that honors Solomon's profound legacy, in the special issue of *Sophia* on Robert C. Solomon and the Spiritual Passions (2011, 50/2: 281–301), which she guest edited. It is presented here with some revisions. And my gratitude also goes out to: Shannon Magree ('Ravenswood'), Nina Rühle, Joseph Prabhu, Chris Chapple, Gayatri Chakravorty Spivak; the Bilimoria, Sharma, Singh, Giborees, Kelvin & Tuttle, Chauhan, Komesaroff families; Jayant Bapat, Rashmi Desai, Steffie Lewis, Rich & Denis, Peter Wong, Greg Bailey, Patrick Hutchings Esq, Joe Loizzo, Robert Thurman, John Koller, Sue Ren & Xing Xiang, Ian Weeks, Max Charlesworth, caring colleagues and staff at Deakin and Melbourne Universities, at NIAS, NIMHANS, SSRI (Bangalore); J. N. Mohanty, Shivesh Thakur, H.H. Dalia Lama, Jay Garfield, Hope & Stephen Phillips, (the late) Hazel Rowley, Ed Casey, Sridhars (Stony Brook), Sridhars (Bangalore), Brahmaputra, Mahboob, Ammas (Parthi), Chris Zvokel, Patrick Olivelle, David Carr, Laurie Patton, Thee Smith and friends in Emory, Ganga-Vidya-Vikram, Tinara Benson, Devi-Rasa, Maya, Lisa; *Sophia* workers: Natassia Kaufman, Serena O'Meley, Amy Rayner, Sherah Bloor, Sara Kerr,; Maxine Therese, Panayiota Karnis, Maureen Voicer, (late) Selva Raj, (late) Jagdish Sharma, Surabhi, Elizabeth Ann Kaplan, Hugh Silverman, Peter Smith; and last not least (*presentia in absentia*) Renuka M. Sharma also contributed to my understanding and coming to terms with this more challenging of creaturely emotions. Of course, there have been other interlocutors, support-givers, and carers, in parts of the world, too numerous to name here, whose insights, questions and wisdom, have added succor to the arduous journey. To be sure, an inner journey that never does really have an endpoint: one is always 'On The Way', as Heidegger reminded us poignantly in the context of Dasein's ontic-ontological quest for meaning of being, non-being and self-actualizing authenticity. I have journeyed through this 'thrownness' that I found myself unwittingly confronted by, with the same philosophical-cum-spiritual passion that I have and despite all do remain engaged in my other intellectual pursuits.

Beck, Aaron T. 2000. A cognitivist analysis of depression. In *The nature of melancholy: From Aristotle to Kristeva*, ed. Jennifer Radden, 317–23. New York: Oxford University Press.

*Bhagavad-Gītā*. 1985. In the *Mahābhārata*, I, trans. and ed. J.A.B. van Buitenen. Chicago: Chicago University Press.

Bilimoria, Purushottama. 2003. Perturbations of desire: Emotions disarming morality in the 'Great Song' of the *Mahābhārata*. In *Thinking about feeling: Contemporary philosophers on emotions*, ed. Robert C. Solomon, 214–232. New York: Oxford University Press.

Bregman, Lucy (ed.). 2010. *Religion, death and dying*, Bereavement and death ritual, vol. 3. Santa Barbara/Denver/Oxford: Praeger.

*Brhadāranyaka Upanishad*. 1996. In *Upaniads*, 3–94 (trans: Olivelle, Patrick). New York: Oxford University Press.

Charlesworth, Max. 2003. A dedicated life that illuminated many hearts and minds: Dr. Renuka M. Sharma, 11 December 1958–31 October 2002. Obituary. *The Age*, Melbourne, May 18.

Demos, Virginia, and Samuel Kaplan. 1986. Motivation and affect reconsidered: Affect biographies of two infants. *Psychoanalysis and Contemporary Thought* 9: 147–221.

Derrida, Jacques. 2001. Letter to Francine Loreau. In *The work of mourning*, ed. Pascale-Anne Brault and Michael Naas, 94–104. Chicago: University of Chicago Press.

Freud, Sigmund. 1986 [1917]. Mourning and melancholia. In *The standard edition of the complete psychological works of Sigmund Freud*, vol. 14, 239–260 (trans: Strachey, James). London: The Hogarth Press.

Gielen, Uwe P. 1977. A death on the roof of the world: The perspective of Tibetan Buddhism. In *Death and bereavement across cultures*, ed. Collin Murray Parkes, Pittu Laungani, and Bill Young, 52–71. New York/London: Routledge.

Gustafson, Donald. 1989. Grief. *Noûs* 23: 457–479. Stable URL: http://www.jstor.org/stable/2215878.

Heidegger, Martin. 1977a [1929]. What is metaphysics? (Was ist Metaphysic?) (trans: Krell, David F). In *Martin Heidegger: Basic writings*, ed. David F. Krell, 95–112. New York: Harper & Row.

Heidegger, Martin. 1977b [1954]. What is called thinking? (Was heisst Denken?) (trans: Wieck, Fred D. and J. Glenn Gray (1968)). In *Martin Heidegger: Basic writings*, ed. David F. Krell, 345–367. New York: Harper & Row.

Heilman, Samuel C. 2001. *When a Jew dies: The ethnography of a bereaved son*. Berkeley: University of California Press.

Hutchings, Patrick. 2011. Hazel Rowley: Obituary. *Sophia* 50/1: 313.

Jenkins, Janis H., and Marvin Karno. 1992. Meaning of expressed emotion: Theoretical issues raised by cross-cultural research. *The American Journal of Psychiatry* 149: 9–21.

Klein, Melanie. 2000. The depressive position. In *The nature of melancholy: From Aristotle to Kristeva*, ed. Jennifer Radden, 297–310. New York: Oxford University Press.

Kleinman, Arthur, and Byron Good (eds.). 1985. *Culture and depression: Studies in anthropology and cross-cultural psychiatry of affect and disorder*. Berkeley: University of California Press.

Kristeva, Julia. 1989. *Black sun: Depression and melancholy* (trans: Roudiez, Leon S). New York: Columbia University Press.

Lamm, Maurice. 2000. *The Jewish way in death and mourning*. Middle Village: Jonathan David Publishers.

Leonard, Richard S.J. 2010. *Where the hell is God?* Mahwah: Paulist Press.

Lewis, C.S. 1976. *A grief observed*. London/Greenwich: Faber & Faber/Seabury Press/Bantam Books.

Lutz, Catherine. 1985. Depression and the translation of emotional worlds. In *Culture and depression: Studies in the anthropology and cross-cultural psychiatry of affect and disorder*, ed. Arthur Kleinman and Byron Good, 63–100. Berkeley: University of California Press.

Malpas, Jeff, and Robert C. Robert C (eds.). 1998. *Philosophy and death*. London/New York: Routledge.

Márquez, Gabriel Garcia. 1993. *Strange pilgrims twelve stories* (trans: Grossman, Edith). New York: Alfred A. Knopf.

Masel, Deborah. 2011. *Soul to soul: Writings from dark places*. Jerusalem: Gefen Publishing House.

Moller, Dan. 2007. Love and death. *Journal of Philosophy* 104: 301–16.

Nash, Ronald Alan. 1989. Cognitive theories of emotion. *Noûs* 23: 481–504.

Nussbaum, Martha. 1997. Emotions as judgments of value and importance. In *Relativism, suffering, and beyond: Essays in memory of Bimal K. Matilal*, ed. P. Bilimoria and J.N. Mohanty, 231–251. New York: Oxford University Press (expanded version in Nussbaum, 2001).

Nussbaum, Martha. 2001. *Upheavals of thought: The intelligence of emotions.* Cambridge: Cambridge University Press.

Obeyesekere, Ganantha. 1985. Depression, Buddhism, and the work of culture in Sri Lanka. In *Culture and depression: Studies in the anthropology and cross-cultural psychiatry of affect and disorder*, ed. Arthur Kleinman and Byron Good, 134–151. Berkeley: University of California Press.

Parkes, Collin Murray, Pittu Laungani, and Bill Young (eds.). 1997. *Death and bereavement across cultures.* New York/London: Routledge.

Poe, Edgar Allen. 1845. The raven. *Evening Mirror.* New York, January.

Radden, Jennifer (ed.). 2000. *The nature of melancholy: From Aristotle to Kristeva.* New York: Oxford University Press.

Rosaldo, Renato. 2004. Grief and a headhunter's rage. In *Death, mourning, and burial: A cross-cultural reader*, ed. Antonius C.G.M. Robben, 167–178. Oxford: Blackwell Publishing.

Rosenblatt, Paul C. 1997. Grief in small-scale societies. In *Death and bereavement across cultures*, ed. Collin Murray Parkes, Pittu Laungani, and Bill Young, 27–51. New York/London: Routledge.

Rushdie, Salman. 2001. *Fury: A novel.* New York: Random House.

Shakespeare, William. 1992. In *Hamlet*, ed. Cedric Watts. Hertfordshire: Wordsworth.

Sharma, Renuka M. 1993a. *Understanding the concept of empathy and its foundations in psychonanalysis.* Lewiston: The Edwin Mellon Press.

Sharma, Renuka M. 1993b. Empathy—A retrospective on its development in psychotherapy. *The Australian and New Zealand Journal of Psychiatry* 26: 377–390.

Shepherdson, Charles. 2007. Emotion, affect, drive: For Teresa Brennan. In *Living attention: On Teresa Brennan*, ed. Alice A. Jardine, Shannon Lundeen, and Kelly Oliver, 57–77. Albany: State University of New York Press.

Smith, Stan (ed.). 2004. *The Cambridge companion to W. H. Auden.* Cambridge: Cambridge University Press.

Solomon, Robert C. 1976. *The passions.* Garden City: Doubleday.

Solomon, Robert C. 2002. Review of Martha Nussbaum, *Upheavals of thought: The intelligence of emotion. Mind* 111: 897–901 (Cambridge: Cambridge University Press, 2001).

Solomon, Robert C. (ed.). 2003. *Thinking about feeling: Philosophers on the emotions.* New York: Oxford University Press.

Solomon, Robert C. 2004. On grief and gratitude. In *In defense of sentimentality*, 75–107. New York: Oxford University Press.

Solomon, Robert C. 2007. *True to our feelings: What our emotions are really telling us.* New York: Oxford University Press.

Stocker, Michael. 2003. Some considerations about intellectual desire and emotions. In *Thinking about feeling: Contemporary philosophers on emotions*, ed. Robert C. Solomon, 135–148. New York: Oxford University Press.

Taylor, Mark C. 2004. A letter to the editor and supplement. *The New York Times.* http://www.nytimes.com/2004/10/14/opinion/14taylor.html.

Wilkinson, Steven. 2000. Is 'normal grief' a mental disorder? *The Philosophical Quarterly* 50: 289–30.

# Chapter 13
# The Lost Art of Sadness

Padmasiri de Silva

**Abstract** The dominant psychiatric traditions have failed to clearly comprehend that 'sadness' is a basic facet of the human predicament and not a clinical disorder. It is true that grief and mourning are often grave departures from routine life, but it is not a morbid condition and there is no need to hand over the mourner for medical treatment. In grief counseling some of the richer facets of grief are seen: grief being a time for deep reflection on issues of the meaning of life and for commemorating the contributions of the lost one and make one's love alive. Moving out of the conceptual and scientific issues concerning 'depression' and 'sadness', this study moves into the practical concerns of managing sadness and grief. The author's own contributions to grief management using Buddhist resources and the mindfulness-based emotion focused therapy are presented in detail. The study also refers to the current revolution in emotions studies and presents a close look at the emotion profile of 'sadness'.

> Sadness is an inherent part of the human condition, not a mental disorder. Thus to confront psychiatry's invalid definition of depressive disorder is also to consider a painful but an important part of our humanity that we have tended to shunt aside in the modern medicalization of human problems. As science allows us to gain more control over our emotional states, we will inevitably confront the question of whether normal intense sadness has any redeeming features or should be banished from our lives. Such a momentous scientific and moral issue should not be spuriously resolved by using a semantic confusion in the DSM that mistakenly places states of intense sadness under the medical category of disorder. We can only adequately confront the complex and important concerns involved if we clearly differentiate normal sadness from mental disorder (Horowitz and Wakefield 2007: 225).

> Although grief involves grave departures from the normal attitude to life, it never occurs to us to regard it as a morbid condition and hand the mourner over to medical treatment. We are rest assured that after a lapse of time it will be overcome, and we regard any interference with it as inadvisable or even harmful (Freud 1957: 164–165)

P. de Silva (✉)
Monash University, Melbourne, VIC, 3171, Australia
e-mail: pdesilva@alphalink.com.au

K. Higgins and D. Sherman (eds.), *Passion, Death, and Spirituality*,     175
Sophia Studies in Cross-cultural Philosophy of Traditions and Cultures 1,
DOI 10.1007/978-94-007-4650-3_13, © Springer Science+Business Media Dordrecht 2012

It is…on account of the griever's refocus on the whole of life of the diseased, that grieving tends, to be a time for reflection. While commentators often note that grief is associated with social withdrawal or depression, they rarely discuss its reflective tone. But people in grief regularly experience a very reflective time,…in thought about the deceased, about the meaning of life and death, about the passage of time (McCracken 2005: 145).

The expression of grief due to the contraction of the grief muscles, is by no means confined to Europeans, but appears to be common to all races of mankind (Darwin 1998: 185).

# Introduction

This study is basically focused on what may be called the 'lost art of sadness' and the importance of grief and its positive, reflective, and dedicatory qualities that lead to a process of self-healing. Freud in examining the nature of grief in his reflections on 'mourning' differentiates it from melancholia and clearly rules out the claim that mourning is a medical disorder. Even in the case of melancholia, Freud at times sees this experience as common to all humanity, but following the analysis of Horowitz and Wakefield, (Horowitz and Wakefield for short) we can see conceptual clarity in the statement that "Sadness is an inherent part of the human condition, not a mental disorder" (Horowitz and Wakefield 2007: 225).

While one strand of melancholia is depression, the other strand contained in Burton's *anatomy of melancholy* may be described as 'existential angst'. Burton described 'depression' as of "deep reach, excellent apprehension, judicious, wise and witty" (Burton 1927: 277). Depression has two faces, one, a clinical disorder, and the other face described by Michael Ignatieff as more "a discourse to be understood than a pathology to be corrected," which according to him is "a paradigm lost" (1987). During the development of psychology and psychiatry as empirical sciences, this perspective appears as a lost paradigm, though it has an ideal home in existentialist thought (see de Silva 2007a, 2008b). The existential therapy of Irvin D. Yalom is a more sophisticated revival of this perspective, backed with a great number of clinical studies (Yalom 1980). In looking at issues of meaning and death, he integrates the voices of Dostoevsky, Tolstoy, Kafka and Camus. It appears to me that this 'second face' of melancholy has entered the field of contemporary psychiatry through Yalom's classic and excellent study, *Existential Psychotherapy*. The interface between Buddhism and existentialism has been discussed in my *Explorers of Inner Space* (de Silva 2007a, b).

I shall present a perspective from the Buddhist encounter with 'grief, lamentation and distress,' which provided sustenance to my own journey through grief and sadness (de Silva 2008a, b: 82–98). The mishandling of sadness, and sadness become 'malignant sadness' may lead to depression (Wolpert 1999). The management of grief and sadness is a basic theme of this study. Secondly, while sadness is a visible front of suffering, there lurks an invisible and unarticulated silent form of suffering described as 'ennui' or boredom, which illuminates the path of what I call 'pedestrian depression,' different from clinical depression. Like sadness, boredom is a neglected emotion and its logic illuminates the Buddhist analysis of suffering (*dukkha*).

Another very crucial concern here is to address not merely the conceptual issues about sadness, but the practical need for the management of sadness in the light of current Western therapeutic traditions, and even more important, Western therapeutic traditions which have integrated mindfulness techniques. Alternative therapeutic orientations are not very much explored in the Horowitz and Wakefield study. But therapeutic perspectives often reveal their underlying attitudes toward sadness, and these also include perspectives across cultures.

My own therapeutic orientation, which I used in counseling, may be described as *mindfulness-based emotion focused therapy*. While gaining much from the celebrated work of Leslie Greenberg in developing emotion-focused therapy, I have also integrated the use of mindfulness practice into therapy. This perspective emerged initially in my personal journey through grief and sadness but developed through a professional practice of counseling for many years (de Silva 2010).

> If we are to understand depression then we need to understand emotion, for depression is, I believe, sadness that has become pathological…depression is a disorder of emotion (Wolpert 1999: 74).

## The Pervasiveness of Human Suffering

Three important emotions and their significance have been submerged by the overpowering preoccupation with 'depression' as a clinical disorder during contemporary times: these emotions are sadness, melancholy (as existential *angst*) and boredom. These emotions are part and parcel of normal suffering (*dukkha*), and understanding them with insight and wisdom may paradoxically result in a new sense of awakening in the individual. This is the central message of the present study.

> Freud showed real profundity when he stated that the aim of psychoanalysis was to replace neurotic unhappiness by normal unhappiness. A psychiatry based on a purely hedonistic ethics, a psychiatry that does not recognize that periods of anxiety and periods of melancholy are a necessary part of every human life, such a psychiatry will be no more than a superficial affair. Our task is not merely to relieve but to interpret (Drury 1973: 22).

Drury, writing on the danger of words, is critical of the current medicalisation of the word 'depression,' and this comment sums up the Buddhist perspective on the normality of human suffering (*dukkha*), which is the first noble truth. Similar sentiments have been expressed within some contemporary therapeutic traditions:

> Some mental health problems are pathological in the traditional sense. But short of giving nearly every citizen one or more syndromal labels, no amount of progress in the area of psychological disease will remove our need to explain and address the pervasiveness of human suffering. Most humans are hurting—just some more than others. It is, in effect normal to be abnormal (Hayes et al. 1999: 6).

Hayes and his colleagues also observe that this assumption of destructive normality is held by many religious traditions both east and west—that human suffering is the normal state of affairs. *It has also been observed that there are many forms of psychological disorders that do not constitute 'clinical disorders'*—loneliness, alienation, boredom, meaninglessness, low self-esteem, existential angst, and pain associated with such issues as sexism, bullying, domestic violence and divorce. Some of the people who go through these ailments add an extra load of suffering by repression, denial and deception.

But there is a kind of paradox, which is that once you look at sadness, loneliness and alienation with a different stance, and see them as 'normal suffering', they cease to be suffering—but become a fresh path of awakening. This perspective also implies *that normal people will gain by counseling.* Most of my clients were close to normal life. In fact, I have referred to my therapy as "the magic of the ordinary" and the "elegance of small things" (de Silva 2008a, b). The therapeutic exercises are woven around simple routines in daily life. The real magic is in the focus on the moment-to-moment flow of life, where like ants we build all the qualities of industriousness, diligence, vigilance and compassion to oneself and others.

I am always struck by these words of Sigmund Freud when he claimed neither to be a prophet nor a saint, but said that he aimed at transforming "hysterical misery into common unhappiness'" (Freud and Breuer 1895: 305). During the time of the Buddha there was no clinical concept of abnormality but he saw that a whole culture may be driven by craving, addictions, self-indulgence and reactive behaviour, ranging from anger to aggression. In fact, in the present article, I shall illustrate how different forms of boredom sway through the working life of people. That it is necessary to review the distinction between our concepts of normality and abnormality with reference to mental health; that many people are subject to forms of suffering that do not constitute 'clinical disorders,' such as loneliness, boredom, meaninglessness and existential angst and the increasing number of people subject to depression and suicide: these facts have been highlighted by the emerging therapeutic tradition of action commitment therapy (ACT) (Harris 2006).

## Mourning and Melancholy

Freud's essay "Mourning and Melancholia" is a brilliant piece of work embedded with many insights, but as Jennifer Radden says, in spite of its brilliance it has a kind of opaqueness and ambiguity. This ambiguity is partly due to the fact that there are number of strands of thinking in this study. Reading through it is more like trying to figure out threads of meaning in a complex poem. But it is perhaps the earliest study in the literature of psychiatry, developing on the valuable studies by Karl Abraham, that focuses on the importance of understanding grief and sadness as different from clinical depression.

According to Radden, there is an interesting tension in Freud, between the notion that on the one hand, melancholic propensities are rare and pathological, and on the other hand, that they are common, and even a part of the human condition. The notion of considering melancholy as a universal condition is something that Freud owes to a tradition of writing exemplified in Burton's *Anatomy of Melancholy*

(Burton 1927). Radden considers that melancholy was also associated with genius, creative energy and exalted moods. While there was a central link between grief and melancholia, the tendency to associate melancholia with the human condition is found in Freud's passage extending melancholia beyond loss by death to include "all those situations of being wounded, hurt, neglected, out of favour, or disappointed, which can import opposite feelings of love and hate into their relationship or reinforce an existing ambivalence" (Freud 1957: 161).

While these different strands of thinking embedded in Freud's thinking on melancholia are interesting, Horowitz and Wakefield say that Freud made a clear distinction between normal grief and melancholia. Commenting on the previously cited passage from Freud, Horowitz and Wakefield say, "He asserted that symptoms associated with mourning are intense and are 'grave departures from the normal' in the sense that grief is greatly different from usual functioning. Nevertheless, grief is not a 'morbid condition': it is not a medical condition that represents the breakdown of a biologically normal process. Thus it does not require medical treatment." (Horowitz and Wakefield 2007: 74). Horowitz and Wakefield also observe that grief is a self-healing process and that the mourner will return to a normal psychological state. Both mourning and melancholia are states of profound dejection, loss of interest in the outside world, and an inability to enjoy pleasures. But leaving out such symptoms, mourning is a normal reaction to loss, while melancholia is a pathological state. It has also to be mentioned that Feud shifted from a somatogenic explanation of mental health issues to a psychogenic account. Starting his profession as a neurologist, he was a pioneer in moving to a psychogenic explanation of mental sickness.

## Depression and Boredom

'Boredom' is described under several terms: anguish, ennui, tedium, doldrums, humdrum, apathy, listlessness. As Otto Fenichel has shown, boredom emerges in leading a normal life that is normatively constrained. Fenichel described 'boredom' in this axiom: "when we have to do what we do not want to do or not do what we want to do" (Fenichel 1951: 359) He considers boredom as characterized by an urge to activity, accompanied by an inhibition of the activity. The work on 'boredom' has been mainly in the area of education.

Erich Fromm, who during the later part of his life had some interesting correspondence with the German monk Venerable Nyanaponika in Sri Lanka, offers some interesting insights on the relevance of Buddhism to what he calls "*la malaise du siècle*". In the *Art of Listening* (posthumous publication) he describes this malady: "No symptoms at all, but feeling unhappy, strange, not even sleeplessness, life has no meaning, no zest for life, a feeling of vague malaise" (Fromm 1994: 67). He says that the misery which is experienced by many people lies to a large extent not in the fact that they are sick but rather that they are separated from everything that is interesting and beautiful in life. They sit and fret about their problems, their sins, their mistakes, their symptoms. They say, "I am depressed". Fromm says that instead of concentrating on their problems, they need an increasing enlargement and intensification of their interest in life.

Fromm considers 'boredom' as the sickness of our times, and it is strange that there has not been any useful study on boredom and depression in the context of therapy. Fromm refers to the analysis of the whole character of the person rather than his symptoms, and describes such a study as 'character analysis'. He says that the style of neurosis varies with the change of cultural patterns. After completing the therapeutic perspectives on sadness, I shall explore issues pertaining to managing boredom.

## The Emotion Profile of Sadness & Working with Emotions

Solomon says, "But that trauma is not the whole of grief. The other side of grief, its precondition is love. Thus I want to argue that grief is not only bemoaning the loss. *Grief is also a way of keeping the love alive*" (Solomon 2007: 74–78). He also says that there is a commemoration factor in grief. People dedicate novels, name buildings, create fellowships and so on. Solomon also observes that grief is not a single emotion as such. Kubler-Ross describes a whole enriching process going through denial, anger, distraction, guilt and sorrow. Thus profound grief gets refined by going through this process. Looking at the Maori rituals, Solomon considers grief not just as an interruption of life but as a continuation of the rhythms of life.

My focus is basically on the management of emotions—emotion focused therapy (EFT). The best exponent of EFT is its pioneer Leslie Greenberg.

> Thus promoting emotional processing in cognitive approaches, arousal of fear by imaginative stimulation in behavioural approaches, emotional insight in psychodynamic approaches, increased depth of experience in experiential approaches and communication of feeling in interactional approaches are all aspects of working with emotion that are seen as important within each perspective (Greenberg and Paivio 2003: 1).

All these approaches are important in looking at the management of sadness. I have shown in a paper presented at a Mahidol University conference on Buddhism and science the basic resemblances and differences between the EFT of Greenberg and my own version of Mindfulness-Based EFT (de Silva 2011, in press). The new revolution in emotion studies has integrated the *affective, cognitive, motivational* and the *attentional* dimensions of emotions. A full-blown emotion has all these facets including the physiological aspect of emotion. The Buddhist guide to mindfulness practice known as the *Satipatthana integrates* all these facets: the body, feelings, perceptions, thoughts, thought patterns and phenomena (both physical and psychological) and the underlying technique is the use of mindfulness/attention (*sati*).

In dealing with sadness, we start with the calming of the body; then we look at the emergence of feelings of pleasure, pain and neutral—if we 'put our breaks' here, painful feelings would not develop into sadness or anger; the focus on thoughts and thought patterns deals with what cognitive therapist call the 'autopilot', breaking through automatic and conditioned thought processes. We also look at the meaning-giving dimension of cognition, which helps us to differentiate sadness from its close neighbours, as well as emotion clusters, like the entry of anger into sadness. It is an extremely fascinating bit of lab work, looking at the chemistry of these basic emotions.

In primary sadness there is the experience of parting and separation, loss, the feeling of being left out of attachments, and difficulties in communication. Communication is a very important facet of 'sadness,' and inhibition of genuine communication can be damaging. Apart from the loss of a loved one, shattered hopes, loss of job, and getting uprooted from patterns of comfortable living, as we witness in the context of recent natural disasters, are the many contexts for sadness. In secondary sadness, it is more complex with feelings of being hurt, grief—feelings of being damaged, wounded, ignored, unrecognized, rejected (Greenberg and Paivio 2003: 163). Basically, the distress centers on an irrevocable loss, and there is an emotional need for sympathy and understanding. Collapsing into tears and feeling hopeless is natural, but the most important therapeutic step is *acceptance*.

> The goal in mindfulness therapy is to help the patient relate to his emotional life, and all of his experience, in a different way. It is not an attempt to eliminate sadness, worry, or anxiety, but to help the patient see things in a different light when they do arise. Thoughts and feelings are not in our control, but come and go on their own (Bien 2006: 69).

1. In Greenberg's EFT awareness and acceptance is the starting point. The therapist "works with the client to help the client approach, tolerate and regulate, as well as accept their emotions" (Greenberg 2010: 22).
2. Emotional expression: The client must also be in live contact with their emotions, and thus develop effective exposure to previously avoided feelings. While arousal and tolerance of emotions in necessary, optimum emotional processing involves the integration of cognition and affect.
3. Emotion Regulation. When emotions such as sadness, fear, shame and powerlessness, overwhelm people, there is a need to help people regulate their emotions by getting them some 'distance' from them. Any attempt to regulate emotions by preventing themselves from feeling the disturbing emotions—withdrawing, avoiding, using distraction strategies, transforming emotions by psychosomatic complaints or seeking stimulus enjoyment to drown them—are all counterproductive. In Buddhist practice, loosening the personal identification and seeing sadness as an *impersonal* process that emerges, stays for a while and passes away is recommended.

In fact, at this point Greenberg integrates mindfulness practice into EFT. Important means of regulating emotion include regulating breathing and mindfulness—the non-judgmental observation and description of one's emotional states. Naming and labeling are techniques used in mindfulness practice. Basic emotion regulation skills include naming the emotion, describing the emotion in one's body, clarifying the event that evoked the emotion, and understanding one's interpretation of the situation and the actions prompted by the emotion (Greenberg 2008: 206).

4. Reflection on emotional experience at the level of deep experience is recommended.
5. Transformation of one emotion by another is the final method, quoting Spinoza, "an emotion cannot be restrained nor removed by another emotion unless by an opposed and stronger emotion" (Spinoza 1963: 195).

## Buddhist Pathways for Managing Negative Emotions

1. *The Method of Restraint* takes a preventive stand instead of damage control. The ability to 'step back' and make a choice is a mature achievement in emotion management. This is useful in the case of emotions such as anger and lust, where the motivational roots are important and one can be aware of emotional triggers without any reactivity. Restraint would be useful in trying to handle one's sadness in a thoughtful manner. But in the case of sadness, especially grief at the loss of a loved one, there is no choice; it just comes like an avalanche.
2. *The Method of Remedying.* The reference to Spinoza reminds one of the method of antidotes in remedying a negative state. The four divine states of loving kindness, compassion, altruistic joy and equanimity are crucial and presented as antidotes for sadness. Loving kindness first begins by directing it towards one self and then reaching others, from the lost one, and others in the family, and towards a more universal feeling with other beings. The ability to embrace all parts of oneself without guilt and self-hurt and the ability to connect with others helps one to break through feelings of separateness and egocentric concerns. While compassion and generosity may be practiced in our daily life, they also amount to a meditative state with positive therapeutic value. Equanimity balances love and compassion by bringing in balance and realism, as well as a sense of acceptance of the tragic as part and parcel of the nature of things.
3. *Transforming negative emotions* instead of demonizing them is a technique in which grief may be converted into patience, resilience, a sense of realism, forgiveness, courage and so on. This is what Carl Jung described as emotional alchemy, converting brass into gold. Venerable Nyanaponika observes that one should not throw away negative emotions, and he quotes from *The Little Locksmith*: "If you throw away a thing it is gone. Where you had something you have nothing. Your hands are empty, they have nothing to work on. Whereas almost all those things that you throw away, are capable of being worked over by a little magic into just the opposite of what they were" (Nyanaponika 1986a: 55).
4. *Liberation from an emotion by insight.* Here one can use the componential theory of emotions, where emotions are seen as constructions out of bodily sensations, feelings and thought patterns, and if you have a hard look at them gradually you see them emerging and passing away, and with a hard look they appear empty and evaporate. Here the notion of impermanence is applied to these "seemingly rock-like phenomena".

5. *Dedication Through Gratitude (Katannu Kataveti).* Solomon refers to the reflective and dedicatory qualities of grief, where you bring to your mind the good things by the person whom you have lost. The things you do on behalf of those whom you have lost, especially in the case of parents, are not considered as duties in the Kantian sense; they emerge in the context of reciprocity, what parents do for children and what children do for parents, especially in the context of aging followed by death. Gratitude, generosity practiced in the name of the lost one, and compassion work together and are woven into rituals in Buddhist practice in Thailand and Sri Lanka

6. *Living a good life* is considered as the best way of respecting those who have departed. A moral life with openness, candour and vibrancy brings trust and confidence in one's own life.

I have not given a narrative of my personal journey through life (de Silva 2008a, b: 82–98), but all these methods cited above have been integrated into my own journey through grief, crisis, sadness, distress, enabling me to come back strong, inspired, positive and with confidence and trust in my own self. Such a process of rejuvenation is possible for people in grief and crisis. This turning point took me to professional counselling, which became a mission in my life.

In addition to emotion-focused therapy, I have also been integrating recent work on cultivating emotional balance (CEB) into my research and writing (Wallace 2007; de Silva 2010). One's experience of sadness has to strike a balance between a 'deficit' and 'hyperactivity.' If a person displays the necessary energy by way of motivation, sees things clearly and handles issues of meaning at the cognitive level, feels without any deadness or passivity on the affective level, and maintains a good attentional level, there is no deficit. If a person gets agitated by grief due to the addition of anger, shame and fury, there is hyperactivity. If the way that the person handles his grief leads to more suffering and confusion, his response to grief is dysfunctional. This is a very brief summary of grief in the context of cultivating emotional balance.

## Buddhism and Depression: Anthropological Studies

Horowitz and Wakefield's study indicates that some anthropologists appear to deny the standing of depression as a universal category across cultures. The Sri Lankan anthropologist Gananath Obeysekera claims that the Sri Lankans view symptoms of hopelessness, meaninglessness and sorrow as a culturally conditioned philosophy of life and not an illness:

> How is the western diagnostic term "depression" expressed in a society whose predominant ideology of Buddhism states that life is suffering and sorrow, that the cause of sorrow is attachment or craving, that there is a way (generally through meditation) of understanding and overcoming sorrow (Obeyesekera 1985: 13).

Horowitz and Wakefield maintain that here Obeyesekera is clearly talking about normal sadness, and he does not in this context discuss cases of chronic depression, which might be described as a clinical disorder (2007: 197). Catherine Lutz's celebrated study of the Ifaluk culture contains similar observations on the genius of this culture in managing sadness through grief and loss. The term 'fago' in this culture covers the emotions of compassion, love and sadness: "Fago speaks of the sense that life is fragile, that connections to others are both precious and liable to severance through death and travel, that love may equal loss" (Lutz 1995: 235). While accepting the great value of this study, Horowitz and Wakefield comment:

> Lutz provides an excellent description of normal sadness among the Ifaluk. Her critique ought to focus on the overexpansive definition of depressive disorders in Western psychiatry, which might mistakenly classify these responses as dysfunctions (2007: 198).

As far as my analysis is concerned, independent of the question about the universality of depression as a clinical disorder, Lutz's groundbreaking anthropological study illuminates the power of cultural meaning systems to absorb what I call the lost art of sadness. The same may be true of Sri Lanka, though modernization and social changes have added new variables to the issues of suffering, sadness and depression.

In fact, the tradition of mindfulness-based cognitive therapy for depression developed by Segal et al. (2002) and Williams et al. (2007) is not cited in the Horowitz and Wakefield study. Using the mindfulness approach to therapy, which emerged on Asian soils and was transferred to the west—does it make any difference to managing depression? The approach of Segal and his colleagues differed from Aaron Beck's earlier approach to depression in not disputing and analyzing negative thoughts, but rather "holding thoughts and feelings in awareness rather than trying to change them" (Segal et al. 2002: 6). It is an innovative eight-session program, using the objective scientific study format for validation. Horowitz and Wakefield were looking at depression as a clinical disorder, especially depression relapses, focused on guilt, remorse and negative self-critical thinking, but Segal, Williams and Teasdale were attempting to restore mindfulness in routine life, as far as possible. While some, like Morgan (2005: 133), have used a technique which is more phenomenological and subjective, their focus is on clinical depression. Thus to explore our main theme, the restoration of the need to understand the logic of sadness, we need to go to mindfulness-based grief counseling (de Silva 2008a, b: 82–98; Kumar 2005).

There is no doubt that the Horowitz and Wakefield study is a groundbreaking contribution to the restoration of the loss of sadness. But a further interesting issue is the extent to which these studies of depression, both in the objective scientific tradition and also in the experiential tradition with a phenomenological import, throw new light on the medical category of depressive disorder. There is some attempt, like that of Zeig (2008: 31), not to reify 'depression' as a 'thing,' but to see it as a construction made of a number of components, and as a process. And this approach perhaps helps us to understand that depression is mishandled sadness, or sadness become pathological (Wolpert 1999).

Concluding these thoughts on the anthropological studies and mindfulness-based counselling, what could be said with some certainty is that the Horowitz and Wakefield study has clearly established the status of 'sadness' as what Paul Ekman described as a basic emotion, as well as its difference from depression as a clinical disorder. As Ekman says, understanding the logic of sadness and its different varieties helps us to understand the nature of clinical depression:

> If sadness dominates depression, we speak of retarded depression; if agony is more prominent, it is an agitated depression. People who are depressed not only feel helpless to change their lives, they feel hopeless. They do not believe it will ever get better. In addition to sadness and agony, guilt and shame are strongly felt, for depressed people feel they are worthless...anger directed inward or out, and fear are often manifest (Ekman 2003: 93).

## Boredom

Boredom has a profile of its own and if you understand boredom well, that is one dimension along which you may not merely manage sadness but find positive pathways to overcome it. As Cheshire Calhoun says, issues of value and meaning are important in understanding boredom, as value constraints play a crucial role in boredom (Calhoun 2011). Boredom may also be described as an attentional crisis.

## Boredom as an Attentional Crisis

> To realize that boredom does not come from the object of attention but rather from the quality of attention is truly a transforming insight. Frits Pearls, one of those who brought Gestalt therapy to America, said, "Boredom is lack of attention". Understanding this reality brings profound changes in our lives (Goldstein 1993: 80).

If you have an ability to be immensely interested in something that is exhilarating and beautiful in life, there is no room for the infiltration of boredom into your mind. Whatever the object, it is the subjective state of exhilaration that is within you that is important– it may be music, art, gardening, cooking or reading. One dimension along which one may manage sadness is to have an increasing enlargement and intensification of interest in life. There have to be values and goals that energize one's life, and a dear one that one has lost may be considered as a source of inspiration. In my personal journey through grief, I found these words of Tolstoy very inspiring: "Only people who are capable of loving strongly can suffer great sorrow, but this same necessity of loving serves to counteract their grief and heals them" (cited in Worden 2001: xi).

The boredom associated with sadness may be compared with another form of boredom, just to see its special nature. There is a kind of boredom which emerges out of the manic quality of life with all its "time-compression effect": increased stress at work, sleep deprivation, burn out and workaholism. Alan Wallace in developing the concept of cultivating emotional balance says:

> An attentional deficit is characterized by the inability to focus on a chosen object. The mind becomes withdrawn and disengaged even from its own internal processes. Attentional hyperactivity occurs when the mind is extensively aroused, resulting in compulsive distraction and fragmentation. And attention is dysfunctional when we focus on things in afflictive ways, not conducive to our own or others' well-being (Wallace 2007: 8).In contrast, people who are genuinely immersed in whatever they do, and motivated by intrinsic rewards enjoy the experience.

Whatever the type of boredom, Mihaly Csikszentmihalyi, who is an expert on the psychology of the 'flow' experience, says that those who enjoy life and work have curiosity and interest in life, persistence and low-self-centredness, and are attracted by intrinsic rewards (Csikszentmihalyi 1990). Boredom is a window onto the properties of time, and novel, creative and meaningful ways of spending time is the answer. To understand the boredom that comes with loss and grief, we need to see it in terms of an attentional crisis.

## Emotional Integrity & Spirituality

> Emotional integrity is essential to the good life, fully embracing our being for others as well as our need to live in accordance with our (and others') values (Solomon 2007: 268).

Following this trend of thought on emotional integrity, Solomon says that whatever is the nature of different spiritual traditions, the real valuable spiritual tradition integrates the whole discourse on the rhythms of our emotional life as a central concern and brings thought, reflection and wisdom to their fold. It is in the spirit of these reflections of Solomon that I have devoted a great part of my life looking at the rhythms of our emotional life within fold of the Buddhist culture, in which I have grown through crisis, anxiety, sadness, and passivity and emerged strong, confident and a with tremendous sense of contentment (de Silva 2008a, b). There was also catharsis, rejuvenation, insights and the expansion of gratitude flowering in the divine states of *metta* (loving kindness), *karuna* (compassion), *mudita* (altruistic joy) and equanimity and emotional balance (*upekkha*). As Martha Nussbaum says,

> …an education in common human weakness and vulnerability should be a profound part of the education of children. Children should learn to be tragic spectators and to understand with subtlety and responsiveness the predicament to which human life is prone. Through stories and drama, they should learn to decode the suffering of others, and this decoding should deliberately lead them into both lives both near and far, including the lives of distant humans and the lives of animals (Nussbaum 2003: 24).

The Story of *Kisa Gotami and the Mustard seed* is a kind of 'dramatalogical' model of Buddhist reflections on the theme of grief and death, often presented to children in Sunday school. Kisa Gotami was completely struck by the tragic when she lost her infant child, and she went all over the village to find some medicine to bring the child back to life. Having completely failed in this mission, she listened to a person who said the Buddha may be able to help her. Gladdened by this possibility, she met the Buddha when he was giving a sermon. The Buddha, excusing her for the disturbance, said that he could help her – but she must first bring a mustard seed from a family that has not heard of a death of anyone close to them or their relatives. She went through the whole village but could not find the kind of mustard seed the Buddha wanted. By the time she came back to the Buddha the insight was growing within her to look at her predicament with a sense of realism and equanimity. After listening to a sermon of the Buddha, she was well settled on the path to liberation. Though she could not bring the infant child back to life, there was a profound process of healing within her. She also became skillful in cultivating emotional balance. This is a beautiful story in grief counselling and recovering "The Lost Art of Sadness".

## Humour and Emotional Sensibility: The Tragic and the Comic

> Having gone through grief, let's lighten up and go to what seemed to be the opposite pole of the painful-to-pleasant spectrum of emotions, laughter… What emotion is it that is being expressed in Laughter? (Solomon 2007: 79).

It is striking to me that these remarks immediately followed Solomon's analysis of grief as an emotion. I was able to discuss his interest in laughter and humour at a symposium on emotions, as a tribute to Solomon held at the University of Melbourne (de Silva 2008a, b). This is a brief summary of the different facets of humour. A very profound analysis of humour has been made by one-time British philosopher and later Buddhist Monk Venerable Nanavira:

> When we laugh at a comedy or weep at a tragedy what we are really doing is busying ourselves with all the little crevices that have appeared in our familiar world in the course of the day, which if neglected, might become wider and deeper and eventually bring our world crushing down in ruins about us. Of course, we don't actually admit to ourselves that this is what we are doing (Nyanavira 1987: 62).

Søren Kierkegaard also saw the link between tragic and the comic and he focused on incongruence with his concept of irony. The Freudian theory linked humour to repressed facets of the unconscious.

"Laughter is first and foremost a bonding gesture," says Solomon, "and the emotion it expresses may be any combination of love, affection, comraderie, and solidarity", and he qualifies this by saying that there is a "problematic solidarity of racism, sexism, and shared prejudices" (Solomon 2007: 83). Solomon is critical of both the Freudian perspective and theories of incongruity and opts for what may be called the resonance theory. It is interesting to note that Solomon's theory of humour falls in line with what is described as the resonance theory of humour by Daniel Goleman. The resonance theory of laughter may be summarized in Goleman's words:

> Of all emotional signals, smiles are the most contagious: they have an almost irresistible power to make others smile in return. Smiles may be so potent because of the role they

played in evolution: smiles, laughter, scientist speculate, evolved as a nonverbal way to cement alliances and signify that an individual is relaxed and friendly rather than guarded or hostile (Goleman et al. 2003: 10).

## Concluding Thoughts

To have started with grief and sadness and ended up with laughter and humour is (perhaps) a pointer to the fact that life and death exist side by side. To reflect on grief in the context of death and loss, it may be said, as Matthieu Ricard observes, "Keeping death in mind is to enrich our life", and in this manner we grow, enrich and heal our lives. It is a spur to diligence and keeps us away from vain distractions (Ricard 2007: 253–254). Developing emotional skills is a pathway to happiness.

## References

Bien, Thomas. 2006. *Mindful therapy*. Boston: Wisdom Publishers.

Brodsky, Joseph. 1995. Listening to boredom: Extracts from, 'In praise of boredom'. Dartmouth College Commencement Address. *Harper's*, March 1995.

Burton, Robert. 1927 [1621]. In *An anatomy of melancholy*, ed. Paul Floyd Dell and Paul Joirdon. New York: Farrar and Reinhart.

Calhoun, Chesire. 2011. Living with boredom. *Sophia* 50(2011): 269–279.

Csikszentmihalyi, Mihaly. 1990. *Flow: The psychology of optimal experience*. New York: Harper-Perennial.

Darwin, Charles. 1998. *The expression of emotions in man and animals*. London: Harper Collins.

de Silva, Padmasiri. 2007a. *An introduction to Buddhist psychology*, 4th ed. London: Palgrave-Macmillan.

de Silva, Padmasiri. 2007b. *Explorers of inner space: The Buddha, Krishnamurthi and Kierkegaard*. Ratmalana: Sarvodaya Vishvalekha.

de Silva, Padmasiri. 2008a. *Introduction to mindfulness-based counselling: The magic of the ordinary & elegance of small things*. Ratmalana: Vishvalekha-Sarvodaya Publishers.

de Silva, Padmasiri. 2008b. Theories of humour: A Buddhist perspective. *Conference on Asian and Comparative Philosophy, A Symposium on Emotions*. Tribute to Robert C Solomon. University of Melbourne, Melbourne. Unpublished paper.

de Silva, Padmasiri. 2010. Mental balance and four dimensions of well-being: A Buddhist perspective. In *Global Recovery: A Buddhist Perspective*, UNDV Conference Proceedings. Published by Mahachulalongkorn Rajamahavidyalaya, Bangkok.

de Silva, Padmasiri. 2011. Mindfulness-based emotion focused therapy. *Mahidol University conference on the interface between Buddhism and science*. Nakhon Pathom: Mahidol (unpublished paper).

de Spinoza, Benedictus. 1963 [1677]. In *Ethics*, ed. James Gutman. New York: Hafner.

Drury, M.O.C. 1973. *Danger of words*. London: Routledge and Kegan Paul.

Ekman, Paul. 2003. *Emotions revealed*. London: Weidenfeld & Nicolson.

Fenichel, Otto. 1951. On the psychology of boredom. In *Organization and pathology of thought*, ed. D. Rapaport, 349–361. New York: Columbia University Press.

Freud, Sigmund. 1957 [1917]. Mourning and melancholia. In *Collected papers*, ed. E. Jones, vol. IV, 152–70, authorized translation under the supervision of Joan Rivere. London: Hogarth Press.

Freud, Sigmund, and Joseph Breuer. 1895. Studies in hysteria. In *The complete psychological works of Sigmund Freud*, vol. 2. London: Hogarth Press.

Fromm, Erich. 1994. *The art of listening*. London: Constable.

Goldstein, Joseph. 1993. *Insight meditation: The practice of freedom*. Boston: Shambala Publishers.

Goleman, Daniel, et al. 2003. *Primal leadership*. Cambridge: Harvard Business School Press.

Greenberg, Leslie. 2008. *Emotion-focused therapy*. Washington, DC: American Psychological Association.

Greenberg, Leslie. 2010. *Emotion focused therapy*, Workshop Handbook. Sydney: IEFT.

Greenberg, Leslie, and Sandra C. Paivio. 2003. *Working with emotions in psychotherapy*. New York: Guilford Press.

Harris, Russel. 2006. Embracing your demons: An overview of acceptance and commitment therapy. *Psychotherapy in Australia* 12: 2–8.

Hayes, C.Stephen, Krik D. Strosahl, and G. Wilson Kelly. 1999. *Acceptance and commitment therapy*. New York: Guilford Press.

Horowitz, Allan V., and Jerome Wakefield. 2007. *The loss of sadness*. Oxford: Oxford University Press.

Ignatieff, Michael. 1987. Paradigm lost. *Times Literary Supplement*, 4 Sept 1987, 939–940.

Kornfield, Jack. 2001. Difficulties and hindrances. In *Seeking the heart of wisdom*, ed. Joseph Goldstein and Jack Kornfield, 38–56. Boston: Shambala.

Kumar, Samit. 2005. *Grieving mindfully*. Oakland: New Harbinger Publications.

Lutz, Catherine. 1995. Need, nurturance and the emotions in a Pacific atoll. In *Emotions in Asian thought*, ed. Joel Marks and Roger T. Ames, 235–252. Albany: State University of New York Press.

McCracken, Janet. 2005. Falsely, sanely, shallowly: Reflections on the special character of grief. *International Journal of Applied Philosophy* 19: 139–156.

Morgan, Stephanie P. 2005. Depression: Turning toward life. In *Mindfulness and psychotherapy*, ed. Christopher K. Germer, Ronald R. Siegel, and Paul R. Fulton, 130–151. New York: Guilford Press.

Nussbaum, Martha. 2003. Compassion and terror. *Daedalus* 132(1): 10–26.

Nyanaponika, Thera. 1973. *The heart of Buddhist meditation*. Samual New York: Wiser.

Nyanaponika, Thera. 1986a. *The power of mindfulness*. Kandy: Buddhist Publication Society.

Nyanaponika, Thera. 1986b. *Contemplation of feelings*. Kandy: Buddhist Publication Society.

Nyanavira, Thero. 1987. *The tragic, the comic and the personal*. Kandy: Buddhist Publication Society.

Obeyesekera, Gananath. 1985. Depression, Buddhism and the work of culture in Sri Lanka. In *Culture and depression: Studies in the anthropology and cross-cultural psychiatry of affect and disorder*, ed. Arthur Kleinman and Byron Good, 134–152. Berkeley: University of California Press.

Radden, Jennifer. 2000. Love and loss in Freud's 'Mourning and melancholia': A rereading. In *The analytic Freud: Philosophy and psychoanalysis*, ed. Michael P. Levine, 211–230. London/New York: Routledge.

Ricard, Matthieu. 2007. *Happiness: A guide to developing life's most important skills*. London: Atlantic Books.

Segal, Zindel V.J., Mark G. Williams, and John D. Teasdale. 2002. *Mindfulness-based therapy for depression: A new approach to preventing relapse*. New York/London: Guilford Press.

Solomon, Robert C. 2004. *In defense of sentimentality*. New York: Oxford University Press.

Solomon, Robert C. 2007. *True to our feelings: What our emotions are really telling us*. New York: Oxford University Press.

Wallace, Alan B. 2007. *Contemplative science*. New York: Columbia University Press.

William, Mark, John Teasdale, Zindel Segal, and Jon Kabat-Zinn. 2007. *The mindful way through depression*. New York: Guilford Press.

Wolpert, Lewis. 1999. *Malignant sadness: The anatomy of depression*. London: Faber and Faber.

Worden, J.William. 2001. *Grief counselling and therapy*. Dordrecht: Springer.

Yalom, Irwin. 1980. *Existential psychotherapy*. New York: Basic Books.

Zeig, Jeffrey K. 2008. Depression: A phenomenological approach to assessment and treatment. *Psychotherapy in Australia* 14: 28–35.

# Chapter 14
# Solomonic Justice, Rights, and Truth and Reconciliation Commissions: A Confucian Meditation*

Henry Rosemont Jr.

**Abstract** This chapter focuses first, on the differing and usually conflicting goals of truth and reconciliation commissions; second, how these goals are best achieved by employing the conceptual apparatus of religion; and third, how a Confucian perspective can place the religious dimensions of the work of reconciliation in a secular framework that does not require grounding in any theological beliefs.

## Introduction

Beginning with South Africa after the fall of apartheid, then to East Timor, Argentina, Rwanda, Peru, Sierra Leone and now moving to Kosovo, Bosnia and Herzegovina and Chile again, Truth and Reconciliation Commissions came into being as a way to begin healing the racial, ethnic, and religious strife that have convulsed a number of nation-states, or nations in the making. None of them have been altogether successful thus far, and yet clearly there will be a need for more such commissions in many other countries and areas now or in the near future: Israel/Palestine, Iraq, Afghanistan, Kashmir, Guatemala, El Salvador, Haiti, Sri Lanka, Congo, Northern Ireland, Turkey, and more.[1]

---

[1] Far and away the most well known of these is the first, and people interested in the subject should familiarize themselves with the *Truth and Reconciliation Commission of South Africa Report,* by the Truth and Reconciliation Commission of South Africa and Desmond Tutu (1999). Some general works that bear on reconciliation commissions are Rotberg and Thompson (2000), and Bar-siman-Tov (2007).

H. Rosemont Jr. (✉)
Brown University, Providence, RI, USA
e-mail: Henry_Rosemont_Jr@brown.edu

K. Higgins and D. Sherman (eds.), *Passion, Death, and Spirituality,*
Sophia Studies in Cross-cultural Philosophy of Traditions and Cultures 1,
DOI 10.1007/978-94-007-4650-3_14, © Springer Science+Business Media Dordrecht 2012

Truth and Reconciliation Commissions, however, are not just needed where widespread violence and slaughter have been wrought by a particular group and/or deposed government, as, e.g., in Darfur today. Other countries whose governments have engaged in illegal and/or immoral activities with highly adverse consequences for many innocent people may well also need such commissions. China, for example, will 1 day profit from the employment of a commission to investigate the events of June 4th, 1989, especially in Beijing.

Similarly, it is doubtful that the United States will regain the stature in the world it formerly enjoyed until such a commission investigates the manifold misdeeds of the Bush administration, from the invasion of Iraq to widespread torture, and other possible crimes in violation of the U.S. Constitution, the Geneva Conventions, or Nuremburg Protocols.

Truth and reconciliation commissions, however, should not be seen as all of a piece, because as presently constituted, one or another of the goals of such commissions must be seen as basic; correctly so, because the twin goals are not fully compatible with each other. Establishing the truth of what deeds were done, and by whom, on the one hand, and effecting reconciliation between parties to the conflict(s) on the other, are difficult for any single commission to accomplish. Both efforts seek justice, but the concept must be defined differently for the two goals. The Nuremburg and Tokyo War Crimes Trials were just that: trials. The victors worked mightily to establish the truth of the evils perpetrated by the vanquished, but the goal was to convict the accused, grounded philosophically in the concept of human beings as fundamentally individuals, individuals responsible for their actions.

For example, when people demand truth and reconciliation commissions for Rwandan Hutus or the Cambodian Khmer Rouge, they usually have something like Nuremburg in mind; a not unreasonable assumption given the magnitude of the horrors visited on the victims. Every person of good will must want the perpetrators "brought to justice." But it will be almost solely a retributive justice that is obtained, and it will be seen more or less as vengeance no matter how fair the proceedings. And vengeance seldom generates reconciliation. The latter requires a grounding concept of persons not as fundamentally individuals, but as interrelated co-members of a community.

To illustrate this differing concept of what it is to be a human being I will focus on the classical Confucians, attempting to show that their views have a strong claim on our attention today, and perhaps our allegiance as well. I will further attempt to sharpen the contrast between the two conceptions of personhood by showing the difference between a Truth Commission, which basically functions with a cluster of legal concepts, and a Reconciliation Commission, which requires a cluster of concepts drawn from religion – with the Confucians helping us to also appreciate a different concept of what it is to be religious.

To begin, unlike the civil courts – which seek justice *simpliciter*, and unlike criminal courts – which seek retributive justice of one sort or another – reconciliation commissions have as their major task the healing of deep fraternal wounds within their jurisdiction, and hence their aim must be to achieve *restorative* justice, about which I will say more below. To appreciate fully the Confucian orientation, however, it is necessary to note that the concept of justice with which it is most compatible is *not* the legal one, civil or criminal, nor the more socially-oriented but almost purely rational one made famous by John Rawls in his *A Theory of Justice;* rather the Confucian orientation is closest to the more experientially grounded view of the late Robert Solomon in his *A Passion for Justice,* the title of which makes clear that a true sense of justice involves the heart no less than the head. According to him, "[a] proper conception of justice requires a revised conception of one's self" (Solomon 1990: 70; see also Rawls 1971).[2]

Unfortunately, at present almost all truth commissions incline toward some combination of the civil and criminal court systems, wherein individuals (which includes corporations in the U.S.) are the focal point, and the proceedings are basically adversarial. Such procedures may be important at times for achieving legal justice – usually retributive – but are counterproductive for achieving restorative justice. After critiquing the standard legal models, central to Truth Commissions and grounded in the concept of the free, autonomous individual, the early Confucian alternative, grounded in the concept of responsible human relationality, will be briefly sketched. With some modifications, this Confucian alternative might well serve as a more appropriate theoretical basis for commissions established largely to achieve reconciliation among and between differing groups in a large community or state. In the course of the arguments, a critique of civil and political ("first generation") rights will be proffered, as they stand in the way of achieving social, economic and cultural ("second generation") rights as championed in the United Nations Universal Declaration of Human Rights.[3]

## Human Rights and the Abstract Individual

The Confucian concept I wish to advance has a number of similarities with the way human beings have been viewed in the three Abrahamic religious traditions, wherein each person is defined as standing in a basic set of relations to deity; and because deity created all of us, we stand in fundamental relations with one another – we are all "God's children." But these Abrahamic views, important as they are, cannot conceptually ground reconciliation efforts today, both because deity is construed somewhat differently by Jews, Christians and Muslims – not to mention Hindus, Buddhists, and the adherents of other faith traditions – and also because tens of millions

---

[2] Here is Solomon on Rawls: "...it would take a particularly uncritical reader to miss the overwhelmingly rationalistic frame of Rawls's basic theory, as opposed to the cosmetic plaster that he adds between the structural struts to give his deductive theory some sense of humanity" (Solomon 1990: 301, n.3).

[3] The U.N. Declaration has been published in a variety of places, including The United Nations and Human Rights 1945–1995 (United Nations 1995). The Universal Declaration is Document 8.

of people do not accept the concept of deity at all.[4] At the same time, I do believe that a number of concepts that we have tended to associate with spiritual traditions will need to be at the heart of effective reconciliation efforts.[5]

The view I will advance defines human beings most fundamentally as standing in sets of relations, not with deity, but with other human beings living and dead, a view first articulated in the texts of classical Confucianism, wherein the absence of the concept of a creator deity in no way attenuates, in my opinion, the moral, political insights to be found in them, and as I will argue later, are as genuinely spiritual as the sacred and classical texts of any other religious and philosophical heritage (see Rosemont and Ames 2003a, b).

But before elaborating the Confucian vision I must first sketch briefly the view I want to contrast it with, as it is found in most contemporary legal, economic, political and moral thinking, especially in human rights discourse, namely, that human beings are basically abstract individuals, individuals who above all are free and autonomous, and in addition, are also defined as rational and self-interested.

John Locke basically proffered this definition to argue for a number of universal human rights (throughout Locke 1980, esp. ch. 8), which he employed as a conceptual check on the divine right of kings as articulated by defenders of monarchical power. Much good has come from this individualistic view of persons, and the many gains in human dignity it has brought about are to be celebrated.

There is a dark side to this view, however, which is coming increasingly to the fore as the growing maldistribution of wealth both within and between nations becomes starker, as transnational corporations become less accountable to any political or legal institutions in their search for ever greater profits, and as the policies and actions of the United States, adamant in pressing this unfettered capitalism on the rest of the world, are doing more to exacerbate than alleviate the gross inequalities that contribute so much to the violence in so much of the contemporary world. This dark side of the ethics of the abstract individual is that when freedom is weighted far more heavily than social justice, the political, legal and moral instruments employed in defending and enhancing that freedom virtually insure that social justice will *not* be achieved.

To see how and why this is so, consider the U.S. Bill of Rights, enshrining many of Locke's views as amended by Thomas Jefferson and focusing on freedom: of speech, of association, of worship, and to freely own and freely dispose of property

---

[4] A plethora of books have appeared in just the last three years excoriating any and all beliefs in God. Among the more noteworthy are Harris (2004), Dawkins (2006), Stenger (2007), and Hitchens (2007). I have argued that all such efforts to exorcise the religious ghost from the human machine are fundamentally misguided (Rosemont 2001).

[5] All of the authors mentioned in the last note – and many others – seem to equate religion with fundamentalist readings of sacred texts, especially the New Testament and Quran. In this sense, Confucianism is clearly not a religion; it contains no theology, no concept of a creator god, has no beliefs that contradict any of the laws of physics, geology or biology. But I believe it is a deeply spiritual way of life, and hence of particular value in capturing the religious dimensions needed for the work of reconciliation commissions to be effective, and enduring.

legally acquired. (In law, corporations are also individuals.) Clearly these civil and political rights – "first generation" rights – are linked to the individualistic view of persons: if I am essentially free, and rational, self-interested and autonomous, then certainly no one else, especially a government, should interfere with my speaking my mind, worshipping as I choose, or associating with whomever I wish, as I pursue the projects I have chosen for myself.

It must be noted however, that these civil and political rights are passive, in that they are solely focused on freedom *from*, which can be seen from the fact that I can fully respect all of your civil and political rights simply by ignoring you; of course you have a right to speak, but not to have me listen.

To appreciate the significance of this passivity, or "negative liberty" as Isaiah Berlin defended it (Berlin 1992), we must look to the United Nations Universal Declaration of Human Rights, which in addition to the civil and political, also lists a number of social and cultural rights, such as the right to a job, education, health care, decent housing, and much more (Articles 22–27; see Document 8, 154, n. 3). These "second generation" rights are active rather than passive, concerned as much with freedom *to* as freedom *from*. They are active in the sense that there are certain things I must do if you are to secure the benefits of these rights.

By simply listing all rights *seriatim* the Universal Declaration implies that they are compatible with each other,[6] but they are not, for if I acknowledge your rights claims to housing, health care, a job, and so on, then I must actively help you obtain them so that you may pursue your own projects. But then I would no longer be fully free to self-interestedly pursue *my* own projects, and consequently I am strongly inclined to deny that you have legitimate social, economic and cultural rights at all. That I, too, could secure the material benefits accompanying second generation rights is no counter to this argument if I believe I can secure these material benefits on my own, or in some freely chosen contractual form in conjunction with a few others. Nor can it be replied that I may freely choose to assist you on my own, for this would be an act of charity, not an acknowledgement of your right to these goods.

Unlike most other democratic nations, the US defines "persons" in such a way that the first-generation civil and political rights enumerated in the Bill of Rights can be used to thwart democracy and hinder the achievement of social justice. "Person" is officially defined in the U.S.

> ... to include any individual, branch, partnership, associated group, association, estate, trust, corporation or other organization (whether or not organized under the laws of any State), or any government entity (U.S. Department of Commerce 1996: 12; Chomsky 2000: 117).

---

[6] Many people of good will have insisted on the inseparability of all the rights enumerated in the UN Declaration. See for example, Twiss (1998). I endorse this view politically, but cannot do so conceptually or logically; the inconsistency I raise here I have also raised elsewhere, and it has never been responded to in any way to the best of my knowledge. See also Rosemont "Human Rights: A Bill of Worries," in the *Confucianism and Human Rights* volume cited just above (Rosemont 1998). It is highly noteworthy that the Chinese Ambassador to the United Nations serving on the committee to draw up the Declaration was Carsun Chang, a noted scholar of Mencius; Articles 22–27 are in significant measure due to him.

Such "persons" pay lobbyists very large sums of money to influence legislation that affects them, and they can give the commercial media large sums of money – through giving or withholding advertising dollars – to "spin" the legislation so that it misleadingly appears to be to everyone's benefit, from giving away public lands and resources to lumber and other extraction corporations, to subsidizing the oil companies, defense contractors and other major capitalist enterprises, to giving huge tax cuts to the already wealthiest 1% of Americans.[7]

Consequently, if I am personally well off, and/or hold a managerial position in a large corporation, I will be strongly disinclined to see second generation rights as truly rights, for I will surely be less "free" and not as well off if they were. Rather I will want to elect officials who will see second generation social, economic and cultural rights not as rights but as "hopes" or "aspirations" as the U.S. Senate has done when it consistently refuses to ratify the U.N. International Covenant on Social, Economic and Cultural Rights (United Nations 1966) (as all other developed countries have done).[8] Former US Ambassador to the UN Jeanne Kirkpatrick was more explicit, referring to social, economic and cultural rights as a "letter to Santa Claus," while her successor Morris Abrams described the International Covenant as "little more than an empty vessel into which vague hopes and inchoate expectations can be poured" (see Chomsky 2000: 113).

Thus, without diminishing the great legal, political and moral work that civil and political rights have done worldwide to curb the oppression of citizens by authoritarian governments, and with admiration for the national and international NGOs that police their abuse,[9] it must nevertheless be emphasized that when taken to the personal and corporate levels, respect for first generation rights does not cost very much, requires very little effort, is now a formidable bulwark protecting the rich and the powerful, and has thus become a hindrance to the implementation of social, economic and cultural rights, and of attendant social justice both nationally and internationally.

But only if human beings are defined as most fundamentally free, rational, self-interested and autonomous individuals is it possible to feel morally justified in doing nothing with respect to alleviating the unemployment, inadequate housing, lack of health care, poverty, disease and much else that make for wretched lives on the part of far too many of our fellow citizens (i.e., the miseries second-generation rights are intended to address), a moral stance taken by not a few U.S. governments, and virtually every national and transnational capitalist corporation – which, again, are legally construed as individuals with regard to first generation rights.

This, then, all too sketchily, is the dark side conceptually of viewing human beings most basically as individuals – especially in the moral arena, but also in the

---

[7] Figures compiled form the *New York Times*, April 5, 2006: C4.

[8] *Human Rights: International Instruments*. United Nations Press (United Nations 2002: 10).

[9] Especially, but not confined to, exemplary groups like Human Rights Watch, Amnesty International, Witness for Peace, School of the Americas Watch, and the American Friends Service Committee, among others.

legal – and valuing individual freedom above all else: we too easily lose sight of our sociality, our obligations to others, our common humanity; liberty is purchased at the expense of social justice. In such an intellectual climate, reinforced by international legal and other institutions dominated by the U.S., there is little reason to hope that a more equitable distribution of the world's goods will ever take place, or attendant racial, religious or ethnic violence will diminish – or that reconciliation efforts will be successful.

Now it might seem that by challenging the concept of individual freedom I am at least implicitly championing a collectivism of some sort, Stalinist or Fascist. But individualism and collectivism do not exhaust our social and political possibilities any more than selfishness and altruism exhaust our moral possibilities. These Manichean splits are modern Western conceits, and basically serve as rhetorical support for maintaining the individualistic status quo in some parts of the world, and the collectivistic in others. If all challenges to individuals making individual choices in their own self-interest can be made to appear as subtle endorsements for the gulags, killing fields and labor re-education camps, then obviously we must give three cheers for individualism, drowning out all dissent. But the status quo in the United States is clearly unjust, and to the extent the status quo is defended by appeals to individualism, to just that extent do we need a broader view of what it is to be a human being.

One candidate for such a view, suitably modified for the contemporary world, is that of the classical Confucians, whose texts provide significant conceptual resources for forging new pathways to social justice and to reconciliation.

## Confucian Role Ethics

The texts gathered under the heading of "classical Confucianism" are by no means in full agreement on all points, and there are several tensions within each text itself; they nevertheless present an overall coherent view of the good life for human beings. This life is an altogether social one, and central to understanding it is to see that Confucian sociality has aesthetic, moral, and spiritual no less than political and economic dimensions, all of which are to be integrated.

None of the early texts address the question of the meaning *of* life, but they do put forward a vision of being human, and a discipline in which everyone can find meaning *in* life.[10] This meaning will become increasingly apparent to us as we pursue our ultimate goal, namely, developing ourselves most fully as human beings to become *junzi,* "exemplary persons," or, at the pinnacle of development, *sheng,* or sages. And for Confucians we can only do this through our interactions with other human beings. Treading this human path (*ren dao*) must ultimately be understood

---

[10] This distinction was first made, I believe, in Baier (1966).

as basically a religious quest, even though the canon speaks not of God, nor of creation, salvation, an immortal soul, or a transcendental realm of being; and no prophecies will be found in its pages either. It is nevertheless a truly religious path, yet at the same time a humanistically oriented one; for Confucius, we are irreducibly social, as he makes clear in the *Analects*: "I cannot run with the birds and beasts. Am I not one among the people of their world? If not them, with whom can I associate?" (Rosemont and Ames 1999: §18/6, 212).

Thus the Confucian self is not a free, autonomous individual, but is to be seen relationally: I am a son, husband, father, grandfather, teacher, student, friend, colleague, neighbor, and more. I live rather than "play" these roles, and when all of them have been specified, and their interrelationships made manifest, then I have been fairly thoroughly individuated, but with very little left over with which to piece together an autonomous individual self, free to conclude mutually advantageous contracts with other rational individuals.

While this view may initially seem strange, it is actually straightforward: in order to *be* a friend, neighbor, or lover, for example, I must *have* a friend, neighbor, or lover. Other persons are not merely accidental or incidental to my goal of fully developing as a human being, they are essential to it; indeed they confer unique personhood on me, for to the extent that I define myself as a teacher, students are necessary to my life, not incidental to it. Note in this regard also, that, again, while Confucianism should be seen as fundamentally religious, there are no solitary monks or nuns, anchorites or anchoresses, or hermits to be found in the tradition.

It is thus more accurate to speak of the moral dimensions of early Confucianism than as itself a moral theory, for it is not fundamentally a *theory* – akin to the theories, say, of Kant, Bentham and Mill, or Aristotle; rather is it best described as a *role ethics*.[11]

Our first and most basic role, one that significantly defines us in part throughout our lives, is as children; familial reverence (*xiao*) is one of the highest excellences in Confucianism (Rosemont and Ames 1999). From our beginning roles as children – and as siblings, playmates, and pupils – we mature to become parents ourselves, and assume many other roles and responsibilities as well, all of which are reciprocal relationships, best generalized as holding between *benefactors* and *beneficiaries*.[12] Each of us moves regularly from benefactor to beneficiary and back again, depending

---

[11] Roger Ames and I have begun to elaborate this concept, and contrast it with the moral theories of Western philosophy, in the "Introduction" to our new collaborative work, Rosemont and Ames (2009). We have dedicated the book to the memory of Bob Solomon, our cherished friend as well as highly respected philosopher.

[12] Keeping "superiors" and "inferiors" for *shang* and *xia* virtually guarantees that Western thinkers will take Confucianism no more seriously in the future than they have tended to take it in the past; my view is that a reconstructed Confucian vision is needed today, and that my translation is faithful to the spirit, if not the letter of the classical texts, which is why I have been using these new terms in my papers over the past 20 years. To eschew "superiors" and "Inferiors" for shang and *xia*, should not at all suggest that a great many Chinese of the past – and even some of the present – have not interpreted the terms in that way, especially with regard to women.

on the other(s) with whom we are interacting, when, and under what conditions. When young, I was largely beneficiary of my parents; when they were aged and infirm, I became their benefactor, and the converse holds for my children. I am benefactor to my friend when she needs my help, beneficiary when I need hers. I am a student of my teachers, teacher of my students, colleague of my colleagues.

Twenty-three centuries and half a world distant from these writings are those of Bob Solomon, but they are in many respects very similar in thrust, scope, and sentiment. He says, for example.

> We are not selfish creatures, and this is not because we are remarkably well-bred or well-behaved. It is because selfishness is, for most people, a rare exception in a life that is organized according to the implicit principle that one must fit into one's society and take as one's interests not just the limited benefits to a self narrowly defined but the well-being of those one lives with as well (Solomon 1990: 85).[13]

Taken together, the manifold roles we live as Confucians define us as persons, and constitute who we are. And the ways in which we meet the obligations attendant on these relational roles, and the ways others meet similar obligations toward us, are both the ways whereby we achieve dignity, satisfaction, and meaning in life.

With its emphasis on familial reverence it should be clear that at the heart of Confucian society is indeed the family, the locus of where, how, and why we develop into full human beings. A central government is also important to the good society, because there are necessary ingredients of human flourishing – especially economic – which the family (and local community) cannot secure on their own. The early Confucians saw the state not as in any way in opposition to the family, but rather saw both as complementary; stated in contemporary democratic terms, if we wish to live in a state that insists I meet my fatherly responsibilities, it should insure that I have the wherewithal – i.e., an education, job, etc. – to do so. Similarly, this state must assume responsibility for the well-being of those who have no family networks for support.

As an aside, we may note that if the goal of human life is to develop one's humanity to the utmost, then we have a clear criterion for measuring the worth and quality of our interactions with others in the groups (family, clan, village, school, state) to which each of us belongs; we are not merely to accept them as unalterable givens. Rather we must consistently ask to what extent these groups and interactions conduce to everyone's efforts to realize (make real) their potential. That is to say, while deference and loyalty had to be learned and practiced, remonstrance was obligatory when things were not going well. As the Master said, "To see what it is appropriate to do, and not do it, is cowardice" (Rosemont and Ames 1999: §2/24, 81).

The ideal Confucian society is thus basically communally oriented, with customs, tradition, rituals, ceremonies and manners serving as the binding force of and between our many relationships to one another.

---

[13] Solomon retains the concept of the individual in a way that I believe the Confucians would not, but in my opinion the similarities between his socially embedded persons and Confucian role-bearing persons far outweigh their differences.

This, then, is in woefully brief compass, Confucian humanism in action: interacting with others as benefactors and beneficiaries in an intergenerational context. Confucius himself was absolutely clear on this point, for when a disciple asked him what he would most like to do, he said:

> I would like to bring peace and contentment to the aged, share relationships of trust and confidence with friends, and love and protect the young (Rosemont and Ames 1999: 5/26, 102).

## The Confucian Perspective on Human Rights

Much more, of course, needs to be said about the early Confucian view of what it is to be a human being, but I believe much more *can* be said. The concept of the family can be retained, for example, while making women equals to men, and it can be enhanced by allowing two (or more) nurturers of the same sex to be responsible for child-rearing and care of the elderly – both with state help. Neither sexism nor homophobia is logically implied by the Confucian familial communitarianism or its larger philosophical and religious system.

It is clear that such role-bearing persons will take second generation social, economic and cultural rights very seriously, while necessarily remaining sensitive to the civil and political. If you and I can only flourish as we help each other realize our full humanity as benefactors and beneficiaries, why would I want to silence you, not let you choose your other friends, or follow whichever faith tradition inspires you? That is to say, with role-bearing persons as our philosophical foundation, moving from second to first generation rights is conceptually and attitudinally straightforward.

But the converse does not hold. It requires a major cognitive (and affective) shift to move from respecting civil and political rights passively to actively helping others obtain the benefits attendant on respecting social, economic and cultural rights. And the history of the U.S. provides little grounds for expecting the shift to take place: It is now more than 220 years since civil and political rights became the law of the land, yet over 20% of American children are growing up in families whose income is below the poverty line, three million people are estimated as being homeless, and over two million are in prison. Forty-eight million have no health care, Social Security is being threatened, and private pension plans are being unilaterally abolished while at the same time the wealthiest 400 Americans control more wealth than the lowest 90%. These 400, along with mere multi-millionaires, have also been given substantial tax cuts beginning in 2001. Thus far those cuts have already given roughly $93,500 to every millionaire (about $215 to middle income folk, and of course nothing at all to those at the bottom of the economic ladder). And to protect and increase that wealth, the government now spends more on its military than the defense budgets of all other nations *combined.*

## Reconciliation and Confucian Religiosity

With these two differing views of what it is to be a human being in mind, along with their differing moral and political implications, let me turn now – again, all too briefly – to truth commissions and reconciliation efforts – with their religious implications as well.

Justice must surely be served before reconciliation can take place in a number of cases, but if it is retributive or criminal justice that is basically sought the purely prosecutorial task should be entrusted to the International Criminal Court, not handled intrastate, in order to insure that the proceedings will not be tainted by charges of partisanship and/or corruption. On the other hand, national reconciliation can be effected by a national truth commission *if* reconciliation is kept as the paramount goal of the commission because perpetrators, survivors, and relatives of the victims must participate as actively in the proceedings as the commissioners, whereas with non-restorative justice-seeking truth commissions only the commissioners themselves need be active; perpetrators, victims, and survivors – along with their families – can be passive participants in the proceedings.

If seeking true *reconciliation*, perpetrators must not only be persuaded to tell the truth about the acts they committed against the victims, but if clearly wrong, the perpetrators must also come to acknowledge that those acts were wrong. (And "wrong" here is not a hopelessly relative term of art; if it was – if there was not general agreement *within* a country that terrible things were done to some people by other people over an extended period of time there would be no internal call for the establishment of a truth and reconciliation commission). Moreover, no country, nor any religion, could ever countenance an *external* commission if reconciliation was the primary goal, rather than simply the cessation of hostilities.

Admissions of culpability must thus be made in the old-fashioned religious way rather than in contemporary legal terms, wherein "I did it" is sufficient. Legally, no remorse need be shown or apologies proffered. When a truth commission begins to function like a criminal court in seeking justice, even the "I did it" is unnecessary, for we all have a right – or should have the right – to remain silent: In the presence of our accusers, we may be altogether passive, according to the law in most modern nations.

Following the act of *confession* – telling the truth and acknowledging that what one did was wrong – comes an equally proactive act of *repentance* – again, in the old-fashioned religious sense of the term – a public commitment never to act in that way again, which must be followed in turn by yet another positive act originally religious in nature, of *atonement*: materially and in other ways endeavoring to repair the damage caused by the repentant. These attitudes and actions are far more productive for reconciliation, it seems to me, than attitudes or findings of *guilt*, or actions of a non-rehabilitative kind in the form of *punishment*.

To appreciate why this is so, we must keep in mind that reconciliation requires (at least) two groups to come together, and consequently victims and their families must also participate actively, and at times heroically, in the efforts of a truth commission dedicated primarily to reconciliation rather than simply retributive justice.

This is no more than to say what is obvious, that acts of *forgiveness* no less than confession, repentance and atonement are necessary for reconciliation. The survivors and families of the victims must come to see the offenders as other role-bearing human beings, not merely as individuals to be punished retributively. They must struggle to rid themselves of any desire for revenge; and they must be open to seeing themselves in the future as being possible benefactors and/or beneficiaries in relationship with the offenders.

That is to say, a truth commission seeking only legal justice need not require perpetrators to be active in the proceedings at all, and the victims can remain passive onlookers except to describe what was done to them, and by whom. The greater the threat of severe punishment (retribution) the less likely are perpetrators to tell the truth about their deeds, and/or the more likely they will attempt to justify them in some way ("Ends justify means;" "I was only following orders," etc.). And faced with such behavior, it is little wonder that most victims will be loath to engage in acts of forgiveness. In such circumstances it would be almost a miracle if reconciliation accompanied or followed justice.

But to the extent the Truth and Reconciliation Commission is successful in getting perpetrators to confess – in the old sense – repent, and want to atone, they will, all in all, be seeking the perpetrators' *redemption.* But merely going to jail after conviction of crimes is not redemptive in and of itself for the convict, and will almost never be restorative for the victims and their families if they are only passive observers of the proceedings. But if the Commission does its work well, the victims and their families, by their acts of forgiveness, become *redeemers* for the perpetrators, renewing the significance of their own lives as well as aiding the perpetrators to forge new ones.

Here we may learn a Confucian lesson from China's past, in the form of the duties of the *fumuguan,* the county magistrate. While of course he had to uphold the law, and uphold the penal code, nevertheless in many of his functions he served much more as *arbiter* than as *judge* or *adjudicator,* his main task being to resolve a dispute between clans, families or other neighboring groups in conflict with each other. Truth and Reconciliation Commissioners would be wise, in my opinion, to model themselves on the Confucian magistrates in this way.

Now I hope it is becoming clear that there is a parallel between free, autonomous individuals demanding legal justice from a truth commission when crimes have been committed, on the one hand, and role-bearing persons seeking reconciliation from a truth commission when anti-human behavior has broken the social bonds within or between ethnic, religious or racial communities and families on the other. Certainly free individuals can and do reconcile and role-bearing persons can and do demand legal justice, both rightfully so. But just as second generation human rights encompass first generation rights much more naturally than the other way around, so too, I believe, is the restorative justice attendant on reconciliation broader than legal justice, though in need of it, while legal justice is narrower than reconciliation, and does not require it. Forms of justice other than restorative, grounded in the idea of individual human rights, must surely have a place in the affairs of each nation, but they have no need for the concepts of confession, repentance, atonement, and forgiveness, as all forms of reconciliation do. A Confucian interpretation of these fundamentally religious – but not supernatural – concepts has much to offer the highly conflicted world we are all living in today, in the West and elsewhere no less than in the Confucian East Asia of yesteryear.

I must emphasize that it is a *Confucian* reading of these religious concepts that is being proffered here, not Abrahamic ones. In addition to the lack of theology in the Confucian canon, there is no notion of *vengeance*, for example, which is clearly in evidence throughout the Hebrew Scriptures, the New Testament and Qur'an. Unfortunately for the sense of retributive justice, it smacks strongly of vengeance for the early Confucians as I read them – just as it does for virtually all Buddhists – and is thus not conducive to genuine reconciliation. From the Confucian familial standpoint, then, vengeance can only be seen as retaliation or revenge; would any of us seek vengeance on a family member who had hurt us?

Although the view of human beings I have been advocating is rooted in early Confucianism, it has close parallels in all family-centered cultural traditions and was by no means unknown in the West in the days before the Enlightenment – as, for example, in the writings of John Donne[14] – and, as noted earlier, in the writings of Bob Solomon, who should have the last word here:

> The way to change the world is bit by bit, one small act of generosity after another, hundreds of millions of them adding up to some real global difference... The world may not be just but we ourselves can be, and that begins with the acceptance of all of those mawkish clichés that in our worldly wisdom we have learned to loathe – "opening up one's heart" and "weeping for humanity" (Solomon 1990: 299).

**Acknowledgment** Earlier versions of this paper were read at an U.N. sponsored conference on Truth & Reconciliation Commissions in Sarajevo in August, 2006, at the Beijing Forum in September, 2007, and at the memorial conference in honor of Bob Solomon's life and work at the University of Texas in February, 2008. At the latter I also made a few personal remarks, with anecdotes, about my long friendship with Bob, and made them on behalf of Roger Ames as well, who was unable to attend. I am grateful to the audiences at all three venues for their comments and encouragement.

# References

Baier, Kurt. 1966. The meaning of life. In *Twentieth-century philosophy: The analytic tradition*, ed. Morris Weitz, Paul Edwards, and Richard H. Popkin, 362–379. New York/London: The Free Press/Collier Macmillan.
Bar-siman-Tov, Yaacov (ed.). 2007. *From conflict resolution to reconciliation*. New York: Oxford University Press.
Berlin, Isaiah. 1992. *Four essays on liberty*. New York: Oxford University Press.
Chomsky, Noam. 2000. *Rogue states*. Brooklyn: South End Press.
Dawkins, Richard. 2006. *The God delusion*. New York: Houghton Mifflin.

---

[14] "No man is an island, entire unto itself... Any man's death diminishes me, for I am involved in mankind. Therefore do not send to know for whom the bell tolls; it tolls for thee." Donne (1997: 75).

Donne, John. 1997. *No man is an island: A selection from the prose of John Donne*, ed. Rivers Scott. London: The Folio Society.

Harris, Sam. 2004. *The end of faith: Religion, terror and the future of reason*. New York: Norton.

Hitchens, Christopher. 2007. *God is not great*. New York: Twelve.

Locke, John. 1980 [1690]. *Second treatise on government*. Indianapolis: Hackett.

Rawls, John. 1971. *A theory of justice*. Cambridge: Harvard University Press.

Rosemont Jr., Henry. 1998. Human rights: A bill of worries. In *Confucianism and human right*, ed. William T. deBary and Tu Weiming, 54–66. New York: Columbia University Press.

Rosemont Jr., Henry. 2001. *Rationality and religious experience*. Chicago/LaSalle: Open Court.

Rosemont Jr., Henry, and Roger T. Ames. 1999. *The analects of Confucius: A philosophical translation*. New York: Random House/Ballantine Books.

Rosemont Jr., Henry, and Roger T. Ames. 2003a. Is there a path of spiritual progress in the texts of classical Confucianism? In *Confucian spirituality*, vol. 1, ed. Tu Weiming and Mary Evelyn Tucker. New York: Crossroad Publishing Company.

Rosemont Jr., Henry, and Roger T. Ames. 2003b. *Li* and the a-theistic religiousness of classical Confucianism. In *Confucian spirituality*, vol. 1, ed. Tu Weiming and Mary Evelyn Tucker. New York: Crossroad Publishing Company.

Rosemont Jr., Henry, and Roger T. Ames. 2009. *The classic of family reverence (Xiaojing): A philosophical translation*. Honolulu: University of Hawai'i Press.

Rotberg, Robert, and Desmond Thompson (eds.). 2000. *Truth vs. justice: The morality of truth commissions*. Princeton: Princeton University Press.

Solomon, Robert C. 1990. *A passion for justice*. New York: Addison Wesley.

Stenger, Victor. 2007. *God, the failed hypothesis: How science shows that God does not exist*. Amherst: Prometheus Books.

Tutu, Desmond, and Truth and Reconciliation Commission of South Africa (eds.). 1999. *Truth and reconciliation commission of South Africa report*. New York: Palgrave Macmillan.

Twiss, Sumner B. 1998. A constructive framework for discussing Confucianism and human rights. In *Confucianism and human rights*, ed. William T. deBary and Tu Weiming, 27–53. New York: Columbia University Press.

U.S. Department of Commerce. 1996. *Survey of Current Business*, 76.

United Nations. 1966. *International covenant on social, economic and cultural rights*. New York: The United Nations Press.

United Nations. 1995. United Nations declaration on human rights. In *Nations and human rights*, ed. United Nations, 1945–1995. New York: The United Nations Press.

United Nations. 2002. *Human rights: A compilation of international instruments*, 2 vols. New York: The United Nations Press.

# Part IV
# Spirit and Spirituality

# Chapter 15
# In the Spirit of Solomon: The 'Guise of *Geist*'

Shari Neller Starrett

**Abstract** This chapter argues that focusing on the Hegelian strand of Solomon's diverse legacy not only highlights his unique contributions to Hegel studies, but gives us a glimpse of the ongoing, indomitable spirit of Robert C. Solomon. Particular attention is given to his development of the claim that Hegel's dialectic is not a method, but a metaphor in the mode of the Romantic poets' notion of *Bildung,* which, in Solomon's interpretation of Hegel, highlights an artful image (or "guise") of *Geist* as an ongoing, growing, and intertwined human, lived experience that does not have to have an end, despite the anticipatory suggestiveness and seeming finality of the language of "*Geist*" as Absolute. Experiencing or being moved by the movement of this spirit is 'getting' (and getting into) the spirit of Hegel, and the spirit of Solomon, which doesn't have to end for or with us.

As a grateful past student (California version[1]), a sometimes conversation partner, and reader of Bob Solomon's always spirited outpouring of written work, my goal in this paper is to tug at the Hegelian strand of Bob's thinking by reflecting on his book *In the Spirit of Hegel* just enough to illustrate some of the rich resources of his Hegelian insights and suggest some of his legacy in these insights. There is, of course, much more to what Bob leaves his friends and future readers than this (well illustrated by the diverse articles in this collection of essays honoring the spirit of

---

This is Bob's marvelous phrase. See Solomon (1983: 7).

[1] At the University of California Riverside in the late 1980s Bernd Magnus was my graduate advisor, and both Bob and Kathy were there and on my dissertation committee. It was a truly electric context for which I will always remain grateful.

S.N. Starrett (✉)
Department of Philosophy, California State University,
800 N. State College Boulevard, Fullerton, CA 92834, USA
e-mail: sstarrett@fullerton.edu

K. Higgins and D. Sherman (eds.), *Passion, Death, and Spirituality,*
Sophia Studies in Cross-cultural Philosophy of Traditions and Cultures 1,
DOI 10.1007/978-94-007-4650-3_15, © Springer Science+Business Media Dordrecht 2012

his generous and ongoing engagement with so many people in so many areas of philosophy), but I would like to call particular attention to a few of the ways his provocative readings of Hegel color much of his larger legacy.

In his 2002 *Spirituality for the Skeptic*, in which Hegel plays a big part, Solomon reflects on his book on Hegel, and says, "…my interpretations of Hegel were light on spirit" (Solomon 2002: 5). I disagree, unless, to borrow from Milan Kundera, this lightness is taken in the sense of spirit's "unbearable lightness", or a lightness that is not borne by any static experience. In his 1983 book on Hegel, Spirit found vital expression on nearly every page, although, arguably, more often Bob's spirit than Hegelian Spirit as such (if there is such a thing).

In the introduction to *In the Spirit of Hegel*, Solomon leads off by quoting Hegel's *Introduction to the Lectures on the History of Philosophy*, and since Hegel's focus on history is complemented by Solomon's (and of course, Kathleen Higgins's) undeniable impact on the contemporary study of the history of philosophy for so many readers,[2] the passage he selects from this Hegelian text bears repeating in full:

> … what each generation has brought forward as knowledge and spiritual creation, the next generation inherits. This inheritance constitutes its soul, its spiritual substance, something one has become accustomed to, its principles, its prejudices, its riches… And since each generation has (its own) spiritual activity and vitality, it works upon what it has received and the material thus becomes richer. Our position is the same: to grasp the knowledge which is at hand. To appropriate it, and then to mold it (Hegel 1954: 162).

It is noteworthy that this passage indicates both Hegel's awareness that he is appropriating what he has inherited, and that he is also describing an open-ended process in which he is participating. Solomon's choice of this passage indicates the direction, if not the provocative force,[3] of his reading of Hegel.

---

[2] For me, Solomon is primarily and extraordinarily a historian of philosophy, although if he accepted this, perhaps he would have preferred 'existentialist historian of philosophy'. It is, of course, arguable that Nietzsche or Sartre are more alive in wide span of Bob's work than is Hegel, or that all of the giants of Western Philosophy, shine through at some point in Bob's articulation of his philosophical commitments. The more I think about it, the more I am disinclined to say that one thread is more salient than the others, and that, at least, it may be impossible, for example, to separate the spirit of Hegel from the spirit of Nietzsche in the 'Spirit of Solomon', but it also strikes me that this may have more to do with my own intertwined allegiance to both Hegel and Nietzsche than it does to "discovering" this aspect of Bob's indomitable and unique spirit. Bob once genially accused me of Hegelianizing Nietzsche and Nietzscheanizing Hegel, and over the years I have been inclined to think that this was (either) false, or that it was true and there just was connective resonance between Hegel and Nietzsche, or that mixing the two was just a product of reading them through the lens of Bob's readings, which were always so much more than commentary, and were so infectious. But I am still trying to get beyond Bob's suggestion that seeing them as too interwoven was a problem that I had, and perhaps in writing this I am trying to convince myself, as much as my audience, that via my reading of both Hegel and of Bob, I can identify something that connects all three. But again, it is primarily the Hegelian thread in Bob's work that I am trying to tug on here.

[3] Some (but not all!) of Bob's other provocative insights about Hegel that I will only touch on here include arguments that Hegel is highlighting "freedom of self-realization" and a "realization of self-identity" (1983: 19–20); that "the Absolute is an illusion" (1983: 16).

In his initial comments on Hegel's masterwork, the *Phenomenology of Spirit*, Solomon engages the now familiar question "What is living and what is dead in Hegel's philosophy?"; and his response to this question also bears quoting,

> Napoleon is dead. So is Hegel, the text, however, is alive, brought to life no longer by "the spirit of the times" but by our reading of it, and our thinking about it and its effects on us… and if this approach ignores the spirit of the book, it nonetheless reminds us that we ourselves are the life of that text. (Solomon 1983: x)

For me, reading this now rather than over 25 years ago when it was published, gives me an existential chill (possibly similar to what Solomon in later work would refer to as 'bodily judgment'), by shifting the weight onto thinking about the way readers today and in the future will bring to life not just what Hegel wrote, but what Solomon (and others who now read, digitally view, memorialize, cite him, or make him their own) choose to focus on when trying to stay true to the spirit of the philosopher's projects that they discuss.

I think few readers of Hegel would contest the claim that it is the *Phenomenology* in which Hegel gives his readers his most vital expression of *Geist,* and it is the *Phenomenology* that takes center stage in Solomon's treatment of Hegel, although he does not by any means ignore Hegel's other works. In the first quote cited here we saw Solomon's recognition of Hegel's perspective on the history of philosophy and Hegel's often overlooked emphasis on the process of grasping, appropriating, and molding our own philosophical inheritance which (whether we recognize it or not) is the stuff of *our* soul, *our* vitality, or *our* spirit. In the second passage we saw Solomon passing on his belief that what is living in Hegel for us today is the infusion of *spirit* or a spiritual expression of life in Hegel's writing and that it is an infusion that any reader can experience (and presumably will experience if he or she 'gets' the spirit of Hegel). People who knew Bob, and/or his current readers might be tempted to argue that he infuses his own life passion into all of his own readings of any philosophical piece of writing (if philosophy and life can be separated, particularly for an existentialist philosopher).[4] Surely this is true, but this doesn't exclude the possibility that when he read Hegel, there was a reciprocal, special and lasting infusion of spiritual expression that spilled-over, intensified, or expanded his own philosophical/life/passion/work.

Solomon's work on Hegel is much more than a charitable and celebratory reading, and it is certainly not a detached reading. Some may fault him for this; I do not. His reading is impassioned but also consistently critical, often in a way that resonates with Nietzsche's critical perspective concerning philosophy as unwitting personal confession. For example, consider Solomon's description: "The *Phenomenology* is a grand and passionate vision, a conceptual symphony… it is, first of all, a spiritual

---

[4] I remember a story Bob told me in the 1980s about a conversation he had with Arthur Danto about philosophers marrying other philosophers—in which Danto ostensibly said it was all well and good to take philosophy personally, but you couldn't live it, or in any case you couldn't take it to bed, and Bob's reply was that there was no way to go to bed without it.

autobiography, a passionate confession" (Solomon 1983: x). But, ironically (and I believe this irony was intentional, underscoring a productive tension of oppositions), his book on Hegel is filled with claims that he is redoing Hegel in order to bring him to life for us, i.e. implying that Hegel's spiritual autobiography and his own are both simultaneously at work when Solomon writes *In the Spirit of Hegel*. In more of Bob's words, "Hegel's *Phenomenology* is still an example of the philosophical imagination at its finest, an invitation for us to allow ourselves to use it to our own purposes (Solomon 1983: x). But we also find statements like "Hegel was a horrible writer" (xi), and references to Bob's expressed need "to cut through unnecessary obfuscation to discover truly fundamental ideas (xiii). One could ask, whose fundamental ideas?—without getting a clear either/or answer. Surely one of Bob's (and Kathy's) greatest gifts in discussing historical philosophical figures is to let go of their ponderous language in favor of getting their concerns to hit us where we live, and when Solomon does this with Hegel, he infuses Hegel's spirit with his own commitment to hit us where we live.

In *In the Spirit of Hegel*, Solomon tells us that Hegel is "a very humanist, anti-religious, anti-metaphysical proponent of various human experiences" (Solomon 1983: 27), but the sort of humanist, anti-religious, anti-metaphysician for whom all forms of life were an expression of immanent spirit, that is, for whom any contextual expression of being is an ever-unfolding indication of human thoughtfulness, care, passion. As a strong humanist reading, if it was that simple, Bob's interpretation would probably not be seen as an innovative contribution to Hegelian scholarship. But it is not that simple. Bob acknowledges the significant scholarly influences that impact his humanist reading of Hegel (e.g. Findlay, Harris, Kaufmann) and gives a charitable explanation of what he calls the "two Hegels" of scholars, i.e. the post-Kantian phenomenologist Hegel, who traces lived experience to a final absolute truth, and "a much more radical ...historicist Hegel who sees that the 'necessary' movement and transformation of the forms of experience need not be going anywhere in particular and need not have a reasonable goal in order to have a goal" (Solomon 1983: 14). In a parenthetical remark that follows and illustrates the 'more radical' Hegel's ongoing transformations in life and that is, for me, pure Bob, he adds "(One can reach for the moon, and try to love 'forever')" (15). Current readers can only fruitlessly ask which comes first, Bob's motivation toward such efforts or a Hegelian-inspired motivation, but we can very fruitfully take up the attempt ourselves, keeping alive the quest or spirit of Solomon and/or Hegel.

This Solomonian insight connects up to a stunning set of additional gifts of interpretation that he offers us about Hegel. For example, playing off the last quote from Hegel, he says that the supposed rational progression or movement of the logical oppositions of *Geist*, although shot through with thoughtful, lived concerns –is reason only in retrospect. *Geist* unfolds, in Solomon's words, in "living, desiring, energetic, insecure, ambitious beings for whom experience is as much an adventure as a scientific observation" (Solomon 1983: 10), and not the least of his controversial interpretations of Hegel, that 'the Absolute' is an illusion. I won't focus here on his development of all of his non-standard readings of Hegel, but will instead suggest that they are of a piece with what is one of my personal favorites of his provocations about Hegel—namely, a sustained argument that Hegel's dialectical descriptions in the *Phenomenology* should not be understood as a scientific or logical method, but as a metaphor.

It may be fairly common to read Nietzsche, e.g. his genealogy, metaphorically rather than to say that he has a definitive 'genealogical method', but it is surely far less common to use this interpretative strategy with Hegel. For many of us who teach Hegel, especially at the undergraduate level, the temptation to use dialectical methodology as a way to explain what Hegel is up to in the *Phenomenology of Spirit* is nearly irresistible. And for many of us who have been caught up in Hegelian thought, the internalization of a methodological process of *Aufhebung* or unfolding 'thesis-anti-thesis-synthesis', or at least a progressive, formal movement of conflict toward resolution, has an almost common-sense appeal. I was a grad student without too many Hegelian habits of mind when I first heard Solomon's confident claim that Hegel's dialectic was *not* a method but a metaphor, and it seemed outrageous. His argument is carefully nuanced and I cannot do it justice here. But try as I could I have never been able to let go of it. The upshot of Bob's argument, at least for me, is that Hegelian dialectic is a philosopher's angle on the romantic poet's notion of *Bildung*—traditionally understood as "a metaphor of growth and development," and in Hegel's case of the development "of human consciousness writ large" (Solomon 1983: 22). For Bob, Hegel's dialectic is the philosophical and lived expression of *Bildung*—but he adds a twist to this, telling us that like any really good image it reveals itself in various ways, both to the reader and to the writer. This seems to warrant a more than parenthetical comparison to what in the 1960s (arguably when Bob came of age) was called a 'consciousness raising' process—possibly the paradigmatic expression of the *Zeitgeist* of that time, which was illustrated in so many expressions of its popular culture.

Elaborating on his reasoning for this interpretation, Bob tells us that in the *Phenomenology* we run into the metaphor of *Geist* in the motion of multiple dynamically unfolding human experiences; that is, we run into Hegel's illustrations of experiences of "inner necessity", which, Bob says, are anything but mysterious, since "every author knows what Hegel means when he says that the subject matter develops itself. One begins a novel with a set of characters, or a poem with a central image, and one cannot cancel or change these at will" (Solomon 1983: 25)—i.e. characters develop 'in character,' in context, and one move suggests another. Turning an exquisite phrase, which I used for the subtitle of my paper, Solomon calls this "the guise of *Geist*." Far from referring to something 'otherworldly.' Bob tells us that *Geist* is an artistic and "belligerent demonstration that this is a human world in which all is but a stage for our own self-realization" (Solomon 1983: 7).

For Solomon, the dialectic of *Geist* does not give us A and not A and then resolution or *Aufhebung of this tension*, but instead gives us suggestive clues about how we attempt to grow into ourselves, experiencing tension and desire (cf. trying "to love forever"), and unendingly attempt to create and tie together further experiences. The *Bildung* metaphor, says Bob in yet another controversial interpretation of Hegel, "is the image of the self as a self-enclosed unity" (Solomon 1983: 197)—but a complex unity that is always expanding and transforming itself, and continually attempting to connect itself to others—as a self-alienating process that is both singular (temporally our own) and not singular (historically ongoing).

The dialectic illustrates how any self moves in a continuation of context(s), how a writer describing this process both crafts and watches it take shape, and how it is possible for us, as readers of Hegel, to realize the reason (rational process) of it all after the fact, so to speak, and

> to leave open the central tension in Hegel's philosophy—that is, whether the resolution of contradictions ultimately leads to a single wholly harmonious philosophy, free of all tension and contradictions, or whether the resolution of contradictions, and the need to overcome the limitations of our current 'forms of consciousness' is a perennial process that never comes to an end and never reaches 'the Absolute' (Solomon 1983: 23–24).

Clearly, Bob is favoring the latter, the perennially open aspect of this spirited Hegelian tension, but he is not denying that Hegel relates this process to the anticipatory language of *Geist* as "Absolute". For Bob, as I said before, the Absolute is an illusion, or the artful guise of *Geist*. His reading of Hegel takes an end run around charges of abstraction, and connects us *not* with the so-called arch rationalist who loses touch with the lived experiences of spirit, but instead with a Hegel who artfully weaves his descriptions into the richness of our own experiences. According to Solomon, "Hegel tried to portray his philosophy as a science, when what he proved was that philosophy is an art" (Solomon 1983: ix)—I would add, the art of living a spirited life.

There is so much more to say about Bob's thoughtful and provocative insights on Hegel, and about Bob as expressing the spirit of philosophy, but I want to draw my comments to a close, for now at least, by underscoring something that gives us a glimpse of his living spirit in an aspect of what I have just described. When Bob tells us that the metaphor of dialectic opens up not just for the reader of Hegel, but also for the writer, he gives us Hegel's philosophy as a thoughtful creative process in a way that catches us up in this project, and challenges philosophy and philosophers to find thoughtful, artful ways to make our spirit felt through our words. To my mind, this move pays homage not just to the spirit of Hegel, but to the complex ways in which writing about Hegel helped shape, although surely did not circumscribe, the spirit of Bob Solomon.

# References

Hegel, G.W.F. 1954. The history of philosophy. In *The philosophy of Hegel*, ed. Carl J. Friedrich. New York: Random House.

Solomon, Robert C. 1983. *In the spirit of Hegel*. New York: Oxford University Press.

Solomon, Robert C. 2002. *Spirituality for the skeptic: The thoughtful love of life*. Oxford: Oxford University Press.

# Chapter 16
# "Spirit": A Plea for *Geist*

Richard Schacht

**Abstract**  Robert Solomon and I long ago took up Walter Kaufmann's campaign not only to follow Nietzsche as well as Hegel in keeping the term and concept of "*Geist*" alive, but also to render and use it in English as "spirit" rather than "mind." I prefer to keep and use the German term itself, because I consider "*Geist*" to be a richer term and concept (thanks to Hegel and Nietzsche), and want to be able to use it to pull the idea of "spirit" in that direction. But I share with Solomon the conviction that the language of "spirit" and "spirituality," so understood, is valuable, and deserves a place in our own (Anglophone) philosophical discourse about human reality. I consider what Solomon does with the idea of "spirit," and say something about my own rather different inclination in the matter, which owes something to Hegel's construal of *Geist*, but is closer in spirit (as it were) to Nietzsche's. For me, as for both of them, human *Geist* or spirituality is deeply bound up with human *culture* and the phenomenon they call *Bildung,* through which it is incorporated into human life; and the essential thing about it is the transformation of human life that it involves, from something merely natural into something that is importantly supra-biological even while remaining anchored in and dependent upon our species-specific vitality. It involves the continual innovative restructuring of human experience and activities in ways increasingly emancipated from any sort of biological or merely social-functional imperatives. The language of *Geist* and spirituality is needed to bring and keep this central dimension of human reality in focus, making Solomon's efforts to demystify and promote it an important part of his legacy.

R. Schacht (✉)
Department of Philosophy, University of Illinois, 105 Gregory Hall,
810 So. Wright Street, Urbana IL, 61802, USA
e-mail: rschacht@illinois.edu

K. Higgins and D. Sherman (eds.), *Passion, Death, and Spirituality,*                213
Sophia Studies in Cross-cultural Philosophy of Traditions and Cultures 1,
DOI 10.1007/978-94-007-4650-3_16, © Springer Science+Business Media Dordrecht 2012

What shall we – as philosophers – do with the idea or concept and word *"Geist,"* which we find used so prominently not only in the literature of Christianity (and other religions) but also in the writings of Hegel, and many subsequent German-speaking philosophers? For many among us today, the answer is simple: "Let it go." Let it be just a curiosity of the transition from religious and metaphysical thinking to demythologized, secular, this-worldly, post-religious and post-metaphysical, "naturalistic" if not flatly and completely materialistic or scientistic thinking. Just another lamentable bit of Hegelian mystification and "nonsense on stilts" from the wild and crazy days of German "Idealism" after Kant, before the Germans came to their senses and Neo-Kantianism brought the party to an end.

Something like that is more or less what Feuerbach and Marx thought. There's no need for talk of *"Geist"* any longer – and there are positive reasons to drop it, when we have carried out our "anthropological reduction" of Hegel's *Geistesphilosophie* into a scientifically-minded and -modeled philosophical anthropology. For them, and for many others after them, it's *"der Mensch,"* not *"der Geist,"* that we should be talking about.

Nietzsche might seem to agree that *"Geist"* must go. After all, he certainly was a champion of something like that "reduction" of the religious and metaphysical idea of unearthly spirituality into an enriched concept of earthly humanity, calling for us to "naturalize" our understanding of ourselves as *"Menschen"* as we "de-deify" our understanding of the nature of which human reality is a part (Nietzsche, GS §109), and to "translate ourselves back into nature" as *"homo natura* [natural man]." (Nietzsche, BGE §230).[1] But he in fact was differently disposed, making extensive use of the language of *"Geist"* in the course of his "de-deifying" naturalistic reinterpretation of our human reality. To paraphrase his Zarathustra (in "On the Despisers of the Body"):

> Body am I – and *Geist*? Well, yes and no. No – for *Geist* is only a word for something about the body. But Yes – for *Geist* is a word for something *important* that the body has it in itself *to become* (Nietzsche, Z I,4).

In fact, one could even go so far as to explain Nietzsche's favorite maxim *"Wird wer du bist!* [Become who you are!]," along with his notions of life-enhancement

---

[1] I shall follow the standard practice in the English-language Nietzsche literature of identifying citations from his writings by way of the acronyms of standard English renderings of the titles of his books, followed either by Nietzsche's section or aphorism numbers or first by the Part or Book numbers of the works (in Roman numerals) and then by the section numbers (and then sub-section numbers, if any):

BGE *Beyond Good and Evil*
BT *The Birth of Tragedy*
GS *The Gay Science*
Z *Thus Spoke Zarathustra*

In my citations I generally follow the Kaufmann translations, or where they are lacking the Hollingdale translations, but frequently modify them where I consider different renderings of Nietzsche's German to be preferable.

and even of *"Übermenschlichkeit* [the 'over-humanity' of the *Übermensch*]," in terms of that sort of "becoming" or transformation of our merely human and all-too-human reality into something that may aptly and usefully be characterized in that language.

But others may point with dismay or derision to the late-nineteenth-century spiritualism and vitalism of those who saw a duality in the contrast of *"Geist"* and mere *"Leben,"* and turned that duality into a new dualism, or mystified the properly naturalistically conceived phenomenon of "life" into something that is itself no longer fundamentally a transformed piece of nature at all. To those ill-disposed to these developments, the notion of *"Geist"* was as dangerous to keep around as the notion (to which Nietzsche himself was not unsympathetic in some moods) of "God" – even if one protests (with Nietzsche) that "God" properly conceived is only, but nonetheless usefully and importantly, a word for "something about *the world*" – something divine, but purely immanent.

Robert Solomon and I long ago took up Walter Kaufmann's campaign not only to follow Nietzsche as well as Hegel in keeping the term and concept of *"Geist"* alive, but also to render and use it in English as "spirit" rather than "mind." (The choice of the latter rendering, by the old British Hegelians, resulted in the journal and sub-discipline that go by the names of *"Mind"* and "philosophy of mind," and has been a serious and lamentable handicap to the understanding of Hegel, and of human reality, in the English-speaking world ever since.) Solomon and I both thought that Kaufmann was right to try to fix this problem, and to get people used to using the term "spirit" when talking about (and translating) Nietzsche as well as about Hegel, its traditional religious associations and connotations notwithstanding.

That was one of the best things about Kaufmann's Hegel book and re-translation of the Preface to Hegel's *Phenomenology*[2] – although it is one of the curiosities of the book that Kaufmann virtually always refers to Hegel's *Phenomenology* simply as "the *Phenomenology*," rather than as "the *Phenomenology of Spirit*," even on the opening page of his retranslation of the Preface to it. Kaufmann seems to have remained uncomfortable with it, even as he campaigned to overcome that discomfort in others and to liberate and appropriate the term "spirit" for post-religious and post-metaphysical philosophical uses. So also one of the best chapters in his Nietzsche book (Kaufmann 1974) is the chapter on "Sublimation, *Geist* and Eros" – in the very title of which he chose to retain the German term Nietzsche had used – oddly italicizing it but not "Eros."

I actually think Kaufmann would have done us all a favor if he had italicized neither word, and had taken the occasion to Anglicize the former along with the latter.

---

[2] Initially published together under the title *Hegel: Reinterpretation, Texts, and Commentary*, and under Kaufmann's name as the book's author, and with Kaufmann's translation of Hegel's hundred-page Preface to his *Phenomenology* incorporated into it as "Chapter VIII" (Kaufmann 1965); subsequently published separately by the University of Notre Dame Press – Kaufmann (1977) and Kaufmann (1978).

I prefer to keep and use the German term myself, rather than translating it as either "mind" or "spirit," and am carrying on a campaign of my own to get "Geist" adopted in English-language philosophical discourse (un-italicized), as has more or less happened with Heidegger's "Dasein" and "Angst." My reason is not so much embarrassment or discomfort with the word "spirit" as the sense that "*Geist*" is a considerably richer term and concept (thanks to Hegel and Nietzsche), and that we would do better to speak of "Geist" when we are talking about "*Geist*" rather than trying to get people to think what we want them to think when they hear us or read us talking about "spirit."

On this occasion, however, I will be making use of both terms, because like Solomon I do want the language of "spirit" – "spiritual," "spirituality," "spiritualization" and the like – to have a future, and indeed an important place, in Anglophone philosophical discourse about ourselves. Part of what I want to do on this occasion is to take a look at what Solomon seems to have decided to do with the idea of "spirit," and to say something about my own rather different inclination in the matter.

One of Solomon's biggest books is his Hegel book; and he chose a somewhat punning title for it that immediately foregrounded the term "spirit": *In the Spirit of Hegel* (Solomon 1983). That is also indicative, however, of one of his ways of trying to make it possible, acceptable and even comfortable to use the term: namely, to use it mainly in phrases and figures of speech that are familiar and to which objection can hardly be taken, rather than making it do any real philosophical work. Another of his strategies may be seen in his "Glossary of [Hegelian] Terms," about half-way through the book, in which he characterizes "Spirit [*Geist*]" as "the subject-writ-large, including the objects it determines for itself," which "includes all of us and everything in human experience. It is simply the world, aware of itself as a self-conscious and comprehensible unity." (Solomon 1983: 284). This is the strategy of talking about Hegelian *Geist* in a very general way that makes a kind of grand and even edifying *Weltanschauung*-level sense without running any major philosophical risks. At the end of the book, Solomon combines them, writing: "Hegel's emphasis on Spirit in the *Phenomenology* is just this vision of life as a whole, a heartfelt romantic appeal to rejuvenate the 'spirit' that Christianity sometimes tries to teach us, [al]though… Hegel's Spirit has nothing whatever of the 'otherworldly about it…" (Solomon 1983: 638–39) I wouldn't want to argue with any of this. But I also don't want to leave it at that.

Solomon didn't want to leave it at that either. Somewhat surprisingly to me, he doesn't discuss Nietzsche on *Geist* or spirit in his *Living With Nietzsche* book (Solomon 2003). (Neither "*Geist*" nor "spirit" is even in the index to it.) In his more or less contemporaneous *Spirituality for the Skeptic*, however, he shows what he wanted to do with the idea – or at least *one* of the things he wanted to do with it, and the only thing he actually did do with it. This book seems to me to be rather like his version of Kaufmann's *Faith of a Heretic* (Kaufmann 1961). Its title even echoes Kaufmann's. In it Solomon seems to want to think of "spirit" in terms of "spirituality," and to think of "spirituality" simply as a cluster of qualities and characteristics that are humanly possible and admirable without any sort of otherworldly religious or metaphysical means of support. He thus advocates what I would call a "naturalized" version of spirituality; and the point of the book is to show that such a thing is possible, desirable, and important – perhaps even as important as Nietzsche took the ideas of "the enhancement of life" and "higher humanity" to be in the aftermath of the "death of God." In fact, Nietzsche might be taken to consider his own "naturalized" conception of the "higher spirituality" the upshot of "the enhancement of life," and the very essence of "higher humanity," as he conceives of these notions.

Solomon's basic definition in *Spirituality* of the kind of spirituality he is talking about even has a (probably deliberately) Nietzschean ring to it: "spirituality as the thoughtful *love of life*." In his case, however, it would seem that what makes it "spirituality" (as he conceives of it) is not the "love of life" part, but rather the "thoughtful" part – which I take to be his version of or gesture toward Nietzsche's talk about "enhancement" and "higher" sorts of things human. This is how Solomon chooses to indicate what distinguishes his version of "spirituality" from the "love of life" of the barbaric beast of prey; and it enables him to do so without sounding elitist.

I have no problem with just about any of the many things Solomon goes on to mention in the course of the book. I tend to like the things he likes, admire the things he admires, and feel the same way he does about their opposites. But I do have a few problems with his treatment of spirituality in it. One is that he seems to take a kind of "laundry list" approach to it, and to put so many things he likes on the list that his idea of "spirituality" seems to lose coherence. Another is that he stops just where I would have really liked him to get down to business, with the seeming implication that he thinks what he does with the idea of spirituality gives it about as much weight and substance as its naturalistic revision can bear. And a third is that he waters Hegel's conception of *Geist* down to the point that it becomes almost as featureless as the famous Hegelian "night in which all cows are black." (Solomon 2002: 138, 127).

I have already observed that Solomon more or less defines spirituality as "the thoughtful love of life." But he also characterizes it as "the broader more inclusive conception of philosophy" he was seeking in his early years (Solomon 2002: xiv); as "coming to grips with the big picture" (5); as "the grand and thoughtful passions of life and a life lived in accordance with those grand and thoughtful passions" (6); as "the process of transforming the self" (7); as "the subtle and not easily specifiable awareness that surrounds virtually anything and everything that tran-scends our petty self-interest" (12); as "the realization of what is best in all of us" (16); as "a larger sense of life," and "a larger sense of 'us,' not only of humanity but ultimately the world as well" (26); as "wisdom" (57); as "having the right emotions, or caring about the right sorts of things" (70); as "a triad of emotions [...] – of erotic love, reverence, and trust" (72); as something that "begins with [the] acceptance" of "the tragic sense of life" (78); as something that "at its best is a combination of gratitude and humor, a dash of that mock-heroic Camusian confrontation with the absurd, and a passionate engagement with the details and the people in our lives" (87); and much more. These are all excellent things to my way of thinking too. And they all can reasonably be characterized as instances of what might loosely be called "spirituality" (although they had better not all be considered *necessary* conditions or features of "spirituality," or else "spirituality" will be a very rare thing indeed). But it is hard to see what more than this it is that gets them on the list; and if that is all there is to the conception of "spirituality" we are being offered, that is rather less than its billing would lead one to anticipate.

Even so, however, what Solomon has bequeathed to us here is by no means insignificant. His legacy includes a warm and lively expression of his own spirituality, as well as a contribution to the campaign to make it possible to talk about "spirit" and "spirituality" in polite naturalistic philosophical society. And it also includes a challenge to think seriously (as well as playfully and passionately and evocatively) – with our philosophical as well as human hats on – about them, and about Geist along with them, to whatever extent it turns out that "Geist" and Solomonian "spirituality" are not synonymous and coextensive.

It seems to me that Solomon is absolutely right, even if this is all there is to it, in thinking that it would be a mistake to throw out the baby of "spirit" (or of "Geist") with the bathwater of Christianity and New-Age Nonsense. He may be wrong in saying that the idea of spirituality has been "hijacked" by religion (Solomon 2002: xiii), since religion undoubtedly had it first; but he is certainly right in his realization that (as he puts it) it "can be severed from" religion (Solomon 2002: xii) (although I do wish that he had chosen a different word for the extrication he has in mind).

Nietzsche agrees, making extensive use of the language of *"Geist"* with no hesitation or apology, not only in such expressions as *"Der freie Geist"* or *"Freigeist,"* but also on its own, and less figuratively. As in the case of "soul [*Seele*]," he considers it obvious that we should be able to avail ourselves of this language, even as we also undertake to "de-deify" it and avoid reification in our thinking about what we are talking about. Curiously but significantly, the same may be said about what Hegel did when he made *"Geist"* a part of the post-Kantian as well as post-metaphysical and post-religious philosophical discourse he inaugurated (in his case, "appropriating it from religion" would be a more apt way to put it).

For Hegel, *Geist* is the "truth" of Nature; it is that which Nature has it in itself to become, or for which Nature sets the stage and prepares the way. Nature, he contends, is not only what it is as such; it further is the possibility of *Geist* – and that is its highest meaning and significance. *Geist* is the realization of the potentiality of the reality that initially expresses itself as nature to overcome that expression of itself – and what is more, for Hegel (and, I would say, for Nietzsche too, and Solomon as well), that potentiality and its full realization is the only divinity there is. (Yes, Virginia, there is divinity. But just as *"Geist"* is only a word for something about the body, "divinity" or "God" is only a word for something about the world – and more specifically, about what the world has it in itself to become.)

Yet Geist for Hegel, is in itself nothing at all – or rather, it is *no thing* at all. Geist, he says, *is* only what it *does*. It is what it is only in the doing – in the sorts of expression and activity that are its living reality. It is not "something about the body" in the sense of a *property of* the body; but it is something real only in its embodiment, in forms of experience and expression and activity that the body (among other things) makes possible. Hegel's *"Geist"* might better be characterized as "a word for something that requires embodiment as a condition of its possibility." But it is also a word for something that requires *consciousness and self-consciousness* – and therefore inter-subjectivity – as conditions of its possibility. And it moreover is a word for something that requires *objectification* and *social structure* as further conditions of its possibility.

In short, "*Geist*" for Hegel is something pretty complicated, with many different forms and developmental stages to be comprehended – and also to be established and sustained historically. And for Hegel it requires something very important at every step of the way: *mediation*. In fact, it requires two sorts of mediation: *objective* mediation, in the form of physical or social or linguistic or artistic or other such objects we make or transform, and *subjective* mediation, in the form of associated kinds of consciousness and self-consciousness. It also is a living reality only as an ongoing dialectical process of expression and impression, externalization and internalization, objectification and subjectification – within a further dialectical process of intersubjective interaction. It is small wonder that Hegel's *Phenomenology of Geist* is such a blockbuster of a book, and that his *Philosophy of Geist* and its supplementary *Philosophy of Right* together are no less formidable.

Why do I mention all of this? Because it seems to me that we in our philosophical community have hardly begun to mine the wealth of Hegel's thinking with respect to Geist, and have much to gain from taking it seriously even if we disregard the "Absolute-Idealist" system in which it is encased. Solomon was so convinced of this point that he undertook the Herculean labor of writing what I believe to be the longest of his many books – *In the Spirit of Hegel* – as a step in that direction. I would like to think that, had he had the chance, he would have followed up his *Spirituality* book's spirited advocacy on behalf of the very idea of a "naturalized" form of "spirituality" with an attempt to think it through as one of the most important pieces of our human reality. In doing so, I would think that he would have drawn more extensively and intensively upon his Hegelian resources than he does in the *Spirituality* book – and upon his Nietzschean resources as well.

Solomon does talk about Nietzsche in *Spirituality*; but he does not tap those latter resources nearly as deeply and fully in this as I would expect of a kindred spirit – who "lived with Nietzsche" philosophically for as long and as intimately as Solomon did. That is something I am trying and hoping to do myself; for I find Nietzsche to be at least Hegel's equal as a philosopher of Geist, as well as his superior with respect to human reality more generally. Perhaps it is something Solomon himself would have done, had he lived to write a more substantial (and typically Solomon-sized) book on the topic than the introduction to it in which *Spirituality* in effect consists.

Geist, for Nietzsche, is not only an *Aufhebung* phenomenon (as it is for Hegel), in which initial forms of spirituality are *aufgehoben* into more sophisticated and interesting ones. It also is a *sublimation* phenomenon, in which elements of our "natural" nature and psycho-physiological constitution are redirected, channeled and transformed under various sorts of social, cultural and educational conditions, in ways that Hegel never could have imagined, and would have had a hard time swallowing.

Nietzsche also had a view of Geist that was in certain respects much broader than the conception of it that Solomon sets forth in his *Spirituality* book. He was much more sensitive to what might be called the "dark side" of Geist – of its "all-too-human" and even pathological origins and functions, and of the ways in which it can be dangerous and harmful in human life and to human health and flourishing – even though he also placed his highest hopes in it, and accorded the highest of values to it. The Apollonian, Dionysian and tragic arts – and associated forms of culture and sensibility – that Nietzsche discusses in *The Birth of Tragedy* are *geistige* phenomena; but so are those subsequent developments (first Socratic and Euripidean, and then Christian) that resulted in the death of tragedy. "Slave morality" is no less a Geist-phenomenon than is so-called "master morality" – and perhaps is more so, along with the ascetic-priestly mentality that fostered it. Ascetic ideals, otherworldly religions, and a host of philosophical, artistic, social and intellectual tendencies that Nietzsche discusses are *geistige* phenomena as well – as also are the forms of higher humanity that he celebrates.

There is hardly a work of Nietzsche's that is not a gold mine for the philosopher of Geist. He considers it imperative to approach and deal with the topic in a broad range of historical, cultural, social and psychological perspectives. He also had a highly commendable interest in scientific inquiry with respect to the underpinnings of *geistige* phenomena (as well as to their cultural and social-psychological genealogies). For him that interest is entirely consistent with – and indeed is enriching of – his interest in their experiential character and significance. In short: Nietzsche's philosophy of Geist is an important part of his broader philosophical anthropology, and is central to his entire reinterpretive and revaluative philosophical project.

For both Hegel and Nietzsche, Geist is deeply bound up with the broadly educational, developmental and transformative social and historical phenomenon they call *Bildung* – and more specifically and explicitly, with *culture* and its internalization, incorporation, and participation, from language to such cultural phenomena as art and philosophy. Our human psychology may provide the warp of Geist; but it is our human cultural "forms of life," institutions, practices and symbol systems that provide its woof. Both are essential to it and indispensable for it. Even at its most individual and creative, human spirituality is informed by historically and socially developed cultural reality, as well as involving and requiring inter-subjective interaction and recognition.

The essential thing about Geist, for both Hegel and Nietzsche, is what cultural forms and their established norms and created values make possible: the transformation of human life from something merely natural into something more and different than that, and emphatically supra-biological even while remaining anchored in and dependent upon our species-specific vitality. This has occurred and continues to occur though its multifarious normativizations and re-normativizations – in historical, humanly created ways. By means of culture we have boot-strapped our way beyond complete entrapment within the toils of nature – not merely exchanging them for those of what Nietzsche calls "the social strait-jacket," but also (at least for some, and to some extent) in a manner opening a way beyond it. What lies beyond it is the flowering of Geist, in yet more autonomous and potentially creative forms of humanity, at the levels of both personality and "absolute" spirituality for Hegel, and in rather more artistically modeled ways for Nietzsche, under the banners of "higher humanity" and "*Übermenschlichkeit*."[3]

Solomon gestures in this direction in his *Spirituality* book, remarking on several occasions that spirituality is "social" (Solomon 2002: 9). He even drives home the point by saying that "Religion is social, spirituality is social, philosophy also is social." But this is a huge topic, requiring much more attention than he gives it there. And the differences between Hegel and Nietzsche in their accounts of it are as important as the similarities I have been noting. They and Solomon are in agreement, however, on a point that I consider to be both more fundamental than their differences and importantly right: Geist operates not just within the psyche of the individual, but supra-individually – that is, socially and culturally. It is a matter of the dynamics not only of individual psychology, but also of the interaction of social structures, systems and imperatives, and of particular human lives, circumstances, and psychosocial histories.

What Solomon's characterization of "spirituality" significantly misses, to my way of thinking, is a point to which both Hegel and Nietzsche are sensitive: Geist involves the restructuring of human experience and activities in ways increasingly emancipated (for better or for worse) from any sort of biological or social imperatives. Its emergence marks and means the beginning of at least the possibility of a new sort of "autonomy," "self-determination," and creative "self-transformation" of humanity – even if not necessarily of the particular individual (at least until a very late stage of the game, and in limited respects). This is why and how, for both Hegel and Nietzsche, "Geist" is a concept that is both interpretively and evaluatively powerful. It is interpretive of human possibilities, and facilitates their appreciation. And it is both fundamental to and informed by the idea of enlightened creativity that they each, in their different ways, seize upon and celebrate. (This is an idea, I might add, that for them – on my reading of them – is not precluded by the necessities they discern in the reality of which we are a part, and contributes in a major way to their and our human ability to come to positive terms with it in the aftermath of the death of transcendence.)

Solomon has helped to make it possible to talk about such things again in our philosophical community, even if his philosophical sensibility made him reluctant to venture out into such deeper waters. In doing so he did much to help the post-Kantian interpretive tradition attain a new lease on life among us for what is most deserving of it and needed from it. Whatever his views may leave to be desired, that more than compensates, and is a great legacy.

---

[3] I take Nietzsche's figure of "the *Übermensch*" (best translated as "the overman" but better left untranslated) to function in his thinking and writing – primarily in *Thus Spoke Zarathustra* – as a kind of encapsulation and symbol of his idea of the "enhancement of life."

# References

Kaufmann, Walter. 1961. *The faith of a heretic*. Garden City: Doubleday & Company.
Kaufmann, Walter. 1965. *Hegel: Reinterpretation, texts, and commentary*. Garden City: Doubleday & Company.
Kaufmann, Walter. 1974 [1950]. *Nietzsche: Philosopher, psychologist, antichrist*, 4th ed. Princeton: Princeton University Press.
Kaufmann, Walter. 1977. *Hegel: Texts and commentary*. South Bend: University of Notre Dame Press.
Kaufmann, Walter. 1978. *Hegel: A reinterpretation*. South Bend: University of Notre Dame Press.
Nietzsche, Friedrich. 1966 [1886]. *Beyond good and evil*. (trans: Kaufmann, Walter). New York: Vintage.
Nietzsche, Friedrich. 1966 [1872]. *The birth of tragedy*. Together with *The case of Wagner* (trans: Kaufmann, Walter). New York: Random House.
Nietzsche, Friedrich. 1966 [1883–1885]. *Thus spoke Zarathustra* (trans: Kaufmann, Walter). New York: Viking Penguin.
Nietzsche, Friedrich. 1974 [1882]. *The gay science* (trans: Kaufmann, Walter). New York: Random House.
Solomon, Robert C. 1983. *In the spirit of Hegel*. New York: Oxford University Press.
Solomon, Robert C. 2002. *Spirituality for the skeptic*. New York: Oxford University Press.
Solomon, Robert C. 2003. *Living with Nietzsche: What the great "immoralist" has to teach us*. New York: Oxford University Press.

# Chapter 17
# Daring to Be Grateful: Robert C. Solomon on Gratitude in the Face of Fanaticism

Markus Weidler

**Abstract** Because I am tracking some of Robert C. Solomon's most provocative claims about the importance of cultivating our ability to give thanks, the focus of my discussion is on the philosophically complex relation among comportments of gratitude over against certain gestures of fanaticism. On Solomon's view, the phenomenon of fanaticism emerges as socially and culturally more pervasive than is commonly assumed. To see why this is the case, I offer a detailed critical exposition of Solomon's analysis of *death fetishism*, which is featured as the main impulse behind fanatical tendencies and the spiritual destruction they can wreak on any community's *esprit de corps*. At the same time, this exposition goes to show why harnessing the "emotional intelligence" of gratitude is our best bet for obviating fanaticism both in its covert forms and in its most spectacular and lethal manifestations. Finally, this line of inquiry will illuminate why Solomon went so far as to extol gratitude as "the best approach to life itself."

## Introduction: Why Gratitude?

In this essay, I am focusing primarily on Robert C. Solomon's book *Spirituality for the Skeptic*, with a special emphasis on Chap. 6, "Spirituality, Fate, and Fatalism" (Solomon 2002). Here I think Solomon is at his best and philosophically most provocative when he assigns priority to specific comportments of *giving thanks* over the identity criteria for the addressee(s) *to whom* thanks is given. What lends importance to such comportments of gratitude is their power to steer us away from certain

M. Weidler (✉)
Department of Mathematics and Philosophy, Columbus State University,
4225 University Avenue, Columbus, GA 31907, USA
e-mail: weidler_markus@columbusstate.edu

K. Higgins and D. Sherman (eds.), *Passion, Death, and Spirituality*,                 223
Sophia Studies in Cross-cultural Philosophy of Traditions and Cultures 1,
DOI 10.1007/978-94-007-4650-3_17, © Springer Science+Business Media Dordrecht 2012

forms of spiritual starvation, which Solomon had previously discussed under the rubric of "thinking thin." The latter received its first full treatment in the earlier volume *The Joy of Philosophy*, which by the author's own account can be seen as a prototype version leading up to *Spirituality* (Solomon 1999).

More specifically, what Solomon seeks to characterize and then criticize is the *habitus* of "thinking thin."[1] This *habitus* is construed not so much as an individual attitude based on somebody's personal thought contents. Rather, Solomon's conception of thinking thin, as I read it, refers to a socially embodied, detrimental tendency, which encroaches upon the *esprit de corps*[2] of a historically situated group or cultural community.[3]

Over against this tendency, Solomon analyzes certain *interactive* features of giving thanks and finds in them the passage to a spiritually "thick" life. Accordingly, giving thanks emerges as the spiritual remedy to thinking thin, for which Solomon takes his bearings from Kierkegaard:

> Gratitude, I want to suggest, is not only the best answer to the tragedies of life. It is the best approach to life itself... The proper recognition of tragedy and the tragic sense of life is not shaking one's fist at the gods or the universe in scorn or defiance but rather, as Kierkegaard writes in a religious context, going down on one's knees and giving thanks. Whether or not there is a God or there are gods to be thanked, however, seems not the issue to me. It is the importance and the significance of being thankful, to whomever or whatever, for life itself (Solomon 2002: 105).[4]

Probably the most immediate question becomes how Solomon can be so casual about the pivotal concern "whether or not there is a god or gods," after all. In fact, the startling proposal to give thanks "to whomever" may seem to echo some recent

---

[1] I assume that the phrase "thinking thin" is intended as a technical term in Solomon's dictionary. In speaking of "thinking thin" as a *habitus*, I am borrowing an expression from the sociologist and philosopher of culture, Pierre Bourdieu. Generally, the *habitus* refers to a system of organized movements, in which individual agency unfolds in a way that is neither mechanistically determined nor simply a matter of self-transparent deliberation or personal intention. Rather, as a socially ingrained sense for what counts as significant and practically required, Bourdieu sometimes likens the *habitus* to a conductorless orchestra, which allows room for some improvisation within certain collective and material constraints. For details, see especially Bourdieu (1990). Cf. also Chap. 3 in Hoy (2005) and Chap. 3 in Holsinger (2005).

[2] I use this term in a way similar to C.S. Peirce when he insists that *esprit de corps* is a concrete phenomenon like national sentiment or sympathy, none of which ought to be dismissed as mere metaphors. Instead, Peirce recognizes them as manifestations of corporate minds (or "minds of corporations") whose "personalities" can exert a very real influence on individuals. (See Peirce 1998: 236).

[3] What I have stated here in terms of *habitus* and the social embodiment of thinking is, basically, a restatement of Solomon's long-standing commitment to Hegel's tenet of the inseparability of "our collective conscious" and "its collective body," leading up to the central claim that *spirit, our collective self, includes the world as well*. For the full quotation of these pivotal remarks, see Solomon (1983: 203). This Hegelian trope of an embodied group mind recurs in the *Spirituality*-volume, when Solomon stresses that contrary to "our libertarian and existentialist pretenses" our lives are largely a product of the culture and times we find ourselves in (Solomon 2002: 93).

[4] For an earlier, though slightly different formulation of this passage, see Solomon (1999: 142).

suggestions in the philosophy of religion, which explore the possibility of an alternate spiritual way of life as a "practicing agnostic," whose profile has been sketched, for example, by Paul Draper in the context of divine hiddenness (Draper 2001). Solomon, however, pursues a rather different and arguably more radical route, I think, which should be considered in its own right. To begin with, Draper's would-be addressee remains largely modeled on the personal creator god of Christian monotheism. Accordingly, Draper's analysis does not dwell on the personal features (which Draper takes for granted) of Him to whom we speak or give thanks, but rather asks whether any meaningful dialogue in prayer can be sustained even if one party ("God, *if* there is one") is shrouded in uncertainty.

By contrast, Solomon departs from this way of raising the question in two regards. He extends his discussion to include non-personal candidates ("to whomever *or whatever*"). Next, he modifies the object or, more precisely, the scope of our gratitude when he underscores the significance of "being thankful...for life itself." In other words, right from the start Solomon's quest for spirituality for the skeptic is more flexible and more scope-sensitive than comparable inquiries like Draper's. It is more flexible because the reservation of Solomon's skeptic toward clearly identifiable personal interlocutors in divine discourse[5] is not relative to any particular creed, whereas Draper's practicing agnostic issues "hypothetical prayers" to a would-be god that clearly belongs within the Western Judeo-Christian tradition. At the same time, Solomon's spiritual quest is more scope-sensitive because it insists that "the importance and the significance of being thankful" does not pertain to just anything for which we might be grateful (like getting the job we applied for, or recovering from a grave disease). Instead, Solomon suggests the challenge is to be able to give thanks "for life itself," which raises various questions about the sense of *holism* or completion implied by this phrase.[6] Does this mean that we have to be thankful for everything that happens in our lives, including the most harrowing experiences? And, on an Aristotelian note, how can one be thankful for one's life in its entirety, if it is not over yet? (cf. Solomon 1999: 146).[7] To answer these questions we need to take a closer look at Solomon's comparison between the two "existentialist" writers alluded to in the opening quotation, Søren Kierkegaard (1813–1855) and Albert Camus (1913–1960).

As the above passage from *Spirituality* suggests, in his allusion to Camus's book *The Myth of Sisyphus* (Camus 2000) Solomon favors Kierkegaard's emphasis on

---

[5] I use this expression in the sense elaborated in Wolterstorff (1995).

[6] Solomon is well aware of this, and he cautions that any reference to the *whole* of somebody's life should not be taken uncritically. Notably in love and grief, it is an "*edited* life" that people encounter. This observation, Solomon adds, does not gainsay a holistic view of the person's life, but it should make us refrain from any claims toward an all-inclusive perspective. (See the chapter "On Grief and Gratitude" in Solomon 2004: 91.)

[7] Solomon quotes from Aristotle's *Nichomachean Ethics*, book I, Chap. 10. For a fuller treatment of the same passage and Aristotle's pivotal claim that one cannot estimate people's happiness until after their death, see Solomon (1976).

gestures of gratitude ("going down on one's knees and giving thanks") over rebellious gestures ("shaking one's fist at the gods or the universe in scorn or defiance"). As for the latter, Solomon views such gestures of existentialist obstinacy with critical reservation. The most extensive and nuanced treatment of Camus's purported failure in this respect is contained in one of Solomon's last major publications, *Dark Feelings, Grim Thoughts* (Solomon 2006). This book, I think, holds the key to the present discussion of gratitude as it is broached in Solomon's *Spirituality*-volume. Through a joint reading of these texts, I submit, we can distill a piece of analysis from Solomon's exposition of gratitude, which goes to show why the capacity for giving thanks was so important to him that he did not hesitate to extol it as "the best approach to life itself."

Moreover, this textual anchor will help us understand why the workings of gratitude are at the heart of Solomon's quest for an *inclusive*, "nonsectarian" form of spirituality that would bridge the divide between skeptics and persons of faith without positing a false sense of solidarity.[8]

## Orders of Experience and the Snares of Paranoia

The chief challenge in this quest, I take it, is to proffer a perspective of inclusion without conflation. In other words, what makes Solomon's account of gratitude both fascinating and resourceful is his alertness to the following problem: One cannot reconcile religious commitment and skeptical reservation by denuding faith of any substantive content so that it would be "secular enough" for the skeptic to swallow. Likewise, we must not patronize the skeptics with the claim that deep down they are repressed or "closet" theists, so that the only challenge *for them* is to get in touch with their hidden religious selves. Arguably, both of these approaches are arrogant and one-sided, and perhaps the very notion of "reconciliation" is already aiming too high when it comes to efforts to negotiate religious and irreligious, i.e., creedal and non-creedal outlooks on life.[9]

But then, what is Solomon after in his *Spirituality*-volume? What, if any, is the spiritual common denominator whose recognition may aid, enrich, or otherwise

---

[8] For Solomon's understanding of "nonsectarian," see Solomon (2002:26).

[9] The present equation of "religious" and "creedal" (and correlatively of "irreligious" and "non-creedal") may be questioned. Thus one may endorse a notion of religion which is not fettered to any particular, explicit creed. In fact, Solomon remarks that the majority of people's religious beliefs are not rooted in thorough theological study yielding explicit propositions. Rather, these beliefs function "more like club passwords or code words," which does not necessarily constitute a spiritual drawback (Solomon 2002: 13). Still, in light of spirituality's built-in sociality, any religious community has to cultivate *some* creedal reference point for the members to share. This holds true even if such reference point consists, for example, only of faith-inspiring paradoxes of the sort Kierkegaard boldly placed at the heart of being a committed Christian. Cf. Solomon (2002: 9, 12, 16).

"thicken" the lives of those committed to a creed-bound cause as well as of those committed to non-creedal causes? Solomon's answer, as we have seen, is: a cultivation of gratitude. Yet to see why or how gratitude fits the bill, we have to take note of two related insights on Solomon's part before we go into any further detail.

First, the challenge for the Solomonian inclusivist here is not simply to work out some broadly political sketch for peaceful coexistence among believers and unbelievers, exemplified most prominently by Habermas's discourse-ethical model grounded in some "pragmatic a priori of...communicative normativity, a kind of Kantian regulative ideal presupposed in every intersubjective exchange" (Žižek 2001: 89). As Slavoj Žižek and other critics have repeatedly argued, this Habermasian approach inevitably tends to subordinate particular religious, creed-bound commitments to universal, ethical standards. Accordingly, the entrenched opposition between rationalist ethics and irrational religious convictions is reinforced, accompanied by the claim that, when push comes to shove, ethics trumps religion.[10]

This point of view entails (for Solomon's quest) the unhelpful stigma that religion is either harmful or superfluous regarding the foundations of peaceful co-existence. By contrast, Solomon, as we shall see, proposes that this territorial view in which believers and unbelievers, respectively, fear the intrusion "from without" by a spiritual other is already skewed – an instance of what Nietzsche famously exposed as slave morality's fixation on a purportedly hostile environment against which it defines its own mission.[11] As an alternative to this moral "reactionism" and spiritual parochialism, Solomon argues that for any of the parties involved, the "enemy," i.e., the threat to a community's thickly spiritual life, is neither strictly external nor strictly internal. Instead, Solomon writes: "spirituality is the continuing trust and insistence...that the world is not out to get you and that the defensive measures of distrust and paranoia are unnecessary and self-destructive" (Solomon 2002: 51). Thus the main concern lies with self-destructive tendencies unleashed by certain forms of (group) paranoia, and how best to keep them in check should their complete or permanent elimination prove impossible:

> To a paranoid, the trust required for opening up to the world seems like utter foolishness and fatal vulnerability. If total trust presupposes a perfect world, total distrust presumes a

---

[10] Habermas may well reject this criticism as unfair or better placed at the door of John Rawls's conception of political liberalism which, according to Habermas, grants the predicate "reasonable" ("*vernünftig*") only to those religious communities that are willing to subordinate their religious convictions to the premises of the state and its constitution, which in turn is grounded in a "profane morality" ("*profane[n] Moral*"). (See Habermas 2001: 13–14.) Alternatively, Habermas opts for the "civilizing role of democratically enlightened common sense, which seeks a way of its own as a third party between science and religion" (13). Similarly, he elaborates in one of his subsequent writings on philosophy's need to present itself in the service of enlightenment and "not as the know-it-all competitor within the legitimate manifold of substantial life projects [*Lebensentwürfe*] by believers, adherents to different creeds, and nonbelievers" (Habermas 2005: 249). All translations of phrases quoted from the German originals are my own [MW].

[11] The *locus classicus* for this account in Nietzsche's writings is: *Genealogy of Morals*, Essay I, section 10, which Solomon quotes in the context of "Emotional Poisons: Paranoia, Envy, and Resentment." See Solomon (2002: 53).

terrible world, a world in which one should never, ever, let his or her guard down and in which the possibility of some larger, spiritual vision is all but foreclosed (Solomon 2002: 47).[12]

To be sure, this comment does *not* advertise the vision of a "perfect world" as the proper alternative to the paranoid vision of a "terrible world." Instead, in Solomon's account these two world-conceptions function as poles between which most people's views on life fluctuate. Accordingly, Solomon makes no pronouncement to the effect that the majority of people are either pathologically starry-eyed or pathologically suspicious of omnipresent threats, i.e., paranoid. What he is suggesting is that our membership in concrete, historically embedded communities cannot fail to make us susceptible to drifting toward either one of these extremes, sometimes (but certainly not always) to the point of a pathological breakdown, where our world comes undone. Solomon is interested in spiritual *tendencies* and how they move between certain extremes, without resting his case on any (statistical) claims about how often these extremes are actually reached by particular persons. Individual cases are not ignored, but their emergence and significance, so Solomon's Hegelian suggestion goes, can be traced only within a concrete communal context.[13]

Second, Solomon's discussion stresses the indelible chance factor involved in the historical development or "crystallization" of such sociocultural complexes broadly conceived, which culminates in the following provocative claim:

> Families and cultures have character as well as individuals. This point may have become politically incorrect, but it is still obviously true. Again, this does not mean that the outcome is inevitable (or for that matter, unavoidable). Germany might well have jettisoned Europe's widespread anti-Semitism and somehow propped up both the Deutsche mark and the Weimar Republic, and either not elected, impeached, or ignored Hitler. But it did not, and those who look at Germany's history and speak of Hitler and the War as Germany's fate are not necessarily speaking either racism or nonsense. (Japanese historians come to pretty much the same conclusions looking at the twentieth century history of Japan. It is not unlikely that our turn will come.) (Solomon 2002: 95)

The notion of a collective fate, central to Solomon's overall approach to community-bound spiritual development, rests on his doctrine of character. This goes to show that Solomon's philosophical program for *naturalized spirituality*[14] is not given to any theological dogma about predestination.[15] He holds that "character as fate strikes a middle position between determinism and chance" (p. 95). As he goes on to elaborate:

> Character can be cultivated, to be sure, but the range of choices, while theoretically unrestricted (I can imagine flying to the moon), is far more restricted in practice than we like to think…

---

[12] Cf. also Solomon's remark that "distrust breeds disharmony and alienation, and extreme distrust – paranoia – makes life unbearable" (Solomon 2002: 45).

[13] For the Hegelian character of Solomon's way of locating the individual's significance within a concrete communal context, see note 3, above. Cf. also the pertinent remarks on Hegel's thought in Geuss (2005: 49).

[14] For the most crucial aspects of Solomon's conception of *naturalized spirituality*, consider in particular Solomon (2002: 5, 7, 41, 42, 52, 87, 99, 137).

[15] Cf. Solomon (2002: 90–91).

> The fact that character is cultivated over a long period of time prevents us from interpreting who we are as simply a matter of chance, although many coincidences and contingencies go into the formation of character...which has a momentum apart from choices. Insofar as a person's future follows from character, we can accept as perfectly intelligible this prominent notion of fate (p. 96).

From this vantage point, we can say that the Solomonian naturalist works as a researcher who postulates general principles of cultural-spiritual development in order to spell out the struggle of different spiritual impulses or tendencies whose interplay has (provisionally) congealed into a particular, historically situated complex. The phenomenon of such emerging complexes is further explicated by Solomon as an *ordering* effected by emotional experience:

> An emotion is not so much an element or item in experience as it is the *ordering* of experience... Emotional experience is not a phenomenon in our heads, so to speak; it is the ordering structure of our being-in-the-world.
> I...want to reject the idea that rational criteria are the external standards by which emotions and their appropriateness may be judged... I suggest instead that emotions constitute the framework (or frameworks) of rationality itself.
> Of course, a single emotion does not do this. It fits (or does not fit) into the framework. But together our emotions dictate the context, the character, the culture in which some values take priority, serve as ultimate ends, provide the criteria for rationality and reasonable behavior (p. 71).

Put in these terms, socially embodied paranoia amounts to a structural corruption of our experiential order, which exploits our community's alertness to the uncertainty and historical contingency of its present condition. Judged by the criteria of such emotional ordering, paranoia is not so much irrational as it is a powerful form of psychotic, social intelligence. In restructuring our experiential habits, it provides a *practical answer*, viz., a concrete response pattern to our fears regarding the historical instability of our highest values. These values are usually enacted and protected by a seemingly robust, but indeed equally volatile social (cultural, ritual) infrastructure such as (non)governmental institutions, church offices, or publicly ordained rites like marriage, baptism, and confession. Commenting in a similar vein, Nietzsche, for example, decries the way "the entire West has lost those instincts out of which institutions grow, out of which the *future* grows..." (Nietzsche 2003: 105). As Solomon puts it more generally: "What distinguishes the emotions from understanding is their motivational and personal nature, not the lack of (emotional) intelligence. The emotions of spirituality constitute a passionate awareness of the existential uncertainty of one's own trajectory in life" (Solomon 2002: 29–30).

For that reason the socially embodied, paranoiac *habitus* cannot be shrugged off as simply irrational but ought to be acknowledged as an expression of a sophisticated capacity for organization, as an action-guiding force that has the power to (re)direct and "emaciate" the spiritual orientation or character of any given community. Of course, this does not entail the crude, monolithic claim that all community members have to be affected equally, at all times, by such paranoid tendencies.

## Death Fetishism – The "Dark" Side of Sisyphus

By exploring the implications of Solomon's understanding of spiritual tendencies, group character, and historical contingency, I submit, we can further clarify the present notion of self-destructive paranoia in the form of *fanaticism* as the ultimate enemy of, and obstacle to, gratitude. Thus extending our observations in the last section about the role of a community's alertness to its contingent conditions and its concomitant sense of "existential uncertainty" (Solomon 2002: 30), we can say the following by way of anticipation and announce the course of investigation for the remainder of this essay: Fanaticism promises to heal our fearful sense of historical contingency with the certainty of death. What does this mean?

To begin with, this uncanny promise does not amount to the deflationary (neo-Epicurean) claim that death is nothing.[16] Rather, it turns death into a fetish which lodges in the fabric of our lives so that, perversely, death becomes the meaning of life. To my knowledge, few authors have brought the complexity of *death fetishism* into relief as sharply as Solomon has. To be sure, the topic of death has drawn a lot of attention in existentialist circles, before and after Martin Heidegger's seminal treatment of it in *Being and Time* (Division 1, Part 2), as one of the classical reference points. Yet Solomon is plowing his own row here, so to speak. That is, his account of how death may turn into a fetish is exemplary, for it provides the centerpiece for his exposition of gratitude. If gratitude, as noted before, constitutes "the best approach to life itself," then turning death into a fetish amounts to the worst approach.

This is how Solomon introduces his working definition of death fetishism:

> Death fetishism…converts death, one moment in the machinery of life, into the meaning of life, the ultimate test of life, even the *point* of life.
>      In his *Myth of Sisyphus*, Camus…notes…that "By the mere activity of consciousness I transform into a rule of life what was an invitation to death." Refusing to commit suicide, according to the young Camus, is what gives meaning to life. If Camus's philosophy is throughout a kind of celebration of life, one cannot help but notice that it is always also a fascination with death (Solomon 2002: 117).

Several things are to be noted about this pithy statement. In terms of author association, one should underscore that Solomon finds Camus susceptible to a fascination with death, which belies his general celebration of life. Solomon does not criticize, much less dismiss, Camus *tout court*. But he does take a sharply critical stance toward one of Camus's most famous texts, *The Myth of Sisyphus*. Despite the latter's well known bravado and machismo (his rhetoric of rebellion and indomitable virility etc.), Solomon detects a very morbid or "dark" tendency at the heart of Camus's *Myth*. This leads to a second observation about the present characterization of death fetishism.

In the above formulation, Solomon's concern about Camus's fascination with death appears centered on its reactive character. There seems to be something amiss

---

[16] Cf. Solomon's charitable criticism of Epicure's dictum that "death is nothing" in Solomon (2002: 117–119).

with a life when its meaning is spelled out merely in negative terms of avoidance, namely, avoiding death. It is almost as if life is merely the photo-negative of death. Death comes first as the primordial threat (or challenge or temptation) and life, as it were, comes second, namely as a "brave" response through an indefatigably repeated gesture of resistance: resisting death by not committing suicide.

The key image of Camus's text at hand (Sisyphus pushing his stone to no end) already illustrates the mind-numbing aspect of this process. In the course of such repetition, there is no room for creativity or growth, which is why Camus's final exhortation "We must imagine Sisyphus happy!" leaves many a reader uneasy, if not completely unconvinced. Solomon, for one, professes to be unable to find happiness in this image or in Camus's general depiction of Sisyphus as the ultimate rebel figure. To appreciate the complexity of Sisyphus's "dark" side, consider how Solomon in *Dark Feelings, Grim Thoughts* zeroes in on the lead character from Camus's *Myth*:

> Sisyphus has the emotional advantage of being "condemned" by the gods. We, on the other hand, condemn ourselves. Camus' literary genius enables him to paint this ghastly scenario in heroic colors; but we must see it for what it is. It is a degrading, spiteful, and hopeless version of the Christian denigration of man… But we seem to like that vision of ourselves. As a counterweight to the existentialist emphasis on responsibility, it lets us off the hook. We can get away with mere *attitude* (Solomon 2006: 58).

Accordingly, we should separate the existentialist's genuine concern about responsibility from the contemporary distortion of that concern through a spiritually perverted cult of attitude. The point Solomon drives home with acerbic poignancy is: *chutzpah* is overrated! But then what does responsibility amount to, and on what grounds could we view Sisyphus's defiance as an expression of fanatical irresponsibility? Is his "emotional advantage" of being "condemned" perhaps related to something even darker than our (pseudo-) existentialist penchant for self-condemnation?

Arguably, the image of Sisyphus is somewhat suspect as a role model for contemporary existentialists, not so much because of the detrimental spiritual tendencies it may induce, but because part and parcel of the protagonist's punishment is his immortality. Sisyphus cannot die, but humans have to. To make Camus's imagery speak to human existence, then, one would have to combine the Sisyphus story with a certain afterlife *fantasy* which, of course, puts the skeptic as well as the advocate of naturalized spirituality on their guard. Deploying a broadly psychoanalytic idiom, I speak of fantasies rather than speculations, because Solomon is at pains to stress that such fantasies mobilize our emotional intelligence in a way that allows them to have *real* effects on how we lead our lives.

Solomon claims not to believe in an afterlife, although he does not dismiss any such fantasy out of hand. "Personally, I do not believe it, although this, I would be the first to insist, is of no interest or importance to anyone but myself. Indeed, it may well be my loss" (Solomon 2002: 113). Yet this is not where the discussion ends. In fact, it is not even where the discussion over death should begin:

> Nevertheless, the belief in an afterlife – any afterlife – is a denial of death in the sense that most concerns me here. Perhaps there is an afterlife. But *What happens after death?* is not

a substitute for the question, *What is death and how should I think about it?*... To think that
life after death answers our concern about death is just another form of denial (Solomon
2002: 113).

As with his proposal that gratitude is important irrespective of the addressee,
here Solomon is again most provocative and at his philosophical best, I think, when
he claims that afterlife stories in their traditional theology-laden dress are completely beside the point, if we are concerned with the this-worldly dangers of spiritual corruption effected by death fetishism. The *present* temptation to fetishize death
remains a perpetual threat for believers and unbelievers alike, regardless of whether
they are (theologically) wedded to some creedal account of life *after* death or not.
In fact, it is this false link between the *future promise* of an afterlife and the role
played by death in our *ongoing* existential fantasy of absolutely indomitable chutzpah, which is ingeniously exploited by Camus's Sisyphus figure.

Bracketing his immortality, for the moment, the first key characteristic of
Sisyphus is that he cannot "win"; his situation is devoid of hope. As Camus sets it
up, there is no room for improvement, growth, or expansion in Sisyphus's condition.
In other words, there is no room at all for what Solomon's Nietzsche described as
spiritual "overflowing" (Solomon 2002: 42–43). His doom is not physical pain but
monotony, mind-numbing repetition. And it is this mind-numbing aspect that Camus
contrasts with the "inflammatory" notion of revolt (Camus 2000: 58, 62, 85).

However, unless such revolt is *recognized* by some divine others, be they hostile
or benign, the corresponding gesture of defiance becomes either completely vacuous or it changes into a vague, self-referential expression of personal discontent. For
example, I can curse my own cowardice in a situation where I wish I had been more
courageous. Yet it seems a stretch of language to call this kind of self-addressed
discontent or even despair, "defiance." What is seemingly paradoxical about Camus's
image of scornful Sisyphus, then, is that it conveys a sense of independence, by way
of defiance, through a gesture which is clearly dependent on an antagonistic audience
that would recognize the hero's revolt for what it is. This paradoxical charm dissipates
quickly though, once we realize that revolt (shaking one's fist) against indefinite repetition (being forced to push a stone forever) would be just as numbing or fearfully
boring as the repetition itself. Within the confines of Sisyphus's fantastic punishment,
it is hard not to imagine how tired – rather than impressed or intimidated – the
on-looking gods would grow of his sight: "Oh well, there he goes again, shaking his
fist. The same old gesture..."

Differently put, Sisyphus's defiance-in-action would *not* pass the acid test of
Nietzsche's conception of self-cultivation by way of self-expansion.[17] To repeat, this
is because the inner logic of this image (unending stone-pushing coupled with
defiant fist-shaking) precludes any spiritual growth: There really is nothing for
Sisyphus to "conquer," no meaningful direction or trajectory along which his
gesture could take on even transient significance. Relentless repetition bleaches out

---

[17] For a succinct statement of this criticism concerning Camus's different figures of the absurd hero,
see Young (2003: 171–172).

meaning for action altogether, it becomes "blind." That is why Camus's imagery is most seductive but also most dangerous when he turns disaster into triumph and asserts:

> The greatness [of being a conqueror] has changed camp. It lies in protest and the blind-alley sacrifice . . . It is a man's demand made against his fate;… Don't assume, however, that I take pleasure in it: opposite the essential contradiction, I maintain my human contradiction. I establish my lucidity in the midst of what negates it. I exalt man before what crushes him (Camus 2000: 82).
>     To a man devoid of blinkers, there is no finer sight than that of the intelligence at grips with a reality that transcends it. The sight of human pride is unequalled (p. 54).

For Camus, this "essential contradiction" consists in the irreconcilable tension between our deepseated (but ultimately inexplicable) human desire for unity and the more or less "benign"[18] indifference of the universe, which does not accommodate our longing in a way that would resolve this conflict. In Sisyphus's fantasy, the universe does in fact "answer" him through the punishment of the gods, but this reply is one of permanent discord. Fate becomes a curse, for he is doomed to reenact his own state of spiritual dissatisfaction.

As Solomon saw clearly, upon scrutiny the image of Sisyphus does not convey the "unequalled sight of human pride" as Camus would have it. Instead, the sheer repetition and monotony of Sisyphus's revolt is nothing but clockwork, which means Sisyphus is spiritually dead – unable to grow in any direction. However, if things were that simple, it would be hard to see how Camus's literary imaginary could have had the immense crowd-appeal it did. The perverse fascination of Sisyphus must lie elsewhere.

Believers and unbelievers are not so obtuse that they would not realize that whenever their emotional "intelligence [is] at grips with a reality that transcends it," they are complicit in that fantasy. Differently put, whether the "higher cause" we are emotionally committed to is a god, a nation, or the charter of human rights, we know that these "gods" would not have any power over us if it were not for our own desire. These "gods" (pagan or Christian) are animated by our own emotions, which means that we can never separate ourselves sufficiently from their image in order to place any blame on them. Bluntly put, deep down we know that our gods are at least in part our own fault, and this makes us oscillate between resentment and despair. We did not choose our gods just as we did not choose the context of our upbringing (cf. Solomon 2002: 93), and so we resent the fact that they are turning on us. At the same time, we recognize them as *our* gods, and so we despair over this (partially) self-inflicted spiritual quandary – a despair whose various stages are the primary subject matter of Kierkegaard's *The Sickness unto Death* (Kierkegaard 2004).[19]

---

[18] As Solomon observes elsewhere, "the world of Camus's hero Sisyphus is populated with gods and goddesses who rather maliciously relish his fate, and whom he can defy. Yet through this "literary ploy" Camus indirectly acknowledges that the universe cannot be merely "indifferent," as he is generally fond of claiming. In fact, Solomon notes, Camus gets closest to admitting just that when he lets Meursault (the protagonist of *The Stranger*) "open his heart to the *benign* indifference of the universe." See Solomon (2004: 105).

[19] Cf. the commentary in Pattison (2005: 61–66).

Despair, to repeat, refers to the shattering realization that not only have your gods irreparably failed you, but you have been complicit in their false promise of salvation by nourishing a desire, or desires, that ultimately cannot be satisfied. Yet at the very moment when the bottom falls out of our world, so to speak, the fanatics among us have a stroke of genius: They turn the tables on the gods who have deserted them, by turning death into a fetish. What would that look like, concretely? As an example of such a fanatical reaction to conditions of utter despair over the irredeemable failure of one's highest cause, consider the case of the "honest Nazi," which I borrow from one of Slavoj Žižek's recent publications.

## Illustrating Fanaticism: The "Honest Nazi"

In *Welcome to the Desert of the Real*, Žižek introduces this figure when he asks us to consider

> the much-celebrated 'honest Nazi', the mayor of a small East German town, who, when the Russians were approaching in February 1945, put on his mayoral uniform and all his medals, and took a stroll along the main street, where the Russians shot him down – in contrast to many others, who quickly destroyed all traces of their Nazi past: is this gesture – of publicly proclaiming one's allegiance to Nazi Germany in the hour of its defeat – really so noble? (Žižek 2002: 73)

Žižek answers his own question in the negative, as he underscores what he takes to be the hypocritical nature of this act. After all, the mayor must have known that the regime, for which he stands up at the moment of its collapse, was "full of compromises with the worst criminals" even at the height of its power (p. 73). In other words, the present variant of proclaiming allegiance to a lost cause is a sanctimonious PR-stunt of sorts. Illustrated by the mayor's posture, the agent makes a spectacle of his fidelity, in which the *formal* quality of his stick-to-it-ness is meant to earn him a great deal of "partial credit," despite the fact that the *content* of the project in the name of which he lays down his life was rotten to the core, throughout its different stages up to its final collapse.

Solomon's present conception of death fetishism, however, goes even further than the (otherwise plausible) charge of hypocrisy in Žižek's account. Of course, we don't know exactly what was going through the mayor's head as he walked down the street to meet his death. Still, in terms of its *performativity*, the "honest Nazi's" final gesture can effectively be used to illustrate what I take to be the essential meaning of death fetishism, considered in conjunction with fanaticism. Extrapolating from Žižek's example along these lines, we can thus detect another level of morbidity in the mayor's comportment.

The first question to ask about the honest Nazi,[20] I suggest, is the following: What if the mayor's final gesture is not hypocritically vesting his "Nazi gods" with

---

[20] I am now omitting the scare quotes around the phrase "honest Nazi," but they should always be imagined to be there.

false glory?[21] What if he is rather accusing his gods for letting him down? Viewed from this angle, the ingenuity of the mayor's figure qua fanatic consists in how he couples hypothetical salvation with actual accusation. For him, as a fanatical adherent to the creed of Nazism, Nazism is categorically assumed to be the only possible path to salvation. What makes the fanatic's stance truly fanatical in this particular context of religio-ideological commitment is his *obsessive exclusivism*: He puts all his hope for salvation in one basket, so to speak. First and foremost, fanaticism – in the sense I take to be most relevant for understanding the critical import of Solomon's plea for gratitude against fanatical tendencies – is characterized by an all-or-nothing approach to eschatological concerns broadly conceived. To be sure, not all exclusivism is obsessive, which means not all exclusivism is fanatical in the present sense of that term. After all, many theistic believers, for example, think of their creed as the only pathway to salvation. We may find such exclusivism (Christian, Muslim, or otherwise) objectionable on other grounds, but applying the title of fanaticism to it without further qualification strikes me as unjustified.

Instead, for exclusivism to count as both obsessive and fanatical it has to be imbued with a particular kind of historical urgency. The fanatic feels personally responsible for making a crucial contribution to the success of his cause. In our illustration, the Nazi fanatic feels summoned to help bring Nazism into its own; or, in more religious language, to help Nazism achieve its final glory. Technically speaking, the fanatical believer views his individual contribution as a necessary (though in the majority of cases not sufficient) condition for the success of his cause, i.e., for realizing its *eschaton*.[22] In this spirit, the fanatic feels the burden of being-in-the-world heavy on his shoulders. Certainly, he won't be able to fulfill Nazism single-handedly. Yet he feels that if he and others like him do not live up to their calling, then a unique historical opportunity is irretrievably lost.

In other words, fanaticism as I conceive it, combines eschatological exclusivism with a particular view of history as a site of unique opportunities, challenges, and responsibilities. From this point of view, the kind of Nazi gods to whom the fanatical mayor-type devotee is obsessively committed have raised the stakes of salvation. They put each of their followers under great pressure by assigning them an immense responsibility, namely, by giving them a unique chance: to help realize Nazism, *now or never*. The Nazi gods, so the fanatic believes, do not offer second chances.[23]

---

[21] Here and in the following, the phrase "Nazi gods" is meant to flexibly designate Nazism as someone's highest cause, i.e. as the ideological matrix that bestows value and meaning onto his or her life. In this sense, adopting Nazism as one's creed may or may not involve explicit reference to personal divine agents. In this regard it is helpful to recall how Žižek spells out the complex meaning of such ideological matrix under the rubric of "the big Other," which is a technical term he imports from the French psychoanalyst Jacques Lacan. (See Žižek 2006: 10. Cf. also Adam Kotsko's concise and accessible comments in Chap. 1 and Chap. 2 of Kotsko 2008.)

[22] In its present use, the term *eschaton* refers to the last order of things or to the "last kind of beings in the order of reality," to borrow J.O. Urmson's phrase. See the entry for *eskhatos* in Urmson (1990: 62).

[23] Many important aspects of this now-or-never attitude are scrutinized in Julian Young's exposition of what he dubs "Nikeism," whose mantra ("Just do it!") becomes ominous when viewed in the context of fanaticism and unique historical opportunities, which the fanatic feels called upon to seize, at any cost. (See Young 2001: 111–114.)

However, the notion of such high-strung salvation-historical responsibility cuts both ways. In terms of possible blame, it is a *double-edged bargain*. According to fanatical reasoning, if my "conscience" tells me that I have done everything in my power to help the cause, the least I can expect from my gods is that this cause does not crumble in front of my very eyes. True, eschatologically speaking, the honest Nazi will allow that the ultimate version of Nazism may be left for future generations to experience. Witnessing the *eschaton* in its full and final glory may not be granted to most of the followers, who contribute their indispensable share but don't live to see the completion of their dream – like Emperor Vespasian and his Flavian Amphitheater, which was to be one of the emblematic sites of a more peaceful Rome after Nero's reign of terror.[24] Yet the one thing that the Nazi gods are not "allowed" to do, from the fanatic's perspective, is to accept his uncompromising devotion to the cause and then push him through an experience of existential disappointment, which leaves him unable to maintain any confidence in the very viability and possible future success of his faith-venture.[25]

Indeed, when it comes to the fanatic's "conscience," that is, his self-estimation as to whether or not he held up his end of the bargain, the situation gets arguably even more involved in light of the following crucial question: Short of hasty self-righteousness, how can the fanatic really know that his devotional commitment was maximal, that he actually did everything in his power to help the cause, in which case it would be the gods who become blameworthy for the cause's failure? The short answer is that the fanatic can't be certain. That is, he cannot simply rely on some inner feeling, regardless how intense, which tells him that he did his best. In this regard the fanatic is unable to take his so-called voice of conscience at face value. Explaining why this is the case requires a slightly longer answer.

## Fanatical Conscience, Performative Proof, and Pure Devotion

As with most, if not all, matters of conscience, there is no objective psychological criterion available that would allow the fanatic to scrutinize the depths of his own mind or heart to verify that his effort has really been maximal, that he did all he could.

---

[24] As the founder of the Flavian dynasty, Vespasian (9–79; emperor 69–79) commissioned the construction of this monumental amphitheater (a.k.a. the "Colosseum"), but only after his death did one of his sons, Titus, manage to have it more or less finished (aside from ongoing decorative work) and opened to the public. One might perceive some historical irony, or at least ambivalence, in the fact that the construction of the Colosseum is associated with a period of Rome's political stabilization and conditions of (relative) peace, while this enormous venue itself became the focal point of an expanding gladiator culture, poised to turn violence into entertainment, in ever more spectacular ways. Be that as it may, Vespasian's persona is generally remembered as marking a politico-historical watershed, and many of the reforms he initiated came to fruition only after his passing.

[25] Here I am using the expression "existential disappointment" in the sense elaborated in Paul Tillich's *Dynamics of Faith* (Tillich 2001: 13).

By way of general comparison, it is instructive to note that here the fanatic faces the same quandary as any staunch adherent to Kantian morality: For Kant a "good will," i.e. unadulterated respect for the moral law expressed by the (variously stated) formula of the categorical imperative, is the only thing of intrinsic worth (see Kant 1993: 7–8). Similarly, for the fanatic the highest ideal, the only thing of intrinsic worth, consists in unadulterated, unconditional or, if you will, "pure" devotion. Yet Kant was quick to point out that we can never know for sure, in any particular instance, whether our presumably good will to abide by the moral law for its own sake might not have been "contaminated" by secondary motives of instrumental reasoning or plain egoism. As he famously put it in *The Grounding for the Metaphysics of Morals*, "the dear self" – i.e. our tendency toward selfishness – can pop up unexpectedly, at any time (pp. 19–20). For the same reason no fanatic, like the honest Nazi, can complacently pat himself on the shoulder and say: "Well, I did everything I could, so the failure to keep the *eschaton* of my highest cause a living vision does not fall on my shoulders. Rather, my gods have let me down. Shame on them!"

However, according to the kind of fanatical emotional intelligence against which Solomon's caveat about death fetishism is directed, there is "performative proof" regarding the purity and unconditionality of one's devotion. And this proof is given through publicly staged self-annihilation. Through the act of killing himself in the name of a now-lost cause, the fanatic combines humiliation and vengeance within a single gesture of protestation.[26] In so doing though, the fanatic's self-directed violence strikes out at an enemy who is neither clearly external nor internal. With Solomon (as with Sartre and his "Portrait of the Anti-Semite"), fanatics always remain co-responsible for their gods, who mark the center of their obsessive optics (Sartre 1989).

But Solomon goes even further when he grants that some (though not all) fanatics are actually aware of this. Fanatics of the death-fetishizing kind, which is Solomon's primary focus here, do not typically seek an easy way out or make convenient excuses for themselves. In the face of traumatic failure, the only way out is death – but with a morbid twist insofar as their suicidal spectacle is performed as an eerie *ex post facto* redemption of sorts. To explain: Here everything rides on the assumption that devotion neither comes about nor dissipates quickly. Rather, devotion, so the death-fetishizing fanatic's general assumption goes, grows over time, gets more and more ingrained in us, and eventually becomes an integral part of our moral fiber. In this sense, devotion can be construed in terms similar to Harry Frankfurt's perspicacious account of people's most deepseated concerns and how they form a relatively robust *care structure* (Frankfurt 2005: 80–94). This care structure, like the fanatic's devotion to his highest cause, cannot easily be modified or overthrown. For this reason Frankfurt argues, contra Sartre, that the moment of self-conscious decision is overrated and that we cannot "reinvent" ourselves spontaneously at any moment.

---

[26] For a nuanced exposition of such ambivalent protest, see Eagleton (2005: 90).

(As a case in point, the young man in Sartre's famous example from *Existentialism is a Humanism* may honestly decide to prioritize his patriotism over the love for his mother, but if the orientation of his care structure points in a different direction, he will not be able to carry out his decision.) Crudely put, the proof of the pudding is in the eating. Accordingly, one of the central claims of Frankfurt's inquiry into "the importance of what we care about" is that performativity, based on our care structure, trumps self-conscious deliberation about whom we think we are or whom we would like to be (see Frankfurt 2005: 84–85).

These considerations about the superficiality of even honest deliberation also apply, *mutatis mutandis*, to the kind of self-assessment expressed in the fanatic's voice of conscience, which would have him believe that he has done everything in his power to contribute to the realization of his creed's *eschaton*. However, the fanatic's emotional intelligence is critical enough to second-guess his own conscience. Like the staunch Kantian, he is aware that secondary (self-congratulatory or self-righteous) motives can easily slip in, below our conscious awareness level. We may think or feel as if we have given it our all, but this judgment could be just the expression of our subconscious vanity. Yet here the fanatic has his morbid stroke of genius: He gives what we may term "performative proof" of his utter devotion by killing himself at the very moment when the failure of his cause has become undeniable (to him).

Once again, illustrated through the honest Nazi's performance, such self-slaying gestures of protestation are hard to interpret with confidence. As noted earlier, it is highly speculative to conjecture about what was going through the Nazi mayor's head, as he was heading down the street toward the enemy's gunfire. But Solomon's provocative point, I take it, was that the Nazi mayor – qua death-fetishizing fanatic – may very well recognize their indecipherability, which is why he "chooses" to let his actions speak for themselves by way of performative proof. The scare quotes in the preceding sentence indicate that, psychologically speaking, the fanatic will have thought contents, of course, which generally qualify as intentions. (He didn't put on his uniform and all his medals and then walk toward the Russians accidentally.) But the crux is that, in terms of his care structure, the meaning of his action will reveal itself only upon completion of the act, and cannot be read from his conscious intentions ahead of time.

Apropos of *ex post facto* redemption, then, the morbid climax of this fanatical logic is that the performative proof of the devotee's maximal devotion becomes manifest only in the devotee's death, which demonstrates that he *would* have been worthy of sharing in the *eschaton*, if any such glorious end state had been in the bargain. According to this logic, the ultimate message issued by the fanatic's death is not only that *his* gods have failed him, but that life in general and human existence in particular is a failure, since it doesn't reward pure devotion. In other words, there is pure devotion in this world, but there are no gods worthy of worship. Hence, life is not just meaningless but an insult to religious sensitivity *tout court*. In *Twilight of the Idols*, Nietzsche famously held that life as a whole cannot be evaluated because that would require a stance outside of life (Nietzsche 2003: 40).[27] The death-fetishizing fanatic bends this insight, for in death as the limit of life he finds a no-place from which to indict life, though such indictment can no longer be attributed to a human subject.

Here the quizzical expression "no-place" is simply meant to underscore the point that the moment of death, which the fanatic turns into a fetish, doesn't offer room for human agency, but only for inhuman revelation. Of course, people (fanatics or not) can ponder, plan, and carry out suicide. But if pure devotion, as explained, is independent of such antecedent "surface intentions," and if all that counts is the elusive moment when death occurs, then we cannot even say that the fanatic "owns" his death – which would steer us back to the initial objection that the honest Nazi's posturing was a PR-stunt. Rather, in the death fetishist's role the fanatic embarks on a course of action that will undo his status as a person, as it transgresses into an *impersonal act* that "won't have belonged" to anyone, once it is carried out. On this reading, what makes the figure of the honest Nazi so perverse, morbid, and dark is that he does *not* aim to issue a message to posterity, by impressing his human (military) enemies or any other recipients of the story with his all-the-way attitude. He does not seek to make a heroic exemplar of himself. Rather, he sets upon a path along which his action will turn into an inhuman performance – an impersonal act of utterly irreconcilable discord, which *embodies* a meaning that is no longer meant for any human or divine audience: Life is not just meaningless, but an absolute failure – like a stupid desire that can never be satisfied.

Death fetishism, then, ultimately amounts to the claim that in death devotion can show itself in all its purity, an impersonal purity which transcends both parties (human and divine) involved in any worshipful relationship. To be clear, nothing that has been said so far suggests that the kind of fanatic illustrated by the honest Nazi wants this catalytic event to happen, in which pure devotion is distilled from death. Rather, following in Solomon's footstep, the preceding considerations were meant to elucidate the workings and inner logic of death fetishism as the fanatic's last resort in the face of trauma. No one, not even the fanatic, volunteers to be traumatized, though many volunteer to die.

## Being Thankful for Life Itself and the Question of Holism

Now that the nuances of Solomon's conception of death fetishism in conjunction with fanaticism have been brought into relief, we can round out our discussion by considering on what grounds gratitude may be viewed as a powerful remedy or safeguard against fanatical tendencies. At the same time, this will allow us to revisit

---

[27] Cf. Nietzsche's similar remark on "perspectival valuations" in *Beyond Good and Evil* (Nietzsche 2002: 35).

the lingering question about the kind of holism that was implied when Solomon hailed gratitude as "best approach to life itself." Recall Solomon's poignant statement with which we began this essay:

> Gratitude, I want to suggest, is not only the best answer to the tragedies of life. It is the best approach to life itself... Whether or not there is a God or there are gods to be thanked, however, seems not the issue to me. It is the importance and the significance of being thankful, to whomever or whatever, for life itself (Solomon 2002: 105).

Cashing in our findings about fanatical response patterns to trauma, we can now interpret the first two sentences as follows. Gratitude is "the best answer to the tragedies of life" in that it offers us an alternative way of responding to the most traumatic experiences in our human existence. It remains up for debate whether all "tragedies of life" entail the occurrence of trauma. Yet it seems plausible to describe those tragedies that undermine our ultimate concern(s) in life – the core values of our care structure, in Frankfurt's idiom – in terms of traumatic experience. And, as the second sentence of the preceding quotation intimates, gratitude's alternative to a fanatical outlook consists in a different "approach to life itself," which Solomon in fact extols as the "best" approach. Put in the philosophical language of Solomon's conception of emotional intelligence, the question thus becomes: How exactly does gratitude "order" our emotions differently with respect to our general approach to, or vision of, life itself?

The answer, I submit, relates to the fanatic's "now-or-neverism" that is, to the eschatological tenet that salvation history burdens the believer with the task of seizing special moments, in which the *eschaton* associated with the believer's highest cause may either be helped along or get irretrievably lost. The advocate of gratitude rejects this construal of salvation history as spiritually damaging – a form of spiritual starvation or "thinking thin," in Solomon's phrase. Such now-or-neverism, the proponent of thankfulness holds, cannot fail to strain and eventually "poison" the spiritual vision of both the individual believer and the cultural community to which he or she belongs.[28]

To see this, recall another succinct formulation which we quoted at the outset from Solomon's *Spirituality*-volume, and which harks back to our preceding observations about group paranoia: "spirituality is the continuing trust and insistence... that the world is not out to get you and that the defensive measures of distrust and paranoia are unnecessary and self-destructive" (Solomon 2002: 51). We already saw that, as far as the fanatic is concerned, the world is in fact out to get him, in the sense that it poses a constant threat that one will miss irretrievable once-in-a-lifetime opportunities. Due to his eschatological lens of now-or-neverism and the double-edged bargain he struck with his gods, he can never let his guard down because salvation history does not offer second chances.

While this eschatological vision appears unbearably stressful on the face of it, one should not overlook those features that may strike many as generally appealing

---

[28] For Solomon's elaboration on "emotional poisons," see Solomon (2002: 53–55).

or, at least, tempting. True, the stakes of salvation history are stressfully raised, but the basic promise of now-or-neverism is that we become active participants in shaping, or co-shaping, our destiny underway to the *eschaton*. In a manner of speaking, we are granted the strenuous privilege of "making history." In this sense, utter stress is the price to be paid for utter significance.

However, Solomon would caution, even those who are generally sympathetic to this trade-off in terms of stressful significance, should heed the more disturbing potential for death fetishism that is smoldering in the background, once the salvation-historical bargain is entered into. As should be apparent by now, neither of fanaticism's two key elements sits well with Solomon's plea for a novel form of naturalist spirituality. First, Solomon, as I understand him, would not approve of the fanatic's *exclusivist* commitment, according to which submission to his highest cause is the only pathway to salvation. This much was already signaled by Solomon's insistence that the kind of non-patronizing naturalist spirituality which could speak to skeptics and believers alike would have to be "nonsectarian."[29]

However, Solomon does not go so far as to simply equate sectarianism with fanaticism. Even if sectarianism with all its dogmatic, exclusivist overtones remains worrisome or objectionable for independent reasons, in and of itself it does not induce death fetishism. The disposition for the latter gets generated only if exclusivism is combined with fanaticism's second key element, namely, double-edged eschatological bargaining. For this reason Solomon's most express criticism zeroes in on the *strategic* dimension of such bargaining as the spiritually most damaging aspect in this context:

> Trust in the world is not motivated by our hopes and expectations. It is a degenerate notion of faith (and trust) that says we have faith in God because we expect something back ... *We do not trust in order to get something back.* Nevertheless, we do get something back, and ... whenever we trust, we reap the benefits of a self-willed comfort in the world, more congenial relationships with others, and the opening up of all sorts of possibilities that distrust or the lack of trust keeps closed ..., authentic trust is *primarily concerned with the integrity of relationships* (including our relationship with the world), not with personal advantage, whether in the short or even the very long term (Solomon 2002: 52) [first italics added].

This passage is key because it illuminates how gratitude and trust interlock within a spiritually thick emotional order that does two things for us: To begin with, by way of gratitude, such emotional ordering keeps us from subscribing to any salvation-historical outlook, which prioritizes "special moments" over life as a whole and thereby generates a now-or-never attitude that pressures us into wanting to "make history." In this sense learning to be grateful for life itself has a prophylactic orientation over against the paranoid vision that we might forsake the *eschaton* at any moment. Specifically, it keeps us from giving in to the temptation of fetishizing death in the face of traumatic experiences. Being thankful for life itself, then, does not mean that we indiscriminately say "hooray" with respect to every detail in our lives, including even the most depressing or embarrassing ones. Rather, it means we

---

[29] Cf. note 8, above.

appreciate the growth character of life, in which the relations that matter most to us develop over time in a way that defies "punctual" evaluation or emotional blackmail.

Gratitude for life means appreciating its trajectory and being free from the desire to trade it all in for a purportedly special all-decisive moment. To use an analogy, being thankful to life is like honoring a long-grown friendship, in which one should never resort to blackmail-style bargaining and say to a friend: "Unless you do X (for me) now, all of our friendship will count for nothing." Similarly, gratitude keeps us from telling our gods: "Unless you reward my maximal devotion now, I will make myself disappear into an inhuman act of self-annihilation so as to give performative proof of the existence of absolutely pure but unanswered desire, that is, proof that life is a failure."

Next, by way of trust, a spiritually thick emotional order enriches our lives along the way, insofar as a trusting approach to the world is rewarding in itself. It makes our relationships with other people and with our environment overall more "congenial," as Solomon put it. Accordingly, an emotional intelligence animated by gratitude and trust is not merely reactive or protective. Rather, Solomon goes on to stress that jointly cultivating these emotions increases our spiritual well-being and the *integrity* of our lives. With an inclusivist gesture that accommodates creed-bound believers and non-creedal devotees alike, Solomon once again draws Kierkegaard to his side when he concludes:

> Nothing is more relevant to our overall well-being than the integrity of our relationships, in particular our relationship to the world as a whole. Insofar as faith is a concern for the integrity of one's relationship to God (as it was for Kierkegaard), it fits our model for authentic trust. But faith can also have such relationship with the world itself, and in the scope of our naturalized spirituality this is much more appropriately called trust than faith (Solomon 2002: 52).

One of the most formidable enemies of integrity consists in the seductions of death fetishism, within an emotional order framed by salvation-historical bargaining. The latter obviates trust in the world, as it infuses our lives with paranoia about missing the right moment to help realize the *eschaton*. Moreover, it "thins out" our faith-commitment or devotion writ large by rendering the relation to our gods or highest causes strategic, according to the logic of *quid pro quo*. For Solomon, gratitude gains critical importance as an emotion with the power to offset these tendencies of spiritual starvation and fanatical indignation. This is why gratitude and fanaticism make for an instructive contrast, according to Solomon's conception of how emotional intelligence can structure our lives in healthy or poisonous ways. At the same time, we noted that gratitude, like any other emotion, cannot bring about spiritual well-being single-handedly. Emotional orders are inherently multifaceted. As a case in point, achieving integrity requires not only gratitude but also trust, along with other emotional qualities,[30] in a complex relation where these emotions are not artificially "added up" but dynamically interwoven so as to reinforce each other.

---

[30] For example, a "good sense of humor" (Solomon 2002: 87).

Still, if death fetishism is the most morbid approach to life, which converts pure impersonal devotion into an absolute indictment, then we can appreciate the proposal that being thankful "to whomever or whatever" is the best approach to life. Once the spiritual dangers of death fetishism have been brought into view, it becomes clear that this claim on Solomon's part is anything but casual.

# References

Bourdieu, Pierre. 1990. *The logic of practice*. Stanford: Stanford University Press.
Camus, Albert. 2000. *The myth of Sisyphus* (trans: O'Brien, J). New York: Penguin Books.
Draper, Paul. 2001. Seeking but not believing: Confessions of a practicing agnostic. In *Divine hiddenness: New essays*, ed. D. Howard-Snyder and P.K. Moser, 197–214. Cambridge: Cambridge University Press.
Eagleton, Terry. 2005. *Holy terror*. Oxford: Oxford University Press.
Frankfurt, Harry. 2005. *The importance of what we care about: Philosophical essays*. Cambridge: Cambridge University Press.
Geuss, Raymond. 2005. *Outside ethics*. Princeton: Princeton University Press.
Habermas, Jürgen. 2001. *Glauben und Wissen*. Frankfurt am Main: Suhrkamp.
Habermas, Jürgen. 2005. *Zwischen Naturalismus und Religion: Philosophische Aufsätze*. Frankfurt am Main: Suhrkamp.
Holsinger, Bruce. 2005. *The premodern condition: Medievalism and the making of theory*. Chicago: University of Chicago Press.
Hoy, David Couzens. 2005. *Critical resistance: From poststructuralism to post-critique*. Cambridge: The MIT Press.
Kant, Immanuel. 1993. *Grounding for the metaphysics of morals* (trans: Ellington, J.W.). Indianapolis/Cambridge: Hackett Publishing Company.
Kierkegaard, Søren. 2004. *The sickness unto death* (trans: Hannay, A.). London/New York: Penguin Books.
Kotsko, Adam. 2008. *Žižek and theology*. London/New York: T&T Clark.
Nietzsche, Friedrich. 2002. *Beyond good and evil*, ed. R.-P. Horstmann and J. Norman. Cambridge: Cambridge University Press.
Nietzsche, Friedrich. 2003. *Twilight of the idols and the anti-christ* (trans: Hollingdale, R.J). London/New York: Penguin Books.
Pattison, George. 2005. *The philosophy of Kierkegaard*. Montreal/Kingston: McGill-Queen's University Press.
Peirce, Charles S. 1998. *Essential writings*. Amherst: Prometheus Books.
Sartre, Jean-Paul. 1989. Portrait of the antisemite. In *Existentialism from Dostoevsky to Sartre*, ed. W. Kaufmann, 329–345. New York: Meridian.
Solomon, Robert C. 1976. Is there happiness after death? *Philosophy* 51: 189–193.
Solomon, Robert C. 1983. *In the spirit of Hegel*. New York/Oxford: Oxford University Press.
Solomon, Robert C. 1999. *The joy of philosophy: Thinking thin versus the passionate life*. Oxford: Oxford University Press.
Solomon, Robert C. 2002. *Spirituality for the skeptic: The thoughtful love of life*. Oxford: Oxford University Press.
Solomon, Robert C. 2004. *In defense of sentimentality*. Oxford/New York: Oxford University Press.
Solomon, Robert C. 2006. *Dark feelings, grim thoughts: Experience and reflection in Camus and Sartre*. Oxford: Oxford University Press.
Tillich, Paul. 2001. *Dynamics of faith*. New York: HarperCollins.
Urmson, J.O. 1990. *The Greek philosophical vocabulary*. London: Duckworth.

Wolterstorff, Nicholas. 1995. *Divine discourse: Philosophical reflections on the claim that God speaks*. Cambridge: Cambridge University Press.

Young, Julian. 2001. *Heidegger's philosophy of art*. Cambridge: Cambridge University Press.

Young, Julian. 2003. *The death of God and the meaning of life*. London/New York: Routledge.

Žižek, Slavoj. 2001. *On belief*. London/New York: Routledge.

Žižek, Slavoj. 2002. *Welcome to the desert of the real: Five essays on September 11 and related dates*. London/New York: Verso.

Žižek, Slavoj. 2006. *How to read Lacan*. New York/London: W.W. Norton & Company.

# Chapter 18
# Solomon on Spirituality

John Bishop

**Abstract** Solomon's thinking on spirituality interestingly connects a range of themes in his philosophical work. What he takes to be spiritual in the primary sense is a certain kind of 'cosmic passion' which implies a judgment about how 'life' or 'the world' is overall. Cosmic trust, for example, takes the world to be fundamentally trustworthy. Such a judgment, I suggest, can be justified even though its truth could not be 'scientifically' established on objective evidence: and I outline a defence of 'doxastic ventures' of this kind based on William James's 'The Will to Believe'. Noting that Solomon's spirituality is naturalist only in the sense that it rejects the supernatural (and not in the sense that it views the world just from a natural scientific perspective), I consider whether it is coherent to adopt such a spirituality without at least implicit theistic or religious commitment. I discuss this question with special reference to the case of cosmic gratitude – thankfulness, not just for good fortune and advantages, but for all of life, including tragedy and death.

Robert Solomon's *Spirituality for the Skeptic* (2002) is a remarkable work. It is, in any case, surprising for an atheist philosopher to be championing a notion typically associated with religious commitment. But what is especially notable is the way the notion of *naturalised* spirituality provides for Solomon an overarching framework connecting the major themes of his extensive philosophical work. Accordingly, much of this book is adapted from previous work: indeed, only the first Chapter is completely new.[1] What Solomon has to say about spirituality both depends upon and unifies his favourite philosophical themes and commitments, bringing them into a pleasing balance.

---

[1] Three chapters are drawn from Solomon (1999), and a fourth is an abridged version of a paper written for a conference on death held in the Bay of Islands in January 1996. In what follows, otherwise unattributed quotations and page references are to Solomon (2002).

J. Bishop (✉)
Department of Philosophy, University of Auckland, Auckland, New Zealand
e-mail: jc.bishop@auckland.ac.nz

K. Higgins and D. Sherman (eds.), *Passion, Death, and Spirituality*,       245
Sophia Studies in Cross-cultural Philosophy of Traditions and Cultures 1,
DOI 10.1007/978-94-007-4650-3_18, © Springer Science+Business Media Dordrecht 2012

Solomon's thinking about spirituality accommodates his existentialism, the need to acknowledge the reality of our freedom. But it also includes his Hegelian sense of the importance of accepting that we do not ultimately control our own destiny, and his belief that we should trust not just other people but, in some sense, the world itself. Solomon's celebrated work on the passions is at the core of his account of spirituality as the *love* of life. But it is the *thoughtful* love of life, so any antithesis between reason and the passions is avoided. In his Chapter on 'Spirituality and Rationality', Solomon provides a critique of 'smart selfishness' – a perversion of both spirituality and rationality – that relates to his work in business ethics. The whole discussion is through and through informed by Solomon's extensive knowledge of the history of philosophy, and his narrative expertise in making it intelligible. His account of spirituality also relates to his philosophy of the self, and the associated ethic of self-transformation: here his use of perspectives from Asian philosophy is apparent.

The conviction that Philosophy should deal with 'the big questions' of life has always been central to Solomon's work. *Spirituality for the Skeptic* deals with these 'big questions', setting out, one may say, an overall 'philosophy of life'. The book has wide scope: though he does not put it this way, Solomon in effect aims to provide a unified answer to the fundamental question 'How should we live?' – a *unified* answer, not a complete or final answer. There has, of course, been suspicion amongst philosophers, especially within the 'analytical' tradition, about attempts at 'big question' philosophising: some have made it a virtue of professional academic philosophy that it should be anything but discussion of 'the meaning of life'. Solomon's *Spirituality* book is an excellent antidote to this suspicion, however, and a model of how 'big questions' philosophy can be done without dogmatism or systematising pretentiousness.

I shall here consider Solomon's discussion of spirituality from more of an analytical philosopher's perspective than he himself takes up. Let me begin with my motives – apart, that is, from my desire to contribute to honouring his work and his memory. First, I am interested in the possibility of a justifiable theism that employs an alternative to the conception of God dominant in contemporary analytical philosophy – a conception distinct from that of the 'personal omniGod', the supernatural omnipotent, omniscient, and omnibenevolent Creator *ex nihilo*. What distance remains between a theist who seeks to make sense of theism without the personal omniGod, and an atheist such as Solomon who recognises the importance of spirituality? Second, I am interested in showing that the concept of the spiritual can be philosophically serviceable, rather than, as many suspect, an amorphous rag-bag. That motivates an interest in trying to define the spiritual, and so I wish to consider whether such a definition does indeed emerge from Solomon's work.

## Spirituality as 'The Grand Thoughtful Passions of Life'

What is it to be a 'spiritual' person? What is 'spirituality' or 'the spiritual'? Solomon gives a wealth of answers to these questions. He does not, however, explicitly attempt an all-encompassing philosophical definition of the spiritual. What is spiritual in the primary sense for Solomon are *certain kinds of passion*, where, on his cognitive account, passions are not separate from, and may even amount to, judgments. Solomon says:

> Spirituality means to me the grand and thoughtful passions of life, and a life lived in accordance with those grand thoughts and passions. (Solomon 2002: 6)

These 'thoughtful passions' include, most centrally, love, trust and reverence. Solomon provides rich accounts of what these thoughtful passions, and their characteristic judgments, involve. He does offer a popular definition of spirituality, using the phrase that serves as his subtitle: spirituality as *'the thoughtful love of life'* (p. 6). The basic form of philosophical definition to which Solomon is committed is therefore clear: what is spiritual are certain thoughtful passions, and a spiritual person is a person who lives life in accordance with those passions.

What is the point, though, of attaching the term 'spiritual' to certain 'thoughtful passions'? Presumably so describing them is not of merely antiquarian interest: it is not that we may simply *replace* the traditional concept of the spiritual with the concepts of the relevant passions. Solomon evidently thinks there is some vital continuing point in recognising certain passions *as spiritual*. But what exactly is that point? It must have to do with *the kind of content* involved in the thoughtful passions Solomon identifies as spiritual. But, then, there surely must be in the background a definition that specifies what kind of content qualifies a thoughtful passion as spiritual.

Does such a definition emerge from Solomon's discussion? Here are some examples of what he says about the contents of the thoughtful passions he classifies as spiritual, taken from three of his Chapters.[2]

> The emotions of spirituality constitute a passionate awareness of the existential uncertainty of one's own trajectory in life. (Solomon 2002: 30)
> … it is that passion, that devotion and enthusiasm in the face of uncertainty, the acceptance of a certain lack of control coupled with responsibility for one's passions, that constitutes the virtue of love and the very heart of spirituality (p. 32).
> In spirituality, one chooses to see the world as beautiful or sublime instead of an industrial resource or a merely contingent set of facts (p. 36).
> Much of the excitement of sex might better be understood in terms of our vulnerability, our openness to others, and ultimately our openness to the world and to our own natural being. In this excitement, too, we recognise the passions of spirituality (p. 37).
> Spirituality includes a generalised erotic love of other people, a love that has learned to appreciate their depth and mystery … (p. 38)
> Spirituality requires reverence. Reverence is a passion that complements love (p. 39).
> With reverence, the perspective of love loses any sense of self-centred indulgence and opens us up to the suprapersonal world of spirituality (p. 39).
> Reverence is ultimately a kind of confidence… [and it] presupposes a commitment to the goodness of the world, a goodness that may be infinitely multifaceted and pluralistic, but that we nevertheless recognise as being much greater and more powerful than we are (p. 42).
> In so far as our trust in the world is based on a sense of entitlement, it is the very opposite of the trust that is involved in spirituality (p. 44).

---

[2] Chapter 2, 'Spirituality as Passion'; Chap. 3, 'Spirituality as Cosmic Trust'; and Chap. 5, 'Facing up to Tragedy'.

Cultivated trust is an essential part of spirituality. But spirituality should not be confused with self-confidence that is limited to confidence in one's abilities and skills for making one's way in the world. Trust in the world includes the acceptance of a *lack* of control and the recognition of one's vulnerability... we cultivate trust even in face of our recognition that a perfect or even a "best possible" world is impossible (p. 46).

... spirituality is the continuing trust and insistence that the world is benign and life is meaningful, that the world is not out to get you, and that the defensive measures of distrust and paranoia are unnecessary and self-destructive (p. 51).

Authentic trust is primarily concerned with the integrity of relationships (including our relationship to the world), not with personal advantage, whether in the short or even very long term (p. 52).

[Spirituality is to be found in an] unflinching recognition [of] an irresolvable tension between our passionate commitments and our awareness that nevertheless our lives are not ultimately in our hands (p. 77).

Spirituality at its best is a combination of gratitude and humor, a dash of that mock heroic Camusian confrontation with the Absurd, and a passionate engagement with the details and people in our lives. The important thing is not to deny tragedy, but to embrace it as an essential part of the life we love and for which we should be grateful (pp. 87–88).

These remarks convey much of great interest about the content of the thoughtful passions that Solomon regards as spiritual. Those passions may seem, however, to exhibit a variety too great to be grasped in a general definition. There may seem to be no more than a family resemblance amongst the passions that count as spiritual.

## Spiritual Stances on the World: The Implications for Ethics

Further reflection may suggest, however, that Solomon's remarks indicate that the spiritual as he understands it has to do with *the connectedness* of things – and with their connectedness in the most comprehensive sense. The spiritual concerns how things are related in 'the whole'. So the *domain* of spirituality will be our mode and style of relating to the world as a whole. What makes certain thoughtful passions count as spiritual will then be the fact that they are essential to spiritual ways of relating to the world. Considered as a definition, this suggestion is, of course, circular: for we now require an account of *spiritual* ways of relating to the world. Nevertheless, this is a step towards the kind of definition which – I suggest – is implicit in Solomon's account of spirituality.

The question of how we relate to the world is at the core, then, of Solomon's notion of spirituality. The spiritual passions involve (a) specific ways of responding to and being in the world, and (b) seeing – or choosing to see – the world in ways which make apt those ways of being and responding. Solomon's discussion of the key spiritual emotions of love, reverence and trust – and also of gratitude – all involve responses to and attitudes towards 'the world' or 'life', understood in a suitably comprehensive sense. Trust, for instance, is *cosmic* trust.[3] It is the insistence 'that the

---

[3] It is important to recognise that the word 'cosmic' is here used in a broader sense than 'belonging to the natural cosmos' or 'pertaining to scientific cosmology'.

world is benign and life meaningful' (Solomon 2002: 51) even though the tragic is not to be denied; indeed, the world may sometimes even be forgiven for it. ('Odd as it may seem, "I forgive you, world" is a surprisingly effective ritual, the implicit animism supporting rather than undermining the gesture' (Solomon 2002: 56).)

This account of the spiritual as concerned with seeing the world overall in certain ways and responding accordingly has interesting implications for ethics. The passions and emotions are open to ethical evaluation – and this evidently extends to those cosmic passions and attitudes that are modes of relating to 'the world' or 'life itself'. Since the cosmic passions are essentially correlated with ways of taking the world to be, it will follow that *virtuous* cosmic passions necessarily involve *good* ways of taking the world to be. It follows, therefore, that part of any complete answer to 'How should we live?' will have the form: 'We should take the world to be thus-and-so.' Cosmic trust, for example, takes the world to be fundamentally trustworthy. But cosmic trust can be a virtuous attitude if and only if it is good and right to take the world to be trustworthy in the way we live our lives. It may thus be that a completed ethics will commend such a practical passional stance towards the world. (Ethics will thus not be confined to theories of right action, or, even, of right character: it will need to include theories of right relationship, including right *cognitive* relationship to 'the world' as a whole.)

## The Epistemology of 'Amplifying' Spiritual Stances on the World

Whether any particular cosmic passional stance *does* get commended by a completed ethics will depend, though, on whether it is *justifiable* to take the world to be as envisaged by that stance. Since there is here an issue about *what is the case*, this justifiability question must include the issue of *epistemic* justifiability. It seems mistaken to presume that questions about reality can be properly settled by appeal solely to the ethical value of responses that make sense only if certain cosmic claims hold true. It may, for example, be virtuous to avoid paranoid or despairing ways of relating to the world: but how could this by itself establish that the world is, in reality, fundamentally trustworthy?

Certainly, the question of epistemic justifiability may not simply be ignored. There would be something wrong with adopting a particular cosmic stance in the face of clear evidence that the implied view of the world was false, even if one derived benefit from so doing. There is nothing admirable about that kind of wishful thinking or 'living in denial'. Solomon's discussion makes it clear that cosmic trust is an attitude that faces up to the tragic: the judgment implicit in cosmic trust must cohere with a proper acceptance of one's dependence on forces far greater than oneself, and of the inevitability of mortality and tragedy. Whatever the claim that 'the world is fundamentally trustworthy' precisely means, then, its truth must fit with our total available evidence about the world: otherwise cosmic trust will not be justified. But neither is the truth of this claim able to be established scientifically on the basis of adequate evidence. No rationally compelling case for adopting cosmic trust will be forthcoming. The context seems thus to be one of *evidential ambiguity*: taking the world to be fundamentally trustworthy is an option for an overall interpretation of the world and our experience of it, but one that cannot be decided on the evidence in accordance with any public and objective evidential practice. It follows, then, that a defining characteristic of a Solomonian 'grand spiritual passion' is that its related overall view of the world is *an extension or amplification* of the scientifically knowable cosmos.

## A Jamesian Defence of Spiritual Stances

The context is thus of exactly the kind in which William James (1956) argued that faith could be justified. We are presented with what James called a 'genuine' option. We may choose whether or not to take the world to be fundamentally trustworthy, and this choice matters significantly, affecting the kind of life we lead. The choice is forced, in the sense that what matters is whether we do or do not commit ourselves to the world's being trustworthy – suspending judgment on the matter, or committing ourselves with some intermediate degree of belief (which are *generally* reasonable responses when the evidence does not decide), are here both forms of choosing *not* to commit ourselves. And the situation is not just that *for the moment* the evidence is mixed – rather this is the kind of overall framing issue that 'cannot by its nature' be settled evidentially (James 1956: 11). In such circumstances, on James's view, it is permissible for us to make a *doxastic venture* – that is, to take to be true in our practical reasoning a claim whose truth we recognise not to be adequately supported on our evidence. Faith can thus be justifiable, according to James – though only if our venture goes beyond what our evidence establishes, not if it ventures against the force of the evidence. James thus advocates a *modest* fideism that places high value on remaining within the scope of epistemic concern and rejects the religious anti-rationalism that often goes by the name 'fideism'.

James's account needs to make explicit important *ethical* constraints on doxastic venture: there is a difference between good and bad 'leaps of faith' (see Bishop 2007a, esp. 163–66). We must avoid conjugating the following irregular verb: 'I am a knight of faith', 'You are an ideologue', 'They are fanatics'. James does make it clear that a leap of faith against the acknowledged weight of our evidence is a bad leap of faith. But he would appear to leave open leaps of faith that are obviously ethically impermissible – faith-commitment to a Nazi worldview, for example. (In the given historical circumstances commitment to the Nazi worldview did present some people with a genuine option, and arguably the question of its truth was in principle beyond evidential resolution.) To deal with this problem, ethical evaluation must be brought into play: permissible faith-ventures have to be morally acceptable, in terms both of their motivation and their content.

Thus, the fact that a certain view of the world is intrinsic to a morally admirable cosmic passion *is* a consideration in favour of the permissibility of doxastic venture in favour of that view of the world. Once all the evidence has been taken properly into account, the ethical evaluation of cosmic passions *can* yield an ethical case for the rightness of taking the world to be a certain way. Of course, this will be so only if a Jamesian modest fideism can be defended against *moral evidentialism* of the kind famously expressed in Clifford's assertion that 'it is wrong, always, everywhere, and for any one, to believe anything upon insufficient evidence' (see Clifford 1879, 177–211). But I will here proceed on the assumption that such a defence can indeed be provided.[4]

We therefore reach a position familiar from Kant: we may properly commit ourselves in practice to certain cosmic claims that escape validation through the resources of our theoretical intellects. Solomon must, I think, agree with that position, even though (so far as I know) he did not concern himself with any attempt to justify faith understood as doxastic venture.

## Does a Spiritual Stance Have to Be Religious?

Solomon would not, of course, endorse Kant's view about *the content* of the cosmic claims that we rightly favour with our faith-ventures. For Kant, properly motivated moral engagement requires that we posit a supernatural agent powerful and good enough to ensure that ultimate happiness is proportional to moral desert. Such a supernaturalist view is anathema to Solomon.[5] So now we need to ask: do ethically sound cosmic passions or spiritual stances require the world to be as conceived by theism or any other religious worldview? Or can a spiritually admirable orientation to the world understand it in a wholly 'naturalist' way, as Solomon supposes?

This question presupposes, of course, that we have a grasp of what the 'ethically sound' spiritual stances are. Solomon's account proceeds largely by describing in commendatory ways certain thoughtful passions, such as reverence and cosmic trust. He uses 'spiritual' as a term of approbation: spirituality is *eo ipso* good, or right, spirituality. But one may use the term more neutrally to refer to a particular set of cosmic passions, along with their implied pragmatic orientations to the world. Then the notion of bad or inadequate spirituality will make sense. Thus, for example, Solomon says that Schopenhauer's view of the world was not a spiritual view at all (see Solomon 2002: 47). Yet Schopenhauer's *is* a view of the world *in the domain of* spirituality, holding that right responses to the world are those that recognise its

---

[4] For my own attempt at such a defence, see Bishop (2007a, Chapter 8).

[5] It is problematic also for theists for whom the Argument from Evil succeeds in removing the sort of personal omniGod Kant seems to need from their stock of live hypotheses. One might concede that the Argument from Evil fails theoretically to establish atheism (for example, because of the availability of a certain kind of 'skeptical theist' response), and yet still find that, relative to certain value commitments which one endorses but recognises not to be required on pain of irrationality, practical commitment to the truth of traditional theism is nevertheless morally ruled out. I explain this possibility in Bishop (2007b). I have also discussed elsewhere whether Christian hope could be of a 'non-triumphalist' type that does not require the kind of righting of all wrongs that Kant seems to need, and which continues to be affirmed by leading Christian philosophers, such as Marilyn McCord Adams. (See Bishop 1998; Adams 1999, 2006.)

essence to be Will (the working out of sheer indifferent forces) – and those right responses include not only pessimism but also compassion for the suffering of sentient beings. We may thus say that Schopenhauer did have *a* spirituality, though perhaps we may agree with Solomon that it was not (altogether) right spirituality. But whether or not we use the term 'spirituality' so that it makes sense to speak of false or inadequate spirituality, the important point remains that there can be real ethical dispute about what are the proper thoughtful cosmic passions and implicated worldviews.

## The Case of Cosmic Gratitude: A Coherent Spiritual Stance for a Naturalist/Atheist?

One might, however, agree that a certain cosmic passion is morally admirable, yet disagree about what view of the world is implied in that passion. There may, in other words, be agreement on the value of a certain spiritual stance, but disagreement about how one must take the world to be in adopting it. So theists and naturalist/ atheists, the religious and the non-religious, may agree that it is good to maintain a certain practical orientation to 'life as whole', while continuing to disagree in their worldviews. It is a very interesting question whether it might be possible to argue from agreement over the value of a given spiritual stance towards a resolution of the disputed metaphysical and religious issues. There is, as well, a related, higher-order, question: in the light of agreement in practical spiritual stance, to what extent and in what way do the metaphysical disagreements really matter?

Let me canvass these issues a little further by considering Solomon's discussion of the spirituality of cosmic gratitude.[6] Solomon's remarks about the need for gratitude occur in Chap. 6 of *Spirituality for the Skeptic*: the Chapter title is 'Spirituality, Fate and Fatalism'. What Solomon says about gratitude thus needs to be placed in the context of what he says about fate. Here is an indicative quote:

> The portrait of fate I have tried to paint is not one of inevitability or mechanical causality. I have said repeatedly that it is not as if it couldn't have happened otherwise. To the contrary, I want to suggest that belief [in] and acceptance of fate has to do with embracing a larger narrative in which one's actions and fortunes have meaning and make sense of one's life. Part of that meaning and making sense, an essential part of that acceptance, is our willingness to feel and show our gratitude (Solomon 2002: 104).

It is important to note that this gratitude is not just for the good things in life or for our good fortune. Solomon says that gratitude is 'the best approach to life itself' (p. 105), and he remarks that

> It is… odd and unfortunate that we take the blessings of life for granted – or insist that we deserve them – then take special offense at the bad things in life, as if we could not properly deserve those. The proper recognition of… the tragic sense of life is not shaking one's fist at the gods or the universe… but rather, as Kierkegaard writes in a religious context, going down on one's knees and giving thanks (p. 105).

---

[6] For my previous discussion of this topic see Bishop (2010: 530–533).

# A Secular Grace?

Can one properly sustain such a claim, however, without viewing the world as providential in a sense rich enough to qualify as theistic?

I am reminded of a story about the hall of residence I belonged to as an undergraduate at the Australian National University. Named 'Bruce Hall' after Stanley Melbourne Bruce, Prime Minister of Australia from 1923 to 1929, this hall of residence followed Oxbridge traditions, including formal dinners with a High Table, everyone wearing gowns, and a Latin grace, as follows:

> *Gratias agamas pro cibo atque sodalitate, nos qui in his aedibus Bruce appellatis, studia ad majorem universitatis gloriam prosequimur.*
>     (We give thanks for food and fellowship, we who, in these halls called Bruce, pursue our studies to the greater glory of the university.)

After I had left Bruce Hall I heard an account of how the grace had been adopted. Unlike the historic Oxbridge Colleges, Bruce Hall was a secular foundation. Its founding Warden, the New Zealand geographer William Packard, felt that, nevertheless, some formal acknowledgement of gratitude would be appropriate. So he asked the classicist A.D. Trendall (also a New Zealander, and then Master of University House, Canberra) whether he might compose a *secular* Latin grace for Bruce Hall formal dinners. The story is that Trendall thought the notion of a secular grace a contradiction in terms, but went ahead and composed one to exemplify the absurdity ('*ad majorem universitatis gloriam*' has the whiff of idolatry unless it is meant as a joke!). Packard did not get the joke, however, and the grace was instituted.

Packard felt exactly what Solomon expresses – that a virtuous community should somehow collectively express its gratitude for food and fellowship. Like Solomon, Packard believed that commitment to the existence of a supreme supernatural being is not required for this stance of gratitude to be held and expressed sincerely. Trendall (if the story is correct) thought otherwise, perhaps taking the view that the virtuous impulse towards gratitude that people naturally feel is what Peter Berger calls a 'signal of transcendence' – an implicit indication of a supernatural Providence to whom gratitude is rightly directed (see Berger 1970). So, who is right? Can there be a naturalist spirituality of gratitude, or is such a spirituality implicitly theistic?

## Gratitude as Distinguished from Appreciation, and Not to Be Detached from a Cognitive Orientation to the World

Solomon recognises that some may question whether gratitude is an apt response to life itself. Gratitude is to be distinguished from appreciation – and perhaps it is only the latter that characterises a proper orientation to the world? Solomon observes that appreciation is correlated with understanding what is to be appreciated as a matter of good luck. Such an understanding, he argues, does see the world as meaningful – but just in the rather weak sense that what happens is not interpreted purely as sheer chance and necessity (Solomon 2002: 104). There is, though, no sense in which we should appreciate our *bad* luck, whereas – as Solomon stresses – authentic cosmic gratitude is a willingness to celebrate and be thankful for the whole of life.

Let us allow, then, Solomon's claim that our attitude to life should be one of gratitude for all of it, rather than simply appreciation of the good bits. How may we resolve the question whether such gratitude is a coherent attitude for a naturalist/ atheist?

One way to support an affirmative answer to this question would be to claim that the ethically admirable attitude of gratefulness can be detached altogether from any amplified or 'transcendent' cognitive commitment about the world. The desirability of taking certain overall practical stances as we live our lives – such as the stance of cosmic gratitude – may then be completely compatible with our accepting a purely natural scientific view of the world.

That attempt to secure the 'naturalist' status of cosmic gratitude, however, goes totally against Solomon's basic analysis of the grand thoughtful passions that belong to the domain of spirituality – since it is *of the essence* of those grand thoughtful passions that they involve some amplified cognitive attitude to the world. Deny this and you are denying altogether that there is such a thing as the domain of spirituality – or, perhaps, you are claiming that all there is in that domain is the stance that takes the world to be no more nor less than a completed evidence-based natural science takes it to be, so that we need have no truck with the amplified, transcendent, understandings of the world that belong to spirituality.

In response to this 'detachment' suggestion, then, the reply will be that you have not properly conceded that it is *gratitude* that is the right response to the world if you think it can be detached from taking the world to be *more* than natural science could show it to be – in particular, to its being *such as to deserve our gratitude*. Such a detached account treats the sense of gratitude as mere benign pathology – a feeling of thankfulness that simply 'comes over us' (some of us, sometimes). But Solomon's cognitive account of the passions is meant to resist any such treatment. And rightly so, surely, when it comes to spiritual stances such as cosmic gratitude – to have such a stance is not merely *to feel* grateful, it is *to judge* gratitude to be the right response to how things really are, part of what is required for living in right relationship with the world.

## Solomon's 'De-Supernaturalised' Naturalism and the Role of the Concept of Fate

Solomon's naturalised spirituality, then – as he himself makes clear – is not a reduction of spirituality to scientific naturalism (the stance that the world is just as natural science depicts it). It is spirituality naturalised only in the sense that it is *de-supernaturalised*. The cosmic gratitude that belongs to the spirituality Solomon approves implies a view of the world extending beyond what natural science shows it to be – but not by deploying the concept of the providence of a supernatural Cosmic Controller; rather, what extends it, Solomon thinks, is the applicability of the notion of fate.

The notion of fate is tied to the notion of narrative significance. Consider these quotes, for example:

> … fate is the larger narrative in which a present choice or event that might otherwise seem meaningless can seem to have profound significance. Fate is, in that sense, a *teleological* phenomenon, the ascription of purpose *in addition to* the causal explanation of what has happened (Solomon 2002: 100).
> Fate provides an explanation, even if a vacuous one. ('It is fate that has brought us together'.) But such explanations do not pretend to account for a phenomenon the way a causal analysis would. They rather underscore the narrative significance of an event (p. 102).

A narrative, of course, is a story we tell – and, as Solomon emphasises, stories about the operation of fate do *explain the point* of what happens to us and what we do in a way that stories that merely record our good and bad luck do not. If gratitude is intrinsically related to understanding the world as fateful, in the sense that our lives are explained within a certain narrative, then two questions arise. First, of what importance is it whether the relevant narrative is true, or, at least, taken to be true? And, second, what kind of a narrative does it have to be to provide grounds for gratitude?

## Theistic and Non-theistic Narratives

Those who think that cosmic gratitude must have the theistic God for its object will answer the first question by insisting that of course the narrative has to be believed to be true. They will answer the second question with the claim that the right kind of narrative will be a narrative of salvation history as found in the theistic religions, in which divine providence works towards a consummation of historical existence, perhaps (on some accounts) achieving universal salvation through the power of forgiveness and reconciling love, but (on any of these accounts) at least achieving final and perfect justice.

What alternative answers may a proponent of de-supernaturalised spirituality give?

Some theists have advocated *non-realism* with respect to theological narratives. We may endorse these narratives, they think, while nevertheless recognising – in our philosophically reflective moments, anyway – that they are true only of a fictional world we have ourselves constructed to express our most fundamental values.[7] Obviously, the same view could be taken with respect to Solomon's narratives of fate. Such a view would not be adequate, however, and would amount only to a

---

[7] Don Cupitt expresses just such a non-realist understanding of theistic beliefs:

> I continue … to pray to God. God is the mythical embodiment of all one is concerned with in the spiritual life. He is the religious demand and ideal … the enshriner of values. He is needed – but as a myth (Cupitt 1980: 180).

This passage is quoted by Charles Taliaferro in a helpful discussion of theological non-realism. See Taliaferro (1998: 40–45).

sophistication of the 'detachment' proposal already dismissed. Authentic gratitude has to involve a specific cognitive attitude to the *real* world, not to a world consciously recognised as a fictional construct.

But perhaps that cognitive attitude need not include belief? It may be possible to venture beyond our evidence in practically committing ourselves to a certain view of the world *without actually believing it be true*. Faith may be a *sub-doxastic* venture: we may take the world to be thus and so while merely hoping that that is how it is.[8] Perhaps it is possible, then, to be authentically grateful in taking the world to be fateful in the appropriate way, yet without actually believing that it is that way – provided, that is, that we do firmly commit ourselves to the truth of the relevant view of the world when we come to act?

I do not rule out such a possibility. But I question how we might find the motivation for such a commitment. Generally, it is only because one *believes* that the world is thus and so that one is motivated to *take it to be* thus and so when one comes to act. Where a faith-venture beyond the evidence is involved, the motivating belief must itself be sustained other than on an evidential basis ('passionally', as William James says; see James 1956, Section II and *passim*) – and typically this occurs through a person's immersion in a historical religious tradition which frames the world in ways which yield providential meaning beyond anything scientifically knowable. For someone like Solomon who not only wishes to de-supernaturalise spirituality, but also, so to speak, to de-religionise it, there is a problem in accounting for how commitment to the required spiritual view of the real world can come to be motivated. One obvious possibility is that, if gratitude is indeed one of the passions of right spirituality, then the required motivation must *ultimately* come from a person's connexion with theistic religious traditions, however much that person has consciously repudiated core aspects of orthodoxy within those traditions.[9] Solomon's de-religionised spirituality might thus ultimately have theistic religious motivational roots. If such a conclusion is uncomfortable, then some alternative account will be required of the motivational source of naturalised spirituality's cognitive commitments.

---

[8] This view of faith has been advocated by Andrei Buckareff (2005). In fact, Buckareff argues that faith can be *only* a sub-doxastic venture, a view that I contest in Bishop (2005). Note that sub-doxastic venture does require belief that the world *could (for all we know) really be* as it is taken to be: there is thus an important if subtle distinction between someone who makes a sub-doxastic venture in favour of a certain meaning-endowing narrative, and someone who takes such a narrative to be a fictional construct. Though (coherent) fictional narratives enjoy merely *logical* possibility, to know them *as fiction* is to recognise that they are *not* (and cannot be, unless by a fluke) true accounts of what is independently real. Sub-doxastic faith-venturing does not, then, simply collapse into the non-realist position just set aside.

[9] This may yet be true even if Solomon takes commitment to the world's deserving our gratitude to be sub-doxastic, since such commitment would seem motivated by the belief that it would be good for the world to be that way and that, for all we know, it could be. Such beliefs about the world are derivable from religious, in particular, theist traditions. Whether they can be derived independently is doubtful.

I see no reason why such a conclusion should be uncomfortable, however. I see no good reason to resist the view that Solomon's account of spirituality is rooted in the theistic religious traditions, even though he plainly (and I think rightly) rejects any need for reference to a supernatural personal omniGod. I shall close with one further argument in support of this conclusion, based once again on Solomon's inclusion of gratitude 'for all of life' amongst the (virtuous) spiritual passions.

Authentic gratitude evidently cannot be grounded in *just any* narrative of fate. Witness the following quote from Solomon's Chap. 6, especially the final parenthetical remark:

> The notion of fate is charming, not because it takes away our sense of responsibility, but because it makes the future – and thus our responsibilities – seem more real. It is as if one's grandchildren are already waiting, as if one has already earned that PhD toward which one is now but a fledgling graduate student, as if the salvation of the world is already settled and it is just up to us to find the means. Belief in fate is thus the equivalent of a kind of optimism, a way of seeing the future as promising. (Of course fate can also be conceived as a kind of pessimism with the idea of the future as doom.) (Solomon 2002: 99–100).

For gratitude to be part of an overall virtuous response to the world, the fateful operations of the world must generally be such as to support an optimistic view. That can be so, I think, only if *something like* a theistic account of salvation history holds good. For me – as I am now suggesting, also for Solomon – the question is whether such accounts can possibly be sustained without taking the world to be under the overall control of a supreme supernatural agency both unequivocally inclined towards and capable of effecting the realisation of whatever those conditions are that would justify the right kinds of gratitude, hope and cosmic trust. An observation Solomon makes in the passage quoted offers an important clue as to a possible means of sustaining such a possibility – namely his remark that the notion of fate 'makes the future more real'. To say that it is 'as if the salvation of the world is already settled and it is just up to us to find the means' is reminiscent of William James's view of the 'melioristic' universe which supports the kind of faith in a fact that is capable of creating that very fact.[10]

It may be, then, that an optimistic theistic kind of spirituality can be defended by positing a world in which it is not an external supernatural controller who ensures salvation but, rather, some real future state of the natural universe itself gloriously realising the goal (or *telos*) for which it has always existed.[11] To the extent that I am right in suggesting that this is what his naturalised spirituality points to, Hegelian influences on Solomon are clearly apparent. The sobering question, of course, is whether the history we have had so far is consistent with supposing that it might yet

---

[10] 'The melioristic universe is conceived after a *social* analogy, as a pluralism of independent powers. It will succeed just in proportion as more of these work for its success. If none work, it will fail. If each does his best, it will not fail' (James 1919: 228–229).

[11] I consider whether such a possibility might yield a recognisably Christian alternative concept of God in Bishop (2007b).

be leading to such a resolution. But if we are in no position to be sure of a negative answer to that question, faith-commitment to an optimistic view of the world that would sustain gratitude, hope and cosmic trust – and also perseverance in moral endeavour – remains at least a permissible and honourable option.

# References

Adams, Marilyn Mc.Cord. 1999. *Horrendous evils and the goodness of god*. Ithaca/London: Cornell University Press.

Adams, Marilyn Mc.Cord. 2006. *Christ and horrors: The coherence of christology*. Cambridge: Cambridge University Press.

Berger, Peter L. 1970. *A rumor of angels: Modern society and the rediscovery of the supernatural*. Garden City: Anchor Books.

Bishop, John. 1998. Can there be alternative concepts of God? *Nous* 32: 174–188.

Bishop, John. 2005. On the Possibility of Doxastic Venture: A Reply to Buckareff. *Religious Studies* 41: 447–451.

Bishop, John. 2007a. *Believing by faith: An essay in the epistemology and ethics of religious belief*. Oxford: Clarendon.

Bishop, John. 2007b. How a modest theism may constrain concepts of God: A Christian alternative to classical theism. *Philosophia* 35: 387–402.

Bishop, John. 2010. Secular spirituality and the logic of giving thanks. *Sophia* 49: 523–534.

Buckareff, Andrei. 2005. Can faith be a doxastic venture? *Religious Studies* 41: 435–445.

Clifford, William Kingdon. 1879. The ethics of belief. In *Lectures and essays of the late William Kingdon Clifford*, vol. 2, ed. L. Stephen and F. Pollock, 177–211. London: Macmillan.

Cupitt, Don. 1980. *Taking leave of god*. London: SCM Press.

James, William. 1919. Appendix: Faith and the right to believe. In *Some problems of philosophy: A beginning of an introduction to philosophy*, 221–231. New York: Longmans, Green.

James, William. 1956. The will to believe. In *'The will to believe' and other essays in popular philosophy, and human immortality*, 1–31. New York: Dover.

Solomon, Robert C. 1999. *The joy of philosophy: Thinking thin versus the passionate life*. Oxford: Oxford University Press.

Solomon, Robert C. 2002. *Spirituality for the skeptic: The thoughtful love of life*. Oxford: Oxford University Press.

Taliaferro, Charles. 1998. *Contemporary philosophy of religion*. Malden: Blackwell.

# Chapter 19
# Bob on Meaning in Life and Death

Kathleen M. Higgins

**Abstract** Robert C. Solomon ("Bob") took a narrative conception of the meaning of life and of death, and this is of a piece with his existentialism. Through the ongoing process of engaging and reflecting, we reposition ourselves and rework our stories, each new version a potential means for responding to the world from a more mature and encompassing stance. Death is meaningful in the context of this narrative, providing the closure to an individual life that gives it a place within a larger whole. Bob's conception of narrative meaning is evident in his own life, and it is that life as well as the thinker who led it that we celebrate in this volume.

When Robert C. Solomon (hereafter "Bob") died on January 2, 2007, we were making our way to the transit lounge in the Zurich airport while en route to Rome. Bob collapsed so suddenly that he was very likely unaware that he was dying. And yet death was on his mind. Only a few days earlier he had begun a book manuscript on the topic of death. The coincidence of this project with the timing of his own death is uncanny, yet there was nothing exceptional in the fact that Bob was thinking about death just before his own demise. He lived his life, in his own words, under "a medical death sentence" due to a congenital heart disorder that doctors had long-anticipated would shorten his life (Solomon 1998: 153). In his childhood and adolescence, Bob had doubted that he would live to see his twentieth birthday. To have lived to the age of sixty-four was, as he thought it, nothing short of a miracle.

If Plato was right that philosophy is preparation for death, then Bob was predestined for philosophy. He lived his entire life in awareness of death's approach. We might see his entire philosophical oeuvre as a meditation on the meaning of life in the face of death. This is not to say that everything that Bob wrote was directly

K.M. Higgins (✉)
Department of Philosophy, The University of Texas at Austin,
1 University Station, C3500, Austin, TX 78712-0310, USA
e-mail: kmhiggins@austin.utexas.edu

K. Higgins and D. Sherman (eds.), *Passion, Death, and Spirituality*,
Sophia Studies in Cross-cultural Philosophy of Traditions and Cultures 1,
DOI 10.1007/978-94-007-4650-3_19, © Springer Science+Business Media Dordrecht 2012

focused on this topic. Bob took great joy in the intellectual acrobatics of philosophical debate on a startling array of subjects. But he was well aware that feats of argumentative prowess did not really prepare one to confront death. In "Death Fetishism, Morbid Solipsism," from which his planned book would no doubt have evolved, he draws attention to the limitations even of the most sensitive abstract accounts of the significance of death.

> Philosophy has provided me with a means to cope with the issue – if not to evade it altogether – in a more subtle, perhaps more hypocritical way…by talking, thinking, writing about death, I have at least managed to face up to death as an abstraction, and philosophical ideas, I believe, can actually have some impact on one's feelings and behavior, on one's actual life… There is no necessary connection between those very sophisticated abstractions afforded only to those who can spend their time reading Heidegger and Sartre, chuckling their way through Zhuangzi or skimming the *Tibetan Book of the Dead* and coming to terms with death… When I am being honest with myself, it becomes clear that all of this talk about "one's own death" has nothing to do with me at all. This lends my glibness a scholarly as well as slightly hysterical air, like a dervish dancing in order not to fall down… I am…fascinated when I read through the (few) analytic writings on death, where so much careful and *sensitive* thought has been forced through the screen of jargon and technical puzzles. But there, too, insulation has become a practice… And so, despite the subject matter and the writer's proximity to it, it is hard to regard such thoughtful analysis as other than one more form of evasion, more cerebral but no less evasive as a way of insulating oneself from the very facts one is considering or 'losing oneself' in the hustle and bustle of the everyday intellectual world (Solomon 1998: 154).

Bob's aim in writing about death was to get past such projects of evasion. When I'd asked Bob what the theme of his death book would be, he responded, "It's all about the story." He did not elaborate, but I take his point to have been the one he makes in *Spirituality for the Skeptic* when he says that a spiritual life involves "the acceptance of death as the completion of life, as the closure that gives an individual life its narrative significance in a larger whole. One's life may be over but life goes on" (Solomon 2002: 108).

Each of us finds meaning in life, as Bob saw it, by bringing our life's fragments into a coherent unity. We each make decisions about what we aim to be, decisions that affect what we become, and decisions about the importance any particular incident has in our life as a whole. A meaningful life is not a series of disconnected events, but one in which interests and concerns become developing threads in a narrative, means by which one gets a grip on oneself and takes hold of one's life. These threads also become thematic means for stitching new events into the fabric so that we see them as making sense in light of what comes before it.

Importantly, the project of endowing one's life with narrative significance is always in a context in which we interact with other people, and our relationships with others are primary bases on which we develop interests and concerns. The story we construct about ourselves involves other people as well, and the story itself is nested within a larger network of stories – those of one's friends and family members, and of all those with whom one interacts, even at great distance. Ultimately, one's own story assumes a place in the saga of one's own society and in the human narrative as a whole. In order for us to find meaning in our personal lives, we need to recognize and attempt to integrate our own stories with this larger narrative texture.

Bob thought that death, like life, should be understood in the context of the larger social narrative.

> One's own death is always, except in the most lonely of cases, a disruption (one hopes, not too minor) of a network of relationships… When I think of my death, I cannot help but think of what others will see in me, how others will see me, how others will think of and remember me. When I imagine myself at my own funeral, à la Freud, it is the eyes of others I am imagining, not my own… When I worry about how I will die, bravely or badly, it is for others that I am concerned.
>
> …it makes a difference to me whether I live or die not because of the phenomenology of experience but because of the particular phenomenology of *social* experience. I want to live because of other people. I want to live because I love, because I am steeped in my projects – social projects, as Sartre above all would be the first to appreciate. I want to live, perhaps because others need me, but, for most of us, because we care for and about others. I am part of their world as they are part of mine.
>
> What I really care about are the people I leave behind… (Solomon 1998: 175–176)

Bob's narrative conception of the meaning of life and death is of a piece with his existentialism. We make sense of our individual lives through the evolving stories we build as we try to draw the threads together into something integral. Not only do we give shape to our individual lives through interpreting them as stories; we also see stories in the lives of others, giving them shapes and meanings that differ in certain ways from the stories that individuals see in their own lives. Because there are tensions between the ways we individually see things, features of our narratives are sometimes challenged by those of others, complicating the project of trying to integrate our individual stories, either internally or with the larger texture of narratives beyond them. This is not, however, a sign that "hell is other people" (Bob certainly parted company with Sartre on this score), but instead an indication of how much we can enrich each other's lives. Difference is essential to human beings learning from each other. We can and do learn from each other's alternative narratives, gaining insight into ourselves as well as being awakened to other possibilities.

The project of making coherent narrative sense of our lives is not an abstract intellectual exercise. We are unavoidably "engaged" in our lives, and thus we find ourselves "on the line" in our efforts to make sense of them. The existential character of Bob's notion of the story is again evident when we consider the relevance of engagement and reflection – the reciprocal moves that Bob describes as thematic in the existentialism of Sartre and Camus (Solomon 2006) – to the story-constructing project. Engaged in our own stories, we are motivated to reflect when events, the narratives of others, and details within our own accounts do not easily fit into the narrative as we have formulated it so far. The reflections to which we are prompted help us to revise our narratives. We grow through these efforts to reintegrate our stories, and these efforts are ongoing, for we continually confront new experiences and interact with others' alternative perspectives. Through the ongoing process of engaging and reflecting, we reposition ourselves and rework our stories, each new version a potential means for responding to the world from a more mature and encompassing stance. Bob's describes his vision of this aim as "emotional integrity," his own version of existential authenticity, and his characterization of this ideal draws attention to the project of developing increasingly rich, complicated, and coherent accounts of our lives in all of their facets.

> Emotional integrity has to do with the unity of our emotional lives... Emotional integrity is
> not just consistency in one's emotional life (where the easiest consistency or unity, to be
> sure, is an exclusive focal point, a single set of beliefs, and a single emotion). Integrity
> implies richness and profundity rather than simplicity... Emotional integrity...necessarily
> involves second-order reflection as well as first-order feeling, and... I would want to allow
> for a mixed, even conflicted repertoire of feelings, emotions and reflections, including dis-
> satisfaction, self-criticism, lack of contentment, and real ethical dilemmas, that is, impos-
> sible choices and engagements... A life without any such sense of conflict is a limited life
> indeed... A happy life with emotional integrity is not a life without conflict but a life in
> which one wisely manages emotional conflicts in conjunction with one's most heartfelt
> values (Solomon 2007: 267–268).[1]

If Bob saw the quest for emotional integrity as the project that endows our lives
with meaning, he saw death as the capstone, "the closure that gives an individual life
its narrative significance in a larger whole," as we noted above. What an individual life
means within the context of the larger human saga depends on the specific shape that
life attains; but the shape of the story becomes determinate only when the story is
closed. One of the paradoxes of the closure that death provides is that the person who
dies never lives to enjoy it. The closure, for the individual, is always the horizon, what
we are "being toward" when we are (in Heidegger's phrase) "being toward death."

Nevertheless, this unattained closure does not prevent us, while living, from taking
stock of our lives as a whole. We simply have to recognize that this "whole" is the
product of interpretive imagination that does not correspond to "the facts" in an
objective sense. This recognition can serve to remind us that the story we tell is in
important ways up to us. In drawing the threads of our lives together, we decide how
they mutually relate and, most importantly, what it all means.

Such taking stock is a central theme in Bob's narrative understanding of spirituality,
"the thoughtful love of life," with certain characteristic emotional orientations.[2]
One of these, which Bob figured as central to emotional integrity, is gratitude.

> Gratitude...is a philosophical emotion. It is, in a phrase, appreciating the bigger picture and
> having a chance to play a role in it, no matter how small. In relationships, gratitude is seeing
> a particular act or transaction as part of a larger ongoing relationship. So viewed, "opening

---

[1] I cannot resist the impulse to mention here that in articulating his idea about emotional integrity,
Bob points out that he had shifted from the rhetoric of emotional judgments to that of emotions as
"engagements with the world because I now see my former emphasis on judgments suggests more
intellectualism in emotions than I intended, despite twenty years of qualifications and explanations." He goes on to say, however, that he remained convinced that "evaluative judgments...are
essential to the emotions" (Solomon 2007: 204–205). I want to emphasize his point that his understanding of "emotions as judgments" was misunderstood and caricatured when it was taken to be
exclusively cerebral. Bob did not equate judgment with conceptual belief about one's circumstances, formulated in analytical philosophy's familiar terms of "propositional attitudes" as "believing-
that $p$." Instead, his sense of judgment was a fuller notion, drawing on the continental tradition, in
which the term has a reflective and an aesthetic dimension, and in which we might see the judgment
as bridging one's own feelings and an external situation. Comparing emotional judgments to kinesthetic judgments, Bob saw the judgments involved in emotion as embedded in an on-going process
of relating and responding to the world and revising one's outlook and behavior. Emotional judgment involves "learning and detailed knowledge about the world and our place in it" (p. 206).

[2] These are discussed in Richard Schacht and John Bishop's essays in this volume.

one's heart to the universe" is not so much personifying the universe as reflecting on as well as feeling and expressing a cosmic gratitude, that is, expanding one's perspective...so that one comes to appreciate the beauty of the whole as well as be absorbed in our own limited projects and passions. That is spirituality. It is, perhaps, the ultimate happiness, and it is an ideal expression of emotional integrity (Solomon 2007: 270).[3]

Gratitude essentially involves taking a narrative approach to one's experience. One needs to tell one's story to oneself in order to appreciate the life that story tells.[4] Bob saw gratitude as providing a philosophical response to life's tragedies, including those involving death.

> Gratitude, I want to suggest, is not only the best answer to the tragedies of life. It is the best approach to life itself... The proper recognition of tragedy and the tragic sense of life is not shaking one's fist at the Gods or the universe in scorn or defiance but rather, as Kierkegaard writes in a religious context, going down on one's knees and giving thanks. Whether or not there is a God or there are Gods to be thanked, however, seems not the issue to me. It is the importance and the significance of being thankful, to whomever or whatever, for life itself (Solomon 2002: 105).[5]

According to Bob, we should be grateful, regardless of whether we believe in a deity to whom we are grateful. As Markus Weidler observes, this unconcern is rather surprising; it does not seem obvious that gratitude can do without an object, or at least a placeholder for an object. Perhaps this is one of the functions that God serves in the spiritual lives of many people, and why the teleological argument for God's existence strike so many people as emotionally compelling. Yet Ronald de Sousa, in a review of Bob's *True to Our Feelings*, takes issue with the idea that thanking God resolves the philosophical problem involved in the stance of gratitude.

> For my part, having long passed the age at which most human beings who have ever lived are dead, I feel gratitude every day for being alive. But if I thought some God was to be thanked for that, as opposed to brute luck, I'd worry about the gross unfairness of it. Why should God privilege me, while condemning millions of innocent people to early and often horrible deaths? Religious gratitude seems to me deeply deplorable, in a way epitomized by the survivor of a plane crash who, while being interviewed by a TV crew, exclaimed, "Now I really know that God exists – because he saved me!" In the event, about half of the other

---

[3] The mention of "opening one's heart to the universe" is a reference to Albert Camus's *The Stranger* (Camus 1988: 122).

[4] One of Bob's favorite passages in Nietzsche is the opening epigram of his autobiographical *Ecce Homo*:

> On this perfect day, when everything is ripening and not only the grape turns brown, the eye of the sun just fell upon my life: I looked back, I looked forward, and never saw so many and such good things at once. It was not for nothing that I buried my forty-fourth year today: I had the *right* to bury it; whatever was life in it has been saved, is immortal. The first book of the *Revaluation of All Values*, the *Songs of Zarathustra*, the *Twilight of the Idols*, my attempt to philosophize with a hammer – all presents of this year, indeed of its last quarter! *How could I fail to be grateful to my whole life?* – and so I tell my life to myself (Nietzsche 1888/1967: 221).

[5] The reference here to shaking one's fist at the Gods in scorn and defiance is to Camus's *Myth of Sisyphus* (see Camus 1955: 90).

passengers had died. That lucky man seemed untroubled by the question: Why should *I* be spared when so many are not? He must suppose that he merits the special attention of the Creator of the Universe – a sentiment that in the guise of humility evinces heights of arrogance beyond Satanic pride. Or else he must assume that God's grace is indeed, as some theologies seem to proclaim, entirely arbitrary. To which the proper response is not gratitude but embarrassment and shame (de Sousa 2007).

Though he largely agrees with Bob's decoupling of gratitude and a specific target, de Sousa thinks Bob's emphasis on responsibility leads him to give short shrift to luck, despite his admission that luck has an under-appreciated place in life. de Sousa, by contrast, thinks it makes good sense to think of "luck" as an acceptable focus for gratitude, a possibility that Bob dismisses.

In the context of defending a narrative approach to making sense of life, Bob did indeed say, "too much emphasis on luck tends to diminish life" (Solomon 2002: 102). I think Bob had other reasons as well for considering luck a non-starter as a focus for gratitude. Bob considered it important that gratitude responds to what is beyond oneself, and I think his generalized sense of gratitude is directed at all the conditions that enable one to be what one is. This is a perfectly coherent idea. The Buddhist notion of *pratītyasamutpāda* [interdependent arising] offers one way of considering this network (although I should note that Bob's sympathies with Buddhism were limited by his sense that it encouraged detachment as opposed to passionate engagement [see Solomon 1994: 255]).

Another reason Bob had for limiting his consideration of luck is that it suggests a dichotomy of lucky and unlucky, which he found overly simplistic (see Solomon 2002: 102). Categorizing events as lucky or unlucky is to consign them to what Julius Moravcik used to call "conceptual garbage pails"; it is a way of pretending to have dealt with a matter and not bothering to think any further about it. Gratitude toward "whomever or whatever for life itself," on the other hand, does not accept this binary thinking. Most importantly, it does not shut down further reflection. It does just the opposite; it necessarily involves appreciatively bringing the various features of one's life to mind.

Despite his somewhat tendentious defense of being grateful to luck, de Sousa recognizes the strangeness of the notion. He notes that we have paradoxical attitudes toward it:

I have sometimes caught myself thinking: "Solomon was lucky to die in the flower of his age, enjoying the height of his intellectual powers." But wouldn't he have been a lot luckier if he had enjoyed them for a few decades longer? The logic of luck is funny like that. We contextualize the event under consideration in a way that takes account of a change in baseline, and what we regard as a baseline is determined by unexpected events that have dislocated the previous baseline (de Sousa 2007).

De Sousa's suggestions here are provocative and deserve considerably more consideration than I will give them. I would like to press the points, however, that it is not entirely clear what luck amounts to, or whether it is actually distinguishable from other possible targets of gratitude. If I am right about how Bob understood the target of the generalized gratitude he recommends, we might describe it as the larger network that sustains us. Would "luck" be an appropriate term for this network? Perhaps this is arguable, although Bob would think that to call this luck is to forego further efforts to make narrative sense of things. Someone who comes close to expressing gratitude toward luck, at least in fiction, is Nietzsche's Zarathustra, when he praises "chance," which he hastens to call divine (Nietzsche 1883–1885/1968: 278). Although Nietzsche seems intent on undercutting teleological explanations in this coinage, he emphasizes the creative possibilities opened when one stumbles upon something "accidentally." It may be luck, but "blind" hardly reflects his sense of it. The luck he has in mind seems to be that of the improvisationalist who fortuitously hits on an accidental configuration that can spur creative development (something with which Nietzsche was familiar as an improvising pianist). When de Sousa speaks of "luck," what sense should we give this and what does it mean to call it blind?

As for the logic of luck, Bob, I am pretty sure, would think that trying to determine what is "lucky" or "unlucky" is much like emotional valence (the binary of positive/negative). Not only are these categories oversimplistic; they are also decontextualized (lucky for what?) and misleading. Bob prefers narratives of fate (among which he would include accounts that direct gratitude toward God) to narratives of luck, even though he does not think that fate is an explanatory principle (see Solomon 2002: 103). "Fate is necessarily part of a larger, more all-encompassing narrative, and although its explanatory value may be slight to nil, its ability to convey meaning is extraordinary" (p. 102). Bob sees the notion of fate as implying a narrative effort to connect the meanings of events together, which the idea of luck forgoes.

Ultimately, whether something is "lucky" is a byproduct of how one tells the story. To consider this point, let us return to de Sousa's example of catching himself thinking about luck in connection with Bob. We might restate the point by saying that de Sousa sometimes catches himself thinking that Bob has an excellent narrative. Fair enough – Bob has a terrific story, and in that he does seem fortunate. One can imagine many twists in his story that would seem less good than the trajectory his life actually took. But even if Bob was fortunate, I don't think it would be right to say that he was "just lucky."

We might, in this connection, recall the Daoist tale in which vicissitudes of fortune lead everyone but the sage to comment "what good news" or "how unfortunate," while the sage responds to all such comments, "Maybe." Some larger context or set of assumptions needs to be presupposed for either assessment. In any case, Bob's views about taking responsibility and constructing one's own narrative are relevant here. To say that he was just lucky would be to ignore the role that his own decisions and actions played in his life and the story he made of it.

The problem with resting content with notions of good and bad luck emerges most starkly if we ask "Was Bob *lucky* to have a congenital heart defect?" The very question seems offensive. Surely no one is lucky to have a birth defect. Was Bob unlucky, then? But that question is incoherent. He would not have been Bob without it.

Bob's story strikes me as heroic, its plot unfolding from dissatisfaction to ultimate gratitude. Bob claimed that "our lives are in our hands," though not completely, and being in our hands means that a lot depends on how we think about them (Solomon 2005). How we think about our lives – the stories we tell ourselves about them – is never forced on us. Bob not only argued this point as the centerpiece of his existentialism; he lived it. This is why John Schwartz takes Bob as a model in a book written for middle-schoolers. Schwartz advises,

> Rent the very cool film "Waking Life," and watch the scene with a guy in a classroom talking about philosophy and, yes, the meaning of life. The guy is Robert Solomon, a real professor of philosophy at the University of Texas.
>
> Bob died a few years ago. He was a good friend of mine, and I miss him every day. I've thought a lot about the things that he taught me, which are summed up pretty neatly by his comment in the film, "It's always our decision who we are."
>
> Bob, by the way, was pretty darned short. And he was born with a weak heart, and lived with a sense that life was a fragile thing. In other words, some people would say that he had been dealt a bad hand, and might not have expected much from life. Bob would have disagreed, though– I never met a happier, funnier guy. I never met anyone who was more deeply engaged in the art of living, and living well.
>
> Bob existed in a no-whining zone, and taught thousands of students that life is not what's handed to you, but what you make of it through your choices. Like he said in the movie, "It's always our decision who we are" (Schwartz 2010: 113–114)

When I think of Bob's own decision in this regard, I am reminded of his last book signing, at Book People in Austin. The book he was signing was *True to Our Feelings*, and Bob was talking about two of his favorite topics, emotion and existentialism. While proselytizing about one of his favorite existentialist themes, the idea that we have more choices than we often think, he told a story about Johnny Weissmuller. Weissmuller, according to Bob, contracted polio in his youth and was told that he may never walk again. He took up swimming in the course of his rehabilitation, and went on to set records in 100 and 200 meter free style swimming and to win several Olympic Gold Medals. He later became famous playing Tarzan in a series of films that were beloved by a whole generation. Referring back to Weissmuller's early bout with polio, Bob said that no one would have blamed him if he responded to his diagnosis by spending the rest of his life nursing his condition. "He might have decided," Bob told us, "'My options are limited, so I just have to take care of myself. I can't push myself too hard.' He might have decided that he couldn't aspire to much beyond staying alive. But that's not how he wanted to live."

At the signing, I smiled, thinking that this was really Bob's kind of story – a tale of someone making an unexpected choice, given the circumstances, and the consequences being profound and admirable. It was only later that I realized that Bob was really telling his own story. Bob could have decided that his options were limited and that he should just take it easy in the hope of prolonging his life. No one would have blamed him if he decided to think of himself as "someone with a heart condition." But that's not how Bob wanted to live. Instead, he decided to live as dynamically and enthusiastically as he possibly could.

The Bob we commemorate here is the Bob who decided to brim with life as opposed to considering himself an invalid, the Bob whose local obituary was titled "A Thinker Who Had 'A Whole Lot of Fun'" (Salomon 2007). Our reflections on Bob's thought and life (replete as they are with mirthful recollections and poignant anecdotes) demonstrate that his life retains narrative significance, not only as a freestanding story, but within a much larger whole. In this respect, his life and his death have the meaning that he intended.

# References

Camus, Albert. 1955. *The myth of Sisyphus and other essays* (trans: O'Brien, Justin). New York: Vintage.

Camus, Albert. 1988. *The stranger* (trans: Ward, Matthew). New York: Knopf.

De Sousa, Ronald. 2007. Review of Robert C. Solomon, *True to our feelings: What our emotions are really telling us*. New York: Oxford University Press, 2007. In *Notre Dame Philosophical Reviews 2007.10.09*. URL: http://ndpr.nd.edu/news/23181-true-to-our-feelings-what-our-emotions-are-really-telling-us/.

Nietzsche, Freidrich. 1883–1885/1968. *Thus spoke Zarathustra*. In *The portable Nietzsche*, trans. and ed. Walter Kaufmann. New York: Viking.

Nietzsche, Freidrich. 1888/1967. *Ecce homo* (trans: Kaufmann, Walter). Together with *On the genealogy of morals* (trans: Kaufmann, Walter and R J. Hollingdale). New York: Vintage.

Salamon, Jeff. 2007. A thinker who had 'a whole lot of fun.' *Austin American-Statesman*, 5 Jan.

Schwartz, John. 2010. *Short: Walking tall when you're not tall at all*. New York: Flash Point.

Solomon, Robert C. 1994. The cross-cultural comparison of emotions. In *Emotions in Asian thought*, ed. Roger Ames and Joel Marks, 253–308. Albany: State University of New York Press.

Solomon, Robert C. 1998. Death fetishism, morbid solipsism. In *Death and philosophy*, ed. Robert C. Solomon and Jeff Malpas, 152–176. New York: Routledge.

Solomon, Robert C. 2002. *Spirituality for the skeptic*. New York: Oxford University Press.

Solomon, Robert C. 2005. *The passions: The intelligence of emotions* [videorecording]. Chantilly: The Teaching Company.

Solomon, Robert C. 2006. *Dark feelings, grim thoughts: Experience and refection in Camus and Sartre*. New York: Oxford University Press.

# Bibliography

Original Books

1972.     *From rationalism to existentialism.* New York: Harper & Row. 2nd ed., Lanham, MD: Rowman and Littlefield, 2001.

1976.     *The passions.* New York: Doubleday-Anchor. Revised and reissued as *The passions: Emotions and the meaning of life.* Indianapolis: Hackett, 1993. German translation, 2000.

1979.     *History and human nature.* New York: Harcourt, Brace & Jovanovich, 1979. Reissued as *The bully culture: Enlightenment, romanticism and the transcendental pretense, 1750–1850,* Lanham, MD: Rowman and Littlefield, 1992.

1981.     *Introducing the existentialists.* Indianapolis: Hackett.
          *Introducing the German idealists.* Indianapolis: Hackett.
          *Love: Emotion, myth and metaphor.* New York: Doubleday-Anchor. Reissued edition. Prometheus (Buffalo), 1990.

1983.     *In the spirit of Hegel.* New York: Oxford University Press, 1983.

1985.     *It's good business* (with Kristine Hanson). New York: Atheneum. French translation, 1989.

1987.     *From Hegel to existentialism.* New York: Oxford University Press, 1987.

1988.     *About love: Reinventing romance for our times.* New York: Simon and Schuster, 1988. Reissued by Hackett (Indianapolis), 2006.
          *Continental philosophy since 1750: The rise and fall of the self.* Oxford: Oxford University Press.

1990.     *A passion for justice: Emotions and the origins of the social contract.* New York: Addison-Wesley. Reissued by Rowman and Littlefield (Lanham, MD), 1995.

1992.     *Ethics and excellence: Cooperation and integrity in business.* New York: Oxford University Press. Chinese translation, 2005. Portuguese translation, 2006.
          *Entertaining ideas: Popular philosophical essays, 1970–1990.* Buffalo: Prometheus.

1993.     *Up the university: Re-creating higher education in America* (with Jon Solomon). New York: Addison-Wesley, 1993. on-line edition, www.cybereditions.com, 2000. Japanese translation, 1997.
          *The new world of business: Ethics and free enterprise in the global nineties.* Lanham MD: Rowman and Littlefield. Revised and reissued as *It's good business: Ethics and free enterprise for the new millennium.* Rowman and Littlefield, 1997.

K. Higgins and D. Sherman (eds.), *Passion, Death, and Spirituality,*
Sophia Studies in Cross-cultural Philosophy of Traditions and Cultures 1,
DOI 10.1007/978-94-007-4650-3, © Springer Science+Business Media Dordrecht 2012

1996.        *A short history of philosophy* (with Kathleen M. Higgins). New York: Oxford
            University Press. Polish translation, 1997. Slovenian translation, 1998. Dutch
            translation, 1999.

1997.        *A passion for wisdom: A very brief history of philosophy* (with Kathleen
            M. Higgins). New York: Oxford University Press. Spanish translation, 1999.
            German translation, 2000. Portuguese translation, 2001. Dutch translation, 2004.
            Korean translation, 2004. Japanese translation, 2004. Persian translation, 2009.
            Chinese translation 2007 (Taiwan), 2009 (PCR). Greek translation forthcoming.

1999.        *A better way to think about business: Getting from values to virtues and integrity.*
            New York: Oxford University Press. Spanish translation, 2000. Portuguese
            translation, 2000.
            *The joy of philosophy: Thinking thin versus the passionate life.* New York: Oxford
            University Press. Dutch translation, 1999. Chinese (Taiwanese) translation, 2010.
            Italian translation, 2008.
            *What Nietzsche really said* (with Kathleen M. Higgins). New York: Random
            House. Korean translation, 2001.

2001.        *Building trust: In business, politics, relationships, and life* (with Fernando Flores).
            New York: Oxford University Press. Chinese translation, 2002. Portuguese
            translation, 2002. Dutch translation, 2002. Japanese translation, 2004.

2002.        *Spirituality for the skeptic: The thoughtful love of life.* Oxford: Oxford University
            Press. Dutch translation, 2004.

2003.        *Not passion's slave: Emotions and choice.* New York: Oxford University Press.
            *Living with Nietzsche: What the great 'immoralist' has to teach us.* New York:
            Oxford University Press.

2004.        *In defense of sentimentality.* New York: Oxford University Press.

2006.        *Dark feelings, grim thoughts: Experience and refection in Camus and Sartre.*
            New York: Oxford University Press.

2007.        *True to our feelings: What our emotions are really telling us.* New York: Oxford
            University Press.

2008.        *The little philosophy book.* New York: Oxford University Press. Spanish translation,
            2008. German translation, 2009.

Edited Books
1972.        *Phenomenology and existentialism.* New York: Harper and Row. Reissued in new
            ed. by Rowman and Littlefield (Lanham, MD), 2000.

1973.        *Nietzsche.* New York: Doubleday-Anchor, 1973. Reissued by University of Notre
            Dame Press (Notre Dame, IN), 1981.

1974.        *Existentialism.* New York: Random House, 1974. 2nd ed. by Oxford University
            Press (New York), 2004.

1984.        *What is an emotion? Classic readings in philosophical psychology* (with Cheshire
            Calhoun). New York: Oxford University Press. Spanish translation, 1989.
            Reissued in revised edition (sole author) as *What is an emotion?: Classic and
            contemporary readings,* 2003.

1988.        *Reading Nietzsche* (with Kathleen M. Higgins). New York: Oxford University
            Press.

1990.        *What is justice? Classic and contemporary readings* (with Mark Murphy).
            New York: Oxford University Press; 2nd ed., 2000.

1991.        *The philosophy of (erotic) love* (with Kathleen M. Higgins). Lawrence, KS:
            University Press of Kansas.

1993.        *From Africa to Zen: An invitation to world philosophy* (with Kathleen M. Higgins).
            Lanham MD: Rowman and Littlefield. 2nd ed., 2003. Chinese translation, 2004.
            *The Routledge history of philosophy,* Volume VI: *German idealism* (with Kathleen
            M. Higgins). London: Routledge.

1999.        *Death and philosophy* (with J. E. Malpas). London: Routledge.

             *Wicked pleasures: Meditations on the seven deadly sins.* Lanham MD: Rowman
             and Littlefield.

2003.        *The Blackwell guide to continental philosophy* (with David Sherman). New York:
             Blackwell.

2004.        *Thinking about feeling: Contemporary philosophers on emotion.* New York:
             Oxford University Press.

Textbooks

1977.        *Introducing philosophy.* New York: Harcourt, Brace & Jovanovich; revised
             editions 1981, 1985, 1989, 1993, 1997, 2000. New York: Oxford University Press,
             2002, 2005, 2007, (with Kathleen M. Higgins and Clancy Martin) 2011.

1982.        *The big questions: A short introduction to philosophy.* New York: Harcourt, Brace
             & Jovanovich; revised editions 1985, 1990, 1994, 1998, 2001; Wadsworth
             (Belmont, CA) 2002, 2005; with Kathleen M. Higgins, 2010. Chinese translation
             2004.

1982.        *Morality and the good life.* New York: McGraw-Hill; revised editions 1991, (with
             Jennifer Greene) 1999, (with Clancy Martin), (with Clancy Martin and Wayne
             Vaught). 2004, 2009

1983.        *Above the bottom line: An introduction to business ethics* (with Kristine Hanson).
             New York: Harcourt, Brace & Jovanovich; revised editions (sole author) Harcourt
             Brace (Fort Worth) 1994; (with Clancy Martin) Wadsworth (Belmont, CA) 2004.

1984.        *Ethics: A brief introduction.* New York: McGraw Hill. Revised as *Ethics: A short
             introduction,* Brown and Benchmark (Madison, WI) 1992; as *A handbook for
             ethics* Harcourt Brace (Fort Worth) 1996; Wadsworth (Belmont, CA), 2002; as *On
             ethics and living well,* Wadsworth 2005. Indonesian translation 1987.

1988.        *Twenty questions: An introduction to philosophy* (with G. Lee Bowie and Meredith
             Michaels). San Diego: Harcourt, Brace & Jovanovich. Revised editions 1992,
             1996, 2000; Wadsworth (Belmont, CA) 2004, 2006, 2010.

1994.        *World philosophy: A text with readings* (with Kathleen M. Higgins). New York:
             McGraw Hill.

2004.        *Since Socrates: Readings from the history of philosophy* (with Clancy Martin).
             Belmont CA: Wadsworth.

2007.        *Honest work: A business ethics reader* (with Joanne Ciulla and Clancy Martin).
             New York: Oxford University Press; revised edition, 2011.

2010.        *Ethics across the professions: A reader for professional ethics* (with Clancy
             Martin and Wayne Vaught). New York: Oxford University Press.

New Edition

2005.        Friedrich Nietzsche, *Thus Spoke Zarathustra,* a new translation by Clancy
             W. Martin, Introduction and Supplemental material by Robert C. Solomon and
             Kathleen M. Higgins: New York: Barnes and Noble.

*Bob's books have now been translated into **18** languages: Arabic, Chinese, Dutch, French,
German, Greek, Indonesian, Japanese, Korean, Persian, Polish, Portuguese (Brazilian),
Romanian, Slovak, Slovene, Spanish, Swedish, Turkish.

Video Lecture Series

1993.        *No excuses: Existentialism and the meaning of life* [videorecording]. Alexandria,
             VA: The Teaching Company.

1993.        *Love and vengeance: A course on human emotions* [videorecording]. Alexandria,
             VA: The Teaching Company.

1996.        *No excuses: Existentialism and the meaning of life* (extended version, 16 lectures)
             [videorecording]. Alexandria, VA: The Teaching Company.

1999.        *The will to power: The philosophy of Friedrich Nietzsche* (with Kathleen
             Higgins, 24 lectures) [videorecording]. Alexandria, VA: The Teaching
             Company.

1999.          *No excuses: Existentialism and the meaning of life* (revised version, 24 lectures) [videorecording]. Alexandria, VA: The Teaching Company.

2000.          *Great minds in the western tradition* (with Michael Sugrue, Darren Staloff, and others) (lectures on Nietzsche, Mill, Husserl, Heidegger). [videorecording]. Alexandria, VA: The Teaching Company.

2005.          *The passions: The intelligence of emotions* [videorecording]. Chantilly, VA: The Teaching Company.

Film Appearance (Animated)

2001.          *Waking life* [videorecording]. Richard Linklater, director. 20th Century Fox Home Entertainment, [2002].

**Articles:**

1968.          Is life phenomenal? *Pacific Philosophy Forum* 6 (1968): 95–99.

1969.          Approaching Hegel's *Phenomenology. Philosophy Today* 13: 115–125.

1970.          Hegel's concept of 'Geist.' *Review of Metaphysics* 23: 642–661. Reprinted in *Hegel*, ed. Alasdair MacIntyre, 125–149. New York: Doubleday, 1972; and in Solomon, *From Hegel to existentialism*, 3–17. New York: Oxford University Press.
                 Normative and metaethics. *Philosophy and Phenomenological Research* 31: 97–107.
                 Sense and essence: Frege and Husserl. *International Philosophical Quarterly* 10: 378–401. Reprinted in *Phenomenology and existentialism*, ed. Solomon, 258–282; *Analytic philosophy and phenomenology*, ed. Harold Durfee, 31–54. The Hague: Nijhoff, 1976; *The philosophy of Frege*, I: *General assessments and historical accounts of Frege's philosophy*, ed. Hans Sluga, 80–103. New York: Garland, 1993; and Solomon, *From Hegel to existentialism,* 205–220.

1971.          Aristotle, the Socratic principle, and the problem of *akrasia. Modern Schoolman* 49: 13–21.
                 Existentialism and irrationalism. *The Australian Rationalist.*
                 Hegel and systematic philosophy. *Philosophical Forum* 2: 500–510.

1972.          Wittgenstein and Cartesian privacy. *Philosophy Today* 16: 163–179.

1973.          Emotions and choice. *Review of Metaphysics* 28: 20–41. Reprinted, with an appendix, in *Explaining emotions*, ed. Amelie Rorty, 251–281. Berkeley: University of California Press, 1979; *What is an emotion? Classic readings in philosophical psychology,* ed. Cheshire Calhoun and Robert C. Solomon, 305–326. New York: Oxford University Press; in shortened form in *What is an emotion? Classic and contemporary readings,* ed. Robert C. Solomon, 224–235. New York: Oxford University Press.
                 Nietzsche, nihilism and morality. In *Nietzsche*, ed. Robert C. Solomon, 202–225. New York: Doubleday. Reprinted in Solomon, *From Hegel to existentialism*, 87–104.

1974.          Beethoven and the sonata form. *Telos* 19: 141–146.
                 Freud and 'unconscious motivation.' *Journal of the Theory of Social Behaviour* 4: 191–231.
                 God and rationality. *Canadian Journal of Philosophy* 4: 283–292.
                 Hegel's epistemology. *American Philosophical Quarterly* 2: 277–298. Reprinted in *Hegel*, ed. Michael Inwood, 31–53. New York: Oxford University Press; and Solomon, *From Hegel to existentialism*, 18–36.
                 Husserl's private language. *Southwestern Journal of Philosophy* 5: 203–228. Reprinted in Solomon, *From Hegel to existentialism*, 184–204.
                 On Cartesian privacy. *The Southern Journal of Philosophy* 12: 527–536.
                 Reasons as causal explanations. *Philosophy and Phenomenological Research* 34: 415–428.

Sexual paradigms. *Journal of Philosophy* 71: 336–345. Reprinted in *The Philosophy of Sex and Love,* ed. Alan Soble, 4th ed., 21–29. Lanham, MD: Rowman and Littlefield; and a number of other texts and volumes.

Freud's neurological theory of mind. In *Freud: A collection of critical essays,* ed. Richard Wollheim, 25–52. New York: Doubleday, 1974. Reprinted in Solomon, From Hegel to existentialism, 137–157.

1975.    Doubts about the correlation thesis. *British Journal for the Philosophy of Science* 26: 27–39.

Hegel's humanism. *Frontier.*

Sex and perversion. In *Philosophy and sex,* ed. Robert B. Baker and Elliston, 268–287. Buffalo: Prometheus. Reprinted in Solomon, *From Hegel to existentialism,* 122–136.

A small problem in Hegel's *Phenomenology. Journal of the History of Philosophy* 13: 399–400.

Truth and self-satisfaction. *Review of Metaphysics* 28: 698–724. Reprinted in Solomon, *From Hegel to existentialism,* 37–55.

1976.    Is there happiness after death? *Philosophy* 51: 189–193.

Psychological predicates. *Philosophy and Phenomenological Research* 36: 472–493.

1977.    Husserl's concept of the noema. In *Husserl,* ed. Frederick A. Elliston and Peter McCormick, 168–181. Notre Dame, Indiana: Notre Dame University Press. Reprinted in Solomon, *From Hegel to existentialism,* 221–237.

Kierkegaard and 'subjective truth.' *Philosophy Today* 21: 202–215. Reprinted in Solomon, *From Hegel to existentialism,* 72–86.

The logic of emotion. *Nous* 11: 41–49. Reprinted in Solomon, *Entertaining ideas,* 131–138.

The rationality of the emotions. *Southwestern Journal of Philosophy* 8: 105–114.

1978.    Camus's *L'Etranger* and the truth. *Philosophy and Literature* 2:141–159. Reprinted in Solomon, *From Hegel to existentialism,* 246–260.

Emotions and anthropology: The logic of emotional world views. *Inquiry* 21: 181–199.

A pronoun is a small world. *Chicago Review* 29: 9–22. Reprinted in Solomon, *Entertaining ideas,* 24–26.

The secret of Hegel (Kierkegaard's complaint): A study in Hegel's philosophy of religion. *Philosophical Forum* 9: 440–458. Reprinted in Solomon, *From Hegel to existentialism,* 56–71.

Science, ethics and the impersonal passions. In *Science, ethics and medicine* (Vol. 3 of *The foundations of ethics and its relationship to science,* ed. Tristram Engelhardt, Jr., and Daniel Callahan, 311–332). New York: The Hasting Center.

Sociobiology, morality and culture (report on group discussion). In *Morality as a biological phenomenon,* ed. Gunther S. Stent, 283–308. Berlin: Dahlem Konferenzen, 283–308; U.S. edition: *Morality as a biological phenomenon: The presuppositions of sociobiological research,* 253–274. Berkeley: University of California Press, 1980.

Teaching Hegel. *Teaching Philosophy* 2: 213–224.

1979.    Paul Ricoeur on passion and emotion (with a reply by Ricoeur). *Studies in the philosophy of Paul Ricoeur,* ed. Charles E. Reagan, 1–20. University of Ohio Press.

1980.    Nothing to be proud of (emotions and intentionality). In *Understanding human emotions,* ed. Fred D. Miller, Jr., and Thomas W. Attig, 18–35. Bowling Green, OH: Bowling Green State University Press.

1981.        The end of man. *Mankind* (June). Reprinted in Solomon, *Entertaining ideas,*
            45–53.
            The love lost in clichés. *Psychology Today* 15: 83–94.
            Sartre on emotions. In *The philosophy of Jean-Paul Sartre,* ed. Paul Schilpp,
            211–228. Carbondale: Library of Living Philosophers, 1981. Reprinted in
            Solomon, *From Hegel to existentialism,* 261–275.
1982.        Aristotle on Anger. *Proceedings of the World Congress on Aristotle.* Athens:
            Ministry of Culture and Sciences.
1983.        Emotions' mysterious objects. In *Emotion: Philosophical studies,* ed. K. D. Irani
            and Gerald Eugene Myers, 19–41. New York: Haven.
            Hegel and Marx today (in Hebrew). In *Contemporary philosophy,* ed.
            Weinschweig. Jerusalem: Yachdav Press.
            Thoughts on the meaning of (fetal) life. In *Abortion and the status of the fetus,*
            ed. William B. Bondeson, H. Tristram Engelhardt, Jr., Stuart F. Spicker, and
            Daniel H. Winship, 209–226. Dordrecht: Reidel.
1984.        Love and feminism. In *Philosophy and sex,* ed. Robert Baker and Frederick
            Elliston, 2nd ed., 53–70. Buffalo: Prometheus, 1984; and in *Philosophy and sex,*
            ed. Robert Baker and Kathleen J. Winninger, 57–72. Buffalo: Prometheus, 1998.
            Beyond postmodernism. *Krisis* 1: 151–153.
            Getting angry: The Jamesian theory of emotion in anthropology. In *Culture theory,*
            ed. Richard A. Schweder and Robert A. Levine, 238–254. Cambridge: Cambridge
            University Press.
1985.        Ant farm. In *Reflections on America, 1984: An Orwell Symposium,* ed. Robert
            Mulvihill, 114–129. Athens, GA: University of Georgia Press.
1986.        Literacy and the education of the emotions. In *Literacy, society, and schooling,*
            ed. Suzanne de Castell, Allan Luke, and Kieran Egan, 37–58. Cambridge:
            Cambridge University Press. Reprinted in *Literacy: Language and Power,* ed.
            D. Diane L. Vipond and Ronald J. Strahl, 123–139. Long Beach: California State
            University Press, 1994; and in Solomon, *Entertaining ideas,* 299–313.
            A more severe morality: Nietzsche's ethics. *Journal of the British Society for
            Phenomenology* 16: 250–68; and in *Nietzsche's Affirmative Philosophy,* ed.
            Y. Yovel, 69–89. Dordrecht: Martinus Nijhoff, 1986. Reprinted in *Critical
            assessments: Friedrich Nietzsche,* ed. Daniel W. Conway, III: 321–339. New York:
            Routledge, 1998. *The existentialists: Critical essays on Kierkegaard, Nietzsche,
            Heidegger, and Sartre,* ed. Charles Guignon, 53–72. Lanham, MD: Rowman &
            Littlefield; in Solomon, *From Hegel to existentialism,* 105–121; published as *Une
            morale plus severe: l'ethique affirmative de Nietzsche* in *Krisis* 8 (1991): 71–94.
1987.        The ego in Germanic philosophy. *Philosophical Exchange* 18: 5–38.
            Heterosex. In *Sexuality and medicine,* I: *Conceptual roots,* ed. Earl E. Shelp,
            205–224. Dordrecht: Reidel, 1987.
1988.        On emotions as judgments. *American Philosophical Quarterly* 25: 183–191.
            The rediscovery of emotion in philosophy: critical review of Ronald de Sousa,
            *The rationality of emotion* (Cambridge, MA: MIT Press, 1987) and Robert
            Gordon, *The structure of emotion* (Cambridge: Cambridge University Press,
            1987). *Cognition and Emotion* 2:105–113.
            Sex, contraception, and conceptions of sex. *In The contraceptive ethos: Reproductive
            rights and responsibilities,* ed. Stuart F. Spicker, William B. Bondeson, and
            H. Tristram Engelhardt, 223–240. Dordrecht: Reidel, 1988.
            The virtue of love. In *Midwest Studies in Philosophy* 13, ed. Peter French, 12–31.
            Notre Dame: University of Notre Dame Press. Reprinted in Solomon and Higgins,
            eds., *The philosophy of (erotic) love,* 492–518.

1989.      The emotions of justice. *Social Justice Research* 3: 345–374.

Emotions, philosophy, and the self. In *Emotions in ideal human development*, ed. Leonard Cirillo, Bernard Kaplan, Seymour Wapner, 135–149. Hillsdale, NJ: Erlbaum.

1990.      Emotions, feelings and contexts: A reply to Robert Kraut. *Dialogue* 29: 277–284.

Environmentalism as a humanism. In *Business, ethics, and environment: The public policy debate,* ed. W. M. Hoffman, R. Frederick, E. S. Petry, 125–34. New York: Quorum. Reprinted in Solomon, *Entertaining ideas*, 236–247.

In defense of sentimentality. *Philosophy and literature* 14: 304–323. Reprinted as What's wrong with sentimentality? In Solomon, *Entertaining ideas*, 77–86.

Nietzsche, postmodernism, resentment. In *Nietzsche as postmodernist: Essays pro and contra*, ed. Clayton Koelb, 267–293. Buffalo: State University of New York Press.

Phenomenology: Self-presentation. In *American phenomenology: Origins and development*, ed. Calvin O. Schrag and Eugene F. Kaelin, 390–392. The Hague: Kluwer.

1991.      Bioscience as a social practice: Some preliminary remarks. In *Bioethics – society,* ed. D. J. Roy, B. E. Wynne, R. W. Old, 283–291. New York: John Wiley and Sons.

Business ethics. In *A companion to ethics,* ed. Peter Singer, 354–365. Oxford: Blackwell. Revised version in Solomon, *Entertaining ideas*, 255–267.

E-type judgments, emotions and desires. In *Perspectives in personality* III-A, ed. Dan Ozer, Joseph M. Healy, Jr., and Abigail J. Stewart, 169–190. London: Jessica Kingsley.

Fear. In *Here and now*: *Essays in honor of Raymond Dynevor Bradley,* 177–187. Vancouver: Simon Fraser University Press.

On kitsch and sentimentality. *Journal of Aesthetics and Art Criticism* 49:1–14. Reprinted in Solomon, *Entertaining ideas*, 314–321.

1992.      Beyond reason: The importance of emotion in philosophy. In *Revisioning philosophy,* ed. James Ogilvy, 19–47. Albany: State University of New York Press.

Corporate role, personal virtues: An Aristotelean approach to business ethics. *Business Ethics Quarterly* 2: 317–339. Reprinted in *Ethical issues in business*, ed. Thomas Donaldson and Patricia Werhane, 7th ed., 71–83. Englewood Cliffs, NJ: Prentice-Hall, 2002, and other texts. Translated and published in Japanese and in Spanish.

Corporate roles, personal virtues: An Aristotelean approach to business ethics. *Business Ethics Quarterly* 2: 317–339. Reprinted in *Applied ethics*, ed. E. R. Winkler and J. Coombs, 201–221. Oxford: Blackwell, 1993.

Existentialism, emotions, and the cultural limits of rationality. *Philosophy East and West* 42: 597–622.

Fate and the liability crisis. In *Entertaining ideas*, ed. Solomon, 278–285.

1993.      Atomism, art and Arthur: Danto's Hegelian turn (with Kathleen M. Higgins). *Danto and his critics*, ed. Mark Rollins, 107–126. London: Basil Blackwell. Reprinted in *Bigaku Kenkyu* 1 (2001): 69–94

Beyond selfishness: Adam Smith and the limits of the market. *Business Ethics Quarterly* 3: 453–460.

Corporate role, personal virtues, moral mazes: An Aristotelean approach to business ethics. In *Business, ethics and the law*, ed. C.A.J. Coady and C. Sampford, 24–51. Canberra ACT (Australia): Federation Press, 1993.

Environmentalism as a humanism. *Free Inquiry* 13: 21–22.

Hegel's *Phenomenology of Spirit*. In *The Routledge history of philosophy VI: German Idealism*, ed. Robert C. Solomon and Kathleen M. Higgins, 181–215. London: Routledge.

The philosophy of emotions. In *A Handbook of Emotions*, ed. 2008, ed. Michael Lewis and Jeannette M. Haviland, 3–15 (New York: Guilford Press, 1993); 2nd ed., 2000, 3–15; 3rd ed., 2008, ed. Michael Lewis, Jennette M. Haviland-Jones, and Lisa Feldman Barrett, 3–16.

What a tangled web: deception and self-deception in philosophy. In *Lying in everyday life*, ed. M. Lewis and C. Saarni, 30–58. New York: Guilford Press.

1994. Business and the humanities: An Aristotelian approach to business ethics. In *Business as a humanity*, ed. Thomas J. Donaldson and R. Edward Freeman, 45–75. New York: Oxford University Press.

Community and coercion in the university. In *Science and the powers*, ed. Lars Gustafsson, Susan Wells Howard & Lars Niklasson, 69–113. Stockholm: Swedish Ministry of Education and Science.

The corporation as community: A reply to Ed Hartman. *Business Ethics Quarterly* 4: 271–285.

The cross-cultural comparison of emotions. In *Emotions in Asian thought*, ed. Roger T. Ames and Joel Marks, 253–308. Albany, NY: State University of New York Press.

Recapturing personal identity. In *Self as person in Asian theory and practice*, ed. Roger T. Ames, Wimal Dissanayake, and Thomas P. Kasulis, 7–34. Albany: State University of New York Press.

Sympathy and vengeance: The role of the emotions in justice. In *Emotions; Essays on emotion theory (Festschrift for Nico Frijda)*, ed. Stephanie H. M. van Goozen, Nanne E. Van de Poll, Joseph A. Sergeant, 291–311. New York, Lawrence Erlbaum.

1995. Are the Three Stooges funny? Soitainly! In Solomon, *Entertaining ideas*, 139–147. Reprinted in *Aesthetics in perspective*, ed. Kathleen M. Higgins, 604–610. Fort Worth: Harcourt Brace, 1995.

Humor and humiliation in the Three Stooges. *Proceedings of the American Society for Aesthetics, Pacific Division*.

Justice as vengeance, vengeance as justice: A partial defense of Polymarchus. In *Morality and Social Justice*. ed. James Sterba, 251–300. Lanham, MD: Rowman and Littlefield.

One hundred years of *ressentiment:* Nietzsche's *Genealogy of Morals*. In *Nietzsche, Genealogy, Morality*, ed. Richard Schacht, 95–126. Berkeley: University of California Press.

Some notes on emotion, 'East and West.' *Philosophy East and West* 45: 171–202.

1996. Ethical leadership, emotions and trust: Beyond 'charisma.' In Kellogg Leadership Studies Project Working Papers, Kellogg Foundation; and, as The myth of charisma, in *Ethics, The heart of leadership*, Joanne Ciulla, 87–107. Westport CT: Praeger, 1998. Reprinted in *The ethics of leadership*, ed. Joanne Ciulla, 200–212. Belmont, CA: Wadsworth, 2003.

Nietzsche *ad hominem*: Perspectivism, personality and *ressentiment.* In *The Cambridge companion to Nietzsche*, ed. Bernd Magnus and Kathleen M. Higgins, 180–222. Cambridge: Cambridge University Press.

Nineteenth-century philosophy. In *Best books: Experts choose their favourites*, ed. Chris Murray, 21–22. Oxford: Helicon.

Postscript to a philosophy of the future. *International Society for Philosophy* 28: 113–119.

Self, deception and self-deception: A cross-cultural philosophical enquiry. In *Self and deception, a cross-cultural philosophical enquiry*, ed. Roger T. Ames and Wimal Dissanayake, 91–121. Albany: State University of New York Press.

Virtue ethics and business ethics. *Business ethics in Australia and New Zealand*, ed. Klaus Woldring, 22–41. Melbourne: Thomas Nelson.

1997.          Beyond ontology: Ideation, phenomenology and the cross cultural study of
               emotion. *Journal for the Theory of Social Behavior* 27: 289–303.

               Building trust. In *Trust and business: Barriers and bridges*, ed. Daryl Koehn,
               in *Journal of Business & Professional Ethics*. Chinese version published by
               Shanghai Academy of Social Sciences Press in May 2003.

               Competition, care and compassion: Toward a non-chauvinist view of the
               corporation. In *Women's Studies and Business Ethics*, ed. A. L. Larson and
               R.E. Freeman, 144–173. Oxford: Oxford University Press.

               In defense of the emotions (and passions too). *Journal for the Theory of Social
               Behavior* 27: 489–497.

               In defense of sentimentality (expanded version). In *Emotions and the arts*, ed.
               Mette Hjort and Sue Laver, 225–245. New York: Oxford University Press.

               Racist humor: Notes toward a cross-cultural understanding. In *Proceedings of the
               Pacific Rim conference in transcultural aesthetics*, ed. E. Benitez. Sydney: Sydney
               University.

               Shame. In *The Blackwell dictionary of business ethics*, ed. Patricia H. Werhane
               and R. Edward Freeman, 579–581. Malden, MA: Blackwell.

1998.          Creating trust (with Fernando Flores). *Business Ethics Quarterly* 8 (1998):
               205–232.

               Death fetishism, morbid solipsism. In *Death and philosophy*, ed. Jeff Malpas and
               Robert C. Solomon, 152–176. London: Routledge.

               Is it ever right to lie? The politics of deception. *Chronicle of Higher Education* 44
               (1998): A60.

               The moral psychology of business: Care and compassion in the corporation.
               *Business Ethics Quarterly* 8: 515–534. Reprinted in *The next phase of business
               ethics: Integrating psychology and ethics*, ed. J. W. Dienhart, R. F. Duska, and
               D. J. Moberg, 417–438. Amsterdam: JAI/Elsevier Science, 2001.

               Nietzsche and the emotions. In *Nietzsche and depth psychology*, ed. Jacob
               Golomb, 127–145. Albany: State University of New York Press.

               The politics of emotion. *Midwest Studies in Philosophy* 22, 1–20.

               Rethinking trust (with Fernando Flores). *Journal for Business and Professional
               Ethics* 16: 47–76.

               The virtues of a passionate life: Erotic love and 'the will to power.' In *Social
               Philosophy and Policy* 15: 91–118; also in *Virtue and vice*, ed. Ellen Frankel Paul,
               Fred D. Miller, Jr., Jeffrey Paul, 91–118. Cambridge: Cambridge University Press.

1999.          Business ethics and virtue. In *A companion to business ethics*, ed. Robert E.
               Frederick, 30–37. Oxford: Blackwell; rev. ed. 2002.

               Game theory as a model of business. *Business Ethics Quarterly* 9: 11–29.

               Justice v. vengeance: On law and the satisfaction of emotion. In *The passions of
               law*, ed. Susan A. Bandes, 123–148. New York: New York University Press.

               Nietzschean Virtues: A personal inquiry. In *German philosophy since Kant*, ed.
               Anthony O'Hear, 81–108. Cambridge: Cambridge University Press.

               Peter Singer's expanding circle and the liberation of ethics. In *Singer and his
               critics*, ed. Dale Jamieson, 64–84. Oxford: Blackwell.

2000.          Business with virtue: Maybe next year. *Business Ethics Quarterly* 10: 339–341.

               Historicism, communitarianism, and commerce: An Aristotelian approach to
               business ethics. In *Contemporary economic ethics and business ethics,* ed. Peter
               Koslowski, 117–147. Berlin: Springer.

               A lover's reply (to Roland Barthes). In *Philosophy and desire,* ed. Hugh
               Silverman, 143–158. New York: Routledge.

               Nietzsche's virtues. In *Nietzsche's postmoralism,* ed. Richard Schacht, 123–148.
               Cambridge: Cambridge University Press.

          Trusting. In *Essays in honor of Hubert L. Dreyfus*, II: *Heidegger, coping, and cognitive science*, ed. Mark Wrathwall and Jeff Malpas, 229–244. Cambridge: MIT Press.

2001.     Art and sentimentality in a trans-cultural context. In *Frontiers of transculturality in contemporary aesthetics*, ed. Grazia Marchianò and Raffaele Milani, 399–403. Turin: Trauben/Casalini Libri.

          Justice as a virtue. In *Social and political philosophy: Contemporary perspectives*, ed. James Sterbam, 169–186. New York: Routledge.

          El papel esencial de las virtudes en la empresa. *Empresa y Humanismo* 4: 355–374.

          Teaching the joy of philosophy. *Teaching Philosophy* 24: 205–218.

          What is called thinking? Teaching the joy of philosophy. *Philosophy* 24:205–218.

          What is Philosophy? The status of non-western philosophy in the profession. *Newletter on the status of Asian and Asian-American philosophers and philosophies.* American Philosophical Association Newsletters 1: 27–29.

          What is philosophy? The status of world philosophy in the profession. *Philosophy East and West* 51: 100–104.

2002.     Back to basics: On the very idea of 'basic emotions.' *Journal for the Theory of Social Behavior* 32: 115–144.

          Emotions, cognition, affect: On Jerry Neu's *A tear is an intellectual thing.* *Philosophical Studies* 108: 133–142; electronic version, December 2005 (Springer).

          Nietzsche as existentialist and as fatalist: The practical paradoxes of self-making. *International Philosophical Studies* 34: 41–54.

          Nietzsche on fatalism and 'free will'. *Journal for Nietzsche Studies* 23: 63–87.

          On 'positive' and 'negative' emotions (with Lori D. Stone). *Journal for the Theory of Social Behavior* 32: 417–435.

          Reasons for love. *Journal for the Theory of Social Behavior* 32: 1–28.

2003.     Emotions, thoughts and feelings: What is a 'cognitive theory' of the emotions and does it neglect affectivity? In *The philosopy of emotions*, ed. Anthony Hatzimoysis, 1–18. *Royal Institute of Philosophy Supplement* 52: *Philosophy and the emotions*, Cambridge: Cambridge University Press.

          Nietzsche. In *The Blackwell guide to continental philosophy*, ed. Robert C. Solomon and David Sherman, 90–111. New York: Blackwell.

          On fate and fatalism. *Philosophy East and West* 53: 435–454.

          Real horror. In *Dark thoughts: Philosophic reflections on cinematic horror*, ed. Steven Jay Schneider and Daniel Shaw, 230–259. Lanham MD: Scarecrow Press.

          Sympathy as a 'natural' sentiment. *Business Ethics Quarterly* 3: 453–460.

          Victims of circumstance? A defense of virtue ethics (with a reply by Gilbert Harman). *Business Ethics Quarterly* 13: 43–62. Reprinted in *Taking Sides*, ed. Lisa Newton and Maureen M. Ford, 9th ed., 25–38. Guilford, CT: Dushkin, 2006; and in *Religious perspectives on business ethics: An anthology*, ed. Thomas O'Brien and Scott Paeth, 111–131. Lanham, MD: Rowman & Littlefield, 2006.

2004.     Aristotle, ethics and business organizations. *Organization Studies* 25: 1021–43.

          Emotions, thoughts and feelings: Emotions as engagements with the world. In *Thinking about feeling: Contemporary philosophers on emotions*, ed. Robert C. Solomon, 76–88. New York: Oxford University Press.

          On the passivity of the passions. In *Feeling and emotion: The Amsterdam symposium*, ed. Anthony Manstead and Agneta Fischer, 11–29. Cambridge: Cambridge University Press.

          Pathologies of pride in Camus's *The fall. Philosophy and Literature* 28: 41–59.

Sympathy as a 'natural' sentiment. *Business, science, and ethics*, ed. R. Edward Freeman, 53–58. Ruffin Series. Bowling Green: Philosophy Documentation Center.

Thinking in the shadow of death. *The Philosopher's Magazine* 27: 27–29.

Aristotle, ethics, and business organizations. *Organizational Studies* 25: 1021–1043.

2005.    Erotic love as a moral virtue. In *Virtue ethics: Old and new*, ed. Stephen Gardiner, 81–100. Ithaca, NY: Cornell University Press.

Name that feeling: Sabini and Silver on emotional experience. *Psychological Inquiry* 16: 41–44.

Sympathie für Adam Smith: Einige aktuelle philosophische und psychologische Überlegungen. In *Adam Smith als Moralphilosoph*, trans. Christel Fricke and Jörg Heininger, 251–276. (German only). Berlin: de Gruyter.

What's character got to do with it? A reply to John Doris. *Philosophy and Phenomenological Research* 71: 648–655.

2006.    Emotions in continental philosophy. *Philosophy Compass* 1: 413–431.

Emotions in phenomenology and existentialism. *A companion to phenomenology and existentialism*, ed. Hubert L. Dreyfus and Mark Wrathall, 291–309. Malden, MA: Blackwell.

Free enterprise, sympathy, and virtue. In *Moral markets: The critical role of values in the economy*, ed. Paul J. Zak, 16–41. Princeton: Princeton University Press; SSRC top ten downloaded article on the web, 2006.

Hegel en Jena: Liberación y espiritualidad en la filosophía. *Apuntes Filosóficos* 29: 225–246.

Nietzsche's fatalism. In *A Companion to Nietzsche*, ed. Keith Ansell Pearson, 419–434. Oxford: Blackwell.

Philosophy as the queen of the sciences, emotions research as her bastard child. In *Bridging social psychology: The benefits of transdisciplinary approaches*, ed. P. A. M. Van Lange, 207–211. Hillsdale, NJ: Erlbaum.

Success. *The Philosophers' Magazine*, 35: 20–26.

2007.    Existentialism vs. pessimism. *Chronicle of Higher Education*, 53:21 (January): B5.

2008.    Are we victims of circumstances? Hegel and Jean-Paul Sartre on corporate responsibility and bad faith. *Cutting-edge issues in business ethics: Continental challenges to tradition and practice*, ed. Mollie Painter-Morland and Patricia Werhane, 1–20. New York: Springer.

Business ethics, corporate virtues and corporate citizenship. In *Handbook of research on global corporate citizenship*, ed. Andreas Georg Scherer and Guido Palazzo, 116–133. Cheltenham: Edward Elgar.

Educating emotions: The phenomenology of feelings. In *Educations and their purposes: A conversation among cultures*, ed. Roger T. Ames and Peter D. Hershock, 113–130. Honolulu: University of Hawaii Press.

Facing death together: Camus's *The plague*, in *Art and ethical criticism*, ed. Gary L. Hagberg, 163–183. Malden, MA: Blackwell.

The many dimensions of religious emotional experience. In *Religious emotions: Some philosophical explorations*, ed. Willem Lemmens and Walter Van Herck, 230–246. Newcastle: Cambridge Scholars.

The politics of emotion. In *Bringing the passions back in: The emotions in political philosophy*, ed. Rebecca Kingston and Leonard Ferry, 189–208. Vancouver: UBC Press.

2009.    Self, deception, and self-deception in philosophy. In *The philosophy of deception*, ed. Clancy Martin, 15–36. New York: Oxford University Press.

2010.    Foreword: 'Acceptable risk' – On the rationality (and irrationality) of emotional evaluations of risk. In *Emotions and risky technologies*, ed. Sabine Roeser, vii–xiii. Dordrecht: Springer.

**Comments, Forewords, Notes, Abstracts, Brief Replies**

1968.       Sumner on Metaethics. *Ethics* 78 (April 1968): 226–227.
1971.       Nietzsche as analytic philosopher. *Modern Schoolman* 48: 263–266.
1972.       Metamuddles: A reply to Robert L. Simon. *Philosophy and Phenomenological Research* 32: 557–558.
            Psychic processes and the unconscious. *Methodology and Science* 3: 78–80.
1974.       Comment: A change in the weather [on Camus]. *Metaphilosophy* 5: 276.
1975.       Minimal incorrigibility (A comment on Frank Jackson). *Australian Journal of Philosophy* 53: 254–256.
1976.       Comments on papers by William Alston, Donald Davidson, G.E.M. Anscombe, and Richard L. Gregory. In *The philosophy of psychology*, ed. S. C. Brown, 133–134 and 242–243. London: Macmillan.
1977.       Reply to comments by Audi and Quinn. *Southwestern Journal of Philosophy* 8: 129–132.
            The rationality of emotions. *Southwestern Journal of Philosophy* 8: 105–114.
1978.       Phony feelings (Abstract of a reply to Ronald deSousa). *Journal of Philosophy* 75: 697–699.
1979.       Full Back Cover Description, G. W. F. Hegel, *Phenomenology of Spirit,* trans. Miller. Oxford: Oxford University Press.
1982.       Emotional cookbooks: Comment on J. Panksepp, Toward a general psychobiological theory of emotions. *Behavioral and Brain Sciences* 5: 444–445.
1984.       Abstract of comments: Nietzsche's ethics. *Nous* 18: 88–89.
            I can't get it out of my mind (Augustine's problem): Reply to Robert C. Roberts, Solomon on control of the emotions. *Philosophy and Phenomenological Research* 44: 405–412.
1986.       Emotions, feelings, and contexts (A reply to Robert Kraut). *Journal of Philosophy* 83: 653–654.
1989.       Nietzsche and Nehamas's Nietzsche. *International Studies in Philosophy* 21: 55–61.
1991.       Business ethics for the new millennium. Published as La teoria dei giochi come modello per gli affair e l'etica degli affair, *Etica ed Economia* I/2 (1991): 11–39.
1992.       Always the philosopher. *Falling in love with wisdom*, ed. D. Karnos and R. Shoemaker, 154–156. New York: Oxford University Press. Reprinted in Solomon, *Entertaining ideas,* 20–23.
1995.       Comments on other essays. In *Morality and social justice,* ed. James Sterba, 107–109, 155–156. Lanham, MD: Rowman and Littlefield, 1995.
            Marketing Heidegger: Entrepreneurship and corporate practices. *Inquiry* 38: 75–81.
1996.       The passionate life. *Proceedings of the International Society for Research on Emotions.*
1998.       Between disciplines: Why philosophy is important for emotions research. *Affect Science* 12:3.
            *Uncompromising integrity: Motorola's global challenge.* Fourteen Business Ethics Case Commentaries (with Thomas Donaldson, Richart T. deGeorge, William J. Ellos), ed. Robert B. Textor and R. S. Moorthy. Motorola Schaumburg IL: Motorola University Press.
1999.       Emotions and the 'will to power.' *Proceedings of the International Society for Research on Emotions.*
2000.       President's column. *Emotion Researcher* 14/3: 2–3
2001.       President's column (Reflections on September 11th). *The Emotions Researcher* 15/3: 3–4.

2001.          President's column: Defining our terms. *The Emotion Researcher* 15/2: 3–6.
2002.          Foreword to Mitchell D. Ginsberg, *The inner palace*. San Francisco: Blue
               Dolphin, i–vi.
               President's column: Meeting in Spain. *The Emotions Researcher* 16/1: 3–4.
               President's column: 'Nasty' emotions. *The Emotions Researcher* 16/4: 3.
               President's column. *The Emotions Researcher* 16/3: 3.
2003.          President's column. *The Emotions Researcher* 17/1: 3.
               President's column: Is pride a positive emotion? *The Emotions Researcher* 18/2:
               9–10.
               President's column. *The Emotions Researcher*, 18/3: 3.
2004.          President's column. *The Emotions Researcher*, 19/1: 3–4.
               Foreword to Herbert Fingarette, *Mapping Responsibility*. La Salle, IL: Open
               Court, ix.
               Foreword. In *The psychology of gratitude,* ed. Robert A. Emmons and Michael
               E. McCullough, v–xi. New York: Oxford University Press.

Book Reviews
1968.          Review of Hans Jonas, *The phenomenon of life: Toward a philosophical biology*
               (New York, Harper & Row, 1966). *Philosophical Forum,* 1–3 (1968).
1974.          Review of Louis Mackey, *Kierkegaard: A kind of poet* (Philadelphia: University of
               Pennsylvania Press, 1971). *Philosophical Review* 82: 244–247.
1975.          Decidophobia [Review of Walter Kaufmann, *Without guilt and justice*
               (New York: Peter H. Wyden, 1973).] *Michigan Quarterly Review* 15: 240–244.
1977.          Review of Tracy Strong, *Friedrich Nietzsche and the politics of transfiguration*
               (Berkeley: University of California Press, 1976). *Studi Internazionali Filosofia* 9:
               229–231.
1980.          Review of Robert Nisbet, *The history of the idea of progress* (New York: Basic
               Books, 1980). *Chicago Review* 32: 120–123.
1981.          Review of Charles Taylor, *Hegel and modern society* (Cambridge: Cambridge
               University Press, 1981). *Teaching Philosophy* 4: 92–94.
               Review of Evan Simpson, *Reason over passion* (Waterloo, ON: Wilfrid Laurier
               University Press, 1979). *Philosophical Topics,* 12: 270.
1982.          Review of Paul Edwards, *Heidegger on death: A critical evaluation* (LaSalle, IL:
               Hegeler Institute, 1979). *Canadian Philosophical Reviews* 2: 12–14.
               Review of Russell Vannoy, *Sex without love: A philosophical exploration* (Buffalo:
               Prometheus, 1980). *Philosophical Review* 91: 653–656.
1984.          Review of Edmund Husserl, *Shorter works* (Notre Dame: University of Notre
               Dame, 1984) and Martin Heidegger, *The basic problems of phenomenology,* trans.
               Albert Hofstadter (Bloomington: Indiana University Press, 1982). *Teaching
               Philosophy* 7: 154–156.
               Review of Peter Singer, *Hegel* (Oxford: Oxford University Press, 1984). *Teaching
               Philosophy* 7: 248–250.
1986.          Review of Roger Scruton, *Sexual desire* (New York: Free Press, 1986).
               *The Philadelphia Inquirer.*
               Review of Willard Gaylin, *Rediscovering love* (New York: Viking, 1986), and
               Barbara Ehrenreich et al., *Re-making love* (New York: Doubleday, 1986).
               *Philadelphia Inquirer.*
1986/1987.     Review of Alexander Nehamas, *Nietzsche: Life as literature* (Cambridge, MA:
               Harvard University Press, 1986). *Teaching Philosophy* 10: 148–149; and in
               *Philadelphia Inquirer* (May 11, 1986).

1987.       Incest: The ultimate taboo. Review of W. Arens, *The original sin* (Oxford: Oxford
            University Press, 1987) and James B. Twitchell, *Forbidden partners* (New York:
            Columbia University Press, 1987). *Philadelphia Inquirer* (April 12, 1987);
            reprinted in Solomon, *Entertaining ideas*, 187–191.
            Review of Ronald Hayman, *Sartre: A life* (New York: Simon & Schuster, 1987)
            and Annie Cohen-Solai, *Sartre: A life* (New York: Pantheon, 1987). *Philadelphia
            Inquirer.*
            Review of Maggie Scarf, *Intimate partners* (New York: Random House, 1987).
            *Philadelphia Inquirer.*
            Review of Irving Singer, *The nature of love*, III (Chicago: University of Chicago
            Press, 1987), and Francesca M. Cancian, *Love in America* (Cambridge: Cambridge
            University Press, 1987). *Philadelphia Inquirer.*
1988.       Revenge: Analyzing an eye-for-an-eye ideology, Review of Pietro Marongiu and
            Graeme Newman, *Vengeance: The fight against injustice* (Totowa, NJ: Rowman
            & Littlefield, 1987). *Philadelphia Inquirer.*
            Review of Irving Singer, *The nature of love,* II: *Courtly and romantic* (Chicago:
            University of Chicago Press, 1986). *Nous* 22: 467–470.
1989.       Review of Arthur Danto, *Connections to the world* (New York: Harper & Row,
            1989). *Teaching Philosophy* 12:420–423. Reprinted in Solomon, *Entertaining
            ideas,* 33–36.
            Review of Laurence Dickey, *Hegel: Religion, economics, and the politics of spirit,
            1770–1807.* (Cambridge: Cambridge University Press, 1987). *History of European
            Ideas* 10: 251–252.
            Review of Edward R. Freeman and Daniel R. Gilbert, *Corporate strategy and the
            search for ethics* (Englewood Cliffs NJ: Prentice-Hall, 1988). *Teaching Philosophy*
            12: 189–192.
1990.       Review of Bijoy H. Boruah, *Fiction and emotion* (Oxford: Clarendon, 1988).
            *The Review of Metaphysics* 43: 620–621.
1991.       Review of Hubert Dreyfus, *Being-in-the-world: Heidegger's "Being and time,"
            Division I* (Cambridge: MIT Press, 1991). *Philosophy and Literature* 15: 359–361.
            Review of James L. Collier, *The rise of selfishness in America* (Oxford:
            Clarendon, 1991). *The Philadelphia Inquirer.*
1992.       Reaching out — to world philosophy. Featured review of *Rationality in question:
            On eastern and western views of rationality,* ed. Schlomo Biderman and Ben-Ami
            Sharfstein (Leiden: E.J. Brill, 1989), and David A. Dilworth, *Philosophy in world
            perspective: A comparative hermeneutic of the major theories* (New Haven: Yale
            University Press, 1989). *Philosophy East and West* 42: 163–171; reprinted in
            Solomon, *Entertaining ideas*, 37–41.
            Critical review of Noël Carroll, *The philosophy of horror* (New York: Routledge,
            1991). *Philosophy and Literature* 16 (1992): 163–173. Reprinted in Solomon,
            *Entertaining ideas,* 119–130.
            Review of Stuart Zane Charmé, *Vulgarity and authenticity: Dimensions of
            otherness in the world of Jean-Paul Sartre* (Oxford: University of Massachusetts
            Press, 1991). *Ethics* 102: 884.
            Review of John Kenneth Galbraith, *The culture of contentment* (New York:
            Houghton-Mifflin, 1992). *The Philadelphia Inquirer.*
            Review of Alan Soble, *The structure of love* (New Haven: Yale University Press,
            1990). *Dialogue: Canadian Philosophical Review* 10: 478–480.
1993.       Featured Review of *Culture and modernity: East-west perspectives,* ed. Eliot
            Deutsch (Honolulu: University of Hawaii Press, 1991). *Philosophy East and West*
            43: 565–572.
1994.       Review of Jean-Paul Sartre, *Notebooks for an ethics,* trans. David Pellauer
            (Chicago: University of Chicago Press, 1994). *Ethics* 104: 417–418.

1996.          Emotions, ethics and the 'internal ought': A review of six books. *Cognition and Emotion* 10: 529–550.

               Review of Dale Jamieson, ed., *Language, mind and art: Essays in appreciation and analysis in honor of Paul Ziff* (with Kathleen Higgins) (Dordrecht: Kluwer, 1994). *Journal of Aesthetics and Art Criticism* 54: 386–387.

               Featured review of William Lyons, *The philosophy of mind* (London: Dent, 1995). *Philosophy East and West* 46: 389–399.

1997.          What is an emotion? — Review of Paul Griffiths, *What emotions really are: The problem of psychological categories* (Chicago: Chicago University Press, 1997). *Philadelphia Inquirer.*

               The philosophical life: Is it worth living that way? — Review of Richard Shusterman, *Practicing philosophy: Pragmatism and the philosophical life* (New York: Routledge, 1997). In *Philadelphia Inquirer.*

1999.          And now for something completely different — Review of Charles Spinosa, Fernando Flores, and Hubert Dreyfus, *Disclosing new worlds* (Cambridge, MA: M.I.T. Press, 1997). *Business Ethics Quarterly* 9: 169–177.

               Review of Paul Griffiths, *What emotions really are: The problem of psychological categories* (Chicago: Chicago University Press, 1997). *Philosophical Review* 108: 131–134.

2001.          Review of Jon Elster, *Alchemies of the mind: Rationality and the emotions* (Cambridge: Cambridge University Press, 1999). *Philosophical Review* 110: 104–107.

2002.          Review of Martha Nussbaum, *Upheavals of thought: The intelligence of emotions* (Cambridge: Cambridge University Press, 2001). *Mind* 111: 897–901.

               Review of Peter Goldie, *Emotions* (Oxford: Clarendon, 2000). *International Philosophical Quarterly* 42: 259–260.

Professional Service Articles and Books:

1975.          Graduate study in continental philosophy in American universities. *Teaching Philosophy* 1: 159–174.

1984.          A survey of graduate study in continental philosophy in the United States. *Teaching Philosophy* 7 (1984): 337–346.

1995.          Course syllabi for teaching business ethics. In *Business ethics, regulation and law: Business administration reading lists and course outlines,* ed. Richard Schwindt, 245–250. Vancouver: Simon Fraser University Press.

Encyclopedia Entries

1978.          Sexual identity (with Judith Rose Sanders). In *Encyclopedia of bioethics,* ed. Warren T. Reich, IV: 1589–1596. New York: The Free Press/London: Collier Macmillan.

1988.          Existentialism. *Academic American encyclopedia* VII: 332. Danbury, CT: Grolier.

1992.          Ethical dilemmas. In *Encyclopedia of career change and work issues,* ed. Lawrence K. Jones, 106–108. Phoenix: Oryx Press.

1995.          Camus, Albert and Sartre, Jean-Paul. In *The Cambridge dictionary of philosophy,* ed. Robert Audi, 101–102 and 709–711; 2nd ed. (1999) 116 and 812–813. Cambridge: Cambridge University Press.

               Sexual Identity (revised, with Linda Nicholson). In *Encyclopedia of bioethics,* ed. Warren T. Reich, 2nd ed., V: 2378–2386. Kennedy Institute, New York: Macmillan 1996.

1995/2005.     Entries on Camus, Albert, Fear, Master and Slave, Nihilism. Passion/ Passion and emotion in the history of philosophy, Progress, Resentment, Revenge, Shame, Subjective truth, and Subjectivity. In *Oxford companion to philosophy,* ed. Ted Honderich, 118/128, 270/291, 529–530/563, 623–659, 647/683–684, 722/761, 771/814–815, 816/722, 825/869, 857/900, 857/900. Oxford: Oxford University Press.

1996.         Emotions. In *The Blackwell encyclopedic dictionary of business ethics*, ed.
              R. Edward Freeman and Patricia Werhane, 197–199. Oxford: Blackwell, 1996.
              Entries for authenticity; Camus, Albert; existentialism; facticity; in itself/for itself;
              Kierkegaard, Søren; perspectivism; and Sartre, Jean-Paul. *A dictionary of
              philosophy*, ed. Thomas Mautner, 39, 63–64 141–143, 145, 205–206; 224,
              316–317, and 378–380. Oxford: Penguin 1996.
1998.         Entries for Emotions and The philosophy of emotions. In *The concise Routledge
              encyclopedia of philosophy*, ed. Edward Craig, 237–238. London: Routledge.
1999.         Business ethics and virtue. In *A companion to business ethics*, ed. Robert E.
              Frederick, 30–37. Oxford: Blackwell.

              Camus. In *A companion to philosophers,* ed. Robert L. Arrington, 184–186.
              Oxford: Blackwell.

              Emotions (with Kathleen Higgins). In *The encyclopedia of aesthetics*, ed. Michael
              Kelly, II: 102–105. Oxford: Oxford University Press.

              Philosophy. In *Encyclopedia of human emotions*, ed. David Levinson, James
              J. Ponzetti, Jr., and Peter F. Jorgensen, II: 509–514. New York: Macmillan.
2003.         Emotions. In *The encyclopedia Britannica*, 2003.
2004.         Emotions. In *The new dictionary of the history of ideas,* ed. Maryanne Clive
              Horowitz, II: 649–651. Detroit: Scribner's.

              Existentialism. In *The new dictionary of the history of ideas,* ed. Maryanne Clive
              Horowitz, II: 761–765. Detroit: Scribner's.

              Hegel, Georg Wilhelm Friedrich, 1770–1831. In *The encyclopedia of the romantic
              era, 1760–1850,* ed. Christopher John Murray, I: 481–483. London: Fitzroy
              Dearborn.

              Nietzsche. In *Encyclopedia of leadership,* ed. George R. Goethals, Georgia J.
              Sorenson and James MacGregor Burns, III: 1091–1095. Thousand Oaks: Sage.

              Phenomenology. In *The new dictionary of the history of ideas,* ed. Maryanne Clive
              Horowitz, IV: 1754–1757. Detroit: Scribner's.

              *Phenomenology of spirit,* 1807. In *The encyclopedia of the romantic era,
              1760–1850,* ed. Christopher John Murray, II: 870–871. London: Fitzroy Dearborn.

              Philosophy. In *The new dictionary of the history of ideas,* ed. Maryanne Clive
              Horowitz, IV: 1775–1779. Detroit: Scribner's.

              Sexual Identity (revised, with Jennifer Greene), *Encyclopedia of bioethics,* ed.
              Sterling G. Post III, IV: 2434–2442. New York: Macmillan.

# About the Editors

**Kathleen M. Higgins** is Professor of Philosophy at the University of Texas at Austin. Her main areas of research are continental philosophy and aesthetics, particularly musical aesthetics. She has published a number of books: *The Music between Us: Is Music the Universal Language?* (2012), *Comic Relief: Nietzsche's* "Gay Science" (2000), *What Nietzsche* Really *Said* (with Robert C. Solomon 2000), *A Passion for Wisdom* (with Robert C. Solomon 1997), *A Short History of Philosophy* (with Robert C. Solomon 1996), *The Music of Our Lives* (1991, 2011), and *Nietzsche's "Zarathustra"* (1987; rev. 2010). She has edited or co-edited several other books on such topics as Nietzsche, German Idealism, aesthetics, ethics, erotic love, and non-Western philosophy. She has been a Resident Scholar at the Rockefeller Foundation's Bellagio Study and Conference Center (1993), and a Visiting Fellow of the Australian National University Philosophy Department and Canberra School of Music (1997). She is a frequent visitor at the University of Auckland in New Zealand.

**David Sherman** is Professor of Philosophy at the University of Montana. His research focuses on German Idealism, existential phenomenology, and the Frankfurt School. He is the author of *Sartre and Adorno: The Dialectics of Subjectivity* (SUNY 2007) and *Camus* (Blackwell 2009), and he is a coeditor of the *Blackwell Guide to Continental Philosophy* (Blackwell, with Robert Solomon 2003) and *Reading Negri* (with Pierre LaMarche and Max Rosenkrantz, Open Court 2011).

K. Higgins and D. Sherman (eds.), *Passion, Death, and Spirituality*,          285
Sophia Studies in Cross-cultural Philosophy of Traditions and Cultures 1,
DOI 10.1007/978-94-007-4650-3, © Springer Science+Business Media Dordrecht 2012

# About the Contributors

**Robert Audi** writes, teaches, and lectures in ethics and related areas. His books in ethics include *Business Ethics and Ethical Business* (Oxford 2009), a short introduction to the field; *Moral Value and Human Diversity* (Oxford 2007), a wide-ranging introductory treatment of normative ethics and the theory of value, with applications to institutions in business, education, government, and the media; *Practical Reasoning and Ethical Decision* (Routledge 2006), which offers a theory of practical reasoning and its relation to ethical theory and decision-making; *The Good in the Right: A Theory of Intuition and Intrinsic Value* (Princeton 2004), which defends a comprehensive view in both theoretical and normative ethics; and *Democratic Authority and the Separation of Church and State* (Oxford 2011), which offers a theory of the relation between religion and politics. Audi has served as President of the American Philosophical Association (Central Division 1987–1988), as Editor-in-Chief of *The Cambridge Dictionary of Philosophy* (1995 and 1999), and as Director of many National Endowment for the Humanities summer seminars and institutes and of many other national seminars, the latter mainly in ethics. He is presently Professor of Management and John A. O'Brien Professor of Philosophy at the University of Notre Dame.

**David Bevan** (Ph.D. King's College London) is Professor of Management (organizational behavior) at Grenoble Graduate Business School; Academic Director of the Academy of Business in Society (EABIS); Senior Wicklander Fellow at the Institute for Professional and Business Ethics (DePaul); and a member of the Editorial Board at the *Professional and Business Ethics Journal*. His research interests are focused on organizational behavior through a lenses suggested by a range of Continental authors. He has designed and delivered courses in Applied Ethics and Sustainability in numerous universities and business schools including King's College London; Royal Holloway, University of London; EDHEC, Lille and HEC Paris.

**Purushottama Bilimoria** (Ph.D., LaTrobe) is Professor of Philosophy and Comparative Studies at Deakin University in Australia, Senior Research Fellow, University of Melbourne, Visiting Professor and Lecturer at University of California, Berkeley and Dominican University, San Anselmo, and Shivadasani Fellow of Oxford University. His areas of specialist research and publications cover classical Indian philosophy and comparative ethics, Continental thought, cross-cultural philosophy of religion, diaspora studies, bioethics, and personal law in India. He is an Editor-in-Chief of *Sophia, Journal of Philosophy of Religion*, published by Springer. He also edits a book series with Springer, Sophia*: Cross-cultural studies in Culture and Traditions*. Recent publications include *Indian Ethics I* (Ashgate 2007; Oxford 2008); "Sabdapramana: Word and Knowledge (Testimony) in Indian Philosophy" (revised reprint, DK Print World 2008); "Nietzsche as 'Europe's Buddha' and Asia's Superman," (in *Sophia*, 47/3, 2008); *Postcolonial Philosophy of Religion* (with Andrew Irvine, Ken Surin et al., Springer 2009). He teaches and publishes on Hindu religious philosophies. He also works in political philosophy, on topics pertaining to the ethics of rights, theories of justice, capabilities, education and gender issues in the Third World, particularly South Asian, contexts.

**John Bishop** is Professor of Philosophy at the University of Auckland. He is the author of *Natural Agency* (Cambridge University Press 1989) and *Believing by Faith* (Oxford University Press 2007), and of journal articles in the areas of Philosophy of Religion and Philosophy of Action.

**Arindam Chakrabarti** did his doctoral research under Michael Dummett and Peter Strawson at Oxford. He has taught at Calcutta, Delhi, London, and Seattle and now teaches at University of Hawaii. He has published numerous papers on analytic philosophy of language, Indian philosophy, metaphysics and epistemology. Besides his book *Denying Existence* (2010), he has published two books in Bengali and one in Sanskrit on contemporary Western philosophy, and is writing a book on the moral psychology of the emotions. His three favorite philosophers are Abhinavagupta, Kant and Wittgenstein. In the last week of his life, Bob Solomon expressed excitement about the possibility of co-authoring a book with him tentatively titled *Retaliation – For and Against.*

**Padmasiri de Silva** has obtained a Ph.D. in Comparative Philosophy and an Advanced Diploma in Counseling. He is currently Adjunct Research Associate at Monash University. He was formerly Professor and Head of the Philosophy and Psychology Department, University of Peradeniya, Sri Lanka (1980–1989). He has held visiting positions in the National University of Singapore, the University of Pittsburgh, and Waikato University. He is the author of number of books on Buddhist ethics and psychology and on counseling.

**Ronald de Sousa** was educated in Switzerland, England and the United States. He is Professor Emeritus of Philosophy at the University of Toronto, Canada. He is the author of *The Rationality of Emotion* (MIT 1987), *Why Think? Evolution and the Rational Mind* (OUP 2007), and *Emotional Truth* (OUP 2011).

**Janet McCracken** is Professor of Philosophy and former Dean of the Faculty at Lake Forest College, just north of Chicago, IL. She learned a lot of what she knows about teaching from her experiences as a teaching assistant for Bob Solomon at the University of Texas. She is the author of two books, *Taste and the Household: The "Domestic Aesthetic" and Moral Reasoning* (2001) and *Thinking About Gender: A Historical Anthology* (1997). She lives in Lake Forest with her husband, Chad, also a philosophy professor, and their four cats.

**Kelly Oliver** is W. Alton Jones Professor of Philosophy at Vanderbilt University. She is the author of several books, including most recently, *Knock me up, Knock me down: Images of Pregnancy in Hollywood Film*, *Animal Lessons: How They Teach Us to Be Human*, and *Women as Weapons of War: Iraq, Sex and the Media*.

**Jesse J. Prinz** is Distinguished Professor of Philosophy at the City University of New York, Graduate Center. His research focuses on the perceptual, emotional, and cultural foundations of human psychology. He is author of *Furnishing the Mind: Concepts and Their Perception Basis* (MIT 2002), *Gut Reactions: A Perceptual Theory of Emotion* (Oxford 2004), *The Emotional Construction of Morals* (Oxford 2007), *Beyond Human Nature* (Penguin/Norton 2011), and *The Conscious Brain* (Oxford 2012).

**Jenefer Robinson** is Professor of Philosophy at the University of Cincinnati, author of *Deeper than Reason: Emotion and its Role in Literature, Music and Art* (Oxford University Press 2005), editor of *Music and Meaning* (Cornell University Press 1997), Area Editor for Aesthetics, *Encyclopedia of Philosophy* (2006, 2nd ed.), and past president of the American Society for Aesthetics. Her articles on the theory of emotion and on issues in aesthetics on have appeared in various books and journals, including *The Journal of Philosophy, The Philosophical Review, Australasian Journal of Philosophy, Erkenntnis, Philosophy, Behavioral and Brain Sciences, Emotion Review, Journal of Literary Theory, British Journal of Aesthetics*, and *Journal of Aesthetics and Art Criticism*.

**Henry Rosemont, Jr.** is George B. and Wilma Reeves Distinguished Professor of the Liberal Arts Emeritus at St. Mary's College of Maryland, and Visiting Scholar in Religious Studies at Brown University. His most recent book, with Roger T. Ames, is *The Chinese Classic of Family Reverence* (2009).

**Richard Schacht** is Professor of Philosophy and Jubilee Professor of Liberal Arts and Sciences (Emeritus) at the University of Illinois. His interests relate closely to developments in the post-Kantian interpretive tradition, especially as they pertain to the understanding of human reality and possibility. He has long shared Robert Solomon's particular interest in the thought of Hegel and Nietzsche. His books include *Alienation, Hegel and After, Nietzsche, Making Sense of Nietzsche,* and (with Philip Kitcher) *Finding an Ending: Reflections on Wagner's* Ring.

**Shari Neller Starrett** is a past chair and member of the Philosophy Department at California State University, Fullerton. She counts it one of the great fortunes of her life that Bernd Magnus, Bob Solomon, and Kathy Higgins were all on her dissertation committee at the University of California, Riverside. She has published articles on Hegel and Nietzsche, and has recently been researching Arendt and Beauvoir.

**Christine Swanton** teaches in the Philosophy Department, University of Auckland New Zealand. She is currently working on the virtue ethics of Hume and Nietzsche. Her book on virtue ethics, *Virtue Ethics: A Pluralistic View*, was published with Oxford University Press in 2003 (paper 2005).

**Markus Weidler**, a native of Berlin, Germany, received his M.A. and his Ph.D. in philosophy from the University of Texas at Austin. After teaching at the University of Auckland, New Zealand, for two years, he joined the faculty of Columbus State University in 2007. He has published and continues to work in the areas of twentieth-century continental thought and contemporary philosophy of religion.

**Patricia H. Werhane** is the Wicklander Chair of Business Ethics and the Executive Director of the Institute for Business and Professional Ethics at DePaul University, formerly the Ruffin Professor of Business Ethics and Senior Fellow at the Olsson Center for Applied Ethics in the Darden School at the University of Virginia. Professor Werhane has published numerous articles and is the author or editor of over twenty books. She is the founder and former Editor-in-Chief of *Business Ethics Quarterly*, the journal of the Society for Business Ethics, and she is an Academic Advisor to the Business Roundtable Institute for Corporate Ethics.

# Index

CPSIA information can be obtained at www.ICGtesting.com
Printed in the USA
LVOW071820241112

308665LV00005B/111/P